Chasing the Glory

ALSO BY MICHAEL PARFIT

The Boys Behind the Bombs

Last Stand at Rosebud Creek

South Light: A Journey to the Last Continent

MICHAEL PARFIT

Chasing the Glory

TRAVELS ACROSS AMERICA

Macmillan Publishing Company

NEW YORK

Collier Macmillan Publishers

LONDON

Macmillan Publishing Company
866 Third Avenue, New York, NY 10022
Collier Macmillan Canada, Inc.

Permissions acknowledgments appear on page 355.

Library of Congress Cataloging-in-Publication Data
Parfit, Michael.
    Chasing the glory/Michael Parfit.
        p.   cm.
    ISBN 0-02-594731-1
    1. United States—Description and travel—1981– 2. Parfit, Michael—
Journeys—United States. 3. Air travel—United States. I. Title.
E 169.04.P35 1988 917.3'0492—dc19   88-12906   CIP

Macmillan books are available at special discounts for bulk purchases for sales promotions, premiums, fund-raising, or educational use. For details, contact:
    Special Sales Director
    Macmillan Publishing Company
    866 Third Avenue
    New York, NY 10022

Design by Jerry Kelly

Maps by Heather Saunders

10 9 8 7 6 5 4 3 2 1

Printed in the United States of America

To Eric George Parfit
and
Dorothea Hagedorn Parfit
with love

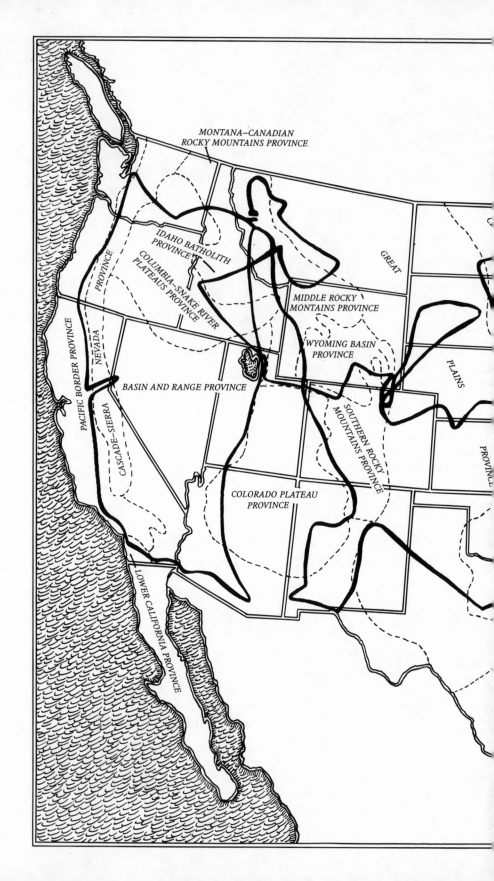

MONTANA–CANADIAN
ROCKY MOUNTAINS PROVINCE

IDAHO BATHOLITH
PROVINCE

COLUMBIA–SNAKE RIVER
PLATEAUS PROVINCE

MIDDLE ROCKY
MOUNTAINS PROVINCE

WYOMING BASIN
PROVINCE

PROVINCE

PACIFIC BORDER PROVINCE

NEVADA

BASIN AND RANGE PROVINCE

CASCADE-SIERRA

SOUTHERN ROCKY
MOUNTAINS PROVINCE

COLORADO PLATEAU
PROVINCE

LOWER CALIFORNIA PROVINCE

GREAT

PLAINS

PROVINCE

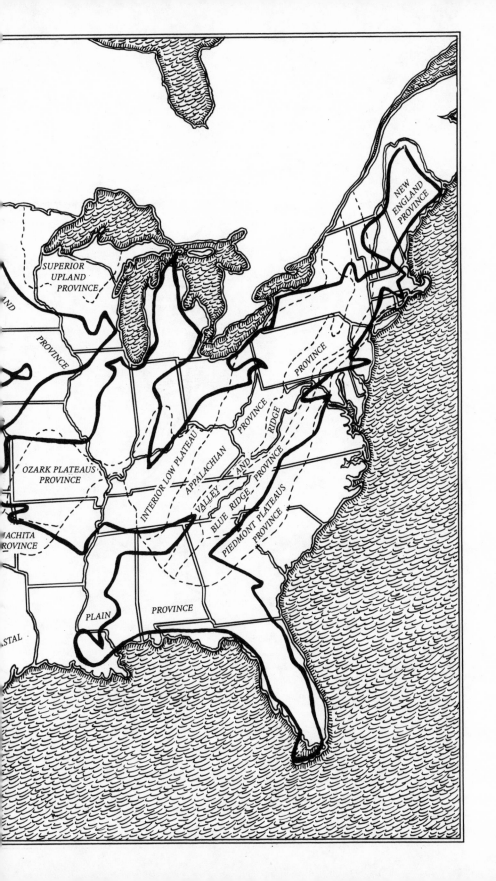

AUTHOR'S NOTE

Nonfiction is Truth. That's what those of us who practice it like to think. After all, except in a few cases in which someone needed protection, and a couple of fanciful inventions, all the names in this book are of real people. All the places exist. All the events are based on fact.

But this is not truth. It isn't truth in the same way that the six-o'clock news and the morning paper aren't truth. These things are collections of evidence.

I say all this because we writers and journalists are always embarking upon crusades to uncover the truth of some event or circumstance. It can't be done. Truth exists in the moment of living, and after that all that remains is evidence. And the evidence is so scattered by the constant explosion of existence that anything you find is fragmentary.

But if this isn't truth, what is it? In a specific sense this book is a record of pieces of a journey that I took over the course of several months above and on the United States, reconstructed with all the accuracy my memory, notes, research, and language can provide. In a more general sense it is something a few people are pleased to call "creative nonfiction," which sounds like a contradiction, but isn't.

Creative nonfiction is not the invention of facts that are then presented as truth. People who write careful nonfiction are appalled at the creation of composite characters or events that are presented to the reader as fact. Creative nonfiction is simply the attempt to surmount the barrier that the exposition of verifiable facts builds between the reader's understanding and the recorded experience itself. Straight nonfiction, if one can make the distinction, is concerned primarily with providing the reader with necessary information: the physical dimensions of a landscape, for instance, or the causes and effects of air pollution, or the voting record of a politician. Creative nonfiction attempts to describe things the way one's own memory would capture them, in intense, bright patches of recollection colored by the layers of emotion, perspective, and experience that go into real living. Without changing any of the facts, which are its backbone, creative nonfiction implies the use of all the devices in the literary bag of tricks, such as symbolism, metaphor, character, dialogue, plot, dramatic tension, even calculated obscurity, to assemble the evidence in a more lifelike form.

Creative nonfiction has been going on forever. Storytelling started off as creative nonfiction and degenerated into fiction only when storytellers cheated. That's the big difference between this kind of thing and a novel: I can't make a character out of five people, I can't put the action in Calcutta because that would be more romantic, and I can't make dialogue up out of thin air. It's often frustrating as hell: Why didn't this person put his feelings more clearly? Why didn't those two meet at the end of all that conflict and fight it out? And there is one more constraint: Sometimes I learn fascinating things that would cause great pain to someone if they were published, pain far more costly to the individual than the corresponding enlightenment might be worth to the public. A novelist would change names and circumstances and write it all down. But I can't do that, either.

But think of what I can do: If I were writing fiction I might once in a while make an imaginary event or scene or person come to life, which is a feat in itself. But when this nonfiction works I have instead tapped into the vein of life itself, and echoed the pulse of blood. Nothing is more exciting in the business of words.

Because so much of this kind of work depends on the way facts are accumulated, some details of method should be described. This book's perspective was made possible by three factors:
1. I can fly a small airplane with my feet.
2. I can touch-type.
3. My airplane is slow.
This may sound odd. The point is that in level flight in relatively still air a light aircraft can be directed precisely on course using only the rudder pedals. This allowed me to put a small portable computer on my lap and type notes while flying across America. These notes were necessarily sporadic: The first responsibility of a pilot is to observe the sky for other traffic, not to watch the landscape. But the lack of speed

of my airplane made the ground go by at a slow enough pace so I could get in my glances and make my notes.

Other notes of encounters and events on the ground were made in more traditional ways, with tape recorders, notebooks, and cameras. Some of the stories referred to in this book were originally researched during the course of other flights around the country on assignment for *New Times Magazine, Smithsonian Magazine,* or *Sports Illustrated,* over the course of a decade of writing and fifteen hundred hours of flight.

There must also, alas, be a further clarification of the circumstances that made this book: I did not have sponsors. No commercial entity provided me with film, fuel, radio equipment, charts, underwear, an airplane, or any other service or product that I used on my journey. I purchased what I needed at the parts store and the fuel pump, and asked for no favors.

Why is it necessary to say this? Because it seems that this is no longer standard operating procedure for all those who would call themselves journalists, reporters, or writers. Travel magazines, for instance, are riddled with corruption: writers receive free room and board, free airline tickets, free lunches, a free pat on the back from the public relations people who give them all these things, and a free smile to go with the words "Of course feel free to write it as you see it." Once when I questioned this policy I aroused the editor's ire. "You will learn," the editor said angrily, "that there is a difference between quality and purity." Books, too, are becoming more and more beholden to benefactors: A fine book of photographs, *A Day in the Life of America,* will forever be tarnished for me by the fact that it was sponsored by a whole raft of American corporations, from Kodak to Apple Computers, whether or not the corporations actually exercised editorial influence.

There are projects in this world for which it is necessary to have sponsors because the dimensions of the enterprise are too large for any individual. Charles Lindbergh's flight to Paris was one; the Voyager's flight around the world was another. The very first transcontinental flight, which involved a Wright experimental aircraft and a support train, was sponsored by the Armour Company. The plane, which was repaired so often that the only original parts to reach the West Coast (along with the repaired pilot) were the rudder and the oil-drip pan, was painted all over with the name of the soft drink Vin Fiz, and even carried a bottle of the stuff bolted to a strut.

But a flight exists separately from the promotional cargo. A book is not as lucky. Freedom from that kind of constraint allows me to thank people without looking over my shoulder. There are many to thank. Hundreds of people across the country participated in this book. My thanks to all of them. Many who are not within these pages gave much time and effort. I think particularly of Reeve Lindbergh and the good people of the Charles A. Lindbergh Fund who helped me with my research on Lindbergh's 1927 flights around the United States. I'd also like to thank Chuck Stone, the manager of the Lindbergh Historic Site in Little Falls, Minnesota. Many geographers assisted me in various states, including Peter Hugill at Texas A&M., D. W. Meinig at Syracuse University, several faculty members at the University of Montana, and, of course, John Brinckerhoff Jackson, who appears elsewhere here. This book goes back a long way: for providing ideas and assignments that led to some of my many flights around this country, I am grateful to Frank Rich, Jonathan Z. Larsen, Cal Fentress, Scott Kaufer, and Jane Amsterdam, who all worked for a while at the late *New Times Magazine*; to Ed Engberg and David Fritzen, both formerly of *Islands Magazine*; to Myra Gelband, Margaret Sieck, and Linda Verigan at *Sports Illustrated*; and to Constance Bond, Jim Doherty, Don Moser, Paul Trachtman, Timothy Foote, and Jack Wiley, among others, at *Smithsonian Magazine*.

Many thanks to Carol Finley, who transcribed endless tapes; to Vickie Dubbs, who put up with the uneven tempers of creation, and to Christine Roesch, who overcame the implacable obstructionism of my computer. Without Barry Lippman's clear-cut analysis of early drafts, this book would have languished forever in the doldrums of uncertainty, and without Connie Bourassa-Shaw's painstaking reading of the first version, and the encouragement given by her and Dick Shaw, the whole thing might have died. My children, Erica and David, put up with my absence and my tape-recorded voice for months and still seemed to remember me when I came home. And there are not enough words or flowers in the world with which to thank Debbie, my wife.

PROLOGUE

As you rise from a cloud into sunshine, you are encircled by light. As you climb, you emerge from the light, and you see it below you, a brightness around your shadow on the cloud. The drops of water in the mist split the light that comes to your eye so you see a luminous circular rainbow, dazzlingly bright, faintly blue on the inside, shading out to pink. The first time you see this light surrounding your own image, it is difficult not to think of yourself as holy.

In the Chinese province of Szechwan, people used to make a pilgrimage to the top of Omei Mountain. The pilgrims stood on the cliff edge and looked out, and if the sun was behind them and the mist below, they would see the bright circle around the shape of a human figure. There, too, it made people feel divine. They thought the shape was the Buddha. Some who beheld the Buddha, chased the Buddha. They sought nirvana. They threw themselves into the arms of the light. The evidence of the rocks did not deter them. The light compelled them to fly.

In Western civilization, because people also saw the haloed shape from a mountain in Germany, it has been named "The Specter of the Brocken." But it has a good common name. It is called a *glory*.

PART *1*

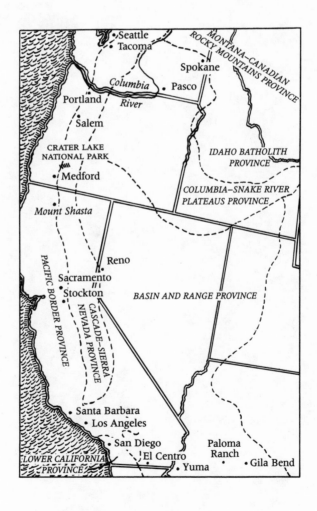

CHAPTER ONE

Ten days before I left my home in the mountains, when the urgency of departure was already upon me, I stood with Phil Timm in his shop on the shore of Flathead Lake, in western Montana, with the big six-cylinder engine of someone else's airplane standing there, painted golden, between us on a stand.

Phil held a connecting rod in his hand. The rod had the shine of metal and thin grease. It had heft. It was cast and machined. It seemed naked, wrenched from the place it belonged. It looked like a shining human bone.

Phil is tall, white-headed, with a slight bend to him that makes him look as if he has just come in through a low door. He often looks as if he had just seen something confidentially amusing on the other side of that door. "Come on up," he says to me on the telephone sometimes, "I'm just sitting here with my legs hanging down. We'll wave our arms and talk loud." Now he looked at the connecting rod and said, "What really gets to me, is that this thing stops. Every revolution. And everything connected to it stops." Hundreds of engines, thousands of connecting rods, had passed through his hands, and still Phil was in awe of the way it all worked. He slid the rod into the cylinder. "It's amazing," he said. Like femur to pelvis, the metal slid together, as if grown that way.

Phil Timm's first experiments with flight involved an umbrella and the family cat. Later he tried to build a hot-air balloon with feed sacks and baling wire. "We had a small fire," he told me once. "The usual catastrophe that one lad of my high rank and smell could create. So I dropped that program."

For a year or two he turned to projects that kept him on the ground.

He built a Model T Ford from parts when he was thirteen. At first it didn't have an engine. He'd coast it down a hill, and pull it back up with a horse, and then coast again. Then one winter day he saw an old engine in the back of someone's garage, lying there on straw like a calf. He hung around, a skinny kid with admiration in his eyes, saying, "I sure like that engine."

The man who owned the garage looked at the skinny kid with the curly hair.

"Phil," he said, "if you'll get that thing out of here today, I'll give it to you." So Phil went out and made a sled, got his horse, and hauled that engine down the road. He got it put together, then went down the road to the natural-gas pumping station, where engines big as houses pressurized gas to get it into Kansas City. The lubricating oil ran through the engine and out into a catch basin for disposal, but it still looked as good as new. A friend's father worked there. The skinny kid admired the blue oil, and said, "I'd sure like some of that oil."

"How about five gallons?" said the friend's father. Phil had no idea how much five gallons was. "Sure," he said. Took him half a day to drag that can home. He put the oil in the engine, and his father and a friend cranked it until it started.

He was excited. It was running! His father and friend were also excited. Oil was gushing out of the engine on all sides.

"You're losing your oil!" his father said.

"That's all right," Phil said, "I've got lots."

"You forgot to put in any gaskets."

"Gaskets?" Phil said. "What are gaskets?"

Gaskets, his father said, are made of cork. They are made at a factory. Phil did some research. Cork was the bark of trees. It came from Portugal. How was he going to get some cork? He kept saying to his father, "I'd sure like some gaskets."

But his father was wise to the skinny kid. No gaskets were forthcoming. So finally Phil compared the feel of cork and cardboard, and cut some gaskets out of a box, and got in trouble for using his mother's best shears. The engine's bell housing had to have felt gaskets, and he made those, too, and got in trouble for cutting up his father's hat. But the engine ran. So at thirteen, he told me sixty years later while we stood beside that golden engine, he had learned something important for his life. "I learned as much from those gaskets as anything. You see, those gaskets were made in a factory, but I could make gaskets too."

I have learned as much from Phil Timm as from anyone. When Phil was eighteen, he built an airplane. It had a Model A engine in it, and it had gaskets made of cork. He taught himself to fly in it, landing and taking off on a strip next to a golf course while a friend gestured instructions at him. Later a wind blew it over and wrecked it, but he went on to flying machines made in factories, flying and fixing and teaching and flying, all his life. Then, in the fall of 1986, I became his student.

One afternoon, long before we stood in the shop with the engine, Phil and I and my old single-engine Cessna Cardinal, whose engine was purring along inside its cocoon of cork gaskets, flinging its pistons and connecting rods back and forth to turn the crank and propeller at 2,700 rotations per minute, rose from a layer of stratus above the Flathead Valley into clear sky, and Phil let me look at the world for a minute before I put the training hood back on again and concentrated on the instruments. The world was clean and wide, with the edge of the mountains standing like islands in the white sea of cloud, and wisps of high cirrus floating above us, and the whole landscape of moisture and rock and light ours to embrace. He had let me see it because he couldn't stand not to share this gift. Now, when I put the hood back over my face and got on with the business of following needles to the invisible radio path in the air that would return us to the earth, he said into the intercom, "I love it." Later, as we descended between luminous cloud layers as if we were a part of the shimmer of the day itself, he said, "Pilots are lucky. They get to see things no one else gets to see."

CHAPTER TWO

There is one miracle under the sun and stars: life. But flight comes close. I rise like an angel, I see the world like God. Anyone who says that flight makes you feel small is wrong. No wonder eagles are arrogant. They think their wings are miles wide. Me, too. Expanded by aluminum, I embrace mountains. I splash down the Flathead River, a mile at a stride, kicking pike into the trees. I see the earth as it is. It is magnificent. It is mine.

In 1973, while I lived in a log house in Idaho with neither running water nor electricity, trying to come as close as possible to the beauty of what I thought of as the natural life, I borrowed $900 and bought a half interest in a 1946 two-seat airplane and learned to fly. Friends thought this was inconsistent. So did I. It was great.

Since then, pursuing my job as a writer of nonfiction, I have flown all over the continental United States, Alaska, and New Zealand. Those trips were all straight lines, from one place to another, using the plane for its speed. But from the moment I left the earth for the first time, I knew that someday I would climb into an airplane, take off, and wander across the landscape, using flight for its other gift: a way to see. At last, on a recent February morning, after almost fifteen years, that time came.

There was a storm in Nevada the day I left home. From western Montana I saw it: an edge of high, thin cloud across my sun. It was cold in Montana that day. The snow below was clean and light, like dust. My daughter wore her blue jacket in the cold when I went to hug her good-bye at the elementary school, where she was bouncing a basketball by herself in the playground while the boys played their exclusive game right next to her. She hugged me three times, in that blue jacket, with the little fringe of dark hair down over her dark eyes. Or maybe it was I that hugged her three times. Twenty-five thousand miles makes a long time to be gone. You're proud in the sky, but you're not invincible. You want to remember good times, just in case.

Flight came as easily as stretching in the morning. My old Cessna airplane gathered itself and lifted the load of motorcycle, sleeping bag, filing cabinets, computer, coat and tie, jug of water, briefcase full of hopeful plans, and hopeful me. We climbed. I glanced at the dials that monitor the machine. It was like checking my heartbeat. 2,700 RPM: Okay. Blood pressure: in the green; okay. Airspeed: 90; climbing.

An airplane lives by haste. Only a rush of wind keeps it aloft. Pause, and it falls. Hasty now, hasty as I would be for the next three months, hasty to see it all, I crossed U.S. Highway 93, which carried trucks and commuters going from this countryside to the city of Missoula. I crossed rectangular fields, laid out in lines by the idea that was born in the days of Thomas Jefferson. Climbing, hasty, I crossed the fenced-off hill where bison live as in a museum.

With altitude the haste was concealed by distance. The ground seemed to move slowly. Time grew. I had lots of it, and space to use it. From this murmuring mechanical platform in the sky, the American landscape stretched on and on ahead, field and mountain, patterned everywhere by human beings and their machines.

Was it coincidence that I turned forty just two weeks before I took off on a young man's journey around America? Probably not. But I didn't feel the need to explore the matter. So far, forty doesn't seem so bad; contemplation might ruin the illusion. So: I'm forty. I'm five feet nine, 155 pounds. Brown hair, blue eyes. Wife: Debra. Children: Erica, ten, and David, eight. I missed them before I even left. I like to run, to race on foot, to play basketball and softball, to walk among mountains, and to fly. I'm a writer of nonfiction, a reporter. I'm not a metaphysician. I think in simple sentences. When profound ideas hit me it is usually because someone else has tossed them out of an upstairs window. I have covered enough controversy and heard enough wildly divergent explanations for the world to beware when someone tells me what the world means. To me the world means what it is. What is it? Yes.

It is beautiful.

I have loved the landscape since I can remember, cherishing the particulars of many places that were, too briefly, home. Connecticut's deep woods, saturated by green; northern Michigan's fresh-water wind;

the chaparral smell of California; the aroma of Idaho sagebrush after a
rain; the emerald and amber glow of a Montana fall. It's a love as
demanding as any other; I cannot get enough. I have flown back and
forth across this nation many times in the past ten years, and everywhere I go is so beautiful that I can't bear to leave it. I long to go back
to it. It seems that loving many landscapes is like having too many
women on your mind: emotions diverge into restlessness and longing.
Ah, to see the prairie; to see the Snake River; to see those dry hills of
the Southwest again; to see those silver waterways of the northwest
corner; to see the green and golden hills of the South in autumn; to
see the stone-walled forests of Maine, just once again! To see that face!

Now that restless affection took me away from the most recent of
those places in which I had put down tenuous roots, to explore the
whole landscape of the nation and the people who lived in it. Two
centuries ago this land was raw and dramatically new. One century
past it was still so wild its wildness is said to have formed the whole
psyche of the nation. What is it now? Every landscape, the geographer
John Brinckerhoff Jackson has written, "is a reflection of the society
which first brought it into being and continues to inhabit it." What is
our landscape now, and what does it have to say about us?

So at the age of forty I left home, with pain in my body from
missing my family already, with the exhilaration of flight once again
running through my hollow bones, looking for the way the people of
America treat their land and the way it reflects them. The journey
would bring all of those special places to me under my wings. But
would it make me sane? Songs of passion forever beg for one more
night, in hope that time will stop; if I sleep again in the arms of the
land, will the restlessness end?

Pilots love history. The machines they live by are made of it.
Don't tell me equipment is inhuman: every piece of metal I depend
upon so completely was shaped by hand and mind. Like a kid with
Roman numerals after his name looking at his face in a mirror beside
old photographs, I examine the plane I fly and see heritage in the
curve of the wing, in the slant of the empennage, in the proud nose.
These is tragedy in that past—a lot of it. The wing bears that shape
because someone died showing that it should not be another shape.
There are slots in the tail of my aircraft because others crashed. We
look back in affection for those who were crushed by gravity against

the earth, and for those who, living, lifted us. So it's inevitable that this journey of mine followed a path of history.

In the summer of 1927 Charles Lindbergh came home from Paris, hero of the world, and made a tour of the forty-eight United States to praise the business and machinery of flight and to make aviation real to the people. He flew twenty-two thousand miles. He landed in every state, spent time at eighty-two cities, and flew over about two hundred more. He made solemn speeches in public and, in private, played practical jokes on the men who went with him in a Department of Commerce advance plane. The line he drew seemed to wander aimlessly, going back and forth from city to city and state to state, but it tied the country together, and gave Lindbergh a brand-new view of America.

"That tour let me know my country as no man had ever known it before," Lindbergh wrote years later. "I saw New England's valleys dotted by white villages, the crystal waters of Michigan's great lakes, Arizona's pastel deserts, Georgia's red cotton fields, the cascades and deep forests of the Oregon Northwest. I saw three great mountain ranges running north and south: the Appalachians, the Rockies, the Sierras—walls of a continent, holding rivers, warning off oceans. I saw waves foaming on the rocks of Maine, cloud layers pressing against Washington's Olympics. I saw California's 'Golden Gate,' Louisiana's delta, Florida's wide sand beaches hundreds of miles in length."

Since then millions of people have looked down on America. Pilots of small aircraft have crisscrossed every square inch. Airliners have worn ruts along the jet routes in the air above 18,000 feet. But people aren't looking out the window anymore; small planes zing straight from corporate headquarters to sales meetings while the men and women within play with more novel tools like lap-top computers; and up in the 747 the seasoned traveler pulls the shade down across the dazzling day and snoozes, oblivious to the grand parade of river and mountain and cloud. So following Lindbergh was like walking the Oregon Trail. The route was old but fresh. On the map of the United States, the line of his flight turned and twisted and doubled back. He flew everywhere, saw everything, spent hour after hour in the air.

It was irresistible. I would drift along in this low and bumpy sky like a wheeling bird, down where you can still smell the air, where you can still land where you wish and talk to the people whom chance brings you across the fields.

In sixty years light airplane design hasn't changed much. The plane I flew on Lindbergh's route has an aluminum instead of a fabric wing, but it looks a lot like the *Spirit of St. Louis:* a high wing, a single engine out front, and a tail and elevators in back. My plane is a 1968 Cessna Cardinal, a four-seat airplane that was never very successful for the Cessna company because of substantial design flaws. The model was discontinued in 1978. The plane's unpopularity allowed me to afford it. I bought it in 1977 for $8,900. Fortunately the plane has been modified to eliminate those design flaws, and now does a pretty good job of getting up off the ground and sailing along at about 135 miles an hour, only slightly faster than the *Spirit of St. Louis.* It is propelled by an Avco Lycoming 0-360 engine that develops 180 horsepower at sea level at 2,700 RPM. The engine does not particularly like any of the grades of aviation fuel presently available, which became a problem later, in Peoria, Illinois. Inside the cockpit are various makes and models of radios and other electronics that I traded for, scrounged for, and borrowed for over the years.

I do not have a cute name for my airplane. Sometimes I call it The Cardinal when I am away from it. On flight-plan forms it is C-177, its Cessna model number. On the radio it is officially known by its Federal Aviation Administration registration number: N29601. This is usually shortened after the introductory transmission to Cessna 601. Because this is sometimes stated "Six Oh One," I was once tempted to have someone stencil on the fuselage the phrase "Half Dozen of the Other" but was restrained by the shackles of my literary sensibility.

It is no doubt symbolic of modern times that I think of my plane as a number instead of a name. But the number is what they call us on the radio, and I'm so familiar with it that I can pick "Six Zero One" out of a babble of transmissions from two different radios, just as if a sergeant in a crowded mess hall had called my name. So not only have I failed to tack a humanizing nickname on the machine, but the machine, by making me jump to its number, has half mechanized me.

Six Zero One and I, equipped with these radios and the training that Phil Timm gave me, can fly inside clouds when we need to, but on this trip we avoided them as much as possible. When you're inside a cloud you can't see much of the country. And that's what an airplane so wonderfully allows you to do.

Flying is like standing up in a room full of children and finding out that you're a giant. You think you see everything, and the squabbles down around the floor look small. "My early flying seemed an experience beyond mortality," Lindbergh wrote. "There was the earth spreading out below me, a planet where I had lived but from which I had astonishingly risen." The astonishment never changes. The plane climbs. The pilot stares. The earth is suddenly revealed. In its patient swiftness the plane holds the land away from itself, and the pilot is an artist standing back to view the composition. At last, it seems, you see things as they are.

Look: Those trees that filled the eye from the county road and made a forest in your mind; they are just a five-acre grove that hides three hundred acres of grain. Those mountains that dominate the view from the bedroom window; they are just foothills against an escarpment of rock that rises beyond. This important block of houses that contains your own special lighted window; it is lost in a flood of roofs and white walls, and tiny yards. And look what is in those yards!

Voyager, voyeur. I am a spy. I see the world as it is, and I look down into everyone's backyard. So you think you locked your gate, you grew a hedge of trees, you fenced, you built back up in the canyon? Here I come. I see the great American backyard: junkyards, graveyards, woodyards, stockyards. I see it big, I see it little: cornfields, cattle, rivers, laundry, cities, children, roses.

Since I learned to fly in 1973, I have never known a land until I have flown with it. I don't mean arching high above in a jet. I mean ducking through the passes in its mountains; bounding on the humps of warm air thrown up by its fields; slipping along in the low space between its winter storm clouds and its iron-gray ground; watching nervously for its 2,000-foot radio antennas in its thick summer haze; seeing the way its rivers coil. Flight close to the land gives you both the big view and the detail, and shows you how they connect.

Nothing about this fair and troubled land escapes my view. I stand back a flier's pace from the picture Americans have painted together and see the beauty, whole.

In every airport gas station in the country, hung on the wall among cartoons about air traffic controllers and the signed T-shirts of new flight school graduates, there's a copy of a sonnet. It is history as well as poetry, so pilots, a sentimental lot, are suckers for it. It's a pilot's cliché, a set of words so powerful that they have become too familiar. They express the nature of human flight. They were written by a boy born in 1922, whose name was John Gillespie Magee. He was still almost a child when he wrote them, and still almost a child when flight killed him.

"Daddy," John Gillespie Magee said to his father when he was four years old, "if we ask the Lord not to let me be afraid, and I *am* afraid, what?" When he was a young schoolboy at a boarding school in Great Britain, the nights were no less disturbing. "I can't sleep at night when I'm worried," he wrote home, ". . . so I . . . get up and walk around in the small hours of the morning." The small hours were beautiful: ". . . I don't think words can describe my sensations at standing by an open window watching the moon when 'all this mighty heart is lying still'—when the only sound abroad is the stirring of the wind in the elms on the close. I sometimes wonder why men were made to sleep at night."

The earth was so beautiful it hurt. When he was thirteen a girl and a teacher inspired him to try poetry. What an idea! He flailed away with his pen. He seemed to be in a hurry to live.

> *What agony of Beauty! How the sad*
> *Long look of moonlight touches all this place.*

Another:

> *. . . And I must live, to see the colours start*
> *To life; when all the world is young in May,*
> *And honeysuckle rushes to the heart . . .*

He was self-centered and temperamental; he flashed from depression to arrogance overnight. Religion haunted him, like the loveliness of the earth. He was an agnostic for a while, then returned to his parents' Christianity. He fell in and out of infatuation with girls, but kept his love of natural beauty and his love of the meaning and rhythm of words, the one a net with which he struggled to catch the other. The beauty always escaped.

After boarding school in England he was returned to the United States, his home. He hated it. He thought in his anguish that his talent for words was fading. He wrote a friend, "They won't let me back to England: the poetry is dying in me."

He was eighteen years old. Then something strange happened. Restless for England, he enlisted in the Royal Canadian Air Force, and found in the air, behind the roar of an engine, the joy he had missed. "I had fun this morning rolling through, looping around and circling a puffy little cloud." . . . "Every time I go up I can't bear to come down while I have any gas left."

In 1941, the last year of his life, he returned to Britain. "The first time I met P/O J. Magee I thought to myself what a sissy what have they given me now," wrote his British batman. "I called him Longfellow Magee so did the other members of the staff. Had a nasty habit of throwing his things about, very hard to wake up. . . . As time wore on he changed sir believe me sir he changed." Yet, wrote a family friend, "It was the same John we had known as a boy of twelve, when he might be laughing and crying almost in the same breath . . . the same eagerness, the same excited lilt in his voice. . . ."

In the sky his poetry came back to life. He had trained; he was ready. He was ready for war; he was ready to write. At last the lines were disciplined, the images precise and unaffected. In the sky he had found his power.

In September 1941, when he was just three months past his nineteenth birthday, he wrote his parents, explaining various flying terms—"Prang," "Hunted Bird," "Operational." On the back of that letter were written fourteen lines. "I am enclosing a verse I wrote the other day," he explained in the letter. "It started at 30,000 feet, and was finished soon after I landed. I thought it might interest you."

"Oh, I have slipped the surly bonds of Earth," the sonnet began, "And danced the skies on laughter-silvered wings . . ." The poem was called *High Flight*. Today *High Flight* still comes closest to revealing the secret of life in the sky. All pilots, when they try to explain what they have discovered, reach, half embarrassed, for the familiar words of John Magee:

> . . . *Sunward I've climbed, and joined the tumbling mirth*
> *Of sun-split clouds, —and done a hundred things*
> *You have not dreamed of—wheeled and soared and swung*
> *High in the sunlit silence. . . .*

John Magee flew his Spitfire out of a cloud one day in December, during training, collided with another plane, and made his silence complete. So he died up here where his life had become whole, in the place where he had learned the great and subtle gift of flight: that here you no longer just watch the surpassing beauty of this world; at last you live within it.

Up, up the long, delirious, burning blue
  I've topped the wind-swept heights with easy grace,
Where never lark, or even eagle flew—
  And, while with silent, lifting mind I've trod
  The high untrespassed sanctity of space,
Put out my hand and touched the face of God.

Arrogant, I began to cross America. Precambrian stone lay in ridges below: endless crumpled centuries, wooded. On a field of snow my glory appeared, pink and dazzling, a rainbow at the end of the rainbow. It is always there, with me, ahead of me, barely visible under clouds; a halo below me when I fly above clouds; a patch of brightness on grass or snow or desert when the sky is clear. I have always chased the glory. It has always been elusive. It slides ahead of me, away from me. It mocks me, and entrances me. Now, at the beginning of my trip, there it was: a flit, a flirt, like Tinker Bell. Should I dive into it now and find my peace? Should I chase it around the world?

The glory slipped off the snow and vanished ahead. I followed.

If I ask the land to solve my life, and I am still afraid, what? Arrogant human being with wings of feathers and wax, I clawed my way into heaven itself, looked full at the face of Earth, and put out my pagan hand.

CHAPTER THREE

Near San Diego, California, night rose from the east like a storm, like a sea. It was a tide of deep blue darkness. It flowed west, its edges bruised pink. It filled the valleys first, flooding out shadow and relief, and last, drowning all detail. While day was still mine and the mountains', the valleys had lost all but its reflection. In this rising darkness the valleys became more profound. They plunged to indistinct depths that seemed impossible, like chasms of the sea. Then that sea of night rose and the landscape sank. Slowly the world faded, and became as it had begun.

"And the earth was without form, and void; and darkness was upon the face of the deep." The world was all mystery. As a biologist might put it, I began my journey afloat in the primordial soup.

The traveling had officially begun the day before. But I had looked forward to it for so long that it took time to make it real. I whizzed out of the Pacific Northwest like a squirted seed. It was too much my own backyard. Spokane, Pasco, Seattle, Portland, Eugene, Sacramento. Mount Rainier, Mount St. Helens, the Columbia River, Mount Hood, Mount Shasta. I spent one night with friends, and strode tall across the green world, up among the volcanoes and the clouds. Because this part of the country was so familiar it would shape and color the whole trip, but I rushed to cross it. I ran across the yard of the Northwest, shedding friends and family and memories like warm coats, and at last broke into the clear. The trip wasn't real until it got dark east of San Diego, over the mountainous desert of California.

Flying a single-engine plane in the dark makes a forced landing much more exciting. Some pilots refuse to do it. But my engine is reliable, and I can't resist the night.

When you drive in the dark, the highway blinds you. It binds you to the strip of the road. In the air no headlights shine to close my irises' window; I open to the darkness. Inside, the plane is a dim red-lit room, where instruments tell their stories. Outside, the earth is primitive and strange. Human life passes beneath in swirls of glitter, as remote as galaxies, and in the light of moon and stars the land itself is moving silver shadows and blackness.

In the night and early dawn over the Atlantic, Charles Lindbergh saw visions, "vaguely outlined forms, transparent, moving, riding weightless with me in the plane . . . emanations from the experience of ages, inhabitants of a universe closed to mortal men." They spoke to him, though he could never remember what they said. "In them are solitude and companionship, proximity and distance, a call to death, a guidance to life." In my long solitude across the United States, I, too, had companions. Though they weren't as unearthly, sometimes they, too, spoke.

"Keep your eye on that little jewel," Phil Timm said when I let the heading drift. Every pilot takes his instructor with him through the years, so there was Phil, always gently amused no matter what the error, talking to me about flight. "Well, that was a flat tire." . . . "If you did that your face would be so long you could eat out of a butter churn."

The two young men of the 1927 tour flew with me also: Charles Lindbergh and Donald Keyhoe, the Department of Commerce representative who covered the same route in another plane and had to coordinate the whole thing. Lindbergh, at twenty-five, was an exuberant young man, laughing and pulling practical jokes on his companions, then speaking seriously to endless crowds. "Someday," he would say, "there will be as many airports as railway stations." Keyhoe, a tiny man next to Lindbergh's tower, had big ears and a matter-of-fact outlook. After the tour he had written a book and a magazine article about it. He marked the route with terse observations: "Mount Shasta," he said as we passed the white volcano. "A very beautiful scene." Keyhoe wore a small, vain mustache that Lindbergh plotted against, and a hat that Lindbergh tried to destroy.

Sometimes I heard the voice of the Charles Lindbergh of later years, no longer safe in his sanctuary in the air, looking at the land change beneath him and, restlessly, fiercely, building and rebuilding his concern for human progress out of calamity to try to make a philosophy large enough to fit the battered globe. When we flew across a landscape torn by military operations, sliced by roads, or stained by smoke, I'd hear him. "Few men have seen with their own eyes, as I have in the past fifty years, how serious is the breakdown of American's land surface," he said. He was always formal, reading from his books. "I have seen fencing pushing westward, enclosing once open land. I have seen bird and animal life disappear. I have seen towns and cities spring up where there were none before. Forest land converted into agriculture, farm land in turn become suburban subdivisions, mountains slashed through with power lines and superhighways, rivers and lakes fouled by pollution, the skies over even small towns hazed by smog— all evidence of human thoughtlessness about their environment."

Behind his voice, in the background, was the steady eloquence of John Brinckerhoff Jackson, a quiet man, famous only among geographers. I had met him through his many essays on the American landscape. John Jackson looked down with endless affection on the same marks made by human beings on the land, and saw them differently: "I find these things interesting, because people like ourselves have produced them, and we ought to be able to understand them."

An instructor, a tour guide, a famous aviator, a geographer. Such were my ghostly companions. In the way you learn to care for the faces in dreams, they became the friends this lonely journey did not otherwise allow.

They were joined by a racy woman I called Macho Irene. She whispered in my ear every time I opened a chart. "MICHL!" she said.

Many of the charts I carried didn't mention the land at all. Does that have anything to say about how modern Americans think of their home? Lindbergh used 50-cent Rand McNally road maps, and followed rivers, railroads, and valleys. The routes most pilots travel today are more abstract. They are instrument airways defined by radio waves and drawn in blue ink on white charts. On these charts the land itself is ignored. Once in a while a faint stain indicates Lake Michigan, perhaps, or the Atlantic Ocean. Other than that, the land looks just as it did that first night of my journey—invisible. You are told how high you have to fly to miss all the rocks and radio towers, and that's enough.

I also carried a set of charts designed for the few private pilots left in this corporate air. These are called Sectional Charts. They are magnificent; you can tell by the shapes of the mountains and the curve of the streams where you are. But I was often guided by the blue lines of the instrument routes, and by Macho Irene.

Irene introduced herself into my world of imaginary companions some time ago on the airway northwest out of Waco, Texas. She works for the Federal Aviation Administration, at an office called a FIFO: Flight Inspection Field Office. There are several Federal Aviation Administration FIFOs around the country. FIFOs are responsible for drawing the instrument routes. There are dozens of places on any route that can be marked electronically. They're called Intersections. Like road intersections on the ground, these invisible electronic mileposts have nicknames. FIFO comes up with the names. I think of Irene as a slender young specialist who reads *Garfield* and Immanuel Kant on the side. She has a soft Texas drawl. She's pretty, and tough as a longhorn heifer. She eats chili for breakfast. Her boss knows what she's doing, but he doesn't dare cross her.

Most of the time, Irene is serious and bureaucratic. She is diligent. The names have to be five letters long, so she calls the intersection at Carmel, California, CARME. Saugus becomes SAUGE. All is appropriate.

But sometimes Irene works late. Nobody else is in the office. Irene smiles and scribbles, and some weeks later a revised chart comes out, and an intersection near a winery is called GRAPE; a line of intersections on an airway near Charleston, West Virginia, becomes SALTY SWIFT BITES. Eastbound from Chicago you cross CUBBS, turn right over the lake and go over BAITE and MUSKY. She signed her own name on Airway Victor 15 between Waco and the navigation station called Scurry Vortac. You cross MACHO nineteen miles out of Waco, and IRENE nine miles later. She loves it. She sits there, deskbound, thinking of some pompous 747 captain on his way west to Knoxville reading back a clearance: "Roger, will report MUMMI."

That first night in the dark, I flew southeast in the red cocoon of the cockpit above scattered lights of farms. The day before I had flown near one of the longest stretches of Interstate 5 where drivers doze on endless straightaways between silent towns. The intersection there was called BORED.

Not I. Night is full of mystery. The planet is unformed. Anything can happen. Sometimes it does.

➤ There is only one place now in the continental United States over which you can fly high on a clear night and not be surrounded by electric light: the vast collection of wilderness areas between Boise, Idaho, and Missoula, Montana. I have many times cast away the friendly illumination of the Snake River Valley and ridden north out into that darkness, knowing of the unforgiving teeth of the land below, and seeing—or hearing about—strange lights.

Once, waiting anxiously for the moon to rise and give me at least a chance of making a forced landing if the engine quit, I looked and looked in vain for a glow in the east that would tell of its arrival, then looked away for what seemed like ten seconds. When I looked up the whole moon was right *there!*, sudden as an explosion, close as the spotlight of the law. Another night the wilderness was smothered in a haze of smoke, with a few stars shining faintly red above. A crescent line of fire crackled through the invisible woods. It looked like a tear in the fabric of the earth, revealing hell.

One night, when I was westbound for McCall, Idaho, the strangeness was out there in someone else's air. For me it was a routine flight—which is to say it was wonderful and dramatic, but not unusual. Flying west from Bozeman, Montana, I crossed Salmon, Idaho, shortly after sunset and watched the lights of the small town drift slowly back and disappear behind the black shoulder of a mountain. I checked the lights, listened more critically to the engine, and set out on an hour of darkness. The sun had gone down in the haze of smoke from thousands of slash fires burning in the Rockies, leaving the western rim of the world glowing red. Jet contrails streamed upward in the last light like dying solar flares. Against that sky the land beneath was formless.

I was at 12,500 feet, and above all turmoil, of either air or stone. I had no sense of movement, no landmarks to count: Space and time, in this air tonight, were the same.

The moon was half full. As the sky grew darker it began to illuminate the earth, but it could not penetrate the wilderness. Occasionally, looking down, I watched the slow passage of a bluff of stone as it slid past beneath me like a great fish sounding—barnacled, tarnished, and old. Once the mass below was briefly seamed by a river, which, reflecting the moon for a second, shone, then vanished. A mountain lake in a forest blinked a last glance at the fading sky, then slept, leaving the image of a pale eye and black lashes.

The only company was, as usual, the radio. Other pilots, seldom identified by place, talked to Salt Lake City Air Traffic Control Center. The communications were brusque:

"Five Nine Yankee, level at eleven."

"Eight Eight Four Two Uniform, descend and maintain two five thousand."

"Roger. Four Two U."

The sound of my engine, muffled by earplugs, rumbled its steady comfort behind the sound of this aerial routine: the mail chugging west, an airliner headed for Chicago, a tired writer heading for a place he briefly called home.

There was an interruption:

"Salt Lake, this is Seven Eight Mike. Request."

"Roger, Seven Eight Mike. Go ahead."

The voice was laconic.

"Ah, Salt Lake, do you have any traffic in our area?"

"Seven Eight Mike, negative traffic," Center said.

The voice was somewhere between Boise and Elko, flying through a void almost as dark as mine. He acknowledged. There was silence for several seconds. Then 78M came back on the air, almost conversational, with a layer of controlled tension in the voice.

"Maybe I'd better explain," he said. But he was not a radio rambler; this was a professional pilot with something to say. "The reason I asked about traffic was that we saw something out here."

"Roger," Center said, noncommittal. There was another pause. How many other pilots flying in this night so separated from the earth were listening? The airliner, the mail plane, maybe fifteen others: a widespread collection of small rooms populated by men and women absorbed in watching red-lighted instruments tell their humming tale of distance vanquished, momentarily drawn to listen to another kind of story. No one interrupted. I started taking notes on my flight-plan form. Seven Eight Mike went on.

"We saw something that looked like it had its landing lights on. It also had a red light that was not blinking. It was about two thousand feet below us. The aircraft, if it was an aircraft, then turned and went away from us at a very high rate of speed."

The transmission ended. The night was again silent. Center said, "Roger."

Seven Eight Mike spoke again:

"When I say a very high rate of speed, I mean an extremely high rate of speed. The aircraft, if it was an aircraft, traversed a very great distance in very short order."

Center said something about making a report and gave 78M a phone number in Oregon to call when he landed. Then, before he accepted a clearance to change and go to another altitude, 78M, maybe defending himself before the silent audience of other pilots he knew were on the frequency, made one more reference to the unexplainable something he had seen:

"There were two other persons in this aircraft who saw the same thing."

That was all. Routine folded in again, like flesh healing a scratch. The airliner going to Chicago climbed to heights unimaginable to me, the mail plane landed in Boise, and very slowly I flew west. The pale green lights of farms appeared over the black edge of the wilderness, and I began to descend.

I said good night to Center, reduced power, and listened to the increased wind of my descent wash over the aluminum skin of the plane. I flipped a switch, and my landing lights built a tunnel in the darkness and let me escape from the night.

I have since felt more like the alien in the swift ship than the American pilot. On the first night of my journey, I looked down into the formless landscape, and saw the place as a stranger. My companions had deserted me. I was utterly alone, in spite of the abstract presence of other pilots talking quietly on the radio over Palm Springs or Las Vegas or the border of Mexico. They spoke another language. "Roger, heading 050, vector Billings," I was alone, a visitor from another galaxy, looking down in wonder with my memories of a home made of red iron plains or steaming liquid, where my people worshiped ice. Down there curious yellow lights glimmered beside some living substance that twisted and glittered up out of a black haze of dangerous breath. I was alone, a visitor from heaven, and down in those canyons were the inhabitants of the planet I was coming to visit, the planet to which I fell from orbit. I tumbled down across its ridges and looked down, far down, to the mystery of their precarious lives.

"Good evening," said a young man from the Child Evangelical Fellowship, handing out a brochure. "How are you this evening?"

"Fine," I said, and took a brochure. He smiled.

Thus I made contact with the natives.

I had ridden in from the west. It was evening. I was tired and elated. To the east the lights of San Diego dwindled away into the desert of California's southeast corner. I rode down out of the radiance through darkness and solitude past PILLO Intersection into a strangely gaudy airport, which was festooned with neon. The unexpected blaze of color turned out to be the Sea Dragon ride at the California Mid-

Winter Fair, across the street from the airport at El Centro, California. I stepped out of the plane into a warm breeze that smelled of alfalfa and manure. Ha! I was pleased. What could be more American than a state fair? 4-H lambs, country bands, rodeo. Night had brought me a bauble, a catalog of the present.

"There's bike racing over there tonight if you're into that," said the woman at the airport.

"What?" I said. "No rodeo?"

She laughed. Bitterly, I thought.

"We had horse racing here one year," she said. "They hated it."

I took my first risk of the journey: I crossed Highway 86 on foot. I survived. I went into the fair.

Just inside the gate the Trinidad Calypso Steele Drum Band was playing warm-weather music. Across the walkway a hypnotist drew more spectators than the band. He had persuaded a pretty woman that her nose was made of rubber. She stretched it a foot. Inside the arts-and-crafts building were displays of winning photographs and landscape paintings. They were of lighthouses, surf, meadows. Not much desert. Out on the midway the Sea Dragon, a huge neon Viking ship, swung back and forth near the bumper cars. It was a giant, hurtling pendulum. People screamed. At the Imperial County Republican Party booth the politicians were already packing up to go home. "There are about twelve thousand Republicans in the county," said the man there, "and about nineteen thousand Democrats. But it goes Republican." A woman spoke up:

"We have a lot of minorities here—"

The man interrupted.

"Who don't vote."

I circulated among the display buildings.

The young man from the Child Evangelical Fellowship was there again. I had seen him before, but he didn't remember. "How are you this evening?"

"Okay," I said, and took another brochure. He smiled.

America: chickens played tic-tac-toe in a cage. A highway patrol accident demonstration machine crashed again and again. I passed up the opportunity to see Smidget, the World's Smallest Horse. I had a bowl of stew at a booth run by a couple from Montrose, Colorado, then sat on a bench with almost no one else to listen to Lloyd Mabrey sing ballads from a stage. Mabrey turned out to be from Parachute, Colorado. Imperial Seed and Feed had planted an entire garden inside the Preble Building, near a big sign that read "California Agriculture: Growing Technology." That display included photos of helicopters spraying chemicals, of a tractor the size of a tank, of concrete irrigation canals, and of farm land seen from a satellite. "Farming from Space," the sign said. The historical museum showed a photograph of the first power pole, put up in 1938. There was a diagram of the way water made its way from Hoover Dam through the Colorado River, through Davis Dam, Parker Dam, Imperial Dam, and the All-American Canal. Outside, a fountain gushed murky water beneath a wooden drill-rig derrick. All night the sound of the dirt bikes roared around inside the metal buildings as if the machines were racing on the roof.

Attracted by live things, I hung around a large aquarium that contained three dignified carp. They wore silver scales and a supercilious look. They were weed eaters. They could afford to condescend: They cost $3.75 each, wholesale, which is more than the most elegant trout; and they were bred to eat, not fry.

Since 1971 irrigation canals had been clogging up with a weed called hydrilla, an escapee from home aquariums that loved a tepid, slow flow. The irrigators had tried scraping the stuff out, poisoning it, burning it, but the hydrilla proliferated like California crabgrass. Finally the Imperial Irrigation District, the largest single employer in El Centro, hired on almost 60,000 of these triploid grass carp, which are genetically sterilized fish interested in nothing but the consumption of hydrilla. So far, the program looked like a success. The fish superciliously gobbled hydrilla. They grew corpulent, like butlers. The hydrilla disappeared. Newspaper editors headlined stories "Nothing to Carp About."

The booth was one of the most popular at the fair. By the time I got to the fish display, Larry Hulsey, an irrigation district supervisor there to explain the carp, was already tired of the questions. Someone asked one more time if they were catfish. He looked at him seriously.

"Yeah," he said. "We cut off the whiskers."

Hulsey liked the haughty, metallic creatures in his tank. Even though they were alive, they fit the culture:

"They're a real eating machine," he said.

"Good evening," said the child evangelist. "How are you this evening?"

"Good night," I said. He smiled. The dirt bikes howled in the rafters.

I went home to The Cardinal. People who looked inside the plane were often amused. "Hey!" they said. "It's a hippie-wagon airplane!"

For ten years I have lived in the plane whenever I travel, so the process of taking the motorcycle out, putting up the curtains Debbie made me, and unrolling the foam pad and sleeping bag made a familiar, friendly routine. The plane is not large: I slept where the back seat and baggage compartment would be, which gave me a little more room than a two-man pup tent. I shared this space with a cooler, two file boxes full of useful information about the places ahead, my backpack, a briefcase of charts and instrument-approach books, and another briefcase that contained notebooks, books, and my Radio Shack laptop computer—a low-power, rudimentary piece of equipment almost as obsolescent as the plane itself, but just as useful. My money went into fuel, which averaged $1.85 a gallon, so I ate cereal and milk from the cooler for breakfast and dinner, and lunch somewhere where they gave you a stainless-steel tray and tanks of food for $3.95.

It was close to midnight when I climbed into the plane and shut the door. I sat there in the bag with my back against the front seat, typing my journal into the computer. The lights of the Sea Dragon rose and fell outside the window. I read a chapter of *The Lord of the Rings* aloud into my tape recorder to send to my kids. The desert wind shook the little room, and the jets from El Centro Air Station rumbled in the distance. America seemed to hum with the sound of engines. I thought, as I dozed off, That's the American Song.

The journey had begun. So much for preconceptions. No 4-H lambs. No rodeo. It had begun with a blaze of lights, a roar of machines, a cold eye from a mechanical fish, and a fistful of religious brochures. America.

CHAPTER FOUR

Morning blew into El Centro the color of steel, sharpened to an edge of storm. The earth took shape. It was broad and dry. Mountains lay on the horizon, showing their ribs. I took off. I searched the desert for the marks of heathens.

I flew rectangular patterns across scarred landscape. Back and forth I turned, leveled off, turned again. Thermals and wind kicked at the plane. A funnel of dust whirled across the sand below: a dust devil. If I flew through it, I would be thrashed. My road was rough enough already; another pilot on the radio canceled a charter flight: "It would not be a very pleasant trip for the lady," the voice said. "She'd wind up with her head in a bag."

I turned again, back parallel to the last run, and went thumping across the dry land. Where was it?

I flew beyond history. Somewhere out there were designs upon the landscape left by people who were gone long before Europeans brought the force of written order to the past. They danced here and left their dead here, and honored their spirits here, and chased their glory here, and left behind only marks on the earth. I had come to look for the marks of the mysterious past. But where were they?

I was in the Basin and Range Province. Province? That was how I chose to slice up the country in order to comprehend it. There are other ways to divide the United States and conquer its immensity. Most people cut it into fifty-two pieces, counting states, the District of Columbia, and Puerto Rico. You could count four: the continental states, Alaska, Hawaii, and Puerto Rico. A few years ago Joel Garreau, a *Washington Post* editor, looked at the North American continent and persuasively described nine nations: Quebec, New England, the Foundry,

Dixie, the Islands, MexAmerica, the Breadbasket, Ecotopia, and the Empty Quarter. But I was interested in the land and how Americans live with it, and the land divides itself up naturally into sections geologists call provinces.

There are forty provinces in North America. Twenty-four of them are all or part in the continental United States. These group themselves in seven major divisions: the Atlantic Plain, the Appalachian Provinces, the Interior Plains, the Interior Highlands, the Rocky Mountain System, the Intermontane Provinces, and the Pacific Mountain System. All would pass under Six Zero One and me, sooner or later.

In my haste to get out of the Pacific Northwest I had crossed several provinces. Already these sections, which seemed arbitrary in a text, made sense. The tilted blocks of the Northern Rockies were completely different from the incredible jumble of stone in the province made up of the Idaho Batholith and its granite neighbors; all they had in common was elevation and snow. The Columbia-Snake Plateaus were vast, dry, and empty, blackened by flows of lava and scoured, in the north, by prehistoric floods that came booming out of the east and created a place now called the Scablands. All along the Cascades-Sierra Nevada Province, which I had flown beside for a whole day, volcanoes stood like sentinels of the kingdom of stone, over whose shoulders I looked and saw armies. The Pacific Border Province was the land of the Willamette River, the Sacramento River, and the San Andreas Fault, where the country shaded down from green to brown. In the night I had slipped east from San Diego over the northernmost granite ridge of the Lower California Province, into the least populated province, Basin and Range.

The Basin and Range Province is a huge expanse, 300,000 square miles of dry salt, desert basins, and parallel mountain ranges. From El Paso, Texas, to Phoenix, Arizona, to Salt Lake City, Utah, to Klamath Falls, Oregon, to Palmdale, California, flying across the Basin and Range Province is like sailing over a windless sea that is stirred by a distant storm: long swells of rock rise from long smooth alluvial fans of gravel out of calm valleys where old lakes lie as if petrified, turned to salt. From the ground the view is different. The valleys lie endless and shimmering with heat. The mountains, wrote Nevadan David W. Toll, "are like sleeping women, sprawled languorously across every horizon."

These women are bony. The heat has parched them. Not much flesh on these ladies.

The province is almost all desert, an empire of sagebrush and mesquite. You see mirages there, or you see marks people put on the ground centuries ago.

And marks laid down last week. It was silent below me on the desert as I circled, looking for old patterns. But like the ceiling at the fair, the desert roared with the echoes of machines.

People who think the desert is pristine have not seen it from the air. American deserts, from Washington's Scablands to the timeless, time-bound landscape of New Mexico, look like pieces of paper that have been in the company of a pencil, a ruler, and my eight-year-old son for half an hour. Straight lines of dirt roads crisscross and lie parallel to one another. They look as if they were made by feuding neighbors who refuse to follow one another's tracks. Among them are curlicues and circles, holes, converging trails dug by cattle gathering from all points to a well, and the Cat scrapes made by miners' bulldozers. Deserts have recently been marked by new patterns drawn by the random romping wheels of three- and four-wheel all-terrain vehicles, pickups, and dune buggies. These tracks, which cover almost every square inch of land where they have been introduced, go around in figure eights and circles. The drivers are determined to chase, but have no glory.

West of me as I paced my rectangular search pattern through today's tumultuous sky was a small town called Glamis, which lies south of a pit made by a gold mine. During weekdays this town has a population of nine people, but on long weekends a flood of pickup trucks carrying all-terrain machines pours over the mountains from the cities to the west. The population of the neighborhood swells to around 100,000, and the song of 10,000 engines rises to the sky.

From the air the dunes that take the brunt of the all-terrain attack were a pale brown haze twenty miles away. In this light, there was no horizon. It dissolved. The day threatened: to the west a blue-gray band dropped right down into the bland horizon. It was raining in San Diego. During my search pattern I crossed a big canal, but it was dry. It looked as if it would never be wet again. Near it was a big chunk of land once cleared, now going back to desert, then a second canal made of concrete, full and green; it needed carp.

Ray Wilcox had showed me photographs and had given me directions. The directions were good, but it was still difficult to find his treasure. I had met Wilcox in El Centro. He was a big man, with a beard and a dry way of talking that fit the climate. He cared about the landscape. To him the off-road vehicles were the tools of vandals. They were like alien creatures introduced into an ecosystem in which they had no predators. They were taking over his desert and ruining its treasure. He was not thinking about gold, or wildlife. The swarm of machines was steadily erasing what to him was the desert's most precious thing: the curious patterns and shapes drawn on the land by early Americans.

Wilcox was the architectural services assistant for the Imperial Valley College Museum. The museum has cataloged 327 marks made on the earth by aboriginals. The marks are called geoglyphs. They're stick figures, or spirals, arrows, snakes, rocks lined up in ranks, or curious squiggles without any regular pattern. They are probably ceremonial dance patterns, spirit guardians, power symbols, and figures out of myths of the creation. They were messages to God.

The signs are made possible by the nature of this landscape. The desert here is paved by a long process that is not clearly understood: a hard-packed layer of stones covers a few inches of soft, light brown loam, making a pavement that sheds water like tarmac but is easily broken, like skin. "In '76," Wilcox said, "one storm raised the level of the Salton Sea by five feet. There was millions of dollars of damage to the agricultural lands. But the desert . . ." He paused. "It didn't even bother it."

The surface of this pavement is stained red-brown by desert varnish, a deposit of iron and manganese that was laid on the stone in wetter centuries. The pavement and the varnish are disturbed more by one rubber tire than by a storm. The single pass of a vehicle rubs off the varnish, cracks the shell of pebbles, and makes a track. No one knows how long it takes for the scar to become repaved: all the vehicle tracks ever made here are still here. So are the patterns cut into the desert by people hundreds of years ago with feet or sticks. The signs remain, vivid light weals in the red stone of the pavement.

These shapes were discovered by plane when an Army Air Corps pilot flew over huge stick figures near Blythe, California, in 1927; they are best seen by plane today.

Or so Wilcox said. I flew my search pattern for a full half hour, and still didn't see any. But there were other marks. Among the aimless wanderings of the three-wheelers was another layer of the past: many of the wide double tracks were made by tanks, and the holes were dug by explosive shells.

"Patton!" As I searched I could hear Wilcox jabbing his finger at a photo of a geoglyph with a splash of craters nearby. "His training group was here from '42 to '44. People think he came here to train tankers, but his main purpose was to find out what the water consumption of a human being was in desert conditions."

Patton saw this place first from the air, flying his little Stinson Voyager here in April of '42. He liked it. "There were no civilians whatever in it to raise objections to training or get in the way of practice with live ammunition," a biographer wrote, "the only living things were coyotes and rattlesnakes. The terrain included many concealed approaches and abounded in surmountable and insurmountable obstacles . . . In summer the temperature rose to 120 degrees; there was absolutely no water."

Perfect. This was Patton's kind of country.

The men of the I Armored Corps were allowed one canteen of water a day. They had to run a mile in ten minutes every twenty-four hours. They had to be able to march eight miles in two hours. "In two and a half years here," Wilcox said, "he lost twenty-seven people."

I carried a gallon of water in the plane. It was not enough. If I had been forced down, I'd have been dust in a day. Wilcox carried two canteens and five gallons of water in his truck when he went out. He wanted to live through the weekend. I looked down at the tracks of suffering. Those men marching, those men locked in tanks, were still here, trapped by the landscape, trapped in each endless hour of that life. They cursed. They sweated. Outside it was 120 degrees; inside the tanks it was 150 degrees. They sipped hot water, and blew holes in the land.

It was a tortured landscape. Car tracks, Cat tracks, trails, Patton's craters, pockmarks, a scattering of holes of the bullets fired by military pilots practicing strafing. Every path was double, and every yard of ground had its path or its crater.

Then, at last, there were the geoglyphs.

It was like suddenly learning how to notice a watermark in paper. They emerged like a secret message hidden among squiggles. How could I have missed them? They were all over the place. They looked like short trails, each leading a few yards from one beaten place on the pavement to another. On desert pavement I had been flying across for thirty minutes, seeing nothing, geoglyphs popped out everywhere, now that I could recognize them. There was a square one; there was one that looked like a long path with bumps on it; there was a spiral.

"They would take this desert pavement," Wilcox had said, "and move the surface rock to the side, exposing the silt and sand underneath. Most of the glyphs were probably used for some kind of dance ceremony, so they're well compacted. Plants will not grow on them."

Among the mechanical scrapes of Caterpillar tractor and all-terrain vehicle and tank, none of these old marks was dramatic. There was no huge sketch of a creature or a man. But all were foreign to the machine-made straight lines and perfect curves. The geoglyphs were sinuous. They were like something knitted by hand. They had the suppleness of human bodies, of the tracks made by urgent feet.

The desert was like a magnetic tape, its iron oxides arranged into a recording. I flew across and played it back, hearing the stories of centuries of people on the land. Roar! The land was assaulted by a subhuman creature of three wheels with beer breath and a 5,000 RPM voice. Boom! One layer down in the record, hundreds of sweaty, thirsty young men pounded the desert in practice for the greatest war that mankind would ever know. Over there on the slope was the roar of their machines, the wail and crash of their weapons. Here was the momentary quiet of a campsite; I could still see the rectangular patches where the tents stood.

The ghosts of this desert overlapped: the toys, the tanks, the explosions; young men dashing around on knobbed tires and laughing; young men listening to the shallow slosh in the bottom of the day's canteen, wondering what would become of them. But back of them the desert played a quieter song, and shapes of somber men and women danced up tiny spirals of dust along the pale tracks they drew on the stony pavement as they sang, as they prayed, as they looked toward the sky and the mysterious future.

CHAPTER FIVE

Come ride! Come ride! Come ride with me to freedom! In the early morning at the southeast edge of the state of California, I found a horse, drawn large in the pavement. Next to it a thread ran across the stones: a trail. Once the trail was a thoroughfare for people crossing the unbounded desert. Now it was used mostly in the dark, with stealth.

The first thing I saw was the horse's head. It was prominent and bright. It lay on dark bench beside the bump at the corner of California that is called Pilot Knob. The horse was only a dent in the red-brown pavement, until I looked carefully. I hardly recognized it from the top, then I turned, and suddenly it had a shape and a great long sweeping tail that dissolved away in the stone wind. Wilcox had told me how to find it. He thought the horse was probably four hundred years old, made about the time the Spanish came to present the people who lived here with a steed no less magic than the airplane. The horse is unique among geoglyphs. Almost all the other geoglyphs are symbolic: stick figures, diagrams. This one is representational, a shape made with awe.

I circled the horse. The artist had to imagine looking down on his work. What vision is involved in making so strong a picture that cannot be seen by one's own eye? Did the artist cut the pavement for an hour or days, then climb the cliffs of Pilot Knob to get a distant look, the way I stand back in the plane to look at the picture of America? It would have been a crabbed, sweaty perspective; but this is an undistorted horse. A mystical creature, to demand such struggle, such devotion.

Was the horse the trail's guardian, its spirit, its symbol of freedom? Who still rode him into a new life? The trail used to go down the hill into the valley of the Colorado. Now it goes a couple of hundred yards to the concrete walls and the thick green water of the All-American Canal. There it crosses, but only in its season. Its season is night.

At night the children of the village of Algodones sell inner tubes and plastic garbage bags to an endless stream of northbound travelers who cross the barrier, swim the canal, and hike that old trail past the horse and into the United States while the kids haul the inner tubes back for the next customers. The old trail past the horse is now one-way. Everyone walks it north; if they return it is through Yuma in a barred bus.

I circled the horse, and widened the circle, and climbed. In Algodones fires glimmered and smoked in the cool of the morning. The storm that hung over the desert the day before had swept past far above, and the sky today was blue, and windy. I saw no children in the streets, and no swimmers.

Instead I saw red-striped white wings. There, circling like a hawk in the thermal uplift, was a United States Border Patrol Piper Super Cub.

These were not the wings of freedom. The little plane was a predator. It was hunting wetbacks. It was flown by an agent whose real name is Colonel R. Child, and whose skill lies in finding and following an entirely different kind of mark on the land: footprints.

I found out about this because I followed Colonel Child back to Yuma. I found him in a hangar at the edge of the Yuma airport, where he was taking off his gun. This made me think of him flying the little plane just above the tops of the mesquite trees, blazing away out the window at foreign trespassers on horseback. Western Romance!

I was wrong. He was a tall man in his thirties, with a neat policeman's mustache but an unofficial air. In the four years he had been flying for the Border Patrol, he had never even drawn his gun, and he had never been shot at, as far as he could tell.

"I'll never know," he said, "until I bring back a bullet hole."

The border Child patrols is a place of heat, of the roar of fighters practicing, and of a long straight dusty road, where seismic intrusion devices like those once used by the U.S. Government to detect Viet Cong on the Ho Chi Minh trail record the earthquake of footprints. Every night a truck passes, pulling a rake that smooths the dust. In the morning Colonel Child flies two hundred feet above the road, looking for fresh marks.

"Certain roads I'll cut every morning," Child said. "The biggest way I know a track is that I was there yesterday, and it wasn't there."

Child is thirty-five; he has been in the border patrol for ten and a half years. He flies a thousand hours a year, up and down the border out of Yuma. He has permission to fly down in the military Restricted Area 2301W, along the border between Arizona and Sonora, below two hundred feet. He has been assured that he won't be blown out of the air; but once: "I split two F-18s." Startling, but better than the other way around.

The United States has only two borders, north and south. In the northern Rockies the line between the United States and Canada is a thin line cut through trees, and you can't see it until you're perfectly aligned. You can't find it, you can't find it; and you think it must have passed unseen. Then suddenly there it is—SNICK!—a cut that opens in the landscape like a line drawn with a scalpel—and SNICK!—it disappears again, and all division between the nations is sutured tight once more.

To the south it is different. South of El Centro, at the twin towns of Calexico and Mexicali, the border looks like a fence across a stream of leaves. The little houses and tiny farm fields of Mexico are piled up in drifts against the chain link. When you pass on a cold morning, the California side is bright and clean, with its vast rectangular grid of huge industrial farm fields, and its pure air preserved by the use of electricity generated elsewhere for heating and cooking; Mexicali lies under a pall of blue smoke, as if the leaves smoldered.

Farther east, from the All-American Canal to El Paso, the border is two roads and a fence. You can see it from fifty miles. It's a livid scar across the subtle colors of desert. It is surgery done with a pocket knife. A car kicks dust along the miles, rubbing the sore. Only east of the lonely town of Hermanas, New Mexico, does the border turn to a single track, which wavers; a string stretched between stakes that has gone slack. But there the landscape itself is the most deadly policeman of all.

Child patrols 27,150 square miles, and does not cover the ground where the border wavers. Things are more formal in his direction. Each day deals new cards. Each evening the trucks clear the table of the action of ' ie day before. Each night groups of solitary travelers cross the border with their belongings in garbage bags, as hard and thirsty as Patton's troopers, taking the cards they are dealt and those they have carried. Then in the morning Child picks up his hand of visibility and weather, and makes his choices of direction, and gets in his Super Cub, which is nicknamed "La Mosca." Now it stops being a game. Now he is The Fly, a little, buzzing, pestering creature, looking for footprints on the virgin dust.

I once watched a biologist seated on the hood of a pickup truck spot part of a bobcat track at thirty feet and twenty miles an hour. This must be like that: There's a faint change in the pattern of shade, a hint of dimples, the most tender interruption of the long flow of dust made by the rake. Like the missile that seeks heat, Child is locked in. He can land the little airplane in about a hundred yards, so sometimes he lands to examine the prints. Usually he just turns in the air and follows the steps through the brush. The quarry, the alien, hides beneath the mesquite or the creosote bush shrubs, but there is no place for a man to burrow from this fly.

Like many whose work contains hazard and adventure, Child was without bombast. It struck him as curious that sometimes, out there in the terrible heat of Restricted Area 2301W, people doomed to die of thirst would still run when he circled overhead and called in the truck or the helicopter that would bring water and life—and deportation.

"If we beheaded them or castrated them," he said, "that would be a reason to run. We just give them a ride back. Risking your life doesn't seem like an equitable deal." But the risk is taken every night, and many pay the inequitable price. The human flood pouring north is dried out by Patton's heat. Sometimes the tracks Child follows leads him to a tragedy.

"We keep finding dead bodies," he said. "Once two guys came across, and one came in and said, 'My buddy's down south.' We found him and put him in the back of a truck and brought him back. The guy said, 'Hey, this isn't the guy.' There are a lot of people going down."

Child watches the desert from the sky all day. He sees the geoglyphs. He sees the pale shadows of Patton's camps. In the restricted areas that belong to the armed forces he sees huge blond blossoms of bared soil on the desert floor where tons of TNT have been detonated to simulate nuclear war. But like Wilcox he is single-minded: The desert landscape contains just one glory—the spoor of humankind.

"It's a real expensive game of hide-and-seek, and it's got some funny rules, so there's little job satisfaction in that sense. But the job is never boring. It is not very often I can't find something to chase somewhere. It doesn't have anything to do with what's right or wrong about our immigration policy, but I find that tracking footsteps is very exciting."

➤ It was odd to think that Colonel R. Child, in his two-seat, eighty-mile-per-hour airplane, armed with his unused revolver, was the first line of defense at the border of the United States. Modern warfare gets stranger and stranger. But the twentieth-century equivalent of the Maginot Line was scattered all over the country. I had to avoid it every day. Through the whole journey one of the most dominant forces in the air and on the landscape was the American military presence: training jets, vast armament depots, bases, and restricted areas. It was impossible to follow Lindbergh's precise route without being accidentally shot down or arrested.

Out of Yuma, Lindbergh flew east along the border, but that way was blocked by the United States Marine Corps. This spacious desert air was fenced off north and south by lines drawn on my chart and shaded in blue or maroon: Restricted Area 2307. Restricted Area 2308A. Restricted Area 2301W. Restricted Area 2301E. Restricted Area 2304. Restricted Area 2305. Sells 1 Military Operations Area. Sells Low Military Operations Area. I had to follow a narrow corridor along Interstate 8 or be in mortal danger.

Five hundred thousand square miles of the United States airspace are occupied by the armed forces—7 percent of the country. These are bombing ranges and fighter training grounds, mortar ranges and missile ranges, jeep proving grounds, tank proving grounds, and grounds to prove the mettle of men. Patton still tramps across the land.

The West gets much of it. The armed forces use 40 percent of Nevada's sky, for instance. For the Basin and Range Province by itself the percentage would probably be higher. The armed forces like the desert for the same reasons Patton did: it's harsh, tough, empty. To me, worry about being clobbered by an F-16 has always been as much a part of that landscape as those long, bony, languorous mountains.

Sometimes, to avoid a four-hundred-mile detour, I have to get permission to go through a military operations area. Inside those shaded lines I don't spend much time looking at the ground. The sky demands attention. Most of the time you see nothing, but if you did you wouldn't have much time to get out of the way. I have shared airspace with dogfighting F-4s and low-level B-52s. What do you say when you meet a B-52 over southern Idaho? After you, sir.

The route from my home to my parents' home in California lies right over an array of military operations areas near Reno. The country there looks very much like the land around Yuma, and the use is the same. The Dixie Valley and its neighboring northern Nevada basins

are, like the southern desert, the playgrounds of fighters. Around
Reno, Navy pilots from Fallon Naval Air Station fight each other and
shoot at the ground with their F-4s and F-18s. Restricted Areas 4813,
4816N, 4816S, 4810, 4812, 4804, and the Gabbs North and South
Military Operations areas cover the country just as these other restricted areas here closed off the land near the Mexican border to my
journeys. When I cross the country west of Fallon I have to communi-
cate seriously with Fallon Desert Control, and listen to groups of
fighters called things like "Arrow Zero One" report positions that
sound uncomfortably similar to mine.

These places are not entirely deserted, but they will be. When
Lindbergh flew into Reno on September 19, 1927, none of these
restricted areas was in place, but there were people living in the Dixie
Valley, south of the Humboldt Salt Marsh and between the Clan
Alpine Range and the Stillwater Range. Now, in the name of aviation
and war, they are being run off. The human landscape there is scarred
by disintegration. The country is losing its people: Those few who once
chose to make their homes there for the space and the solitude are
slowly selling their land to the Navy because it is impossible to live
under the barrage of sonic booms.

I spent the night at Yuma International Airport, which is also
the home of the Yuma Marine Corps Air Station. I slept in the plane,
wearing earplugs. The American song here was played by drums,
trumpets, and a thousand-foot bassoon. I had gone looking for a
shower in the afternoon. The search ended at a truck stop where I was
informed tersely that the showers were for truck drivers only; so much
for the elite status of pilots.

Figuring that if I couldn't be clean, I might as well get truly grimy, I
had gone for a run along a road by another irrigation canal. There
small shells lay scattered on the bank as if there had been a light clam
shower in the night. The clams grow in the canals; they're called
Corbicula and are harvested by muskrats, who eat them on the bank
and litter.

Trotting back to the plane on the road, I was blasted by noise. A
black shape thundered overhead: a TA4F Skyhawk taking off. At the
end of the road was a lemon grove and a sign that advertised a housing
development three and a half miles south: Out of the Noise Zone.

I slept in Yuma in the essence of sweat, lemons, and burned jet fuel,
and, drowsing off, found that I had been flying ahead of my mind.

California was still there. I was still back in El Centro, talking to a young black man in the flight service station. I had asked him about the weather and the restricted areas. He had curly hair and a neatly tailored little mustache. He told me that there was precipitation on the radar from Santa Barbara to Oregon, and east to Nevada. I had asked him about the Naval air facility, and he said:

"They fly out of here to Restricted Areas 2507 and 2510, and they be shooting at live targets."

"Air to ground?"

"They be shooting air to ground and air to air, at targets they be towing."

"So you don't want to go flying out there at all, do you?"

"You don't want to go *walking* through there either, because sometimes they be closing it down and going through there to explode the bombs that didn't explode when they shot them. We got lots of activity here; there's the guys from Yuma, and we got a squadron of T-34s come up; they be learning how to fly. And the Blue Angels are here now training. There's so much activity here they be going to make this a full air station, instead of just a facility, which it is now."

He had a nice smile, a secretly delighted smile, as if he knew it was all a game out there, but you shouldn't acknowledge it was a game. It was a smile as if he knew that all this posturing with formations and fighters and shooting at the ground was as antique as a display of swordsmanship by a knight in front of a man with a pistol; that the holes made by gunfire in the desert were no more significant in history than the curlicues of tracks laid down by the all-terrain vehicles or the spirit barriers and dance tracks of the old people. It was a smile that seemed to say it was more likely that the important changes will be made in this landscape by the steady mingling of cultures and races, by the wavering of the long line across the desert between the nations, by the hunted footprints on the sand, by the ghost riders of the ancient horse, than by war.

I woke in the morning at Yuma to an enormous roar. I lifted a curtain. An AV-8B Harrier II, a vertical-take-off-and-landing jet fighter, hovered on the other side of the field. Dust and heat rose around it and made the Harrier itself dance in mirage, as if it were suspended in liquid. Beyond it a vast cloud of black smoke rose from red flame: crash drill on the base.

Inside Six Zero One was a curious smell, a familiar oily aroma. I looked around for the source and found it with dismay. The container

I use to refill my brake master cylinders had leaked in the night. It had dripped from the pocket in the chair by my head. There was a pink stain on my pillow. It looked as if I had been crying MIL-H-5606A hydraulic fluid in my dreams.

CHAPTER SIX

I flew east of Yuma a thousand feet above the interstate, the late afternoon sun behind me, and I got into the spirit of all this military activity. I played with the motor homes, running my shadow and the shine of my glory right up some guy's back and on ahead of him down the road. So, Snowbird! You came down here in your big machine to live in a warm landscape for a while, did you? Missile armed! Motor home in range! Pow! Just vaporized your kids' inheritance.

I ran east, right down on the deck. I was ready. If somebody in an F-4 came along military routes IR218 or VR1267, which were drawn on the chart across my path in gray, like a trail of jet smoke, I'd wax his tail. I was at five hundred feet. The low altitude gave me a sensation of great speed, power, and aggression. *Rat-tat-tat-tat-tat! KA BOOM!* Tanker truck buys the farm.

I flew up the Gila River, against the flow of the sand. The sand was so smooth that I had to look more than once to know it was not light-colored water. The river looked oddly full of sand, gorged on sand, overflowing its banks with sand, braiding sand streams in and out of one another. It was familiar. It looked like Alaska; say, the Copper River. That made sense. Braided rivers form in arid lands and in glacial country, both for the same reason: The heavy load of silt the water carries continually builds the stream bed and forces the water to multiply its channels. Even in its dryness, the Gila flooded sand out into the desert.

I passed fewer and fewer vehicles. Suddenly it seemed that everything had been abandoned. The river by its water, and the land by its people. I passed over the ruins of a World War II air base, a triangular set of runways cracked by weeds. I flew close to a deserted farm, a hundred acres once tilled, now going back to rabbitbrush, cactus, and snakes. I circled an abandoned Stuckey's restaurant. The blue roof was dirty, the yellow sign broken like an eggshell. It looked as if the interstate exit there was made just for the restaurant. The whole arrangement seemed seedy, discredited, lost. What was happening here? What ghost landscape had I drifted into now? There was a roofless, pumpless gas station. Out in the desert south of the interstate was an orange-and-white skeletal tower that must have been over a hundred feet tall, fallen twisted to the stones. What bad future had I blundered into?

I glanced at the chart and was reminded: I was drifting close to Restricted Area 2301W, where people trying to get into the United States die of thirst, and the armed forces blow up hillsides. This was like the Dixie Valley, a war zone. People weren't being run off here, but their hopes had been raised and smothered. Once there were plans to build the MX missile here: Two long concrete tunnels lay hidden up there against the Mohawk Mountains, built with fanfare in 1977 and '78. Buried inside the trenches were the remains of a machine called the strongback, which was designed to shove the missile out of the concrete tunnel. The machine worked; it erupted out of the desert like a vast science-fiction sand worm. But the worm was killed by an attack of logic and the project collapsed. It was not the first of its kind, and probably not the last.

Over the years the money and the soldiers come and go. When the soldiers come it is time to chase the glory: eternal wealth. People buy land and build, hoping that the landscape will change into something vast and man-made and rich. Then the money and the feds disappear, and along the Gila abandoned buildings fall slowly into the desert pavement, to last as long in their ruin as Patton's tent-cities and the geoglyphs drawn by older hopes.

I climbed up from the lowlands of Yuma along the sandy Gila, and slowly the desert grew more saguaro cactus, and more rocks. In the late light the long shadows of the cactus and the shrubs made the landscape look combed. It was a dry and empty land, with a few bedraggled farms. A geoglyph appeared near the interstate; a curious wiggling path with nodes that ended at a pit and a short line of white rocks. A freight train went by, going the other way. Beyond the rails long straight dirt roads led out into the clear distance and the languorous mountains.

The ghostly presence of Charles Lindbergh was in a reflective mood. This was the serious Lindbergh, the solemn face I had seen in so many photographs. "I looked at the desert," he said as we flew over the empty expanse, "and I realized how much I wanted a night of solitude." He was thinking about 1928. He had been the world's hero for a year. Now, to escape reporters, he had found a patch of level gravel in the expanse of the Basin and Range Province, and landed, for once alone. "The wheels banged heavily on hummocks before my plane stopped rolling. I climbed down from the cockpit and walked out among sparse clumps of brush and cactus. How wonderful it was to feel and be a part of the desert I had crossed so often in my plane yet never touched before, to know its heat, its dryness, the tough sharpness of its prickled growths."

He made supper, and watched darkness come. "What peace I found there, on that warm but cooling surface of our planet's sphere!" But the peace was elusive. It did not quiet the conflict that ran through his life. As I flew east we looked out at that broad, still landscape, and the ghost of Lindbergh said quietly, "How easy it should be, how difficult it was, to combine my fascination with a complicated airplane and my love for the desert's natural simplicity."

And hard it is, too, for those who live here. The natural simplicity of the desert is being changed. John Jackson's voice emerged from the rumble of the engine:

"The best place to find new landscapes is in the West," he observed, quoting from an essay he'd written. "Pictures painted on canvas is not what I mean, nor glimpses of pleasant rural scenery, but landscapes as we are now learning to see them—large-scale organizations of man-made spaces, usually in the open country."

When you fly low you do not see far ahead. Your perspective is similar to the view from a car, except that the horizon comes up twice as fast. So I was startled when a faint green glow on the desert's edge suddenly flashed up into a vast panoply of cultivated fields.

Abruptly the desert's boundless aridity was transformed into a game board of perfect oblong fields. The fields were alternately either a lush and luminous green or a glowing brown. The chart told me I was at a place called Paloma, and I had expected a village, another run-down service station, a ruin. Instead, here was mile after mile of manicured green and brown, a grid of irrigation ditches, a single enormous farm, 100,000 acres of green wheat fields and brown fields awaiting cotton: Prudential Insurance Company's grand Southwest landscape.

Paloma was a large-scale reorganization of man-made spaces in the open country. Paloma had an elegant paved airstrip, and I circled the settlement for five minutes, deciding whether to risk wrath and land. The strip was marked as private on the chart. The grounds were extensive. A large farmhouse that would elsewhere be called an estate was surrounded by trees, but this was not unexpected. Farmers are not necessarily poor. It was more strange to see the tidiness of the grounds. It could not be called a farmyard. Farmyards, even the most economical, have ragged grassy places, sheds that have been erected over the years that don't quite match; at least one informal pile of hay; a combine, tractors, a flatbed truck, and a couple of rusty pieces of old equipment that weren't worth the trade-in, lined up in a casual row; and, romping in the hay and giving birth inside the broken baler, half-wild barn cats. But this was more like a military compound than a farm. I did not take an inventory, but the most dramatic difference was the equipment parked in precise rows on concrete. Pulled up to the line east of the residential area, the row of combines looked like the waiting Harrier jets parked on the apron at Yuma, poised for a Klaxon howl calling the troops.

Near the arrayed equipment, on almost as much concrete, were the houses, near rows of tennis and basketball courts. One hundred heads of households live on the Paloma ranch. Between 125 and 400 employees live there, depending on the season. The houses, too, were military, lined up one after the other, indentical: base housing, tidy and sterile as a row of kennels. Hose 'em out when the labor has gone. Was this the farm of the future—an enterprise of size, precision, efficiency, regulation? I circled again, and decided not to land. But as I straightened out the bank and climbed, I noticed, off to one side of the compound, a corral. In it rose a puff of dust. This was the only movement I had seen on the whole place. A bay horse was loping around in the corral, and a man was chasing it. He couldn't catch it. Paloma wasn't entirely under control.

Night was coming on. But I was wealthy with freedom. The tanks were almost full. I could go where I chose. I had enough gas to make Tucson, to make New Mexico. I could spend the evening anywhere. What joy! To float down out of the sky at just any old place, because it looked interesting.

When I drive somewhere, or just stand on the ground at home, I can never quite imagine the freedom of flight; I try to grasp it and somehow get it wrong. Is it wanderlust? No. Is it solitude? No. Is it the grandeur of the landscape? No. Is it the perspective? No. None of those qualities alone, nor their combination. But then I get back in the plane and recollect. Becoming airborne is like returning into a familiar dream: Oh, yes, that's right. That's how it is. Chasing the glory. Wonderful.

Gila Bend looked disheveled and interesting. It did not look like a wealthy town; the baseball diamonds I saw there had dirt infields.

There's a relationship between dirt infields and life. I played baseball for a few years when I was a kid. I played second base on an infield that grew stones and bad hops. In those days the most glorious thing in the world was a grass infield. So as I flew across America, where baseball is important, I gauged the economic condition of a community by how many of its baseball diamonds had grass infields. If the city had an abundance of those bright triangles, it was wealthy. Half and half, and it was a good middle-class community. If most of the infields were dirt, the town needed federal assistance. If there were no grass infields in the whole place, it should be declared a disaster area, and emergency teams sent there with sod.

I approached Gila Bend in the last sunlight, flying east along the interstate. Ahead of me the glory was a beautiful sparkling circle of emeralds, rubies, and diamonds: colored road signs glittering with the sun. Ten minutes later I made the sun set with my descent, coming down into the desert's shadow. I spent the night in the plane, with the light of the airport beacon flashing on the windows.

In the evening a train went past on the south side of the runway, rumbling like a large natural force rolling west, a thundercloud. All night, wind shook the plane and rattled a piece of tin over by the fuel pumps. I slept restlessly. In my dreams the beacon interrogated me. Flash! Flash! Flash! Tell the truth! But there is no truth. Tell the truth! Truth is experience; the rest is hearsay. Tell the truth! Flash! Just before the sun rose a thunderstorm moved through on the south side of the runway, muttering and growling like a train.

The desert smelled sweet and bitter and desperately beautiful in the damp early dawn, but by the time the sun had been up an hour everything was again dry, and I was off to find a shower. A woman at an RV park in Gila Bend was delighted to take my $2.00 and unlock the showers. She noticed the Montana plates on my tiny motorcycle, so I told her what I was doing.

"Hey, Virgil!" she shouted, so the whole town could hear. Virgil was nearby, mowing thin grass. "Look at this," she bellowed. "He came down out of the sky just long enough to have a bath."

I paid my fee and stood in the hot water for twenty minutes, wasting it. Clean at last! I wandered around town. Gila Bend was a wide main street with no real center, and too many closed businesses. It was a town of restaurants, motels, and quick-stop food stores, many of which had just been cited for selling alcohol to three underage kids from the Maricopa County Sheriff's Explorer Cadets Post who were working for the sheriff. It was a town of migrants: Of the nine candidates for city council profiled in the weekly Gila Bend *Sun*, one was a native of Arizona. The immigrant candidates had surnames like Cassel, Brown, Hull, Fox, Campbell, and Conrad; the kids in the high school *Dolls and Dudes Revue* had surnames like Pino, Fernandez, Alvarez, Villegas, Trujillo, and Peña. The only native in that race for city council was Richard Granillo Cantu.

By ten in the morning it was already hot in Gila Bend, even in early spring. It was the hottest place in the United States. "Well, we *were* always the hottest place in America," said Marsha Farnsworth, "until it got popular, and now we have to share it." I talked to her at Farnsworth's Mobil Self-Service as she cleaned the glass case that held the jewelry she sold. "In the gas business you have to do something else," she explained.

"It used to be our business was in the summer," Marsha said. "People had to stop for a drink, to sleep. Now it's the winter. In summer you see the Europeans. They all travel in motor homes now. Used to be the economy of Arizona was copper, cattle, cotton."

"Now it isn't," Robert said.

Marsha, who was in her thirties, was one of those rarities here: a native. Bob had come here in the service. He was from Rhode Island. "I thought Bob was going to take me miles away from here," Marsha said. "I made a Westerner out of him.

"Gila Bend was developed on the river as the Butterfield Stage," Marsha went on. "Then it moved up to the railroad. Now my generation is moving to the interstate." That explained the boarded windows along the old highway through town. The same thing is happening in many Western towns. The interstate is designed to bypass town, where the land is cheaper, and then the muscle and weight of the big highway tilt the landscape, and slowly, against its will, the whole town slides down into the trough beside the pavement: first the motels and the gas stations and the quick-stop groceries, then the shopping malls, and at last the offices and home. In the process some of the home-owned businesses that once lined Main Street are left behind, supplanted by chains.

"People are designer-happy," Marsha went on. "They want McDonald's." She didn't move around the room, but just sitting there or cleaning the cabinet, she looked like an athlete, a basketball player. She had the poise, the sure look in her eye: she knew how to pass and shoot, and how to handle the pressure. She knew where the ball was going, and her life.

She and Bob had left their mark on the desert. When they were courting they would go out exploring the desert in a four-wheel-drive truck. They'd drive around on the Air Force base, out in the restricted areas. They don't go there anymore. "Used to be just three GIs for security on the whole base," Bob said. "Now you go out there and they'll get you in ten minutes." Now they go four-wheeling on public land administered by the U.S. Bureau of Land Management.

But Marsha was contemptuous of the assault of the off-road recreational vehicles, which pours into this landscape from both east and west. "The strangest part of it," she said, "is they get out of the city and they think they're in the country, so they open the door, and all the trash falls out of the car, and that is where it stays. They have no respect."

Marsha looked at Bob with those poised, wary eyes. "One of these days I don't think the BLM'll let you go anywhere around here," she said.

He said, "Why?"

"Because it scars the desert—all that four-wheeling." She cleaned fingerprints off the glass. She was one who noticed, who had respect. She said, "I don't know where we're going to go to get away."

Somehow we got around to water, a topic close to the surface of conversations anywhere in the Southwest. "When my grandfather was here the Gila River ran from bank to bank," Marsha said. Now the water ran elsewhere. As I had ridden the motorcycle into town I had crossed over a wide concrete canal so full of water that it backed up against the top of the bridge and boiled out under it on the downstream side. I had looked down at the thick green water for a few minutes, already thirsty. The main irrigation district feeder canal from three reservoirs in my own valley was not as large as this. This thing must be part of a major federal project. I glanced over at the other side. Wrong.

"No trespassing," the sign said, "Paloma Ranch." The ranch has what may be the largest private irrigation system in the world: a thirty-four-mile canal from a privately owned dam on the Gila River, and 312 miles of concrete irrigation ditches. Most of this predates Prudential; Paloma has been a huge farm all this century.

"You've got to realize," Bob said, "that ranch is water rich."

There was talk around town that Prudential might turn that liquid wealth from green and gold fields into a retirement community. When I called John Utz at the ranch itself, he said it was "possible, but not in the near future. It will be farmed for several years yet."

Farmers and the armed forces are not the only organizations that create vast man-made landscapes on the open country. So do hotel chains and housing developers. Marsha thought Paloma might be turned into a new city, or into something like the 640-acre Hyatt Regency resort that had just been build north of Scottsdale. The Hyatt Regency pumps water from its own wells and from the city into a lake and into twenty-eight fountains, twenty-seven waterfalls, nine pools, a spa, and a three-story water sled built in a mock-up of Big Ben. You get a lot of splash in a parched landscape for $175 a night.

Thinking of this, Marsha looked around with disgust. A wonderful dry wind blew heat down the highway, carrying the arid, bright aroma of the desert through town.

"If they want lakes," she said, "they ought to go to Wisconsin."

I flew east out of Gila Bend. The landscape was again desert, but the pavement and red varnish were gone. It was a sandy country of scattered bushes and loose, pale soil. No grand fields; Paloma was far behind. No canals, no irrigation green. I passed a couple of large areas where fields were once hacked out and plowed; but ambition and hope had withered and the new landscape had never been completed. The mesquite had come back.

Sand washes here were blocked every mile or two with small dams, but the only thing pooled up behind these dams was tired green grass, and even that was sandy. Sometimes, out near the base of the hills, I saw a white box in the distance: a motor home parked near a grove of mesquite or a tender spot of green. "They're called *Boondockers*," Marsha had said. "They live out there. You see them once every two weeks when they come in for water and food."

I flew low, sneaking along the northern edge of the Sells 1 Military Operations Area. As the day ended I flew over the Papago Indian Reservation, and crossed a village my chart called Kohatk: white buildings and wide white dusty streets. The streets flowed from house to house with no pretense at organization. They looked more friendly in their abandon than the orderly blocks of modern towns; they made an intimate web.

This was boondocking, no mistake. Lifetimes of dryness and wind, and no option to jack your home down on its tires and drive to Wisconsin. I flew over a cemetery, where the crosses faced the sun. The graves were all mounded, the mounds outlined by the low light and the shadow: pillows in the stony earth.

Graveyards are for the living, to soothe stark imaginings. This bleak acre in the desert was good for mine. I live in fear of orderly rows of stones in grass beside a cathedral. When the time comes I would prefer to disappear into the air, or vanish at sea. But if I must go underground, I thought, dig a place for me with a backhoe somewhere like this, in shallow sand, with the creosote bushes dancing in the dry wind and the coyotes singing. Sooner or later, maybe, they would get a chance to gnaw on my bones, and that would be fine. I've never thought of the grave as rest, and I have always wanted to be a part of the howl of the wild.

This ultimate human use of the land reminded me of an alternate means of disposal: the casting of human ashes into the sky. I used to think this might be a good way to become permanently airborne. I lost my enthusiasm for it recently. Phil Timm used to drop ashes for the bereaved. "Awful job. Awful." As I left the Papago cemetery behind and flew over a desert full of dust, I remembered a story I overheard on the other side of the nation.

It was in the quiet office of a flying service near Boston. Charts on the wall. Sunglasses and airsick bags for sale in a glass case. The young pilot was sitting in an overstuffed Naugahyde chair trying to make the day go by faster, talking to the secretary.

"The guy said, 'She said right over the Berkshires,' so that's where I am. It's his wife, in one of these—containers. What do you call it? Urn. So we're over the Berkshires. He opens the window, and he thinks it's like dumping a bucket. He just dumps the ashes out.

"Well. You know. There's a lot of wind. I mean, I'm slowed down, but I'm still doing eighty knots. So the ashes came back in. Everything. All over the inside of the plane."

The young pilot was halfway between a grin and a grimace. This has bothered him. The secretary, who was more worldly, loved it. As for me, I stood just inside the door, trying not to look conspicuous and stop the story before its end. This was fundamental stuff.

"Yeah?" said the secretary.

"Well," the pilot went on, "I guess when they burn somebody it's not just ash, you know, it's like a gravel road. Dust and gravel. We got some of it out the window, and then when we got back down, the guy, this lady's husband, he said, 'I'll pick up the big pieces.' So he did, and I told a line boy to go back and clean the rest of it out of the plane. I told him what it was, and he said, 'I'm not going to do that.'

"So he called somebody else over and this other kid cleaned it out. Didn't tell him what it was. The kid had a terrible time."

The pilot sat there for a few moments. His gaze was inward. Maybe, he was thinking, I should not have started this story.

"Yeah?" said the secretary. The pilot began again, reluctantly.

"Well, so, anyway. Here we are sitting in the office, this guy—the husband—and me. I mean, he was writing a check or something. He still had the urn with the—big pieces.

"So this other line boy comes in—the second one. 'Jesus,' the kid says to us, 'what was all that shit?' "

The hills northwest of Tuscon were disemboweled, their guts dug out and laid in terraces on the lower slopes. Copper mines. Some were closed down or abandoned: empty foundations, empty trailer parks on the red-streaked ground. The land seemed wounded, and in decay. A long valley stretched south, twenty miles, thirty miles, stippled with mesquite and creosote bush, down to the dark lumpy rim of the Baboquivari Range. Across that long expanse, a single pond gleamed in the sun.

I approached Tucson over the busy red scar of the last leg of the Central Arizona Project, the big canal that would soon divert a piece of the Colorado River down from the north. The water would mean more golf courses, more well-watered hotels, more pockets of Wisconsin in the desert.

On an ever grander scale, the face of America is changing. The only reason it seemed so striking out here was that the harsh land of the Basin and Range Province is the last holdout. Here the altered human environment was made up of satellites of new landscape like Paloma, the Hyatt Regency, or Tucson, joined by conduits of change like this new canal. But as I traveled east it became more and more apparent: The American landscape is not just overlaid by a few engineering marvels built under an umbrella of military power—it is a complete rework of the face of the continent.

Dust to lawn. As I flew east toward Tucson, vast yellow Caterpillar scrapers were carving out the channel for the new canal. It was Sunday, but the work was holy. Everywhere on the opened earth tanker trucks rolled across the course of the work, in the wake of the scrapers, knocking down the dust of the old landscape with a fine spray of precious water.

PART 2

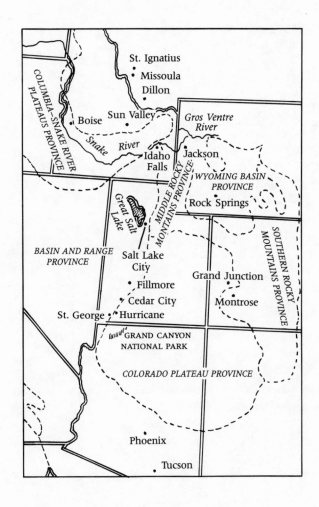

CHAPTER SEVEN

Leaving Tucson, I flew north, under a contrail, and the finger of God pointed down from the sky.

The contrail cast a shadow like a pane of glass; a thin sheet of shade that I couldn't see except on end. But when I crossed the jet's path and looked down it, it suddenly appeared, distinct as a shaft of light from between clouds. A friend would call a light shaft a Catholic Miracle Sunrise. This was Catholic Doom: a shaft of darkness. I looked down at the land and wondered who looked up, startled, at the snuffing of the sun?

From the air the landscape is full of strange things. Darkness points from the sky. Fields of power-generation windmills shimmer on hills like a crop of tinsel. Paired scrapes made by miners' bulldozers march across the desert exactly like the tracks of a vast rabbit. They make the desert look as soft as snow. Dredged river bottom stands out in a Mississippi River backwater in the perfect shape of a question mark.

In the great changed landscape of America, some things seemed so bizarre that I said to myself, "Yup, people at work." But the grandest and most dramatic change human beings have made seemed so normal that it took me a while even to notice it.

From Tucson I made the first of three major detours from Lindbergh's route. I didn't have to follow him to the letter of his log, though I flew over almost every town he crossed. After all, military restricted areas blocked me off from many short legs of the trip, and I was not out to race history around the country; I was there to see the land. And the ghost of Lindbergh would never object; he liked seeing new country as much as old. But this was an enormous jag in the route: I went from Tucson to Santa Fe via Montana.

I detoured mainly because my wife was ill and I had to go home for a while, but also because Lindbergh's route left out one whole geographic province and big chunks of several others, and I wanted to stitch them into the picture.

Weather and terrain bent my route northwest through Utah, and at first I flew along cut off from the landscape by worry and clouds. Then, as I emerged from clouds near the Grand Canyon, I began seeing things.

It was a windy spring day. I came out of a squall over the canyon, beaten up by the turbulence and awed by chasms. Nearby was one of Macho Irene's airway intersections: KLIFF. The cliffs shone in patches of sun. A short rainbow stood beneath a black cloud like a pillar of color. Over the canyon I held myself high up against the heavy sky, sorry to bring the noise of one more damned airplane to the seekers of solitude in the echoing cliffs below. I came north across the red country east of St. George and west of Zion National Park. There, in the wide empty ranch country of Southern Utah, somewhere out over the Uinkaret Plateau, not far from Clayhole Wash, I crossed the concrete foundation of a house built beside a broken windmill.

This was not a typical ruin. Nothing stood on the foundation, but scattered all around it on the dirt were planks. The planks perfectly surrounded the square foundation, a ring of dead gray soldiers fallen outward at attention on the red sand. In some recent past that house had been blown up.

How it happened? Here was a scenario: On some hot afternoon, one of those sharp and shiny days in the dry lands when the light is white iron in the head, someone had come to this house, someone who had lived here too long and had a debt to pay. Out in this solitude, this person or persons arranged the better part of a case and a half of dynamite inside this building, with preference toward those rooms in which the hard light had burned out the color in the pine floor and the reason in the mind. Daydreams of long years were realized that day when the spark took and the old house blew its guts out all over the valley. A line of four Mormon brothers stood there beside the plunger as the planks were flung out in their fatal ring, and the gray smoke drifted out into a dust devil and whirled away across the chained fields of dead juniper, like the spirit of the mother broken by the harsh land and the loneliness. The four lean men put their big hats back on silently and without a word turned and each climbed into his pickup truck and drew a long plume of dust down the empty roads; and the four plumes blew to the four corners of the bleak land. And an old man in a back room on a straw cot in the cheap rest home in Colorado City or Hurricane heard the distant rumble and cackled with laughter until he cried.

Western Romance! The house was probably blasted for a firemen's drill.

I crossed a gray-green landscape of dry grass and juniper, where a red road cut through it like a weal. The Colorado City airport looked half made, a strip bulldozed out of the red soil that petered out at the west end. A creek flowed west between pale red rimrocks. The belly of the cut was deep red, with a trickle of red water and dry leafless trees. One cottonwood blushed green next to a corral at a fence line. The sagebrush grew only in the washes, so the wriggles of drainage seemed to flow with vegetation.

I rode the bucking airplane up past Hurricane and crossed low over a strange mesa. A plateau hung above the valley of Interstate 15. From below it would have appeared just as an indent in the cliff, its curiosities hidden from the cars on the road the way a ham on the table is hidden from the cat. But from above it was a wide, flat bench.

The center of the stone table was occupied by a long, straight railroad track, which emerged full grown from a steel shed at the north end of the plateau, ran straight for about two miles, and vanished off the edge of the cliff.

This was great. I could invent scenarios here too.

I looked down. The earth trembled. Whistles sounded in the distance. A four-engine unit train pouring black smoke and howling and pulling a hundred black cars loaded with Carbon County coal from the mines up by Price, Utah, emerged from that shed the way a chain of flags is pulled by a magician from someone's ear. The train, going full speed right out of the garage, rumbled down the two miles of track, snorting and bellowing and dusting the embankment with coal, and shot over the precipice at the end with a great clamor of screaming engines and clashing cars. Quiet returned to the hilltop. A wisp of black dust rose, and five minutes later a ghostly whistle haunted the mountainside.

No?

I circled the singular track, making no other sense of it, then saw the trailer. The trailer was great too.

It was one of three. A dirt road wound over to it from an unknown access, and made a circular driveway for the trailers. They were loosely arranged in the shape of a T, with the road at the top of the figure. All were alike: about ten by forty, blue with white roofs and doors, each topped by an air conditioner. They stood among piñon pines and junipers on light brown sandy soil near a cliff that dropped off 150 feet of sheer sandstone to a fall of gravel and stones and a wriggle of steep washes, in which no rolling body would come to rest. Two of the three trailers were near the edge. The third was over it, hanging out in the breeze.

I circled, looked carefully, and took photographs. It was no illusion. This trailer was installed on a long slab of sandstone that leaned out from the cliff, but whoever put the trailer there was not content with living on the edge. He had to be over it. The entire area of the trailer that might be called the living room—ten or fifteen feet of the thing—hung out past the stone, into space. The windows looked out at no shrubs, no yard, no stone, no support—just air. The trailers had all been removed from their wheels, so I assumed this one was anchored at the grounded end, but I quickly populated it with guests at a cocktail party, who were all bunched as far as they could from those terrible windows for fear of tilting the whole thing and going for a short flight. The guests talked brightly about valleys, Kansas, and the reassuring values of religion, and left when they had the chance.

It was a wonderful place, the ultimate perch. A trapdoor would have an incredible view. You could drop cherry pits and kill hawks.

Reluctantly, I turned north and settled into the long run against wind and squally rain, normal parts of life; but up near Fillmore, Utah, I saw the footprints of a giant shuffling across the ground.

It was desert; open country too low and hot for the piñon-juniper woodlands of the hills. The prints were long and narrow—five feet wide, twenty long—and close together, and looked as if the giant had been shuffling along half sideways. They marched in an uncompromising straight line almost due west, an even pattern of pale rectangles on the ground at a precise angle to the direction for their collective line, much as these slashes //////// lie at an angle to the line they make across the page.

I was used to the Cat scrapes that miners' bulldozers make: shallow blade-wide trenches, each terminated with a mount of pushed-up dirt. These were nothing like that. The pattern of earth and brush was not disturbed; it was just discolored.

No, these were not a giant's footprints. This was the track made by a UFO shaped like a tractor tire. Still hot from its penetration of the atmosphere, it had landed and rolled on edge across the Utah desert, singeing the grass.

I circled the tracks, too, making notes and taking pictures, and came up with no better explanation. So I let the plane lead on away north, through a rattling haze of snow pellets, and watched the wide emptiness of desert become the controlled order of farms, and the spacious arrangement of farms congeal into tight subdivisions, and the subdivisions clot into the urban constrictions of Salt Lake City. On the farms I began to see long, earthen pyramids, but at least I knew what those were: root cellars, built to keep the spuds cool and comfortable while the farmer negotiated the sale. Nothing strange about this place.

Or maybe there was.

If I had been riding that interstellar tire, if I had come across space to this broad valley, the strangest thing would have been the most familiar. If I had come rolling in from a far galaxy, even in dizziness I would have been amazed. I would have seen that all the flat land in this series of big valleys, this expanse of landscape between walls of rock, a hundred miles long and twenty wide, was cut into squares. In my occasional glances through the portholes between the treads, I would have analyzed the surface and concluded that this part of Earth had a few irregular rock outcrops, but that most of it was made out of the tidy assembly of green and brown cubes. The planet had been manufactured by highly organized beings. I would have landed and looked for a place to hide.

It was The Grid. The grid is the single most dramatic human imprint on the American landscape.

John Jackson was pleased to have another view of this phenomenon. He murmured from the back seat, "Our national grid system, the triumph of geometry over topography, will be with us till the end of time."

If I arrived above these lands in my tire long after the human species had died, the American grid would eternally mystify me. The other artifacts on the land—the spreading of reservoirs, the sprawl of cities, the swoop of interstate highways, and all similar marks of the burgeoning human presence on the land—are insignificant compared to the grid. Adventurer from another kind, I would stare from above at the precise remains of the grid with amazement. A whole continent chalked off into all these millions of squares! Why?

To take it! To own it. When the fledgling Congress of the United States looked at its possessions, it had to figure out a way to divide them up. A committee chaired by Thomas Jefferson was formed to develop a system. Drawing on ideas that may have gone all the way back to the Roman Empire, the committee proposed the grid. The grid concept emerged out of the committee and formally divided the public land into thirty-six-square-mile townships, and each township into square-mile sections, and then drew roads down the lines. Like democracy, the grid overthrew a traditional European system, metes and bounds, which had produced acrimony over surveys in the original colonies. "Two hundred feet to the marked rock; thence fifty feet to the oak tree" was replaced by "Northwest quarter of section 15, township 20, range 10."

Like a plague of order, the grid spread across the open land from the germ of the Ordinance of 1785, which was drafted by Jefferson's committee. It moved west from the Ohio River, refined by the ordinances of 1788, the acts of 1796, 1800, 1803, 1804, 1805, and on down the years.

But any rectangular piece of paper glued to a globe will buckle. So the grid is not perfectly tidy. The problem didn't become obvious until the surveyors began to tackle large areas, so it wasn't formally adjusted until the grid reached Indiana in 1819. Though in some places the grid looks as if it was pasted down in kindergarten, usually even the kinks are orderly. The grid is so regular and clean that in the early days of his flying out east of the Rockies, Phil Timm would eyeball the angle at which he needed to cross the grid in order to maintain a heading, and just hold that angle from section to section and township to township, until the field he wanted scrolled up over the horizon. I also remember flying at a set angle to the grid, in low clouds and lowering sunlight, on a course set inexorably—if only I had known!—to a crash. But that right-angle intersection of roads and memory, too, would be part of this journey.

The grid is an instinctive part of Phil's landscape. In later days, when I flew with him under the training hood, instead of correcting the gyrocompass with the magnet that jiggled in its globe of kerosene, he would align us with the grid. We could fly a thousand miles and still trust those Jeffersonian lines.

John Jackson once prowled through the early travel literature of the Midwest to see if anyone had noticed the grid. He himself writes graceful prose; those stylized travel stories, he said with a gentle grimace, were "all but impossible to read." He found one sentence about the grid, written in 1817: "All these lines are well defined in the woods, by marks on the trees." In 1850 a visitor from England, looking at the mess of clearing and the long straight roads and fences, described the land as "ugly and formal." The grid, Jackson once wrote, was the "most imposing example" on the land of the "vision of the new rational, mathematical order [that] began to inspire the designed environment" after the American Revolution.

We looked out at the expanse of rectangles that covered the valley. To Jackson the view was familiar. He always liked the aerial perspective. "It is from the air," he once wrote, "that the true relationship between the natural and human landscape is first clearly revealed."

"It is ironic," Jackson said, as I flew across the revealed grid, "that the rational, mathematical aspect of this landscape has been revealed to us only within the last generation, with the coming of commercial flying. It was there, of course, all the time, but in the abstract."

It has been there ever since people have flown. It was there under Lindbergh, under Phil Timm when he taught himself to fly in the plane he built, in Worland, Wyoming, in 1938, and was under me now. All pilots have seen stretches of land, in the Basin and Range Province or in the Appalachians, where the grid is invisible, existing only on the quadrangle maps drawn by the U.S. Geological Survey. But no human ever saw America from the air as it was so very recently: mile after endless mile of grass or forest unbroken by a single straight surveyed line. Sometimes, even in the generous spaciousness of today's American sky, the knowledge that no one ever had the joy of flight across that free view is a source of grief.

There's nothing free about the land today. In some places, where the earth is a deep brown or red, the roads in the grid are darker than the surrounding fields. Then it looks as if the whole arrangement is a net, flung neatly across the world and nailed down with tension by the big spikes called grain elevators. We have taken possession.

➤ We flew over more root cellars. They stuck up from the grid like tiny schematic models of mountains. The shade of Phil Timm looked at them and was reminded, as he often is, of other times. "Did you ever hear about the time I flew an airplane backwards?" he said, and was off. "I made a trip from Casper, Wyoming, to Denver in a J2 Cub. This would've been one of the first Cubs that were ever manufactured. It had 36-horse opposed flathead Continental engine. You can recognize the fact that at five thousand feet it had lost twenty-five percent of its horsepower just because of the altitude."

I sat back, cruising, to listen to the story. Phil told stories like Mark Twain; you enjoyed getting there as much as you enjoyed the point. This one rambled around the Western states at about the speed of the J2, and, sooner or later, arrived at a root cellar near Horse Creek Station, Wyoming. The wind howled around this root cellar, but the cellar bent the wind into a wave. Phil, struggling with his heavily loaded, underpowered plane, used the wave to climb. "I got a considerable altitude," Phil said, "a hundred and fifty, two hundred feet. You understand, each inch was a prize amount of altitude with this powerful piece of equipment." This exalted height let him get over a low pass, but then things got worse. "About all I could do was maintain minimum speed so I could maintain flight. The fact of the matter is the machine had stabilized, to a degree, about five feet off the ground. But now I'm going at such a slow airspeed, the airplane is being blown backwards." His passenger looked out over his shoulder. "There's a little rise back there," the passenger said, "and the way you are going you will run into it."

Of course, he missed it. He used the lift off the rise to get a few more feet, and made it back to the place he started. And that was the end of the story. A little later I figured out the point: There are many ways to turn the subtle secrets of the land into survival.

So that day as I flew past Salt Lake, root cellars took on new meaning. I could see them all over the place, lifting airplanes. But I kept flying over other things I did not understand. A few miles west of Salt Lake City, an enormous Mississippi River paddle-wheel steamer lay anchored to the dock of a four-acre pond. A ferry? Something stranded, left over from the Pleistocene? I didn't turn. I tried not to look. I just flew on. But after I passed a rectangular lake full of blood, I radioed to Salt Lake Air Traffic Control Center for an instrument clearance and pulled up into the clouds and lived for the rest of the day in the simple gauzy mystery of clouds.

◆— I was home for four weeks. During that time I spent a few hours on the telephone trying to find out something about what I had seen in Utah. Some answers came without much effort, and some were harder to find.

The big boat in the small pond was the easiest. A couple of calls resolved it into the Jordan Queen, a three-story restaurant. It stood out there on its pond without complaint, never restless for the great river, because it was never a boat. It seated seven hundred people, and served such traditional Utah dishes as halibut, Cajun creole, and prime rib, while Stephen Foster music played in the background: "Old Black Joe."

The lake of blood was a pond at Western Zirconium, a company that uses the dry air of Utah to help the process of extracting zirconium and hafnium, metals used in the nuclear power industry, from beach sand imported from Australia. The pond was full of ammonium chloride. The color depended upon temperature.

The tracks of the UFO on the desert were, it turned out, more likely to be the steps of a giant than I had thought—a giant corporation. Jerry Muhlestein, from the Bureau of Land Management in Fillmore, thought they were probably the marks of a seismic survey. "The markings are from seismograph primer cord line," he wrote me after I sent him a photo. "I have never seen them on the slant like this, however." The solution became even less sure when Paul Carter, at the Cedar City office of the BLM, which covers the area I had been flying over, told me that his people couldn't figure out what the tracks were. "Nobody's been able to identify them," Carter said. The most likely explanation had to be the seismography: Sometime during the previous years, men and machines had marched across there, stamping on the ground with explosives, just to hear the echoes curl around stone or oil. But what if this was not the meaning of the tracks? What if—? I told Carter I'd send all the UFO nuts in his direction.

What about the railroad track on Hurricane Mesa? No, it wasn't a phantom section of the Southern Pacific Railroad. It was military. I should have known. Scratch something truly bizarre and it turns out to be painted olive drab. It was a track used for the testing of ejection seats.

You can't just climb out of a jet when it's coming apart at a thousand knots, so ejection seats must be designed to protect pilots from violent forces. Early ones weren't very good; at the beginning of the supersonic age pilots were almost as worried about being ejected as about being shot. So the track was built on Hurricane Mesa to test new designs. "This was when they didn't have it down too pat," said Ward Wright, a sixty-seven-year-old native of Hurricane who worked as lead mechanic on the mesa for about a decade.

Wright had an interesting way of expressing things. The track was built in Utah, he said, because the Air Force was using a similar facility down at Edwards Air Force Base in California but it wasn't working out. "I guess they had a major down there went down the track and was thrown up only about eight hundred feet and his chute didn't open," Wright said. "It just ruined him."

The Hurricane track was two miles long, and you could fire a rocket sled down it at up to 1,700 miles an hour, though the normal speed was a more modest seven or eight hundred. When Wright worked on the Mesa during the fifties and early sixties, when Coleman Engineering of Culver City, California, ran the operation, he would travel all over the country ordering surplus rockets from military ordnance depots. He would adapt the rockets to his sled, and then the major plane manufacturers—Convair, Republic, or others—would bring ejection seats or whole fuselages up to the mesa and Wright would blast them down the track and see what happened. At the end of the track was a water brake, a gradually deepening pool beneath the track that a scoop on the sled would dig into, throwing up a great cloud of spray. There the sled and fuselage assembly would stop, while whomever had just been launched from the seat would fly out over the edge of the cliff, making pacts with God.

It was fifteen hundred feet down to the rubble above the Virgin River, a gentle ride of several seconds if the chute opened. Who were the lucky folks who got to make the ride?

One was a life-sized mannequin, whose name was Hurricane Sam. Others were chimpanzees who lived in big cages on the mesa. "Powerful animals, those chimpanzees," Wright said. "There are several chimpanzees buried up in those hills. Someday someone's going to dig one up and wonder." The other passengers were bears.

The bears—and the chimps—would be sedated while they were strapped into the straitjackets and parachute harnesses in the ejection seat, but because it was important to monitor all their functions as they careened toward the edge, they would be wide awake by the time the rockets went off. Wright put it differently: "At the time we were ready to fire," he said, "those bears were rational."

He did not say much about their sanity when they reached the ground after that engrossing ride. But at least once, he remembered, a bear retained some sense of reason through the chaos of movement. When he alighted softly among the rocks by the grace of Uncle Sam's parachute, he got the hell out of that straitjacket and ran for it.

And what about the trailer that hung over the edge? It was a relatively recent installation. "I helped put that on," said Mack J. Hall, also of Hurricane. "It's a restaurant. A kitchen, were the workers ate. We just poured a footing and put it on it. It's about fifty feet long, and about twenty feet of it hangs out. I guess it's pretty picturesque. At one time they wanted to put a glass bottom on it so you could look down while you ate."

This was even better than I had imagined. What a pleasant break, sitting there with your hamburger, trying not to tap your feet too hard to the jukebox music, watching the bears fly by.

"One of the wives wouldn't go in there," Wright said. "They had to carry her meals out to her."

After talking to the people in Hurricane I was ready to go back. One of those I talked to was Darwin Stratton, one of three men named Darwin who had worked at the track on the mesa. (Did that have something to do with the monkeys?) When we finished our conversation, Stratton invited me to visit. "Come on down one of these days," he said with a friendly chuckle. "We'll fill 'er full of water and take you for a ride."

I'm ready. No one has ever accused me of being rational.

CHAPTER EIGHT

Like the sea, the air requires that you be wholly present in your life. You take off, the attention the plane demands cleanses you of the multiple confusions of the ground. You emerge from conflict or sadness in the same way that you rise from a cloud, borne up from the bright circle of your glory.

You sail closer to death in the air. It is not that flying a small plane is more dangerous than driving on the freeway. It is simply that when you learn to drive a car you are trained to back into a parking place, but in a plane you are trained how to make a forced landing when the engine quits. You are more aware of the danger of miscalculation. You understand more clearly the way you fence with the odds and chances of living.

In a car your encounters with danger are sudden and unexpected, and dealt with by instinct—Look out! Hit the brakes! Swerve! Whew! In a plane you have plenty of time to think. If the engine quit me at 13,500 feet over Idaho, it would take fifteen minutes to reach the ground. That amount of time would not make the ground any softer, but it would allow me to exercise all my craft to arrange for a gentle meeting of plane and earth. An engine failure is like stalling on the tracks with a car full of children and hearing a whistle from around the shining curve of rails. You make your plans. You act. You do not allow yourself to dwell upon the possibilities.

In April I began my journey again, with all the same gear in the back of the plane but a new uncertainty in the back of the mind. I had been home a month; during that time I had walked in some dark places with my wife. We hoped we had come out on the other side. "No one," the surgeon had said when he had taken the thing out, "dies of thyroid cancer."

So, southbound in April, south of home by two hundred miles, over lava fields covered with snow and the snow covered with the spaghetti of snowmobile tracks, I climbed high above the earth, and set a course toward a vast stone on the horizon, the Grand Teton, and thought about the grid, the military presence in the landscape, the many divergent uses of the land, and death.

This was not the best place for a man who was already thinking somber thoughts. I was going to pass a place that could have been grim for me. Like a wildebeest walking warily near a pride of somnolent lions—the prey keeping watch on the predator—I would pass over the canyon in which I came close to being killed by the land.

It was winter a few years ago. It was snowing. Not hard, but thickly, the kind of snow that softens streetlights, turns the golf course into a toboggan run overnight and, when seen from a window, seems to hold the world in a kindly embrace.

I was an anachronism in this snow, a whirring, frantic bug whose summer metabolism was out of place in this fluid combination of cold air and frozen water. I circled and circled, trapped in this Mason jar of snow, but I had not yet surrendered to the solidity below or the gray chloroform above.

I was flying a Mooney Mite, a single-seat aircraft about the size and shape of a science-fiction dragonfly. It was one of several planes I owned before I bought the Cardinal, each of which was young at the same time of the century I was. This one was made of wood and fabric and was built in 1950, and was powered by a tiny 65-horsepower Continental that looked like an engine pulled out of a Volkswagen Bug. This little power plant held me aloft at 9,500 feet, but the ground below was almost as high, and all around in the snowfall were peaks and ridges that showed on the chart but not through the white shadow: 10,452; 10,073; 11,491; 11,940. At the most I could see half a mile. I had no instruments to allow me to fly in cloud. I was trapped.

I had a small refuge that afternoon: a basin perhaps a mile on a side, a rolling bench of lodgepole pine and grass, rutted by one dirt road, which was deep in snow. I circled this flat place repeatedly, ripping small rents in the peace of the snowfall. Like a plastic yellow-and-blue PT-19 on a pair of strings, like the toy plane I flew and crashed on the school parking lot on weekends when I was a kid, I went around and around dogmatically, aware that should the strings of this vague contact part, I would hurtle away upside down and conclude myself in a mess of broken rubber bands and wings.

At the end of my strings, where the boy holding them would be, were three small houses. It was November, and they were deserted. From my altitude of two or three hundred feet, they seemed faded, stippled on the field with a dry brush, but they offered me slightly more encouragement of survival than did the naked cabin of the plane. A semistraight patch of road, about a thousand feet long, doglegged beside them. If I could put the plane down there, without breaking myself, I might make it. And what choice was there?

I was boxed in. A faint line of cliffs below marked the canyon of the Gros Ventre River, an exit I had already tried. The snow seemed thicker there. Eastward was the ridge I had left two moments ago in sunshine. It was ten thousand feet high. It was invisible. There was pressure in my brain. I must land. I must land.

The landing gear in this old airplane was raised and lowered with a lever at my right hand. I put it down. The plane slowed with the new drag of wheels sticking out in the wind. I circled again. I had no idea of the way the wind was blowing. It was roughly capricious. Without contemplation, I turned for the approach to the piece of road. The snow ahead was deep, smoothing out the rough edges of the ground as if the earth had been hand-rubbed. I was hesitant, one hundred feet above the ground. Should I pull the landing gear back up and sled the plane in on the snow? Was the wind behind me? It pushed me right, away from the road, and the Mite's small rudder was ineffective in a slip. I approached the ground. I felt no fear, no anticipation, just sadness.

Maybe I was going to die here, either by a miscalculation on this difficult crash landing or, injured, from the cold. If so, surely this was a moment that mattered. This was important! I might die here! This was the center of the world, the way the sun seems to concentrate its gaze upon me to make a glory against a cloud. So I must have made some fundamental error here, to get to this place. If I must pay with my life here, there must be something of great importance to be purchased. Surely I had made a vast error. What basic rule of living had I violated? If my life has any significance, this moment was significant. What flaw in my being had drawn me inexorably toward this moment of raw survival or loss? Was I, like a suspect witch, being tested against the nature I revered? If the coals burned my feet, if the rack made me scream, if the snow swallowed me, was my guilt proved?

At Worland, Wyoming, two hours before, I had asked Flight Service for the Jackson weather. Four thousand broken, eight thousand overcast. Slight deterioration forecast. Later, over Dubois, Wyoming, the sun was shining, though there was a sweep of cumulus over the mountains toward Jackson and snow showers along the ridge. The pass looked open, and no doubt, I had thought, I would find, as I had before, that the snow was a light, narrow band along the highest peaks.

It was not so. I had slipped over the ridge, led on by glowing phantoms that said, "It's clear over here," until, leaving me trapped against the slope, the phantoms had faded into uniform obscurity, and I had circled and circled and planned how to land. And now I was gliding, twisting toward the road.

No! It was not right, this approach. I was overshooting my spot, and my landing gear would grab the snow and throw me end over end. Like a shaft of pain, the thought came into my head of Debbie getting a call from Flight Service when I became overdue. "Has your husband called? The last contact we had was . . ."

I still had fuel and power. I advanced the throttle. I raised the landing gear. I leaped toward the Gros Ventre Gorge. Escaping the snare set by my longing to touch the ground, I pursued another phantom glow into the canyon.

As I descended the indefinite ceiling seemed to drop with me. Thickening with snow and evening, the sky grew darker. I could still see half a mile, just to the two walls of the canyon. I could not turn around in this space, and the implacable ceiling forbade a climb. If there were more layers of cloud below, or if the snowfall suddenly began to stick to the plane, I would have no choice but to slow the plane as much as I could, and tumble into the brush in the canyon floor.

But I had three factors in my favor: I knew precisely where I was—this canyon would, if I could get through it, spew me out at the Jackson airport. There was no ice on the plane; and now that my decision was made, my mind was clear to cope with the execution.

The canyon twisted around its river, and I had to make steep turns in turbulence, but slowly the space between walls widened, and suddenly I passed hard over two men in a pickup who were feeding hay to cows on a bench above the river. Neither of them even looked up. In spite of the tightness in my belly, I grinned.

I kept the right wing close to the trees. The canyon wall rose beside me like a curb. Its top edges were indistinct above. I turned with it, turned again, again, again, dropping with the river, down, over stones. The ceiling came down with me, a hand cramming me down into a box.

There's a huge recent landslide near the mouth of Gros Ventre Canyon. I have visited it more than once by car. It tells a story of the age and movement of the planet; it makes the earth fluid in the mind. But when I came around the last curve of rock and saw that slide on the opposite hill, I didn't think about geology. This slide meant that this was going to be a story about life. I had made the right choice. I was safe.

The canyon ended. There was the Jackson airport, sketched in snow-faded charcoal at the edge of the national park.

I was half an hour late on my flight plan. I called Flight Service just in time to prevent the call to Debbie. Inside the office, which was warm and bright-lit against the pale darkness outside, a young instructor looked up from a magazine. He had heard my conversation on the phone. "Came over the hill?" he asked, and then, without waiting for explanations I was reluctant to give, he went on, "I don't know I'd really call that visual flight."

I stood at the window. Snow continued to fall. I had walked on the coals, and I was not consumed. But I was neither absolved nor convicted. It was not a trial. There had been no crime. It had not been so important—just life and death. It was just another day, and now it was ending, and I was still in it. It was snowing. That was all.

Southeast of the Snake River I crossed a mark on the ground that could be understood only by those who had lived there. It was a long concrete slab with walls, perched on the rim of a canyon. It looked like a straight freeway on ramp helicoptered up from Los Angeles to stand out in this dry open country like a monument. In a way that is what it is: It is the spillway for a major dam, but the dam is not there. The spillway is a monument to a man-made natural disaster, the breaking of Teton Dam, which blew out in the spring of 1976 and almost destroyed the villages on the Snake River plain downstream.

In the summer of 1976 I drove through the town of Sugar City, which lies on the Snake River plain not far from here. It appeared as if the city had undergone a nuclear attack. All the houses were abandoned. They looked blackened. Windows and doors were blown out.

Many tilted off their foundations. All around them was debris: broken slabs of wood, ruined cars, a terrible stench. Sugar City had been in the path of a wall of water.

People look at vast constructions of the twentieth century and, contemplating the grandeur of engineering, get philosophical. Instead of proving the permanence of the human presence, as they should, these things seem to draw out our sense of transience and loss. "Someday," we muse, "all these works will be ruins." When you fly over Teton Dam you know the truth in that outlook. Someday is today at Teton Dam.

Death. Fate. Gloom. I stopped in Southeast Idaho, at the east end of the vast Columbia-Snake Plateau Province, where rivers run down into lava and disappear, and springs fed by that vanishing water burst out of the rock in waterfalls hundreds of miles away. I landed at one of the small towns along the Snake. I thought that a breath of that good chilly eastern Idaho wind might break my glum mood. The wind was cold all right. Blew right through me. A young pilot helped me fuel the plane. He offered more good cheer.

"Had a farmer down the road hung himself in his shop couple of days ago," he said. "He had a load of fertilizer and seed and everything and was ready to go, and I guess he got his check from the spud processor and it was about half what he had expected it to be, and he just went into his shop and hung himself."

Help! I didn't shout out loud, but I thought it.

And someone came.

It was Jerry Moore, one of my best and oldest friends. He picked me up at the airport, where I sat waiting like a sack of grain in a depressed market, and took me to his home. He lived on four acres in a nearby town. Jerry's a big man, close to three hundred pounds, but it isn't blubber. I'm about half his weight. To show friendship he punches you on the shoulder or in the ribs. I shake hands. Jerry is an active evangelical Christian, born again in the days I knew him in Mackay, Idaho. I am not. But none of these differences come between us. Something else is more important.

We walked out in the yard, looking around at the land. Far on the north horizon lay a line of blue mountains near the town in which we had both lived: it was the Lost River Range, and the town was Mackay, Idaho. Over the mountains a line of thunderstorms grew. We wandered across the hummocks of Jerry's pasture, where green was beginning to work back into the grass. We had a few words with

Sweet Thing, Jerry's mare. Both of us glanced north, almost surreptitiously, looking toward that place that was once home. We didn't talk about it, except obliquely, just the way we didn't talk about religion.

"You know," Jerry said, "in Idaho I don't think we appreciate what we have."

"Tell me about the American landscape," I said. It was good to see him, and to see those mountains. He slugged me on the arm, and I grinned.

"I guess I wouldn't want to live anyplace else." He was more serious about it than I was. "Oh, I take that back. I really like that country south of Missoula—the Bitterroot. And the Blue Mountains over in Oregon. Near Baker."

We walked around the yard. On the horizon above those familiar mountains the thunderstorms brewed, rising against the lowering spring sunlight. Jerry used to say he would never leave Mackay, and those mountains that filled your life. I used to feel the same way. We looked at his yard. "I took the fence out here. You wouldn't believe the stuff they left out here. Junk! They left mattresses out here."

The pond in the irrigation ditch was dry, a dusty place pockmarked with hoofprints, fringed with dry reeds. "I got a lot of water," Jerry said. "Got twenty-eight shares. But we're at the end of the ditch. Kind of hard to get water down here."

We caught a chicken named Matilda, who was limping around, and cut a tangle of string off her feet. Gulls flew north. Jerry whistled at Sweet Thing, and a peacock in the yard next door went crazy, squawking and screaming. We peered through a knothole in the fence and saw ten peacocks and pea hens strutting around a scuffed yard. Jerry's other chicken, McNugget, ran around in the grass, eating bugs. Jerry looked up toward the mountains to the north and at the thunderstorms and talked about growing up in the Pahsimeroi Valley, a vast dry space between mountains, where he lived by a creek. In season, big trout would come up the stream to spawn, their backs breaking the quick, shallow water. The kids would go down and put set lines out in the evening with night crawlers on 45-pound test line, and bring in the fish in the morning. But his father, the tough old miner, would shoot the trout from the porch.

We played one-on-one basketball on the concrete pad behind the house. Jerry worked up a big sweat. He hadn't grown any smaller. "That's three hundred pounds you're talking about here," he said. "Course I've always been two-eighty, two-eighty-five, so what's ten pounds?" He played hard. Ten years before we had both played for a team in a tiny league up among those mountains on the horizon. It was called Outlaw Basketball. He had weighed as much then. Tough under the basket. Tougher, he might have said, than boiled bat manure. He hadn't lost it. He drove and jumped and the sweat poured off of him, and he beat me.

"Not bad for an old fat guy with a bad heart," he said, giving me a friendly elbow to the ribs.

"How is it these days?"

"Same as it's always been."

Jerry's son Jason scratched his knee on a branch and was crying, and as Jerry cleaned it and patched it, Jason whimpered just like my own boy. If things had worked out differently, they would have grown up together among those mountains. As we walked again in the yard that long line of thunderstorms over Mackay and the Lost River Range grew. Dark thin clouds flew at its leading edge, and clouds boiling high above caught the sun, silhouetted there on the edge of our view each time we glanced north, each of us pining a little for other days, for those mountains.

"I guess this looks just like the Midwest around here," Jerry said, apologizing for the expanse of flatness in the near view.

"No it doesn't. Not at all. No." I grinned.

Each time we looked at the line of thunderstorms the clouds changed shape, and became more dramatic, the air lifting tons of moisture, miles of heat. It was as if a tremendous life was being lived out there between afternoon and dark, fifty miles away, a vast, brief life that we hardly knew. We just glanced at the high wings of this old drama and remarked upon it, and then went back to talking of other things. But we checked the storms as we talked, just to be sure they were there, part of our own hours of living, part of his God, part of my mystery.

The mountains out on the edge of the view were dim, just low blue edges. The storms would rumble through in the night and then die, like time. The mountains would remain. At last we looked at them long. What we shared, what mattered, was that land.

"Nothing like those big old mountains of Mackay, is there?" Jerry said. He slugged me in the arm.

"Nothing."

CHAPTER NINE

Like a wounded body, the world was wrapped in gauze. The clouds below were thin stratus, but here and there were rises and lumps in the smooth white surface, as if the wrap covered the hills of a nose, the hollows of eyes, the rolling sinews of a shoulder. When seen through tears in the fabric, the skin of this old friend was cut and bruised, seamed with gullies, miners' cuts, and roads. There was a dark patch in the thin cloud cover, like an old seepage of blood: somewhere down there was a fire.

I flew south at 15,500 feet, breathing cold oxygen from a bottle through tubes plugged into my nose. I could see over the eastern edge of the clouds, toward the blue and white ridges of the Wind River Range, and I had a moment's glimpse down into blue cloud shadow, and saw a curve of river below layer after layer of clouds.

When you cross clouds it is like watching the curtain close on the first act. There is movement behind the curtain, and you know the scene is going to be different when you emerge on the other side. I flew over the whiteness south of Jackson Hole, with the spine of the Tetons behind. I crossed a mountain whose woods were scarred by the parallel clearings of avalanche tracks. Then the clouds moved below; the curtain closed.

My glory moved across the clouds like a spotlight, searching for actors. Macho Irene whispered in the wings. I came to GRIPS, south of Big Piney, east of SWEAT. Could I come to grips? Once more on the loose, I drifted. I sat at fifteen thousand feet, sucking my bottled air like a baby. The planet was smothered and distant. It looked like Venus. It was beautiful. It was austere.

For a while it was good to be apart from the overwhelming presence of human beings. But the intermission grew too long. I was not out here to look at hills or mountains or clouds. I have seen endless photo books on the American landscape in which the power lines, the roads, the junkyards, the open-pit mines, the subdivisions, the statues, the harvested fields have all been edited out. That's not why I came. I came to chase the glory and see the play.

Forty-six miles on the loran C, north of Rock Springs, I had a glimpse: blue-brown land dusted with snow, a frozen lake, snowmobile tracks on the lake. Forty miles later I had another look between clouds: this time a scattering of trailer houses, parallel lines on the ground, converging out toward the east, an interstate, an old highway, a path through sagebrush under a power line. All headed east, ducking under the cloud, but out there at the point in perspective where they should have met was a billow in the flat cloud—a curious round growth of heat-heaved moisture on a day of cool stratus. It was a power plant blowing steam into the gray morning.

This province was the Wyoming Basin, a vast, open, high, windy place: cold. The Wyoming Basin is rich with energy resources, including coal. That power plant was near Rock Springs, notorious in the recent past: boom town of energy independence, now quietly pumping power to other parts of the nation from its pocket of blight among the Rockies.

Seventy miles south of Rock Springs, the curtain of cloud at last withdrew, and there was the scene: mountains stippled with piñon-juniper woodland; a big brown river. It was a new set on the stage. This was order and wildness mixed: straight lines and shadows of layered cliffs and red rock; precipice and mountain. The high plains of the Wyoming Basin had turned into the maze of flat-topped cliffs and ditches of the Colorado Plateau Province, and what clouds were left had changed from layers of stratus into puffs of cumulus. Among them I bounced around like a Ping-Pong ball on a fountain, riding the warming air down across the Roan Plateau, across the wide valley by Grand Junction where the Colorado and the Gunnison rivers meet, where the national grid asserts itself for a few miles, then south across the parallel canyons and mesas west of Delta and Montrose. Wild country, full of wild animals: I once spent an enforced night in one of those canyons, down by the roaring waters of the Dry Fork of the Escalante River, in the company of a hunter, a scientist, and a wild, invisible lion.

America teems with life that isn't us. I seldom see it from the air. Even elk on an open hillside become specks from two thousand feet.

But in spring and summer lakes are covered with fishing boats, and in fall and winter pickup trucks are parked on high ridges and remote meadows while their drivers prowl the woods with guns. Americans pursue wild things. A deer, a fish, a bear is like a glory running across patchy clouds; a glimpse of something rare and mystical that must be attained. In the West vast acreages of land are managed for what are called wildlife values. These creatures seem important. These wild animals thrill us, drive us, and inhabit the land with their mystery.

To human beings the mountain lion is the wildest creature in the American landscape. It baffles us. It walks alone. It hunts in silence. It kills and eats the largest animals in the woods. It is unafraid. It sees us more often than we see it.

Lions are controversial in every state in which they live. No one seems to be able to agree on how many there are, how they should be hunted, or even how they live. In the states in which they aren't known to exist they're controversial, too, because people keep seeing phantom lions tiptoeing through bayous in Louisiana, or climbing power poles in West Virginia. It's impossible to find a lion without dogs. When you do see one it's usually a fluke.

Jerry Moore once hiked through snow in the mountains and came upon lion tracks. He followed them along a bench below a cliff. They led past the cliff and up a slope and then back along the cliff's top. There on the edge lay the long, fresh impression of the lion's body, where it had crouched, looking down the rock. "I could see where the tail had swished the snow," Jerry had told me. He went to the edge and peered over at what the lion had been watching. There, below, were the tracks of Jerry's own boots in the snow.

"He was like a CIA agent," Jerry said. "I decided at that point that he could do his own thing."

Years later I saw a lion myself. It won that skirmish too.

For two days before the lion trapped Allen Anderson, Don Kattner, and me in the canyon of the Dry Fork of the Escalante, we had been out looking for it and its solitary relatives with aircraft, trucks, and radios. Allen Anderson is a game biologist, an employee of the state of Colorado, who was studying lions. Kattner is a hunter. Anderson, who was fifty-eight when I visited him, is tall, lean, austere, clean-shaven, a man of infinite patience and rectitude, a careful scientist who used to race bicycles in his time off. Don Kattner, who was thirty-seven, is stocky, bearded, flamboyant, hotheaded, a professional guide hired by Anderson as part of a Colorado state study of mountain lions. Kattner hunts for a living and hunts for fun. He calls the big cats simply lions. Anderson uses all the tools of modern wildlife science: radio collars, aircraft tracking, computerized data. After studying the etymology of the various names for the big cat—catamount, panther, cougar—Allen calls them pumas. Kattner runs dogs, and trusts them and his instinct more than the machines. His acronym for the qualities it takes to be a lion hunter is PPC: Persistence, Patience, and Coors.

Our first morning out, Kattner found tracks, and Anderson heard a beeping in his headset. The beeps were in code. They said, "Here is lion number six."

It is strange to listen to a collared lion on headphones. The transmitter emits a rhythmical cross between a tick and a chirp. The strength of this broadcast varies according to distance and the orientation of an antenna, but when you first listen to a lion ticking away somewhere out in those woods you think you're hearing a heartbeat. The sound seems intimate. Suddenly you're there. Your ear is hard against the furred neck. Disembodied, tawny, you pace among the junipers with the breath of meat in your mouth, your nostrils wide to the smell of frightened deer.

To Allen Anderson it was more like tuning in satellites. Lion Six ticked away on 149.909 megahertz. She was a female whose collar was running down. Anderson wanted to catch her to change the batteries. All day we followed that lion, pushing through scrub oak and juniper, while Don muttered about the efficiency of the radio and Allen limped steadily on, wearing the headphones and waving his antenna wand across the landscape. Don's four dogs—Jack, Doc, Turkey, and Tiger, chained together two by two to prevent a wild dash before Don was ready to let them go—paced the ground restlessly, their chains jingling, and sat regularly to get spiny chunks of jumping cholla cactus off their feet. Turkey was the young enthusiast of the group, wide-eyed and restless; Doc was the wise old hand. He kept his nose to the ground, and whenever a piece of cactus got him, he ate it.

Allen was like Doc: stubborn and determined. He had short white hair and the look of a monk; a tall slender abbot of the ascetic life of wildlife research. Persistence and patience suited him too. He suffered from ankylosing spondylitis, a degenerative arthritis that would probably cripple him slowly and lead him to a painful death. Some days he found it difficult even to walk. In the spring a year before he had fallen into one of these many precipitous canyons and torn the tendon right off a kneecap. So he limped as we pushed through the brush, but the work continued. "I just hope that I can finish it," he said.

We started the search for Number Six at about 8:15 A.M., and followed the wand and the lion's electronic heartbeat all day across the gullies and mesas of the Monitor Creek drainage. There were fir trees and high creeks of muddy water down in the canyons, but on the mesa tops ranchers, trying to make more grassland for their cows, had years before torn down the vegetation with chains stretched between bulldozers, so the landscape was a ripped-up mixture of young juniper and scrub oak and old gray lines of slash. During the hours of tramping we talked about dogs, and their lore. I told Kattner another hunter's story of a dog who, when a trail was cold, would lick twigs to moisten the scent and thus find his way to the cat. Kattner was skeptical.

"Aw, bullshit," he observed.

We talked about lions, particularly about the various legal systems under which they exist. Although they are no longer considered varmits, to be killed for bounty, they are legally hunted in most Western states, with legal constraints that vary from a year-round hunting season in Arizona to a temporary but complete ban on sport hunting in California. Anderson was reluctant to comment on the California ban, which was controversial; his own study was related. There was too much emotion in the California dispute: scientists were making unpleasant remarks about other scientists in public hearings.

"It's a funny thing about wildlife and the way people view it," Allen said. "I know some people—fine scientific people—but when they get into wildlife they kind of lose their scientific capabilities."

Kattner, who had grown up in northern California—hunting—was more vivid about the California ban. He didn't feel any need to be scientific: "It was good they closed it when they did," he said, "because the sumbitches were getting down. But now there's lions everywhere."

The two were always at gentle philosophical odds. Once when I visited them in Montrose, Don had been fishing down on the Colorado and had caught an officially endangered fish, which he had to release.

"These endangered species might as well not be in there," he said, with a wry look at Allen, "you can't eat them."

Allen went for it:

"Don, you know there are other reasons for animals besides eating them."

Don grinned. "I know, I know. I meant if they're so endangered, how come I'm catching them?"

Before lions, Allen had studied deer and elk. "To me this is just another facet of deer ecology," he said. "It's certainly been a privilege to work on them."

At 5 P.M., still chasing the lion, we came to a ridge and Allen's wand pointed down into still another canyon, already shadowed by evening.

"It's in the bottom there," he said.

"Don't you believe it," Don said.

"That's what the stuff says," Allen said. He had a scratch on his face from a thorn. White stubble showed on his cheek. He strode on. Don shrugged and followed. The dogs jingled along. But at five to six the sun had gone behind the mountains, and the lion was still beeping from too far south. It was a long walk back to the truck in the dark.

The next day Allen and I spent the morning flying across the same country with a plane that also carried antennas, locating the collared lions one by one, so he could chart their movement. If the lions had been wrecked airplanes broadcasting homing signals, we would have saved no lives; though we located all of Allen's animals, we saw no sign of even one. It was strange indeed to pinpoint lion after lion in a landscape in which I could have wandered for years and never once been aware of their presence. But they were there, along with other lions whom Allen had not yet met. When we landed for lunch there was a message from Don via radio: "Come to the Dry Fork."

"Hell of a canyon," Allen said. We drove up in a pickup whose hood still bore a dusty smear left over from when Allen and Don had boiled the skull of a lion that had died. Don was on the radio. "I'm down here by the creek. Got one treed. He's about fifty feet up in a doug fir. Definitely no collar on him." This was a fresh lion. In the background of the transmission dogs barked and howled. We packed rope and water, but, alas, no food and jackets, and went down into the canyon at about one in the afternoon. Allen had the rifle and a little green pack that contained a collar and the tranquilizing darts.

By two we could hear the dogs in the distance. "Take the trail on the benches," Don had said on the radio, "come up-country about three quarters of a mile, and go down the ridge where the deer horns are on the ground." By two-thirty we were down along the creek, and the dogs' voices were drowned by the noise of the high water, which was the color of sand and ran so hard we could hear the thump and crack of big stones tumbling down its bed. At about three we came through a stand of budding sumac and there was the tree with the lion in it.

The lion was a bundle, crouched on branches close to the trunk. The sun was behind it. It was in shadow. It looked down at the frenzy that Doc, Turkey, and the rest, whom Don had tethered at the bottom of the tree, were making below him. When the lion heard us in the brush, he looked up.

For a moment we stared at each other at fifty yards. I have seen many photographs of mountain lions: broad head, big eyes, vertical dark stripes in the tawny face. This one was the same. It seemed both enormously rare and familiar. It was like making eye contact with a famous person in the street: a shock of connection and then distance. Its gaze was intimate; it was remote.

Something about our movement led the lion to a decision. It didn't like the dogs, but it liked us less. It came down the tree right in the faces of the dogs. As it dropped from branch to branch, it seemed to grow. With its final leap ten feet to the ground, it stretched huge and golden, backlit by the sun.

The lion moved fast. Don was almost as quick. He leaped to release the tethers of the dogs as soon as the lion came out of the tree. The lion hit the ground, made a single leap to the middle of the creek, sprang out of its splash, and was gone.

Doc was right behind, yelping and howling. Turkey was still barking up the empty tree. He never even saw it happen.

Don shouted at Turkey, "You sumbitch!" Turkey came out of his trance and followed Doc. Don followed the dogs. Allen and I trailed after. Soon the sound of the dogs faded and disappeared around a bend in the narrow canyon.

We settled down to walk. Every once in a while a distant howl floated off the rocks, its direction lost in a maze of echoes. I followed Allen upstream, through brush and boulders. The back of his shirt was wet with sweat. There was blood and dust on the back of his hand from a brush with a stone. Trees scratched his face and plucked the hat off his head. He walked on.

The day before, Don had expanded his philosophy of hunting lions: "You've got to put it in your mind," he had said, "and pound it out, day after day." Pounding it out, Allen and I trailed both Don and the lion, but at least we could find Don's footprints. We caught up with him on a little ridge above the creek. "These cats," he said. "You read where they don't have much endurance, but I don't know about that. We chased one for six miles in snow one time, and about two miles of that we had snowmobiles. There! Did you hear that?" Another distant howl.

We pushed on. Thorny wild rose bushes, hung with dried hips, lashed us. Gooseberry spines struck like bees. The creek was roaring sand. The sun went behind a shoulder of the canyon. At a quarter to six Allen pointed out a patch of dirt where, long before, a lion had made a scrape in the valley floor. Then, suddenly, the three younger dogs appeared, silent, casting about among the trees.

Allen said, "Uh-oh."

Doc appeared last, sniffing the ground and peering up into trees, as if hoping against the evidence of his nose to see that severe cat face among the branches.

Don eyed us skeptically. "You fellows might want to get on out of here," he said. "In about an hour it's going to be so dark you can't see anything."

Allen looked at him. It was a look of astonishment. He said nothing. We made no preparations to leave. Then there was a single bawl from Doc, and the dog was on his way again.

"In just a minute," Don said dryly, "he'll lick a twig and find him."

Allen and I sat down among the junipers. Doc howled sporadically, like an aviator giving position reports. A pink light appeared on the higher clouds and grew red. At 6:45 the light was gone. In the dusk Don went across the creek and called Doc in, but fifteen minutes later the dog was gone, bawling again, following some kind of trail up a ledge on the other side. "Once Doc wouldn't get back in the truck," Don said. It grew cold. We built a big fire beside a stone. Don smoked and stared into the flames. He had held that lion treed for over an hour, waiting for us, for the dart and collar.

"I'll tell you," he said. "If it had been a different deal, that sumbitch would have been dead."

Hunched like the dogs in the dust, we dozed, getting up every hour or so to rebuild the fire against the cold spring night. All through that night the lion seemed to enlarge itself in my memory, leaping, backlit, from the tree. He was haloed; he was a glory. If only we had caught him! A silent landscape had suddenly manufactured a bundle of intense and powerful life out of trees and tawny stone. Where had he come from? Where was he now?

Why were people so curious about other lives? The state of Colorado needed to understand lions in order to manage big game and prevent predation on cattle, but that was not what drove Allen Anderson through the thorns and across the chained landscape, day after day, in pain, bearing his radio receiver wand and his books of statistics. Nor did Don Kattner pursue lions with his dogs and his intuition just to bring them death. Science and instinct shared a goal. We chased the glory, where it glowed through the trees. Wilderness, mystery, life.

The wild creatures of the mountains were festooned with radios. Radios were out there everywhere. When Allen was tuning in Number Six, he had had to be careful with the frequencies: deer and mountain sheep out here within radio range also carried radio collars for other people's studies.

We dozed, waiting for morning to set us free. Out there, wild animals carried our transmitters around, telling the secrets of their lives to the most lonely creature on earth. Down in the canyon of the Dry Fork we huddled close to the flames, and our shadows danced, long and black, out into the wilderness.

PART 3

CHAPTER TEN

"I have been plagued by an urge to understand the contemporary landscape," John Brinckerhoff Jackson said, "to understand and love it regardless of its unsightliness."

In late 1944, when he was an intelligence officer in the United States Army during the allied advance into Germany, Jackson went into the hilly Eifel region, between the Rhine River and the border of Holland. He was following an old guidebook of the region, and as he traveled on the road suggested by the guidebook he saw a sign on the road, which read, in German, "To the dam."

There was no dam in the guidebook. There was no dam on the maps drawn by the United States Army. He followed the road sign over the hill. There was the dam. When he went back to headquarters he said, "There's an enormous lake out there. We're not going to get through that."

"There must be some mistake," said the men who drew the maps. "Our maps are right. There cannot be a dam. You're crazy."

"I'd seen it, for Christ's sake," Jackson said. So, determined, he took the day off and drove back through the battered landscape of Belguim to Brussels. There, at the Royal Topographic Institute, he found a map that showed the dam.

It was mid-December 1944. "I went back," he said, "to what I thought would be triumphant vindication. And that was the night that the Germans burst through in the Battle of the Bulge, and nobody was interested in what I had to say."

Later, people became interested. Jackson began the journal *Landscape* after his postwar career as a rancher in New Mexico was ended by a fall from a horse that put him in the hospital for months. The little magazine was never prosperous, but Jackson's published observations on New Mexico and, later, the whole United States became a respected part of the literature of geography. *Landscape*, Lewis Mumford wrote, "has made a unique contribution to the thought of our time. . . . No other magazine, with such modest resources, has done so much to focus attention to this major aspect of man's existence."

"A rich and beautiful book is always open before us," Jackson wrote in the first issue of *Landscape* in 1951. "We have but to learn to read it."

I flew to Santa Fe from Montrose, struggling over houses and farms built at elevations higher than the peaks behind my home in Montana. On the high slopes were enormous groves of aspen, now all gray like a soft beard; downy, like the fuzz on penguin chicks. All along the ridge of the San Juan Mountains, to the south of me, a cloud hung snow showers across the route I wanted to take. It looked like the many soapy hanging rags of a car wash. I decided not to be churned in that machine. I'd fly east to get around it.

South of Gunnison I flew over huge snow-covered hillsides. Ski tracks and snowmobile tracks crossed them in languid curves. The most austere landscapes carry our signs. Then I crossed a ridge south of North Pass, and a vast plain appeared ahead, checkerboarded and polka-dotted with farmland. A single mountain stood engulfed in a snowstorm to the south. It was the northern end of the valley of the Rio Grande.

Little towns lay up against the edge of the hills. At Monte Vista a grain elevator stood out like a steeple in the late sunlight—a church of commerce. A tidy automobile junkyard made cornrows of glitter in the sun. White houses gleamed like scattered teeth out along country roads. Outside Del Norte a sewage lagoon shimmered in the low light. It made pretty patterns, as if the high school girls were doing synchronized swimming in it.

I was changing the stage set again. The Colorado Plateau rose into the southern edge of the Rocky Mountain Province. I crossed these last ridges, the ground opened out—and I was back with the languorous ladies of the Basin and Range Province.

And I was back with the grid. In the mountains the grid is subdued by the unruly terrain. I had forgotten its power. I came out over the flat land, and the hump and swirl of earth were abruptly replaced by lines, and suddenly it looked as if the whole landscape in the valley was manufactured. Oddly, all the straight lines crossing this valley, north and south of Alamosa, bent slightly to the south, as if they were clotheslines hung with fields.

The darkness came on before I got to Santa Fe, so I stopped just north, at the town of Espanola. Frost came with the darkness, and I wrapped myself in the sleeping bag in the plane, read to the kids about trolls and wizards, and thought about Debbie. All we had to share tonight was loneliness. Sometimes all this traveling seemed as deadly as the disease she fought. We'd talk on the phone and hang up, and it was like crashing into silence.

I slept deeply but woke chilled. The morning was clear and cold, but it rained lightly in the plane, dripping off the windshield as I rose over a military drill at the high school at Espanola. A formation of boys stood behind the gym: ROTC. Their figures were foreshortened into stumpy soldiers. They were good troops, arranged each an arm's length from the next, but three faces broke formation to flash a glance upward at the low plane. They were bright in the shadow, luminous young planets shining in the long morning eclipse of the gym. Then at a command the faces vanished, the kids all came to attention, and I saw a flicker of hands as the children saluted the chilly morning.

Along the Rio Grande the grid was broken. Beside the river and up its wide banks there were no broad rectangles. Instead, the land was divided into long narrow strips. Among the grand blocks of the American survey this riverside was a subtle interruption. It was as if an artist who had always worked with slabs of color had changed his whole style to draw a fine and delicate sketch down the center of his work. The sketch was simple: numerous nearly parallel lines perpendicular to a river, dividing long narrow fields colored many shades of green and brown. But this quiet central sketch was profound: it changed the quality of the human mark on this land; it softened it.

This was the old landscape. I looked down into four centuries. It was like looking at the horizontal lines of strata cut by the canyons in the Colorado Plateau, and seeing geologic time. Here, captured in narrow fields, was a pattern of memory, a layering of paths of the mind. These lines of ownership were drawn on the landscape by Spanish settlers long before Americans came along with their Jeffersonian quilt. They were designed by ancient necessities. Irrigation is as old as agriculture in this dry air, and each of these fields ran from the *acequia*, the water ditch, down to the river. Here ownership was never vast, but everyone had a piece of the action that made the land come alive: the fields lay between water and water, one after another, like planks in a boardwalk.

I flew over ragged hills speckled with junipers, and dry washes covered with vehicle tracks that crossed and mingled with the braided flow of sand. A small reservoir reflected pale blue; a trailer park snuggled close to a freeway, its relative.

The big houses of Sante Fe were built up in the hills where the views are, not down on the slices of land by the water where the *acequia* once brought the only wealth there was. The big houses had flat roofs like pueblos, adorned with skylights and solar panels.

The whole city was reddish-brown, earth-tone, sandy. I saw no water. I looked for a river. A committee of important people had made formal recommendations for the preservation and improvement of the Santa Fe River, but I couldn't even find the river where it runs through town. I circled over the new hotels and the old plaza, maintaining a discreet altitude, but where was the famous river? Donald Keyhoe was the quiet man among my companions, the little fellow with the big ears, who so often was the butt of Lindbergh's practical jokes, but at Santa Fe he offered a remark. When he was here, he said, it was "a beautiful oasis in the surrounding land of rock and desert." The river must have been the oasis's heart. Today Sante Fe is a sprawl, tumbling down the alluvial fan like a spill of clay marbles. It is no longer an oasis. It is a metropolis.

At last, there was the river, a thread of water, stones, and brown sand. It did not seem to have much to do with the city. It, too, was like a memory.

John Jackson does not live on the American grid. Near the Santa Fe airport I flew over a village down the hill from the city. It was the town in which Jackson lives, not far from the vast dusty compound of the state prison and close to the horse racetrack. It was a small community on the banks of a creek. Jackson's house, like most of the others at the heart of what is left of this town, stood deep in time, on a narrow strip of watered land between the *acequia* and the stream.

The dirt road rattled my teeth, and shook the headlight right off the motorcycle. It hung on its wire. I had to stop and bolt it back on. Out along the dirt roads down the slope from Santa Fe new houses were scattered around on the open desert like the graves on the Papago Reservation: people choosing to live out in the dry wind.

I got lost out by the horse racetrack but found my way to John Jackson's house at last. The house was a modest adobe set among dry wintry trees. In the yard were a small pine tree with a single red Christmas tree globe in it, a wind goose planted in the lawn, and vines growing up chicken wire. Jackson was watering the plants.

"Forgive the mess," he said, "that's the way I live."

Sometimes when you read someone's work the impression you build of the person opposes the reality. But the ghostly presence of John Brinckerhoff Jackson, the geographer, who traveled with me, was no different from John Jackson the man, whom I met in Santa Fe. He is a small man with a dark, weathered face and large eyes. He wore jeans and a plaid shirt. His writing is carefully measured, eloquent, observant, and utterly unencumbered by bias; so is he. I envied the gift to see so clearly.

I was there in the afternoon. In the mornings Jackson opens a small community school, cleans the place and gets it ready for the day. Some days he works for poor people, cleaning up their yards, hauling junk away in his Toyota pickup. To them he is just a small vigorous workman with a handy truck. Sometimes he has to go away for a few days and can't help with the school, can't work in the yards. The people with whom he works have no idea that on those days he is away delivering a guest lecture at Rice University, at Columbia, or at Harvard.

We sat outside in a cool breeze. An occasional pickup truck passed on the open road, leaving behind a breath of dust. We talked about what you could see of New Mexico from the air: the vast spread of roads near Albuquerque; huge subdivisions with no houses; the terraced mountains where the uranium mines once were; the white dishes of the radio telescopes listening to the stars; abandoned homes and farmsteads.

"But aside from the ruination and the sudden development," he said, "I think that the air view could show what the little irrigation ditch does to the whole valley. These ditches were done in the original years, back in the seventeenth or eighteenth century all by hand and with very crude tools, and I think they represent quite an engineering stunt. And they survived. They used to be the main artery, literally, of the community. The ditch made people come together. They had to elect their officers, they had to get out and clear it, they had to go to meetings. It was about the most indigenous organization of a village that New Mexico had. The church was there, of course, but that wasn't quite the same. They would call the organization the 'ditch.' You go to the meetings of the ditch, and you elect the mayordomo, and then go out and clean the ditch, all of you together. It used to be kind of nice, because at the end of the ditch cleaning there would be a blessing; a priest would come out and bless the ditch for the rest of the year."

The wind goose on the lawn turned in the breeze. Jackson's five acres went down to the creek past a pond he had made from a spring. Tall cottonwood trees stood beside the pond, trees he had planted.

"Well," he said, "that has begun to dwindle, because farmers don't farm here anymore. They have the ditch, and they're glad to have water for their gardens, but the idea of depending on the irrigation ditch to give them a livelihood is gone, so they don't work on it anymore. They don't come to meetings. Nobody wants to be mayordomo anymore."

It was an elegy, not a lament. In that dry early-spring landscape, with the gray trees and the brown grass and the dust, Jackson was like the earth itself, weathered but undefeated, knowing the world's history is of change, not decline.

"I think perhaps desertion is more of an aspect of the landscape than we realize sometimes—because we don't want to look at it," he said. "Many villages have been deserted. Whole valleys have been deserted. It means nothing to us today, but at one time they were full of imagery and full of symbolism to the people who live there. And that is just wiped out. It will happen here too. Things that we think are exquisite and have a marvelous sense of place—twenty years from now they won't be here.

"There is a great deal of talk about community and the virtues of community, and community usually means living together in one place, and sharing experiences, which seems to be totally essential. And yet I have lived long enough even in this little village here to see the community almost disintegrate. The ditches are gone. The school has disappeared. The Catholic Church—there was a time when you had to stay within your parish. Well, that has been abolished, so there you go again, one of the institutions which held us together has disappeared. And the family has disintegrated to some extent. Well, there are a variety of things that make the old idea of community a very repressive thing in retrospect, and here we are living more or less satisfactory lives, it seems to me, without that community."

John Brinckerhoff Jackson is seventy-nine. All his life he has looked with curiosity at the world out of those big blue eyes. He was graduated from Harvard with a BS in history and literature in 1932, but he became interested in geography reading the works of French geographers in France during the war. "That set me on fire," he said, "that geography could be written with knowledge and taste and style, and not be pedantic."

He has written that way about the landscape of the Southwest, and the rest of the world, since 1951, when he published the first issue of the magazine *Landscape*. The eminent geographer D. W. Meinig described Jackson as "an inveterate traveler, crossing the continent and the ocean time and again, doing field work from car, truck, plane, and motorcycle; receptive to the common scene . . . open to change, attracted by new experiences. . . ."

Everything has meaning to his view. When he saw a flat building he thought about how Americans like horizontal space. When he saw a parking lot he thought of it as as place of freedom. He used to ride his motorcycle all over the country—"I was crazy about it." When he rode his motorcycle, he thought about motion. The modern viewer participated in the landscape: the view became alive. This landscape, "seen at a rapid, sometimes even a terrifying pace, is composed of rushing air, shifting lights, clouds, waves, a constantly moving, changing horizon, a constantly changing surface. . . . The view is no longer static . . . the traditional way of seeing and experiencing the world is abandoned; in its stead we become active participants, the shifting focus of a moving abstract world; our nerves and muscles are all of them brought into play. To the perceptive individual there can be an almost mystical quality to the experience; his identity seems for the moment to be transmuted."

A few years ago, when a whole flock of writers—including me— saw only ugliness and blight in the coal-development trailer camps that sprang up in western rural landscapes in the sixties and seventies, Jackson wrote instead about the people who lived in them: "They are wanderers in a landscape always inhabited by wanderers. They never settled down. The way they came out of nowhere, stayed awhile and then moved on without leaving more than a few half-hidden traces behind, makes them forever part of this lonely and beautiful country."

Jackson looked at the trailer camps and saw nomads crossing the landscape the way the Navajos once did; he saw the neon strips on the edges of American towns—the strips where most other observers came, saw, and retched—and noticed in the golden arches and mall signs a powerful expression of the needs and desires of ordinary people. "How are we to tame this force," he wrote, "unless we understand it and even develop a kind of love for it?" This was an admonition to the rest of us. He heeded the thought long ago; for the earth and the works of people he is already unfailingly generous with his affection:

"Wherever we go," he wrote, "whatever the nature of our work, we adorn the face of the earth with a living design which changes and is eventually replaced by that of a future generation. How can one tire of looking at their variety, or of marveling at the forces within man and nature that brought it about?"

"Jackson never purported to be a research scholar," wrote D. W. Meinig. Meinig is a research scholar. I carried his latest book with me. *Atlantic America: 1492–1800.* If I had left it behind, Six Zero One could have carried a passenger. Jackson, Meinig continued, "openly assumed the role of the speculative intuitive interpreter reaching beyond the usual realms of science."

"He is one of those richly creative idiosyncratic people," Meinig said much later when I met him at Syracuse. "He talked about landscape with a kind of clarity and intelligence that transcended anything that the geographers were doing."

Jackson and Meinig are different kinds of men. Meinig is tall, urbane, gray-haired, a man with bushy eyebrows and the personal power to handle the title of the Maxwell Professor of Geography. He writes major books; he consults for *National Geographic*; he has taught professors in colleges around the country. Jackson is small, almost bald, darkened by the sun, a little laborer who works outdoors for the poor people and looks around him at the landscape with wide blue affectionate eyes.

In an essay about Jackson, Meinig once summarized seven points about the landscape he suggested were theme of Jackson's work. They were:

> 1. The idea of landscape is anchored upon *human life*; "the true and lasting meaning of the word landscape: not something to look at but to live in; and not alone but with other people."
> 2. Landscape is a *unity*, a wholeness, an integration, of community and environment; man is ever part of nature, and the city is basically no less involved than the countryside. . . .
> 3. Therefore we must always seek to understand the landscape in *living terms*. . . .

4. Just as the elementary unit of mankind is the person, the elementary unit in the landscape is the *individual dwelling.* . . .

5. To understand the landscape in living terms requires primary attention to the *vernacular,* to the environments of the workaday world. . . .

6. In the broadest view, all landscapes are *symbolic.* . . . They are "expressions of a persistent desire to make the earth over in the image of some heaven."

7. And, evitably, landscapes are ever undergoing *change.*

➤ There was a ham in the oven. "Do stay and have a slice of ham," Jackson said. We sat at a small kitchen table and continued the conversation. He was reluctant to talk about himself. That subject did not interest him. He was still living by the way the landscape is worn by the people who put it on like clothing and live in it. Jackson's life in New Mexico covers almost as much time as it has been since Lindbergh was here. Some of the changes he has seen do not give him joy.

"I went around in those days to village after village and enjoyed them very much," he said. "And I went back recently to a lot of those villages and they were awful. They were slums. The houses were falling down, the irrigation canals were full of beat-up cars and trash. Nobody had a job. It was pitiful. Travelers don't realize when they're in Santa Fe, with its luxury and sophistication, that twenty miles away you can find a slum that is worse than anything in Appalachia. You feel sorry for a community that is simply to expire. The fields are overgrown and the ditches are not used, the houses are falling down. But they live there because that's all they have.

"I've been writing about vernacular houses, which in this state are not picturesque. There are some pretty little adobe houses, but most of them are very shabby, impoverished little houses. And that's the way most people in the world live, and there is just no point in ignoring them, or deploring them. And so I have been trying to study them. New Mexico is ideal for that, because we're so poor and so inefficient and so resigned."

"Do you go and talk to people about their houses?" I asked. I should have known the answer. The knowledge of it haunts every journalist, every sociologist: It is impossible to get to the roots of things with interviews. You have to live it.

"No. I don't. I should. Well, you overhear conversations, you do it yourself. I wince at people going around, people who barge into somebody's house and say do you mind if I take a picture of your kitchen? I just couldn't do that. I just do it from my own experience.

"I work in people's gardens in town. I want something to do, and poor people appeal to me. Poor people need services just as much as anybody who has a pocketbook. There are three places I go just to help them clean up."

John Jackson's home seemed timeless. It was like New Mexico: a place where past and present do not seem divided. The house is made of adobe and is full of old books. Outside, the long narrow piece of land goes down past the pond and an orchard to the stream. But about five slices of land to the east is a large, gaudy conglomeration of structures that leaves a different impression. It is the modern Santa Fe, a place people come for empowerment, or for personal grounding. It is a resort called Sunrise Springs: If you go there for the weekend you can jog or roller skate on the oval track, meditate in the electronic chairs, get a modern massage, or swim in the mystical springs. "Our intention," a brochure says, "is to promote creative expression, self-empowerment, and vision-making."

I dropped in at Sunrise Springs on my way home to the plane. The office was stark white. A young woman behind the desk rattled off the amenities: "We have astrology, we have alpha chairs, we have massage." The special for the night was $42.50, including one hour of massage and half an hour in the alpha chamber. A young man who had managed, by careful study, to assume the least agreeable mannerisms of California youth, came in griping about having to take food to some old dudes in one of the rooms. I went and stood on a deck overlooking the mystical pond. A garden grew herbs in the middle of the jogging track. You could chase the glory here in all kinds of ways. The place was an expression of a persistent desire to make the earth over in the image of some kind of heaven.

⤳ I took two days and flew a loop around New Mexico, to catch up with Lindbergh. John Jackson rode with me again, in spirit. South of Santa Fe the Rio Grande appeared beneath, rolling down from the north, with dusty-looking trees beside it. The river was big and gray-green-yellow in this season. Narrow fields lined it, the old boardwalk going south. A single canoe floated down the water, and the person in it paused to admire life; the still paddle shone.

At Albuquerque I crossed the thousands of acres marked by straight and curving dirt roads of which Jackson had warned. They looked like an enormous diagram of a solid-state electronic circuit board, drawn in the dirt by Caterpillar tractors. A few blocks were packed with glittering bunches of new buildings; crystals growing on a string. In time the magic crystals may grow on all these empty lines; the grid will hum.

"So that," Jackson said dryly, "is something sensational from the air about New Mexico."

Everywhere New Mexico was sensational: uranium mines, terraces up a creek, with long dirt roads; five trucks lined up on the highway, pulling what looked like apartment buildings—big white blocks too large to be trailers, with windows in them—the nomads were still moving; tablelands so cracked and split that they looked like concrete poured a milllennium ago and left to the weather.

New Mexico: "There are ruins like geological formations, disorders of tumbled stone," Jackson said. "There are immense arrays of slowly crumbling rocks that look like ruins. . . . It is the sort of landscape, which (before the creation of the bomb) we associated with the world after history had come to an end—sheep grazing among long-abandoned ruins, the lesson of Ozymandias driven home by enormous red arches leading nowhere, lofty red obelisks or needles commemorating events no one had ever heard of, symbols of the vanity of human endeavor . . . What makes the landscape so impressive and so beautiful is that it teaches no copybook moral, no ecological or social lesson. It tells us that there is another way of measuring time, and that the present is, in fact, an enormous interval in which even the newest of man-made structures are contemporary with the primeval."

New Mexico: I passed another prison; another ruin; I breathed juniper pollen in the rough air. The Cardinal bucked. I sneezed. Slam, bang, woof! I could see Lindbergh's serious face, the one he showed the public. "In planes of the 1920s," Lindbergh said, "the climate you flew through actually came inside the cockpits, bringing a sensual contact with the geography below." Thanks. Six Zero One's the same. Woof!

I made a sloppy landing at Whiskey Creek Airport near Silver City, then, tired from wrestling with the wheel, spent the evening hitting my head against things like the wing and the cabin ceiling; dropping papers, tapes, and pens in inaccessible places; and being betrayed by my machines. My portable printer broke down; my computer broke down; even the little fluorescent light I read by suddenly faded away.

I opened the plane's door, and the wind whipped it closed across my knees. Ow! Damn. I propped it open and sat in the cool breeze, looking around. The motto under the logo of the Silver City *Enterprise* the year Lindbergh flew over this town was "Best Out-of-Doors Country Out of Doors." Is it still? The airstrip was on a ridge top. From there I could see far across the valley to the huge open-pit copper mine at the town of Santa Rita. It was surrounded by amber lights. The plane shook with the wind, and the stars were hard, with narrow dark stripes of cloud against them. The moon was bigger than half, so the mine lights had a feeling of distance in a dark gray world; they didn't just hang in blackness. And off to the right, the south, the two stacks of the smelter stood spotlit, huge, and distant. The plume was partly lighted too; it looked like a bend in the stack, leaning over, as if the stack was wax melting before the hot wind. The planes tied down next to me shifted restlessly on their thin legs. The moon and the yellow lights of the hangars gleamed on their cool aluminum skin.

Late at night, I finished reading to the children into the the tape recorder, and turned off the penlight, but I couldn't sleep. The wind made hooting noises in my antennas, and the plane shook. Slowly I became aware of an undercurrent of noise. It was a distant metallic sound of machines. Maybe it was cars' tires on the highway, or perhaps the sound of the mine over there under all those lights, or the smelter pouring out smoke that blew south. The sound was like the hum of an electric clock. It was the song of America. I lay in the sleeping bag, but the moon shone down through a gap in the curtains on my face, and I kept looking at my watch to see if it was yet time for morning, while America hummed in my ears.

New Mexico: East of Silver City at Santa Rita machines dug into the earth's history to take out copper made there before human time began. In the early morning light I took off and circled the mine. A line of vast Caterpillar dump trucks rolled slowly along roads and down into the hole in the earth like a line of insects lumbering away to drop eggs. The pit was a pool of dusk. Jackson was not distressed by the scar.

"I'm enough of a New Mexican to be glad when we get jobs," he said. "We are so poor; it is just terrible how poor this state is; no promise, no promise here at all."

Along Interstate 10 east of Lordsburg the desert sparkled. As I raced low above it the sand and stones winked bits of light up at me, as if the land were sown with jewelry. "You see," Jackson said, "in New Mexico, things don't rot. They never rot, they never rust. The whole country just glitters with tin cans."

Mountains rose out of desert at all points of the compass. Once again I flew among the broad valleys and long mountains of the Basin and Range Province. White dry desert playas stood out to north and south. This mountain woman wasn't just languorous and bony; she was dead. The long ridges were like meatless rows of vertebrae; the playas were the color of calcium.

New Mexico: A white horizon grew into a sea of white—White Sands National Monument—and the red sandy dirt of another restricted area expanded ahead. It was a target: the White Sands Missile Range.

I approached Alamogordo. Below was the mark of an atomic explosion. At least I thought it looked like one: lines radiating outward from a central point. Charles Lindbergh's ghost shook its head. No. That's not what it looks like. He had seen the real thing, in December 1947. "A gray-ash saucer, a mile or so in width, marks the blasted, radiated, and heat-shriveled earth," he said. "Surrounding it is a black halo of undamaged roots on the outskirts. The straw-colored stippling which glints now and then in sunlight, as we bank, is caused by the unpainted lumber of newly built dwellings. . . ." It was Hiroshima. Both instinct and science recoiled.

But the landscape below me was not the mark of a bomb. Its center was a well, and the lines were made over the years by cattle, coming unerringly from miles away, straight to water.

I climbed to 11,500, and looked out over the ridge of a single lovely peak, east. It was as if I hid inside the perimeter of the mountains, sticking my head up to look over into the vastness of the great plains. Out there the mountains dwindled, falling rapidly lower into a few ridges and then nothing. That was the end of the western mountains, that great succession: the Coastal Range, the Cascades and Sierra Nevada, the Basin and Range, the Rockies. There were no more big shapes in the distant haze, no more high drama on that horizon; the land slid down into a pale white haze and went on forever. That was a strange country to me, down there; I'd be in it the next day. I sat back to enjoy this last touch with the high stone.

A ranch landing strip stretched below next to a ranch house surrounded by trees, an empty swimming pool, and fields with dark
patches in the gray of the soil where they were irrigated. This ranch
was right below that single peak. It was a beautiful spot up in these
mountain foothills, on a red dirt road, with surrounding poplars and a
short school bus parked in the yard.

Suddenly I longed to go down there. I wanted to land and talk to
those people, out in the country of sparse company and open air.
More: I wanted to live there, out on that flat, to listen every day to the
changing tune of that ribbon of water. Suddenly the loneliness of this
journey, of my own long restless wandering through life, never sticking anywhere long enough to belong to it, hit me like a shot of
turbulence. I ached to live there—to belong there, to have lived there
forever, to have stored all my time in this valley.

I circled and circled, at 11,500 feet no larger from the ground than a
hawk. Then I turned slowly out of the bank and flew on north across
rolling high plains of juniper woods and pastures and strange sickly
lakes, back to Santa Fe for the night. Sometimes it is better to wish
forever than to land.

Jackson doesn't travel as much as he once did. He no longer takes to
the adventure of his motorcycle: "I'm getting too old to take off for a
week of just running around from bad road to bad road, and bad meal
to bad meal, but there is still a great deal I wish I could see." But he
does not feel bent by his seventy-nine years. He goes out to see what he
needs to see in his pickup: he recently drove from New Mexico to give
lectures in Illinois and Iowa. He may notice his age less than younger
people do. Not long ago someone came to shoot a documentary about
him, and to conclude the show asked him to sit in the garden under a
tree reading a book. "It was in the late afternoon and the light was
magnificent." The director asked him to close the book, call his dog,
and walk to the house. He did as he was asked; he is a courteous man.
But he thought, This is a picture of an old man living in an attractive
house in New Mexico, in decline.

It is not a true image. A man, like a landscape, only changes. It is
not a tragedy that, in the land that holds its past preserved in its dry
and luminous air, tomorrow will, once again, be different.

"The drama of New Mexico's attraction and conquest is being continued," he wrote not long ago, "and we are in the fortunate position
of being able to observe and record that wave of optimistic expansion
and discovery. It is no less a fact of history than the compromise and

defeat that ultimately overtake our endeavors to live in a region which continues to fascinate us, allure us, and teach us the hard lessons of the passage of time.''

~~ In the morning a tower of windblown cloud stood over the mountains to the north. It was dramatic, but I didn't want to dance with it. It was rounded and falsely soft, like a boxing glove. The wind was the right arm behind it, and the wind was strong. I was going to get beaten up on my way out of the West's hall of majesty. So I got into the air: Let's go and get it over with. Near the prison by the airport an updraft flung me to 9,500 feet. Houses were scattered out in the high hills east of Santa Fe, human life anchored in the landscape, built in the pursuit of an image of heaven.

"Which comes first," John Jackson said, "the blessing or the prayer? It is not easy in this landscape to separate the role of man from the role of nature.''

It was a quarter past nine. My time in the Mountain West was over. In an hour I'd be flat out in Texas. Six Zero One and I tumbled east like a leaf to meet whatever was there.

CHAPTER ELEVEN

The solemn face of Lindbergh changed. It broke into a big grin. It was a grin seldom seen in public. It was a grin of camaraderie, delighted and conspiratorial. He must have worn a grin like that the first time he entirely accidentally sat on Keyhoe's hat. He was talking about Sante Fe.

"We had to get up at 12:15 A.M.," he said "We ate breakfast at one and reached the airport at one-thirty. Then we took off at two-fifteen."

"He did not hide his elation," Keyhoe said, perhaps a bit grumpy. But why wouldn't Lindbergh be happy? He loved it. To ride the machine through the complete darkness of the West was another grand adventure. He had no lights on the *Spirit of St. Louis,* but he and the plane Keyhoe rode in were the only human conveyances in this night air. What a night! The flight made even Keyhoe lyrical.

"The sky was free from clouds and the stars shone brightly," he said. "Below and off to the sides was only a black void, so that we seemed to be floating in space far removed from any planet. Every few minutes a faint flicker of light showed off to the left, as Lindbergh swung his flashlight out of his window to warn us if we happened to be near." It was a night for young men, crossing the wild expanse of a young country in a mechanism that had been invented after they were born. In the dark, they chased the glory.

Alone, in daylight, and older, I was doing the same thing. I ripped along before the wind toward buttes and rain. Beyond, farther east, there were light skies and layers of blue. I looked out at that great plain from my mountain fastness, and it was a place of light and space. Today its strangeness to me drew me on. The Great Plains greeted me with a promise of sunlight and fair weather, within which thunderstorms hid like cells of exuberance. The wind was behind me, and the plane responded willingly to my touch. I rode the rough air like a cowboy on a proud and obstreperous horse, and galloped with the morning into Texas.

Flying is athletic. It involves grace, coolness, coordination. That's why pilots have to get physical exams regularly. But pilots, for all the image, are sometimes solitary, shy people. At least as far as his own body was concerned, Phil Timm was like that. He was already an athlete of the air by the time he got around to his first physical, but it turned out to be one of the great ordeals of his flying career.

"I grew up in a chiropractic home," Phil's amiable ghost said as we headed for Texas. I settled back for the story. "My mother was an absolute crank, and 'crank' doesn't even give a good explanation. I was born in a hospital, but that's as far as we went. My mother figured that any disease that you had was all cured by this silly chiropractic malarkey."

But now a friend wanted Phil, who had been flying for several years, to ferry a plane for him, and "of course he wanted me to be legal. Now this is amusing that I'm going to be legal, because I'm going to get a physical. My first. I had no more license than your dog has, you understand. So all I'm going to get is a physical.

"I go to this doctor's office, fat, dumb, and happy. The office girls were two cute little things. But I had nothing to do with girls. Now the doctor comes by. He is very brisk."

The room in which Phil was placed was in a hall of offices, with doors from one to another so the doctor could stride through from one to another without wasted steps. Phil was in the middle room of three. The doctor came in. He said:

"Take off your clothes."

Phil grew nervous.

"I was so demure," Phil said, "I didn't even undress in front of a mirror. So I took my shirt off and that was undressed."

The doctor strode through again. He said:

"Get your clothes off."

Phil took off his undershirt.

The doctor came through again. He said:

"I thought I told you to take your clothes off. Now I want *all* of your clothes off."

Phil took his pants off. And the doctor came through again, "and behind him is one of these sweet young things. And I'm sitting here. I had finally got my pants off, but I have my shorts on, and my shoes on. I just felt like I was on a stage, with big lights on me."

The doctor said:

"Get your shoes and socks off, and I want those underpants off too."

But that was too much. Phil was done. "Well," he told me, "I ain't gonna take those off. These girls are coming through here, and I'm not quite built for this."

He was briefly saved by some question about his vision; he had to put his clothes on and get another physician's approval. But then it was back to the hall of public rooms, the sweet young things, and the nakedness.

"So now I'm going to get a blood-pressure machine put on," he remembered. "Lord, there must not have been any top in that machine, because I would've blown it if there was. The doctor says, 'Calm down a little bit. Lie down here on your back and rest.' Can you imagine a guy with no clothes on, not even his socks, lying on his back right in the hallway? Where these girls, that I dared not look at, were going by? So how are you going to get your blood pressure down?

"He came back and he took this pencil, he pushes it here, and here, and two places down here, and, man, I pretty near fly out of the place. Then he put it down here on the inside of my leg, and I was about to go bananas. And he would say 'Humph,' and I thought, Humph! Man, I flunked. So eventually he puts this blood-pressure machine back on me. He said, 'You really want to go on that trip, don't you?'

"I said, 'Yes, not only do I want to go, but I'm going, whether I get this physical or not. I'd just kinda like to have it.' "

He got it. The story ended. Phil didn't hit you with a punch line; he let the story trickle away as in real life. In the little group of phantoms that attended my loneliness in the sky I could see Lindbergh's grin; a solemn look from Keyhoe—in this part of Texas he had become lost in the advance plane—and thoughtful amusement on the face of John Jackson. Then the radio broke in:

It was an airliner calling Fort Worth Air Traffic Control Center.

Airliner: Fort Worth, question, over.

Fort Worth: Go ahead with your question.

Airliner: We just wanted to know where we're going.

Silence.

Airliner: Correction. We know where we're going. We just wanted to know if it was all coordinated with you.

Fort Worth (dryly): Roger, it is.

✦ Drops of rain rattled on the Plexiglas. The last mountains were hidden by snowfall to my north; now I crossed buttes and craggy canyons and the beginnings of plains. High clouds swirled in wind-blown blue; the air was restless. Wind stirred even the tiny stock ponds that were starting to speckle the landscape. The day was making thunderstorms out of these raw materials of moisture, wind, and the growing warmth of spring.

A new reservoir tamed the Pecos River almost before it left the hills. On an old 1982 chart in my flight bag this reservoir is not mentioned; if I had been using it, I would have said to John Jackson, "What lake?" "Santa Rosa Lake," he would have said, looking at my current chart. The river, deep and full at this time of year, poured a robust orange-red-brown stream into the lake, and the lake drained the blood out of it. From under the dam a green creek flowed meekly down to Santa Rosa through a canyon cut in heartier days.

Another blocked river: Of all the marks of human beings on the surface, only the grid made a larger impression. Everywhere I looked on the land reservoirs flooded valleys. You can tell them apart from natural lakes immediately; because their waves have worked on their shorelines for only a few years, all their arms are deep-lobed and jagged. Natural lakes have long curves of beach, but reservoirs lap up into the steep sides of gullies. Maps call these bodies of waters lakes, and most are lovely, but to me they will always be impoundments.

Over reservoir and pasture I came to the Great Plains Province, the band of high, dry, flat country that crosses the United States north to south, built of soil washed down from the mountains, once covered with grass and buffalo, and now by the grid, farm fields, and cows.

At first, as I flew east, the grid was barely evident. An occasional straight road shot across vast rolling pastures. But slowly and steadily it annexed more land into its grand organization of connection and division, until, by the time I crossed the many cattle feedlots around the town called Bovina, the grid was in absolute control.

I flew level across one of the most level parts of the country, the flatland called the Llano Estacado, the Staked Plain. This country is so flat that travelers who got here before the grid had to put up stakes to guide them from mirage to mirage toward the invisible mountains. These plains drain poorly; like an imperfect tennis court after a rain, they are splotched with puddles. My chart pointed out "numerous intermittent lakes," but the people here call them buffalo wallows. Occasionally within these puddles are horseshoe-shaped dams scooped out by bulldozers to cup the last of the evaporating water later in the year.

During my circuit of New Mexico I had spent one night in El Paso. That night I had gone to two baseball games. No wonder I was thinking about being an athlete. I went to a high school field in the afternoon, and a minor-league stadium in the evening. The games seemed very different. At the high school game between the Austin High Panthers and the El Paso High Tigers parents hollered and cajoled, *"Lo necessita, Mike!"* "Let's go! *Andale!*" It was a sunny afternoon, and the stadium had no grass on its infield; as the shadow of the light standard grew out into right field the lead changed hands and the parents hollered and cajoled. At the minor-league game the crowd was oddly quiet, and responded mechanically, as a laugh track might, to the constant urging of the announcer. The stadium was lined with stacked ads: Airport Hilton, Buck Rogers Travel, Burger King, Apodaca Bail Bonds, KROD, Romney Implement Company, Jerry's Perfect Pets, Sun Floors ("The best little floorhouse in Texas"), and El Paso Disposal ("We really move our can for you"). In between innings Dr Pepper presented the Little Pepper for the night. The announcer suggested that if I was ever in trouble, I should call Easy Bail Bonds. A pitching change was brought to us by the Iron Skillet. The stadium was surrounded by interstate junctions, multiple layers of road. As the beautiful evening faded behind the silhouette of a mountain and the Asarco smelter stack, the freeway came alive with headlights and gave the game a strange backdrop of constant motion; it was like watching fish in an aquarium.

But the two games were, in the end, the same. When Miguel Vega hit the winning home run for the Austin High School Panthers, and when a twenty-four-year-old lefty named Tim Casey, from Newburg, Oregon, hit a grand slam over the scoreboard for the Diablos, the crowds stood and yelled, just for the power and the joy and the youth of it.

Here in the air it was peaceful. Nobody was on the radio. Finally Cannon Approach, which was giving me radar advisories, asked me for the radio check, just to make sure there was somebody out there.

"Loud and clear."

"Roger, Thanks."

"Pretty quiet up here today."

"Yeah, that's why I called for radio check."

Long pause.

"Is it warm down there?"

"It's about sixty-one. Feels warmer than it did yesterdee. Yesterdee got to eighty-three, but the wind was blowing about thirty, so it seemed colder. It's just right now."

Silence. The sky was full of drama today.

On days like this the conversation sometimes sounded vaguely like a locker room: a private place in the sky where us athletes flicked towels at each other and smirked. Once over North Dakota I heard this:

CENTER: Seahawk One, traffic one o'clock, five miles, altitude unknown.

SEAHAWK ONE: Roger. No contact.

SECOND PLANE: Seahawk One, do you have the football team?

SEAHAWK ONE: Roger that.

SECOND PLANE: Where you going?

SEAHAWK ONE: St. Louis.

Long silence.

THIRD PLANE: You got the balls on there?

SEAHAWK ONE: Roger that.

Long silence.

CENTER TO FOURTH PLANE: Traffic at twelve o'clock. Boeing 727 out of flight level two three zero for one eight zero. He'll be passing underneath you.

FOURTH PLANE: Roger. We won't flush till he's by.

Silence.

FIFTH PLANE: It's getting wild out here, I'll tell you.

✈ Crosbyton, Roaring Springs, Stamford. Names in the log of the *Spirit of St. Louis* became a town on the edge of the West Texas caprock, a dying village near a railroad bridge with no rails, and a tidy community on the edge of a big white freeway under construction. In between were gravel pits, a broad somber landscape speckled with hundreds of light patches where oil wells spiked the ground, and hundreds of polka-dot fields, most brown and waterless.

At Crosbyton I made a wonderfully short landing in a nasty crosswind. I love to land in the least possible distance, with precision. Slow the approach; watch the airspeed, drop the flaps, slow the plane some more; one mile an hour at a time. Hold sixty. Hold sixty. Hold fifty-five. The airspeed needle is restless; calm it, Quiet the clamor of the engine, to just a notch above idle. Gentle the rush of the slip-stream. Caress the controls as they soften in the hand. There; soothe the gust. Gently catch the sink. Encourage the engine; give it a little power. Dance lightly on the pedals; ease down the upwind wing six inches, a foot. Slip, dance, ease a wheel to pavement. Glory.

Landing short is a source of much foolish pride to me; it is one of the few I allow myself in flight. In this ordinary old airplane I can't loop, and I don't buzz, and I'm slower than almost everything, but I can sure as hell land short.

When you are up there in the sky in the easy still air with nothing to do but kick the rudder and bump the stick once in a while to stay on course, all that concern about your physical condition seems ab-surd. But then you land in hard rain and a gusty wind and you know you're an athlete. Nothing is like landing an airplane softly in a bad crosswind, unless it is driving through a crowded lane in a basketball game and laying the ball gently over the rim so it just sighs through the net. In meeting the runway this wonderfully complex body that you own is engaged with a complex machine in a complex and demanding task, matching wits and coordination with the wind itself.

Is it surprising that Lindbergh was exuberant in the air? On the ground he was a sober adult; in the air he was a kid. Once, flying somewhere around these empty landscapes, Keyhoe, riding the other plane nearby, saw him tossing tomatoes from a gift lunch basket forward into the *Spirit*'s prop wash. Over and over he did it, each time watching, delighted, while the red orb hung briefly poised between the force of his throw and the rushing air, then fell aft and away. Life, then, for him, was poised in a similar kind of equilibrium between his body, his machine, and his land. He loved it. He'd spend the rest of his lifetime trying to find that kind of balance again.

Small towns rose from behind the earth's curve and passed beneath: Anson, Avoca, Lueders, Albany. They were scattered piles of pinto and navy beans on a bright tablecloth. I passed Earth. It was near Muleshoe, Springlake, Lazbuddie, Halfway, and Nazareth. The land was a riot of names, color, and patterns: greens, browns, reds, golds, purples; cres-cents, circles, oblongs, trapezoids, triangles. Farmers are like gamblers, like test pilots: They try all possible permutations of crop, irrigation, livestock, rotation, chemicals, equipment, superstition, science, and luck to reach new altitudes of profit, or to get out a dry spin. And what you get from this on the land is a wild individualism all caught and disciplined by the country roads of the grid.

"Attention all aircraft!" The radio woke, barking, out of a long sleep. "Convective Sigmet Two Niner Charlie for Texas is in effect, for a line of thunderstorms from three zero miles southwest of Abilene to two zero miles northwest of Sweetwater, moving northeast. Tops to forty-five thousand feet, possible tornadoes, wind shear, hail to two inches, wind gusts to sixty knots."

This was the first of a season of dire warnings. Weather people are such cheerful folks. That was fifty miles from me. Close, as the plane flies. I could see smooth high clouds on the horizon; the tops, where the hail is made. That was where I was going: Abilene. Right in the track of the storms. Up here in the sky, all alone, I found myself grinning.

As I approached Abilene I hummed the old song about "My Abilene." A flight of military jets was roaring around nearby talking to Abilene Approach. The flight called itself Rambo Zero Three. "Women there," I hummed, "don't treat you mean, in Abilene, my Abilene." People must take that song seriously. When Lindbergh came the people of Abilene had eighty girls they called Spirits following him in cars during his parade. Later there was even one for me. When I landed my old airplane and taxied over to the fuel pumps, a pretty young woman came running out from the office with a short red carpet and tried to get it under my feet before I touched the ground. She didn't make it.

"You got out too fast!" she complained. I offered to get back in the plane and get out again, but she thought that wasn't necessary.

I went for a long run in the afternoon, around a lake and a subdivision where the new rich had been building in the sight of water until the oil boom crashed: fancy houses with For Sale signs and overgrown lots. My landing at Abilene had been as satisfying as at Crosbyton, and now I ran and ran, mile after mile, exulting.

In the evening the stars were slowly smothered. The horizon flickered. The flickering grew like a windblown fire. At nine-thirty, after my day's notes and my reading to the children were finished, the plane began to shake and shudder and yank against the tie-down ropes. I went into the fuel office and called the weather people at the Flight Service Station: Yes, there was a chance of hail. Aluminum is soft—a friend of mine has a hail-damaged plane whose wings are covered with dents—so I stood out on the pavement in the warm wind, waiting. I was not sure what I would do if the sky started stoning my plane, but at least I could shout at it.

The woman who had come out with the red carpet was still on duty. She joined me on the tarmac looking at the storm. She was Allena Hopper, a twenty-three-year-old hostess for Jet West. While Allena and I waited, the clouds boomed and flashed, and two young men also on duty, Brad Wickman and Jim Schoonover, drove around on a four-wheel aircraft tug, moving the expensive twin-engine planes into a hangar. The sky blasted us with a shot of light so bright, all the high-pressure sodium bulbs on the apron thought it was daylight. They shut themselves off. I jumped. Allena wasn't worried.

"The clouds don't look green," she said. "That's what you look for. If it looks green and stuff, that's hail."

She was born and raised in the country near here; these storms were nothing new. She remembered sitting on her porch, counting funnel clouds—There's one. Yep. There's another. Once she saw a tree explode in a field, hit by lightning.

I asked her what she liked about her home landscape.

"I don't know," she said. "The weather can change all the time. I don't know why I like it."

She had been to the West. "You get tired of seeing mountains all the time. You want to see forever and ever."

It was good standing on the tarmac in the warm windy night watching the lightning ripple through the gray-blue heaps it illuminated, standing next to a friendly woman, talking about weather and living and home and watching Brad and Jim rush around on their blazing steed of a tractor, their yellow rain capes flying in the wind. For a while it seemed as if the four of us were off in a different world entirely, the young America of Charles Lindbergh and Don Keyhoe; a fierce, exciting world of youth and drama.

That much I felt, just standing on tarmac as rain began. My happinesses can be small. I chase the glory, and every once in a while know for a few moments that the glory is in the chase.

CHAPTER TWELVE

From Forth Worth I talked by phone to a woman at a bank in Waxahachie, south of Dallas. I said something about Hillsboro. She said:

"Oh, that's a BIG city! Don't you go getting lost in that BIG city, now."

This made me favorably disposed toward Hillsboro. I landed at an airport where turbine-powered crop dusters were whining in and out with the sound of airliners, rode the motorcycle to the town square. A big courthouse, built in 1891, stood in the square among beautiful pecan trees that were leafing out in pale green. It was later in the season here; Hillsboro was at 660 feet above sea level, at the high edge of the Coastal Plains Province. On one side of the square was Big Al's Pizzeria. I was hungry. I went in.

The place was empty except for the considerable presence of Big Al.

I bought a sandwich. A voice somewhere in a back room said, "The Black Knight will slay you! Ha, ha, ha, ha."

"What's that?"

"Video machine."

Big Al got to talking. What else could he do with only that machine for company? His name was Al Jodoin, and he was from Massachusetts. By profession he was a quality-control engineer. He hadn't worked in an office for years. He was restless. A few years ago he and his wife had driven all around the United States in a motor home, and now he was ready to do it again. While they traveled they'd go into a town and look up the Chamber of Commerce and find out what was manufactured there, then they'd go ask the company for a tour.

"We didn't have much money," he said, "and this was all free. We saw 'em making tanks, boats, planes, flutes. Only two plants we couldn't get into. A winery in California and an RV plant in Washington. You know what Chicago is known for? Salt!"

"The Black Knight will slay you!" said the machine.

Al was large, as his sign proclaimed, but without bombast. He wore a Campbell's Soup hat, a short-sleeved shirt, and a big white apron. His beard had gray in it. "I'm forty-six, but I've lived a hard life." There were posters of old movies on the walls. After Big Al told me a few more things that he and his wife had watched being built (cars, violins, plastic bottles), and the machine threatened us a couple of dozen times, Dick Bergman came in to play his daily cribbage game with Al. Bergman had moved to Texas from Minnesota.

"The Minneapolis skyline looks like this," he said, raising his middle finger. "I went back for Christmas three years ago. My mistake."

Dick was small and slender, with curly hair. He had lived near Dallas, and left because, he said, the schools were becoming too dangerous for his kids, and because he liked it out in the farmland, among the gently rolling hills, the reservoirs, and the hundreds of stock ponds I had seen scattered all over the landscape.

"This is pretty country," he said.

"Yeah," said Big Al. "You can go skiing four hundred miles north, go to the desert four hundred miles west, and go fishing four hundred miles south—and you've never left Texas."

"I can't say I've met all nice people here," Dick said. He gestured at Big Al. "Most of them are guys like him."

"The Black Knight will slay you!" said the machine.

Dick made his money in construction. "I think there's a lot more opportunity down here," Dick said, "mainly because Texans by nature would rather be hunting and fishing. Any place in Texas, when the sand bass are hitting, nobody works. You and I are used to deer. Down here they shoot small dogs. A hundred-and-ten-pound deer is a big deer." Dick had made a lot of money building in the Dallas-Fort Worth Metroplex area, but all that expansion had driven him out. "The city's not nice no more. Crime, drugs, problems, the whole thing. In Arlington, where I lived, when I moved there, it was a town of about fifty thousand. About eight years later it was three hundred thousand and going."

"I'm a dropout from Houston," Al said.

Big Al sure wanted to get back on the road. His glory was a big comfortable motor home. He kept talking about how much it would cost, as if considering it would whittle it down. His wife wasn't ready to move again. We discussed what made roots. His wife has furniture, antiques, things she has collected; anchors.

Dick, too, was a man who could get up and leave anytime, and often did. "We've never lived in a house," he said, "that wasn't for sale."

"Hey," Al said, "you've got to have some of my blueberry pizza!"

"The Black Knight will slay you!" the machine warned. "Ha. Ha. Ha. Ha." The blueberry pizza looked like a small hairless creature with purple guts that had been run over some days before. I ate it anyway. It was chewy and sweet and good.

"Got a lot of people here that got good money for their house in the Metroplex," Dick said. "They come down here and bought a house and five acres for $30,000, and put up with the hour drive. Five years ago there were 574 kids in school. This year there were 972 kids registered. Now it's up to 1,070-something. They just built a new school, and they're four classrooms short. The trouble with Hillsboro is that there are too many people like me moving to Hillsboro."

I spent the night after Big Al's at Whitney Lake, a reservoir that had an airstrip. I took off from Hillsboro in the low light of the evening, the sweet light, and crossed over town. The sun was bright on the west side of the courthouse, but Big Al's was in shadow. The countryside was beautiful, with trees in green and brown, and the terraces on the fields etched by deep shadow.

The lake was still and beautiful and innocent; full of water that, released, could corrode the face of all those polished fields in the bottomlands downstream. I landed and sat outside the plane under a full moon yellowed by haze. Armadillos made scuffling noises in the brush. Frogs clanked like water dripping through a long melodic pipe. There was a deep trill of an owl, and the call of a killdeer. A dog barked in the distance, hollow and echoing, as if it was barking down the frogs' pipe. Red slow-pulsing lights glowed on antennas above the horizon. The near trees blended into the more distant trees, so the horizon was undefined close or far, but was all leafy. Beyond it the distance glowed softly, as if some vast vehicle was approaching from over the horizon, but it was only the Metroplex.

Texas is supposed to be different. In many ways it isn't. Americans are at least superficially at home all over their country, which makes wandering comfortable. "Most states are the same," Dick had said. "Most places you go, people are pretty much the same."

I sat in the plane in the dark. It was warm. It was almost summer.

"This all-pervading sameness is by and large the product of the grid," John Jackson said quietly. "It is this grid, not the eagle or the Stars and Stripes, which is our true national emblem. It is imprinted at the moment of conception in every American child."

The grid locks us together: Los Angeles and the Metroplex; Big Al of Massachusetts and Little Richard of Minnesota. It locks us together and frees us to scatter within the pattern. Those two are utterly mobile, free by inclination to wander up and down the right angles of the grid. There they sat in that old building, across the street from the historic courthouse, with its bright brick and its massive clock tower, symbol of law and constancy and roots and permanence. They sat loose.

"My wife said we got to have a mailing address," Dick had said. "I said it only costs five dollars for a P.O. box."

Downtown Dallas is a clot of tall buildings standing out on a plain of low factories and homes. From thirty miles south it looked like a bunch of people who had been standing together in an elevator so long that they didn't know how to spread out.

The morning after the blueberry pizza I left Lake Whitney to attempt The Sidewalk. This wasn't just landing short. This was landing *narrow.* The Sidewalk was a pilots' nickname for the strip at O'Brien Airpark, north of Waxahachie, south of Dallas. This was a patch of concrete 1,200 feet long and sixteen feet wide. Runway 36 Right at Dallas-Fort Worth is two hundred feet wide and two miles long; the stripes down the middle of it look about as wide as the Sidewalk.

So did I have trouble with this? Naw. I was just sweating because it was hot.

I landed on the Sidewalk to get to Waxahachie, where I took a tour of the landscape of illusion. This seemed, at first, to be a lot of fun. Waxahachie could be called the movie capital of Texas: It's a pretty little town from the air, with a courthouse in the square, lots of oaks and pecan trees, with Interstate 35E going past on the west side, a lake with a golf course around it on the northeast edge of town, and Interstate 287 on the other side. Country subdivisions mix with old cotton fields turned to wheat; big motels milk the interstates, and a major subdivision beside the lake and golf course attracts the elite. Waxahachie is getting closer to Dallas every day, or maybe it's the other way around. But to the people who make movies it is off in its own special world.

The first syllable of the town's name rhymes with rocks, not sax. It's a BIG city, about the same size as Hillsboro. It has recently been the location of at least a dozen movies, television specials, and commercials. "We even have our own unofficial film commissioner and movie public relations man," said a Chamber of Commerce publication, "L. T. Felty."

"20 lbs coarsely ground meat; 4lbs suet." That's what you start with to make T's Chili. L. T. Felty, who wrote the menu and has consumed unknown gallons of T's Chili over the years, is vice president and public relations director for the Waxahachie Bank and Trust, and Chili Consultant for the governor of Texas. He's a retired assistant school superintendent, principal, athletic director, and football coach, and he's been a lobbyist for the Texas State Teachers Association in Austin. His chili has left its mark of abundance on him; he is a substantial man. He has a wonderful head of white hair, and bushy white eyebrows, and sneaky-innocent little blue eyes. The movies are not Waxahachie's only source of fantasy. A permanent institution called Scarborough Faire runs a summer playground for knights and ladies near town, and in pageants at Scarborough Faire, L.T. plays King Cole.

King Cole wasn't a Renaissance figure, but L.T. charmed the Faire's organizers into moving him up a few centuries. He could probably charm Waxahachie into looking like northern Michigan if he wanted to, but the movie people take care of that. We drove around town, and he had something to say about things that had happened at every corner. "History has just been sitting there for all these years," he said, as if the past were a natural resource, like oil before the automobile. "Nobody has done anything about it." But it was an odd kind of history I heard from him. It wasn't easy to separate the real past of Waxahachie from history contrived elsewhere.

"This building was used for a big revival meeting. If you've seen *Square Dance*, I came out of that door when I came out. I was following the lead actress. . . . Look down the railroad tracks and you can see where in *Places in the Heart*, where a man got killed. He was the sheriff. . . . That building was built in 1918. . . . In *Nineteen Eighteen*, by Horton Foote, the courthouse was quite a background. . . . *Return to Peyton Place* was shot on that street there, a lot of it. . . . This gazebo here was given to the county and city by *Peyton Place*. . . . Phone lines are sometimes a problem. They'll move them if they have to, but usually they just adjust the camera. . . . That building on the left is the Rogers Hotel. They change its name every time they have a movie. . . . There's where one of the main characters in *Valentine's Day* had a room. . . . Let me introduce you— This is Lynn Lasswell. He's an officer of the bank. He was a preacher in *Places in the Heart.* . . . Over there, under those two pecan trees, that's where my burial plot will be. . . . That old house was in *Trip to Bountiful.* . . . Sometimes they fool me, how good they make it look. They can take a small area and make it look like fields and fields of bluebonnets.''

We drove out through the fields to the Chapman Ranch, where part of *The Trip to Bountiful* was filmed. Like the old Victorian homes in Waxahachie, which were built by cotton money and have attracted Hollywood money, the open land is useful, too, in the harvest of illusion. ''We have flat prairies and pretty good hills,'' he said. ''We have creeks and woods in small areas that are suitable for a production. We have real different terrain, what you want in every direction.''

The bluebonnets were just beginning to blossom in the fields, and L.T. loved it. ''I want you to look left here. See, those fields look just *blue.*'' He stopped beside a fence, got out, and yanked a knot of bluebonnets out of the ground for me to hold. ''The Texas state flower,'' he said. They were beautiful. In the fields the hundreds of bluebonnets looked cool, as if the spring breeze itself had brushed the grass with the color of sky.

Nearby in a field was an old combine, lying bent and rusted on its side. ''Blown over by a storm,'' he said. To him a tornado was just a storm. ''When the machines blow over they just let them lay.'' We drove back toward town. ''The inside of that church has been used for several different productions.'' In the car the bluebonnets quickly went limp and died. Although they held their color for a long time, it no longer seemed to be borrowed from the sky. But they would have looked great in the movies.

Outside town the flowers made drifts of blue on the soft slopes of unplanted fields. At the end of *The Trip to Bountiful,* just before the hymn and the titles, Geraldine Page sits on the porch of the dilapidated building that was actually the Chapman ranch and looks out into the peaceful countryside.

''Pretty soon all this'll be gone,'' she says to her son. ''Twenty years. Ten. This house. Me. You.''

''I know, Mama.''

''But the river'll still be here. The fields. The trees. And the smell of the Gulf. Always got my strength from that. Not from houses. Not from people.

"So quiet," she goes on. "So eternally quiet. I'd forgotten the peace. The quiet. Do you remember how my poppa always had that field over there planted in cotton?"

"Yes, Mama."

"See, it's all woods now. But I expect someday people will come and cut down the trees and plant the cotton, and maybe even wear out the land again, and their children will sell it and move to the cities. And the trees will come up again."

"I expect so, Mama."

"We're part of all that."

The open landscape gives us the hope and the promise of permanence, of cycles and silences bigger than our lives, than our hates. But on the fields around Waxahachie, among the bluebonnets, houses were being built on the old cotton fields, one after another, and everywhere you could hear the growing murmur of the American Song.

What a fine and genial gentleman L. T. Felty was! He gave me a tour of Scarborough Faire, where young men were retouching plywood castles. He gave me a copy of his recipe for T's Chili. "I believe everyone's entitled to one good bowl of chili in their lifetime before they die," he said. He even took me to lunch at the Rotary Club meeting, where a group of white men was served by black waiters. They were the only black people I saw in town. It reminded me of something that Dick had said in Hillsboro the day before: "I think a lot of people in Texas believe that when it comes to colored people, everybody should own one."

Racism is a contortion of human features, and cripples those who lean upon it like some kind of crutch for the ego. Everyone I met in Waxahachie was wonderfully friendly, and then someone said, "People are moving down here from Dallas to live out in the country, to get away from the niggers." Then I met a woman who talked about elegance and art and wore black-faced babies on her earrings. Then someone said, "The population of Waxahachie is seventeen thousand, not including the Mexicans."

The movie *Places in the Heart* is about the courage of a woman in adversity; but it is also about the evil of racism in Waxahachie, Texas, in 1935. L. T. Felty said nothing about this theme. It was part of this town's past and present that didn't need repainting; it was still vivid. It made the whole town seem to be a set, a real live city that worms had infested. They had eaten out the honor and left the facade. The movies tidy up the old Victorian houses, erase the power poles, and multiply the bluebonnets with their camera angles, but they can't hide the shadow of unreasoned hate that stains the landscape of America, North and South. It is no illusion.

I left the Dallas-Fort Worth Metroplex in the dark. The word *Metroplex* sounds as if it describes a big computer. It fits this huge framework of lights. When I got to two thousand feet the lights spread in a dense mat out into a hazy horizon toward Dallas; but the haze obscured that skyline. The Fort Worth skyline was right below me, with the buildings outlined by lights mounted on their tall edges. The outlining lights and the glass of the buildings make them look as if they were transparent; as if the outlines were just sketches made in the air of what is to come.

I rose, and the earth seemed tiled with light. The whole floor of my world was polished with glow and grouted with incandescence. It spread and multiplied out into the distance. The few gaps in the expanse of illumination—a reservoir, a gravel pit—looked unnatural, like chunks dropped out of the world, a disease of obscurity; pools of clotted blackness.

Night makes an infrared photo of a familiar face. You notice different features. A town that seems in daylight to be a nondescript sprawl becomes a crucifix of baubles, where two commercial streets cross with their neon fast-food signs and car lots. Greenhouses stand out among farms like bars of platinum. Busy roads link villages into spangled chains. Lighted parks and baseball stadiums, with their crescents of floodlights on standards, are tiaras, shining crowns scattered out among the subdued amber streetlights of the suburbs. They focus your mind on play; I sailed across the Metroplex on this spring evening and looked down at a crown and the green field beneath it, and saw a moving red speck. Someone was stealing second base.

The expanse of light was multitudinous: the many crowns of the baseball stadiums, the pouring flood of red and white lights of heavy traffic, the packed lights of the multiple downtowns of the cities. Searchlights sliced the haze, dueling like light sabers through the luminous murk. This was the gift of dams and power stations, of all those strands of wire that loop their way across deserts and mountains like gauzy threads of steel binding the land. Coal burned, water fell, the city shone. From where I sat like a god, invisible, high above, seeing everything, the light and the flow of power were clearly related, like linked elements of a myth. Carried here through darkness by pumps, metal, and magic, they poured from one into another; drops of flame glittering by alchemy into diamonds of water. The diamonds became a moving stream, the stream burned, and all was roaring and luminous, replenished endlessly as it endlessly evaporated into the sky.

A vapor made of moisture and light filled the world. The haze stood two thousand feet deep, bright and tangible, each molecule of vapor holding a globe of reflected light. At my elevation I was just above the line of inversion that trapped the haze and the light that occupied it; the illuminated haze ended in a level line. Its surface was as distinct as the skin of water; I sailed on it as on a sea of glow, floating on the tension and density of light itself. The light rolled along, reflected, on the bottom of my wing. The world was upside down. I would have had to spill the buoyant dark out of my wings and tanks, and weigh myself down with 100-watt electric bulbs, all turned on, just to be heavy enough to sink.

But I did not choose to descend. I did not wish to descend. If longing could have held me aloft, I would have followed night around the world, because at night the human landscape is a field of jewels.

Above Dallas I slowed the engine, held my altitude, and soared slowly north. The city was a panoply of goodies, like a department store. Macho Irene had thought so too. There off to my right distance was KMART intersection. Like a kid among the toys, I was happy here. For a while I lived on wishfulness: Oh, do not bring me day! Do not make dust out of this glitter! Let me run my fingers through this treasure and drape diamonds on my shoulders, and pretend there is no morning.

— I spent the night at Ardmore, under a deep orange moon with the top of it rubbed off: a tired moon, a tired color. All night the airport beacon flashed on the window and on the wall of the hangar right next to the plane; a glaring Mobil sign outshone the moon; and the highway roared right next to the airport. All night cars come along at intervals, each with a thunder of engine and a hissing of tires that reflected off the steel walls of the hangar so the sound seemed to come from both directions, as if two cars were rushing breakneck at each other. I half awoke again and again, tense and afraid, waiting for the crash.

CHAPTER THIRTEEN

It was Easter Week. During those special days of the year I worshiped in a house of fishes, and attended baptism at the cathedral of Spavinaw Creek. How different were they? Not much.

The day after I fled from Waxahachie and Texas, I ran for miles along the edge of a reservoir called Lake Murray near the town of Ardmore, Oklahoma. Sweat dried off like the sadness. I liked this state. "People're slower here," said a mechanic as skinny as a reed who helped me reline my brakes. All those short landings wear out brake pads. "You can talk to somebody and they'll shut down and talk to you," he said. The land here was gently rolling, and partly wooded. It suited him.

"I just feel comfortable as long as I'm between the Mississippi and the Rocky Mountains," he said, and I thought suddenly of a home landscape as a familiar room in the dark. As long as you know where the door is, and the chair and the table, and you know a photo of a loved one is on the bureau, even if you can't see them and you never think about them, you're safe.

The mechanic didn't quite shut down to talk, but he slowed to half speed. When I talked about Lindbergh, he thought I was writing history. People always thought other people's past was more interesting than their present. They couldn't imagine that I wanted to talk to them more than to their ancestors.

"There's a wealth of flying stuff around here," he said, while he set the rivets. "Wiley Post learned to fly here. If old Ben Scott was alive, he could tell you the middle name of the Wright Brothers, almost. Once an old gal jumped off an old biplane into the city lake. This place is the grandmother of all kinds of shit."

An airstrip lay at the south end of the lake, and in the early evening I flew down from Ardmore to spend the night in the country. The air was still, and the reservoir was a pool of unstained blue. It was the day before the long weekend, and on one peninsula an armored cavalry of motor homes was already assembled in ranks, with hardly a tree between them. By the airstrip, at the Lake Murray Lodge, the air was cool and lovely. The banks were wooded. I walked by the shore of the lake, and not a ripple creased the lake's luminous skin. High school kids gathered at the lodge in suits and dresses for a big dance beside the lake. I had seen a walleye jump in the morning, but here there were no fishermen. What was the matter with this place? A fish moved out on the surface. The sunset turned the sky and the lake red, and I sat on a rock, listening to the tiny *slip, slip, hush* of water moving against the bank and the *tink*ing of a frog, utterly pleased to be out under the clean sky. But where were the fishermen?

They were inside. The sign said "Fishing Arena." A short pontoon bridge led out to a building like a pool hall on the water. I gingerly opened the door. I looked inside. When I thought about fishing, this was not what came to mind.

In the green light inside sat a dozen people. They sat in patio furniture on a rectangular deck that surrounded a pool of water. A lamp hung down close to the water on a long cord. The ceiling was corrugated tin. The walls were paneled with light brown wood-grained vinyl. The floor was a combination of boards and pieces of green carpet. Six fishermen sat around the rim, their rods braced on a wide red rail. They were accompanied by wives and kids. Outside, the sunset turned to flame, then embers, and we had glimpses of it through the windows. Inside the light was flat white and yellow, and voice murmured reverently beside the water.

The fishermen had paid $3.00 each for the privilege of sitting here. I thought for a moment that the rectangle of water must be netted off from the rest of the lake and stocked, to make the arena pay. I was wrong. It was a fishing boat turned outside in, just a way to get inside on the water.

The fish weren't biting. Nobody said much. I liked the place. It was novel. It could make a novel. A short, lean, quiet, minimalist novel. Nothing much would happen in the novel, but it would be full of unspoken tension and very profound.

I wandered around and introduced myself. Louise Coleman ran the place with her husband, Ron. She had white-blond hair and little shorts, and she'd been making grilled cheese sandwiches since eight in the morning. Matthew Nelms, Mr. and Mrs. Harry Nelms, Jr., and Ruffin Nelms, age six, had come from Dallas to fish. Matthew, a young teenager, flipped a combination fish knife and pliers over and over in his hand. Troy Tindall and Nathan Knight were from Flower Mound, Texas; both were about twelve, and were very worldly. Troy wore a T-shirt with a big red splotch of painted blood in the middle of it. It read, "I [splotch] New York." Mike Wray, had also come up here from Dallas, with his teenage son, Jason, Mr. and Mrs. Jack Barnett had driven down from Oklahoma City. They had brought their son, Tyler. Jack was burly and intent, poised over his pole. His wife was tall and slender and young, and contentedly sleepy. Tyler made sucking noises. He was two months old.

After I introduced myself I sat down to watch. Matthew's pliers clinked in his hand. *Clink, Clink, Clink.* Tyler bubbled and then had to be changed. The Flower Mound Kids went out, came back in, went out, came back in, fished with wads of white bread, went out, came in. They were having a geographical dispute. "Does West Texas look like desert, or *what*?" said Nathan. Once in a while Mike Wray struck violently, and his pole whacked against the ceiling. But nobody caught anything.

At about nine Louise opened up a bag of hog feed and threw pellets into the murky water. "This is the second clearest lake in Oklahoma," she said. "It has a rocky-type bottom." I leaned over the rail. I could see into the water about six feet. *Clink, Clink, Clink,* went Matthew's pliers. Tyler fell asleep. Jack, his father, had brought a wooden framework padded with shag rug. He had attached it to the rail and braced two rods on it. He knew what to do here; he had been coming to this arena since 1968. Once he had been fishing for crappie here and a storm blew away the ramp. He was rescued by someone in a boat. "Caught a ton of fish while I was sitting there."

"Today around noon they were biting real good," Louise said. "We keep it baited with Christmas trees."

"Christmas trees?"

"You know, cedar trees you see in the woods here."

Two cables led down into the water from the roof. The trees were tied to the cables, weighted down with cinder blocks like executed mobsters, and lowered to the bottom.

"The fish like the cedar trees," Louise said.

Every once in a while one of the cables vibrated gently: "That's one of those big fish banging against the tree." The trees gathered fish, but also collected hooks, lines, and sinkers. At the end of the season, Ron and Louise hauled up the trees, and clipped pounds of lead off the branches.

Jack talked about carp. They bit as softly as kittens; those little dips of Mike's rod might be the sucking of a twenty-five-pound fish. "When you rare back and set the hook," Jack said, "it's like trying to set the hook on a runaway locomotive."

Marmalade, the cat, wandered around the deck, and Louise chased it away. Mike Wray's rod dipped an eighth of an inch, and then dipped again. He struck, whacking the ceiling. Nothing. He put the rod back down against the rail. Jason sat beside him, chewing Levi Garrett tobacco, and talking periodically about a stereo he was going to get for his car. I knew how he felt. The machine was insistent. It glowed in the distance. It had a halo. He knew about all the knobs and buttons. It would make him happy.

Mike rebaited his hook.

"I guess most people don't have the patience to do this," he said. "To me it's the challenge of it."

At about ten Louise threw a handful of hog pellets into the rectangle of water, and followed them with wads of white bread. Tiny perch floated up into the bright water and sucked down bits of bread. A tree cable vibrated. Mike's rod dipped again, and he waited, and let it dip once more. Then he struck against the ceiling. Crash! Nothing. Out at the lodge, high school girls in long dresses and thousands of petticoats spun and whirled and looked at the deep stony waters of the lake and fell in love.

The Nelmses picked up their rods and left. The Flower Mound Kids left. By 10:30 Mike Wray and Jack Barnett were the only fishermen left. Louise put some food in a dish for the raccoon and went up to the lodge briefly. Jason Wray watched his father fish and thought about his stereo. Tyler Barnett woke up and wanted to eat. Jack mixed him a bottle of formula. Tyler ate and lay down in his playpen and slept another hour.

Mike Wray struck. The rod bent heavily. He grunted. He held the bent pole with one hand and looked at it. Then he gripped the line and hauled it hand over hand until it snapped. "Thought I had a whopper," he said. The Christmas trees had claimed another ornament.

The silt and algae in the water hid the trees and the bottom from us. It must have been a strange place. It must have been a wild world down there, a place where creatures lived a harsh and violent existence in which human beings were mystical. Dead Christmas trees stood there with their feet in concrete, bearing monofilament tinsel and decorations of lead. Hog pellets fell among the branches. Gossamer lines bearing corn and bread wads and crippled minnows floated down from a source of glorious green and golden light, a permanent Catholic sunset in the night. The wavering shafts of light made patterns on the bottom, and gave the fish luminous shadows that flashed and darted, like glories, among the gifts from heaven.

Jack Barnett's rod dipped gently. He waited. He watched. It dipped again. He struck! He set the hook! It was like setting the hook on a runaway leaf. The fish fluttered to the surface, falling up to its doom. It was a five-inch rock bass. It was shocked and desperate. What right had heaven to be so cruel? Jack grinned, contemplated its trembling, and flipped it back.

The arena settled back down. The night's drama was over. It was eleven-thirty. At the lodge a couple of teachers came out on the steps to smoke and to chaperone the departure of the children. "Not much longer," one said. "At midnight they all turn into pumpkins." In the arena Tyler was just a cute little punkin' asleep in his mother's complaisant arms. She watched the baby dream. He almost smiled, shaping his mouth, a gentle suck, an almost-kiss. Unaware, she shaped her lips. She almost-kissed him back. Jack watched the end of his pole. He glanced at his kid, who seemed happy.

"I've got me a fishing partner, Mama," Jack said, and I abruptly saw all these hopes in his head. It was like looking through the keyhole of that one sentence, and seeing a hall. Far down the hall were Mike Wray and his son, Jason: Mike striking the ceiling, and Jason thinking lovingly about the music machine for his car.

In his arena of religion, which was once a roller-skating rink, Arnold Murray had a photograph of God. It was a shot from a plane of the cloud of ash that rose from Mount St. Helens on that explosive day in May 1981. If you looked carefully at the shape the ash made, you could see a vast human face: gray, weathered, bearded, wise, violent.

Praise the Lord! From Lake Murray to Arnold Murray, it was not too far to fly. "I was born in Oklahoma where the water all runs red," Arnold Murray said later. I flew up red water, and up brown water, past the town where Smith Paul settled in the place "where the bottom land was very rich, and the blue stem grass grew so high that a man on horseback was almost hidden in its foliage." The town of Pauls Valley lay in a tidy rectangle among red fields that had been broken out of the primordial sod by a man named Achols, Echols, or Acres, who used four oxen to each plow, and whose whip rang like gunfire across the dying grass. Outside town a red car roared down a dirt road, weaving violently from side to side like a bobsled in a chute. A kid with joy or anger in his head was trying to make it skid, or roll, and find the glory.

Oklahoma City. Tulsa. Muskogee. From the air only the most enormous cities seem significant. We spend so much time inside the walls of our towns that they loom over our minds. But the cities are just clusters of dark roofs and dark trees on a vast bright landscape of farms, roads, rivers, power-line and pipeline tracks, railroads, and smoke. I flew across the big sandy bends of the Canadian River and the jagged blue expanse of Keystone Reservoir, where the Cimarron and the Arkansas rivers join, and across large black pastures edged with fire, and I hardly noticed the cities where they lay like cloud shadows on the land.

On my way to Arkansas and my meeting with the man of God I stopped in Pawhuska on a whim. It was one of Lindbergh's fly-overs. Pawhuska was in the middle of the Osage Plains, part of the great Central Lowland Province, but it seemed to mark the edge of the open prairie; to the east woods grew like a spreading moss; to the west lay open fields speckled with oil-well patches. I turned onto final approach over a black pump that stood unmoving in a field like a skeleton. I landed and parked, and a pickup truck roared up. Out jumped a lean young man. He rushed over.

"Will you give me a ride?" he said.

His name was Nathan Bain. He was twenty. He was in the construction business. What the hell—I took him up and circled Pawhuska. "That's Bird Creek," he said. "Everybody calls it the Arkansas. This is an outdoorsman kind of place." Bain had a bright, clean young face, and a great smile. His red mesh cap was stained white with Sheetrock mud. There were speckles of white of his shirt.

"It's a rugged life, I'll tell you that. That's a fact. Many nights I've stayed out on the river; you catch a fish, shoot a rabbit, get in a boat and go gigging. It's unreal. You can catch fish in Salt Creek. You get five- to fifteen-pound catfish out there. That's a fact." He ran Bain

Construction and Remodel. "I'm a young guy, but I started when I was fifteen. In this country people that are worth anything have to take the initiative and start when they're young. That's a fact."

He invited me to lunch at the drive-in. He bought me a hamburger and a milk shake. I told him where I was going: Gravette, Arkansas. He loved the way I pronounced it. "Pretty country out there," he said. "Lot of trees."

Back in the air I got to thinking about all of us wanderers floating around the country, thinking we're not tied to the land. But we are. We can't help noticing the shape of it, the subtleties of the dust and the smells, and the opening of the prairie, and the way the creek flows to the Arkansas, and the way the land swells and changes, and the way the winter feels here when the wind gets around to the northwest. We think we're free to come and go, we are not rooted; but we're more comfortable between the Rockies and the Mississippi, or in sight of the sea, or out where we can see forever. We think we can sell the house, rent a post office box, and leave, but we think, too, that knowledge of the land is wisdom, and we feel wise when we can say, I know that country: that's where the river turns south, and in the low water there's this big bar. As the land has filled up with people and machines, that wisdom has not become less important.

On my way out of town I circled over a fenced rectangle where horses and steers ran, kicking up dust. I knew this place, all right. I had followed Bain into town on my motorcycle and caught up to him on the way parked beside the road next to a steer-roping arena. Inside men and women on horses were roping steers, jerking them off their feet and flinging them to the ground. Bain got out of the pickup and stood watching. I thought he was admiring the show. But when I reached him he said something I didn't expect.

"An animal doesn't know what's cruel," he said, his clean young face going all serious. "But look." A steel gate clanged open. A black steer ran for its life. Its horns were strapped to its head to keep the rope from jerking them out. The rider spurred after it, rope overhead. Like a curse catching up, the rope settled, the horse planted its feet, and the steer fell as if it had been shot.

"They've probably killed that calf," Bain said. "I want you to look at this. This is an important thing to a lot of people in Oklahoma. See, this one's a girl." Clang, run, spur, rope, crash. "She's pretty good. Sometimes they break their necks. That's a fact. But there's a lot of stature in Oklahoma to be a good steer roper. I raised hogs and calves, but I'm not a steer roper. I think it's an evil sport. An animal is an animal, but you can only go so far on it. If you're going to write a book about Oklahoma, you might remember that this was a little cruel."

➤ Arnold Murray grew up among the thick waters of Oklahoma; when he saw Arkansas he fell in love with it. "This is the most beautiful place I have ever seen," he said. "The water is clear. The very fact that you could see the bottom amazed me. I said this is it."

I came up into the wooded Ozark hills of northwest Arkansas from Tulsa and Pryor, over the stub end of an interstate that stuck out into the farmland and ended in a big red weal of disturbed dirt aiming through the woods. "It's just Highway 33," said a white-haired man at the airport south of Pryor. "They've spent all my lifetime building that road." I flew east across deepening woods, where marijuana growers hang lines of fishhooks at eye level to discourage trespassers, and where, when my friends Al and Helen Kuettner came to this country a few years ago, a lot of the churches thought the world was about to end in fire.

I came to see Al and Helen, but wound up watching Arnold Murray baptize dish people in Spavinaw Creek. In a complicated way I was working for Al.

I'd do a lot for Al. He has a lumpy bulldog face, with a stubborn lower lip and the attitude to go with it. He has small eyes, receding hair, and a face that looks as if it has been banged around some. Among the events of the century he has covered as a journalist is the civil rights movement in the South during the fifties and sixties. He's old enough to be old, but he's still banging around like a young guy. Years ago I took Al and his son camping and, through my own inexperience, got him into a terrible fix: soaked and cold and miserable through a dark twelve hours that Al later called the worst night of his life. That he remains civil to me is a mystery.

Of course it's his own brand of civility. He lets you know how much he likes you and trusts you by needling you. Al owns the weekly Gravette *News Herald*, and when I helped him in the darkroom for a couple of days he'd say, "Come on, Parfit, get to work." Or: "Good print. Must be the paper." Al showed me his supply of the three things he said were necessary in a newspaper office: a spray can of silicone, a can of wasp and hornet spray and a bottle of Pepto Bismol.

Al wrote about Spavinaw Creek: "In the rolling hills between Hiwasse and Centerton in northwest Arkansas, springs of clear, cold water bubble to the earth's rocky surface, and soon merge into a stream of unending beauty and delight. The French, who explored this region before the Louisiana Purchase, sought a name that would do it justice and chose 'Spavinaw' from words that mean 'young growth.' " Al had written a "Reflections of the Editor" column about the creek's history. It was damned in the twenties and became the first good water supply for Tulsa. "Drink at the sink," a newspaper headlined at the time. "No more mud in the tub." A poet wrote:

> Roll on, roll on, oh Spavinaw;
> Roll on to Tulsa, roll;
> Your springs of wisdom have a heart
> To make a city's soul.

Al loved Spavinaw Creek. So did Arnold Murray. You could see the bottom. You could even see the bottom of the hole in the gravel dug out by a tractor so he could baptize his dish people. Murray appreciated it for more than that. Like most spring-fed waters, Spavinaw was cold; it had bite to it. It flowed swiftly through the hills. People dipped in these waters would remember it. Spavinaw Creek wasn't like any old tepid, chlorinated indoor baptistry.

"It is symbolic in the first place," he said, "and if you lose the symbolism of the flowing, cleansing water, you lose the total symbology. Anyone can take a bath."

Murray had a ten-year lease on Transponder 6 on the Westar 4 satellite. As pastor of his Shepherd's Chapel, which was housed in the old steel roller rink in Gravette, he broadcast Bible study programs from a studio soundproofed with egg cartons. The programs discussed things like the Bible's understanding of the geological age of the Earth and the heathen fertility rite of Easter-egg hunting. They could be picked up on backyard satellite receivers all over the country. "We minister to several million people a day," he said. "Our reserve and strength lie in rural America—the dish people." On this Easter Sunday, twenty-three dish people and their families had come to Arkansas to be baptized, and Al and I went to cover it for the paper.

The pool dug for the baptism was just in front of the new Spavinaw Supper Club. This led to a couple of possible headlines: Brunch and Baptism; Saved Beside the Supper Club.

"Cut it out, Parfit," Al said. The dish people came to the river in a cavalcade of motor vehicles and parked on the bank. Al, always the precise journalist, counted thirty-seven cars and one enormous motorcycle. The first thing immersed was the motorcycle. Its owner rode right into the river as if he didn't want to be separated from it in salvation. Several men hauled it to the shore.

The water was fifty-four degrees, but there was another possible bite in the stream. Spavinaw is sweet and clean, but fishermen who wade it carry a rod and a stick. The rod is for the fish; the stick is for the water moccasins that lie in the shadows, four feet long, thick as your arm. "One of those could put you out of business," said a spectator.

"Father, behold Thy daughter," Arnold Murray said, standing in the water beside a girl of ten. He is six feet, four inches tall; he's a God-bless-you man, with a friendly manner, a ready smile, and a hand always extended for a shake. When I first met him he shook my hand three times in ten sentences. It is a large hand, curiously soft and engulfing. He held the arm of the girl, who held her nose and squeezed her eyes shut. "I anoint you with the oil of our people, on the forehead, and into the service of Jesus Christ our King. I baptize you in the name of Yahveh, the heavenly father, creator of all things; Yahshua, His son and our precious Savior, and the Holy Spirit." Another man stood opposite the girl. The two men leaned the girl over backward, full into the stream, then raised her again. The stream poured off her, chuckled and gurgled, and washed her sins away. "Father," Murray said, his eyes closed, "behold this one, and use her in Your heavenly service."

When Murray was younger and lived in California, he used to put a pack on his back and go live for a while in a desert range northeast of San Diego. The hills are deeply eroded into folds of rock and sand; if you looked long enough in their seamed and dimpled canyons, you would see all the faces you had ever loved or feared. The range is called the Superstition Mountains.

In his twenties, he questioned his religion. "Ministers would say, 'Well, just have faith,' " He had explained this one day when we had talked in the steel chapel. "Hey, that's a cop-out," he had said. "If God is real, he's giving us the answers. So I went to a scholar, and he began to teach me the language and removed brackets placed there by men. I became very hungry to be able to share that with others. It really went from a kitchen table to what it is today."

A crowd stood on the bank of Spavinaw Creek, everyone grinning and smiling and laughing in the spring sunshine, under the budding oaks and sycamores, with the dogwood shining white in the forest behind. The girl ran laughing up the bank. "How was it?"

"Cold."

"Father, behold Thy son." The next man trembled, and put his hand to his nose.

Arnold Murray used to fly to his flock. Then he was called the Shepherd of the Hills. He had a Cessna Skymaster he flew to landing strips back in the hills, "and somebody would pick me up, and people would gather in little old buildings that maybe didn't even have electricity." The Skymaster was a capable machine. "Boy, she was a workhorse. Short-field takeoffs, and stuff like that, and safety—I think that is the safest machine ever designed. To me airplanes are almost people."

The creek washed more sins away. The water moccasins didn't show up. "I anoint you with the oil of our people, into the service of Jesus Christ our King."

Murray has a small farm and an International Harvester tractor. Every year he cranks up the machine and rides across the field, plowing. "I only have three acres," he said, "and I only plow up a strip about fifty feet wide. But if I don't turn that soil in the spring, it's just—you haven't started the year. When I can get my hands in the dirt, the soil, it is a closer walk with God."

Spavinaw Creek flowed on, undisturbed by the lives changing in its flow. "I baptize you in the name of Yahveh, the heavenly father, creator of all things; Yahshua, His son and our precious Savior, and the Holy Spirit."

A man of God, machines, and nature; an American. "God can be worshiped anywhere in America. I love America. I fought for her, I bleed for her. A lot of times we open our program here with 'God Bless America.' People might say, 'He's a religious patriot.' I guess that would be about right."

The snakes in the water, invisible friends of death, did not visit the Spavinaw Supper Club that afternoon. Twenty-three dish people tasted the cold flow, and felt better for it. They had become part of a long tradition. That day's baptismal hole had been dug beside the old stage-road ford through the Spavinaw. People had always come here for baptisms. It was an old place in the short thread of American history, a place of touching the flow of life, where people had come on foot, in horse carts, in automobiles, on motorcycles, for a hundred years, to leave their machines on the bank and duck themselves in the inexorable flow of water, in hope that it would wash away the guilt, the regret, and the consciousness of evil. For a hundred years the running water had carried off the silt that they stirred up with their feet and their anguish. The stream had burbled along just the same whether the baptized laughed or wept.

"I just love it—Nature, God's creation," Murray had said. We had walked through the big metal chapel, where the ashen face of Mount St. Helens hung on the wall. No one would have seen that face if there had not been airplanes. Murray gestured at the photo: "That happened on Pentecost Day." As I prepared to leave, Murray shook my hand occasionally, as if by reflex. I finally asked him about money. "I will not be a minister begging," he said. "There has never been a plate passed in this room, an offering taken. If my teaching will not support itself without begging, then I will quit. I simply say, 'If we have taught you, then share your tithe and offerings.' That's it." He grinned.

"The day they quit giving," he said, "I'm going fishing."

On that spring afternoon joy and happiness abounded on the bank. I watched and listened to the dish people's mystical experience, and, like a good journalist doing the job, I was unmoved. Well, I was not quite unmoved. How could you fail to love them, these hopeful people, engaging in this odd ritual of nature and spirit and mystery, chasing their glory, trying to become new?

Turkey buzzards wheeled overhead, the diners at the supper club watched curiously, automobiles hummed the song of America on the highway, and Murray smiled and laughed like Santa Claus. He shook everybody's hand. A girl walked away up the slope and said, "My jeans feel like concrete." The sins flowed downstream into the water supply of Tulsa.

Al and I drove back to his house.

"I went in up to my knees," Al said to Helen, "but it didn't take."

PART *4*

CHAPTER FOURTEEN

Chicken sheds. Thousands of chicken sheds. Millions of chickens. There were so many long metal poultry barns among the trees in Arkansas that it was amazing that at four thousand feet I didn't hear a roar of cackles.

I followed the Spavinaw's sins downstream past a power plant, to the point where the stream stilled and grew dark behind a dam. What happened to the sins there? Did they build up, like silt?

In the short hours of this day the land changed, and changed again. From the limestone hills and cliffs of the Ozarks, I flew through the long Arkansas River Valley between the Ozark Plateau and the Ouachita Mountains Province, with hills showing faintly in haze on either side, and the chart warning "Rapidly Rising Terrain: Use Caution During Periods of Low Ceiling and Visibility."

The armed forces were chasing the glory in force today. South of Fort Smith were Hog One, Hog Two, and Hog Three Military Operational Areas; they were, in the word of Memphis Center, hot. When I landed at Little Rock a flock of Army King Air twin-engine planes was parked on the ramp. The Army was making plans for more heat. Army fliers wandered through the restaurant in pairs, as if you needed a copilot for eating too.

"What's all the brass doing here?" I asked one pair.

"We don't ask," the pair lied, smiling. "We just fly them."

Little Rock lay at the edge of the Ozarks. It had a modest but thoroughly urban skyline. I should have paid more attention to it. A few months before, when people criticized his new forty-story building in downtown Little Rock, tallest in the city, developer John J. Flake had said, "People flying in here will now look at our skyline and see Little Rock is a strong and vibrant city. . . ." I hadn't noticed. From the air in daylight cities are unimpressive. Compared to the expanse and power of the landscape, a tall building looks like bravado. I paid much more attention to the strong and vibrant Arkansas River.

Below Little Rock the broad valley of the Mississippi opened out, as if rolled. I had crossed into another province: the Coastal Plains, the wide edge of flatland that sweeps down from the lower valley of the Mississippi and around the edge of the Atlantic states' Piedmont Province to Cape Cod. At first, as I gave away altitude to become intimate with the Arkansas, the landscape was ordered into fields—cotton, grain, and terraced rice. Then, as the drop of the Arkansas slowed and the waters spread into broader curves, close to the master river, trees replaced the fields, and the order of the grid sank beneath swamp and forest.

I flew away from the sunset. The landscape behind was tidy and ordered and conventional; dogmatic. Ahead it was wild. After the order of Spavinaw Creek, this place, where big rivers approach one another ponderously, was profligate, pagan: dense forests, muddy water flowing across miles of sand. Behind me were neat woodlands and mowed fence lines, and everybody had a tractor with a Brush Hog to keep the weeds down and a Bible to keep the instincts down; but here forests oozed out across miles of swamp, and the water rolled logs and fields down ahead of it in slow whorls of depth.

Low, in red sunshine, among bugs, smoke, forests, and fishermen, I followed the big brown heathen river. I descended to three hundred feet and rode with the current downstream above the Arkansas from the arsenal at Pine Bluff, where the Army makes and stores chemical weapons. There are about sixty thousand people and forty-six Baptist Churches in Pine Bluff. With that kind of output they ought to have settling ponds for the sins.

The air was sultry. The water moved like an eternal flood. Whorls of current glittered and spun, slow as galaxies, bearing green leaves and tree trunks in their arms. A buoy leaned in the flow, a gurgle behind it. A tug pushed barges upstream. The wake slid toward the shore like the silken scaled humps of a river monster. Foam lay in heaps on the banks. Wet brush was tangled in the trees. Trees had been pushed over. Sand bars shone pink and rippled, ripples within ripples, drying.

The life of the river was as slow as the water. Two white pelicans drifted past on the languid air. Thirty deer stood motionless in a clearing. Vines writhed patiently in the dim edges of the forest. A smell of smoke drifted into the plane from a fire in the woods; its wisp curled slowly up from a place where trees were cut. A rusty barge lay moored to the bank, bearing a trailer. Someone lived there, flood or low water, drinking and sweating Arkansas River mud.

In a backwater hazed with algae, four men fished from a johnboat. They stood at the four corners of the boat like priests, poised on the water. I circled and waved my wings. There was no response. Any gesture would upset the balance, the prayer. In this ritual of faith and power, they must all hook fish at the same moment, and, in unison, must bend and fight and rise and kill.

A blossom of red light flickered and bloomed down among the trees, following me as I moved. It was a reflection off the swamp water. It slide through the woods, flaring up at me. It seemed as if I looked through a pane of Earth at another sun. It was dazzling. If there had been a piece of cloud above me in this flaming evening, would my glory have shone above me in the sky?

At the moment of sunset I met the Mississippi, flood upon flood, in graying haze. I turned upstream toward Helena, Arkansas. Beside the river the levees stood in long broad strips of grass that looked mowed, topped with dirt roads. Sections of these roads were so long and straight that I could have landed on one and slept beside the river and no one would have known.

Levees are strange to a Westerner. They look as solemn and intent as the earthworks of war. They work their way out to the horizon in quiet uniformity, always half a step back from the water, like a line of police cars parked around the corner from the Mafia hideout. They're in control.

They're in control. They're in control. It is necessary to believe. The chart showed all the curves of the big river. Next to them were drawn the curves of the border between Arkansas and Mississippi. That dotted line did not match the river; it buckled away from the flow through oxbow lakes or wooded swampland. Mississippi became a state in 1817, and Arkansas in 1836. In the years since the border was drawn the river has been moved, both by the United States Army Corps of Engineers and by its own restlessness, and a border that was once marked by nature is now preserved only by law. The chart also showed the levees. On the chart the river was blue, the low land was pale green, the railroads were black and the roads were purple, but the levees were gray, the color of pencil, as if made to be erased.

From one day to the next the land appears the same, and from the air the levees looked unassailable, fortress walls arrayed against the water. But the old border between states lies there on banks and in dying pieces of river, like a dead fish, like one of those dry shorelines in Nevada; an artifact of stability on a planet whose every moment is marked by the profound accumulation of change. On the day I passed by and landed at Helena, the levees were in control. But tomorrow was another day.

➤ I fueled up and tried to fly on, but Six Zero One coughed and stuttered when I checked the magnetos at the end of the runway in Helena, so I taxied back to the ramp and tied it down and slept, restless with worry. I wasn't the only one. There was a lot of worry in Helena, Arkansas.

"We had Allied Chemical and Mohawk rug," Jeff Brandon said. "They closed down those two plants, and all that money is gone now." Brandon ran the General Store, a cafe, bar, and quick market out Arkansas 252 at the edge of West Helena, among pecan orchards. The orchards were serene, blossoming into life. This town was not.

"Guy who had this store before me," Jeff said, "had two shifts, two sets of beer drinkers come in. Now, eighty percent of my clientele is either unemployed or retired. Those four folks here, three of them are retired. Pete's working, but he drives chip truck." Jeff took a swig out of a can of Budweiser beer.

"We barely surviving," he said.

"That's right," said Pete. "That's right. All of us."

Pete's last name was Hibbard. He loaded bags of potato chips into a rack. This was not heavy work. Pete looked like a man who would be more comfortable with a sack of seed on his shoulder. Jeff looked like a man who had given up, had abandoned the chase. Jeff was slender, and had a long face, and blue eyes that looked shy and defensive all at once. Right down to the bottom, those eyes were weary. He popped the top off another can of Budweiser and, having dealt with industry, addressed agriculture. He looked at me with those flat, tired eyes.

"This is the first year I didn't plant a crop," he said. "I got completely out. I had a hundred thousand bucks tied up, and was barely making a living. Here I got two thousand tied up, and I'm making a living." He grabbed one of the pages of the blank notepad on which he totaled up customers' purchases. He drew me a picture of a thousand acres of farmland with a column of figures that began at $100,000 and ended up at $75. "These boys who say they holdin' on," he said, "they ain't holdin' on. They losing ground every day."

Earlier I'd talked to Claude Clement down at the Phillips County Cooperative Extension Service. On his desk were displays of wheat, cotton, rice, and soybeans. Clement had come to work here in 1974. "When I came there was thirty cotton gins, and we were growing seventy-five thousand acres of cotton. Last year we had—I believe—we was down to seven gins. In '74 prices were booming, and as far as agriculture was concerned a lot of people thought we was on the road to a great future."

Among the companies that invested in Phillips County agricultural land in the seventies, before the eighties knocked the bottom out, was the Prudential Insurance Company. This seemed to please Jeff. "They was selling land then for eighteen hundred and fifty an acre. Prudential bought about eighteen thousand acres. You can buy pretty good land now for eight hundred an acre."

The jukebox played country songs about loneliness. Five young men came in for lunch. They were roofers on a job. They were cheerful; they had sandwiches and beer. Pete played with a puzzle made of a horseshoe, a ring, and a chain, and was perplexed, until Jeff, with mild exasperation, showed him how to twist and jerk and separate the ring from the chain. The five roofers came over to the counter and told Jeff what they'd eaten and taken from the cases. Jeff wrote it down on the blank pad and took their money. "We work on the honor system here," he said. They could have stolen a six-pack. He didn't care.

Jeff brought out photographs for me to see. One was a shot of himself taken years before in Acapulco. When he showed that one any feeling left in his eyes dried right up. In those days life was better for him. He was farming, he was making money. He wasn't drinking Budweisers in a road store at noon with old men and chip truck drivers. In the photo he was standing next to a sailfish he had caught. When he was hauling in that fish he must have thought he was on the road to a great future. But the fish was mutilated. While he was reeling it in a shark had come up out of the depths and bitten off its tail.

Then Pete and Jeff drifted away from the state of the economy. They started talking about turkey hunting. Pete got all worked up. He forgot the puzzle. He had recently taken a couple of kids with him into the woods.

"So I set them dudes down," Pete said, "and I called turkey, and turkey just walked all around me. One walked right down in front of me. And them boys had not seen one of them! Wasn't no mosquitoes; it was kind of cold, you know, and there hadn't been nothing bothering them, so they fell off to sleep. I found Mike about nine or nine-thirty, and he done got so bad he'd almost fell over on his side."

"I know," Jeff said. "I thought Keith was old enough, but he ain't. When I had him out, he was snoring so bad I couldn't hear the turkey gobbling."

Jeff grinned. Something was working in him. He was coming alive. He reached under the counter and got out a different pile of photographs. They were all pictures of himself and Keith, his nine-year-old boy. Keith was holding a shotgun. Keith was standing beside a heap of crappies. Only a few miles from the General Store was the edge of the St. Francis National Forest, a beautiful place of pines, beech, oak that ran along an anomalous long hill called Crowley Ridge. It was already deep green in this early lowland spring. But more and more hunters prowled the woods. Each year, it seemed, less game fell. A place like that wasn't good enough for Keith. Jeff spent his money to take Keith hunting on private ground.

"If you're not in a club nowdays," he said, "you just almost don't have a good place to hunt." He tapped a snapshot of Keith taken when he was seven. Jeff's eyes had changed. He was getting sentimental. "I pay out a thousand a year in hunting-club dues for that little boy there."

Jeff invited me to come to the General Store on a weekend. "On a Friday or Saturday night, it's a good country place to be," he said. "We only got two rules. One, nobody can drink whiskey in here except me. Two, no matter if you hit somebody or if somebody hits you, you're both going to jail."

A man who was delivering soft drinks laughed.

"You can have a good time here," he said. "Then you can go on to another place, and by the end of the evening you've got a good chance you'll get naked."

For some reason Jeff was irritated by the remark. Maybe it was because he was still thinking about Keith. He didn't laugh. He got out more photos. They were of big dead turkeys and Keith, and little dead deer, and Keith. I thought of Jack Barnett and Tyler sleeping in his mother's arms. I thought of my own son, David, growing up without me through these months. It is a good thing these boy children do not know how important the woods and waters and their own clean little bodies are to their dads. Jeff hadn't given up. He was just chasing the glory in somebody else's name.

Helena wanted a harbor. It is a river city. "People here do seem more river-oriented than in Memphis," Robert Shearon said. He was managing editor of the Helena-West Helena *Daily World,* and had recently moved down the river. "People here seem to be more fascinated with it." While I was there the news passed through town: The *Delta Queen* was coming by. Cars and bicycles and foot traffic found its way to the river, and people stood on the bank and waved as the old paddle wheeler, on a Smithsonian tour, passed on the big brown river.

What everyone in Helena was fascinated with right now was a slack-water port, a major facility to be built by the federal government, if the bill passed. Like dams in the West, the slack-water harbor was an adjustment of the landscape that people here thought was utterly necessary, both for the commerce of the nation and the survival of their town. Some estimates predicted that the harbor would double the population of the county. Like the people of every town faced with this kind of glorious future, residents of Helena thought that if the harbor was built, prosperity would attend them, and the role of the poor would be taken over by strangers. It was a glowing thought.

"They think this twenty percent unemployment will go away if they get this harbor," Shearon said.

"*Twenty percent?*"

"It's awesome."

I stopped at a federal agriculture office in town to find out about agriculture. I carried my helmet and my notebook upstairs to the office. I asked the secretary if I could talk to the head guy. "Just a minute," she said. I sat down. I made some notes. Not much to see here. Linoleum floors. White ceiling. I leaned my head against the wall and slept for ten minutes. Every once in a while a young man emerged, went through a card file on a counter, and glanced at me. After forty-five minutes I got up and asked the secretary if I was going to be able to see anybody. "Probably not," she said. Trying not to be obvious in my irritation, I left. Before the door closed behind me, I heard them talking about me. "Strange fellow," said the young man. He was right.

I worked on Six Zero One with Don Smith, an old-fashioned mechanic, who was almost as strange as me. We got along.

You cannot be hasty in making aircraft repairs. It has to be done right. I have at times been rushed and careless in changing the oil or plugs of my car, but never with an airplane. The connection of the machine to your life is too close.

The problem was in the spark plugs. Private aviation is in such poor economic condition, and occupies such a small part of this oil-based economy, that some of the precise grades of fuel called for in engine design are no longer manufactured, so my engine has to use a richer fuel than necessary. It chokes on the lead. We pulled the eight plugs out of the four cylinders, and Smith sat at his workbench and chipped out hunks of lead. He was a small man, with a gray beard and a wild laugh. He kept his spare parts and tools in racks of plastic trays marked with neatly hand-printed lables: Rivets; Popsicle Sticks; Toothpicks; Clecos; Widgets. He kept loose screws temporarily removed from planes in boiled-out cat-food cans.

Over the years, as planes have been safer and safer, stories of close calls have been dwindling in supply for hangar talk, so Don told me several from a burgeoning new genre: horrible bureaucratic encounters with the Federal Aviation Administration. In his stories he eventually won his points, and each time the government official was bested, Smith threw back his head and filled every corner of the metal hangar with laughter.

Then he told me that he had known Charles Lindbergh. Not as a friend, he said, but an acquaintance. He had worked in Connecticut, at the Danbury airport, and late in Lindbergh's life the famous pilot, whose face was no longer on every newsstand, sometimes went there to fly. "Once he came to the airport to fly an Aeronca Champ, and he was doing a very thorough preflight inspection. Very careful. The young guys were making remarks. After a while I said, 'Do you know who that is?' 'No.' 'Charlie Lindbergh.' Their faces fell."

Don threw back his head and laughed. The hangar rang with it.

While he cleaned the plugs and I tidied up the engine compartment, I was content. The engine was uncowled, like a penitent monk. I stood beside it, confessor to my machine. I patiently followed the run of all the hoses and wires and controls, looking for worn places or loose bolts: throttle, carb heat, mixture, magnetos and harness, oil cooler, oil pressure, exhaust gas probe and cable; cylinder-head temperature probe and cable; propeller governor and control; engine mount. I have done this again and again for ten years; everything was familiar. It was like checking my own body for bruises or cuts after a fall. Nothing inhuman here, this extension of my life, and of the lives of so many before. If you fail me, engine, I may die, but in that extremity it will be my own failure.

We pushed the plane back out of the hanger and ran the engine. It was smooth. Ahhhh. It felt as if I had been cured of a cold. I shut it down and got out with a big smile.

"How much do I owe you?"

"What was that? I don't understand you."

"How much . . ."

Don was shaking his head and grinning.

"You're following Charlie Lindbergh's route, aren't you?"

"Yes, but . . ."

"Just remember that along the way you met a man that knew him."

The engine rumbled smoothly, but the sky was rough ahead. I was trying to get to Chattanooga, but more thunderstorms were forecast, and first I had to find Coon Dog Graveyard.

I climbed out of Helena, crossed the woods of Crowley Ridge going north, and followed the Mississippi again. The St. Francis River flows into the big river just north of Helena; it pours green water into the brown, as if stained by the vegetation of the ridge. In the lowlands beside the water the land itself swirls with that same graceful flow of the river, showing up as changes in the soil color in the fields, or in thin green areas or lakes in the middle of the fields. It is hard for a human to comprehend the power of the forces of the earth. I found it difficult to imagine the size of the river and the depth of time that made this place; I looked at the land and knew that floods and centuries carved those swirls, but the knowledge fought my eyes' belief that the land swirled because it was itself fluid.

Since the swirls here are so pronounced, they even dominate the grid, so the village of Austin seemed to be a rectangular island in a sea of flowing earth.

A lake shaped like a catfish lay beside the river; an island shaped like a dolphin lay out in it. The levee followed the river discreetly, a long, green, angular, mowed line, with a light brown road down the middle of it. A set of multicolored barges was being pushed up the river: five ranks of three barges each; green, yellow, blue, brown.

At the direction of Approach Control, I zigzagged across Memphis. Tank farms, a refinery. The air grew hazy. Subdivisions grew on the vine west of the airport, most with rectangular blocks and lots of trees;

they had been there awhile; modern subdivisions are built on stylishly curving roads. There was a big factory or shopping mall near the airport, and a depot full of freight trains. The river channel wandered away between its fortress walls to the north under the bridges of interstate highways. On the Memphis side was a harbor jammed with barges, and a brown, abandoned golf course near a bridge under construction. The fairways were still visible, but the greens were dead.

I couldn't find downtown. I couldn't find a high-rise building anywhere. Was it just the haze, or is Memphis flat? John Jackson, back with me again, suggested that Americans love horizontal spaces. "It would be more precise," he said, "to say that Americans prefer to *work* on a horizontal plane." It reminded me of what Flake said about the skyline of Little Rock that he had so improved. Did flat Memphis look weak and drab? No. It looked bigger than Little Rock. But maybe it was the haze: there are four buildings of more than thirty stories in Memphis; I just couldn't see them.

I climbed on top of a layer of scattered clouds. My glory flicked across the puffballs like an elusive spirit; a glimpse of halo, then a distant glow down in the growing haze. I left the great river, and the land changed again. I crossed the gently rolling hills and gullies of the edge of an arm of the Gulf Coastal Plain that reaches all the way up to the tip of Illinois, and looked down at winding roads and the homes of people who have fled from the city in pursuit of the glory of rural living: exurbanites.

These homes were easily recognized. They lay among pretty hills and wooded places in too great a profusion to be paying farms, or were strung tightly along country roads like charms on a bracelet. The houses were substantial; no sharecroppers here. But the bits of land were small—five, ten, twenty acres to a home.

A *New York Times* writer named John Herbers, who was born in Memphis, wrote a book about the movement that is creating these homes. It has a *New York Times* kind of title: *The New Heartland, America's Flight Beyond the Suburbs and How It Is Changing Our Future.* The people out here, he wrote, are not back-to-the-land hippies. They're conservative, religious, nonagricultural. They're looking for a whole new kind of life, not on the city's doorstep, but beyond even the glow of its lights. They build in the Appalachians, the Ozarks, the Rockies; anyplace where there are hills, trees, water, and the bright rainbow image of peace.

Back at Gravette, Arkansas, where Al and Helen Kuettner live, the whole countryside is being taken over by a vast exurban development called Bella Vista; as the farms are growing to look more and more like industry, with their huge machines and their chicken factories, city folks are spreading out over the landscape, trying to make it look as rural as possible.

They even want it to look like some other country's countryside, maybe a couple of centuries ago. Bella Vista covered 36,000 acres of Benton County and tacked a Highland Scottish motif to part of its Spanish name: sections near Gravette bore names like Lochinvar, Aberfoyle, Askival, Dunblane, Brim Ness, and Carloway. Streets were named Glasgow Road, Hobkirk Drive, Stronsay Lane, Bosewell Circle, Cromarty Drive, Casswade Circle, or Dalkeith Lane. One of the many reservoirs was called Lock Lomond. Flying over Bella Vista was strange. It did not look familiar. Next to the tight villages built along the streams and highways, where they had been for centuries, Bella Vista looked like a whole new kind of living, a wave of salty ocean washing over clear fresh pools of life. Lochinvar, Aberfoyle, and Askival were going to swamp old Sulphur Springs.

"Cardinal Six Zero One," Memphis Center said. "You have traffic at eleven o'clock. A T-Thirty-four at six thousand."

I glanced out into the haze. There it was, a mile away, five hundred feet below. It materialized swiftly out of a brown horizon, turned solid, bright, swift, and deadly, and zipped past below, waggling its wings at me. It vanished astern, like a dream of metal and power with a Navy star and a gaudy orange tail. Beyond it, my glory danced on a wisp of cloud, but that guy in the little trainer, heading west to become a fighter pilot, had his own.

"So long, Y'l," Memphis Center said, turning me over to the Muscle Shoals advisory frequency. I slipped into the Appalachian Provinces through the back door, looking down among swelling hills for Coon Dog Graveyard.

Coon Dog Graveyard is near Muscle Shoals. People who live there call their town "the Shoals." In 1916 the National Defense Act authorized the construction of Wilson Dam at the Shoals, to provide power for the manufacture of nitrates for arms. The dam wasn't finished in time to help make explosives for World War I, but it provided plenty of ammunition for political wars over how to develop the Tennessee Valley. The dispute was not between the intuitive values of nature and the power of science, the conflict that would so concern Lindbergh. The struggle was about private versus public control of the system, not whether the rivers should be dammed at all. The management of the Tennessee was a glorious dream that still seemed elusive when Lindbergh flew through in 1927. For the first time, people thought, human beings had the power to control an entire river system. What a wonderful chance; if only it could be done!

The conflict was resolved by Franklin Roosevelt in 1933, and Wilson Dam eventually became first in the series of dams built by the Tennessee Valley Authority on the river and its tributaries, part of the great damming of America that made the impoundments I saw every day of my journey. Six dams later Roosevelt spoke at a dedication. He talked about a glory that human beings have chased for a long time. The dams, he said, are "helping give all of us human control of the watershed of the Tennessee River in order that it may serve in full the purpose of men."

"Coon Dog Graveyard came into being on Labor Day, September 4, 1937," a brochure read, "when Key Underwood, for whom the park is named, and two friends buried his famous coon hound Troop. They had spent many enjoyable hours hunting in this area and it was only fitting that Troop be laid to rest here. Since that time over 100 coon dogs have been buried at the site."

A coon dog is an endearing creature, all legs and voice. Some people listen like dreamers for the sound of their song in the woods. Some people look at their sons and think, not of fishing, nor of the gobble of wild turkeys, but of the boy shooting a raccoon out of a tree with a coon hound at his feet. "Coon hunting," the brochure says, "is a great American sport dating back to Colonial days. It is followed today by rugged sportsmen who have genuine appreciation of the untamed beauty of nature and the performance of an intelligent well-trained hunting dog." Coon dogs, like well-trained rivers, serve in full the purpose of men.

At the edge of Coon Dog Graveyard is a statue of two hounds barking up a stone tree. There are picnic tables and rest rooms. Every Labor Day a barbecue is held there, complete with a liars' contest and buck dancing. But these things were hidden from me. Alas, there was no airport within motorcycle distance of Coon Dog Graveyard. I circled and circled, looking under trees for monuments, picnic tables, the statue. I couldn't find it. Besides, I'd never be able to read the gravestones from up here. Reluctantly, I turned the plane away, but I kept the brochure. It had something interesting to say about the grave markers, some as finished as tombstones, some made of sandstone cut by unpracticed hands. These rugged sportsmen were tough men, tough on themselves, tough on their dogs, even after death.

"Only true and tried coon hounds are allowed to be buried in this unusual memorial park," the brochure said. "Epithets carved in many of the grave markers give poignant evidence of the affection and respect of coon hunters for their canine friends."

Here lies King. Miserable cur!

"Caution: Rapidly Rising Terrain," the chart warned. Clouds and mountains became heavy together. In its slow and steady way, flight had brought me to the highlands of eastern America, the Appalachian Provinces. The stone rose, the sky lowered, and I squeezed between, through a blast of rain, across the forest of the Cumberland Plateau, and came out into late sunshine beside the long and elegant ridge of Lookout Mountain, the heart of the Valley and Ridge Province.

"We're coming past the monastery or whatever it is," the aircraft ahead of me said to Chattanooga Tower.

"That's Covenant Presbyterian College." Tower said. "Be aware of hang-gliding activity near the college." The sun shone on the pale stone of the college on the ridge as I descended, and as I crossed the ridge of Lookout Mountain it shone on Chattanooga and a forest of white spires gleaming in the afternoon.

Behind, the cloud rolled like foam. Lookout Mountain rose like a sea swell. I glanced back at that long comber of cloud and mountain from which I had come, and it felt as if I had plunged out of the sand and tumble of the surf onto a green, religious beach. The runway was ahead, the sun shone on me and all those churches, and I was happy. A bright spot of light far ahead crossed the hills restlessly as I moved, but I paid no mind.

CHAPTER FIFTEEN

Pull back the sheet, Sergeant, I can take it. Yup. That's him. Worked him over, didn't they?

I once saw a murdered airplane. I had parked Six Zero One at Whitman Field, north of Los Angeles, where people trapped by poverty and racism stoned airplanes. One group of tie-down spots on the field was nearly empty, because it was within a stone's throw of the chain-link fence. That acre of tarmac looked like some street in Lebanon or Ireland, where people of different shades or religion hate each other across an open space. It was littered with rocks and cans. One plane was abandoned there. I'll never know why. It was a red 1968 Cardinal, like Six Zero One: same make, same year. It was like a relative, a person for whom I had a blood affection, a dead cousin. I didn't like to look at it. I couldn't help but look at it. The wings were dented. The windshield was broken out. The fuselage was gashed. The tires were flat. It was a corpse of an airplane, symbol of the arrogance of flight, killed in the street.

But there was nothing like that here. Of course not. Chattanooga was a kind and friendly city. Friendly! At the airport fixed base operator I was ushered to the shower as if I were the pilot of a Lear and had ordered two thousand gallons of fuel. The FBO had snooze rooms with beds, sheets, and pillows, for pilots stuck overnight. This was great, but I liked the faded green curtains of my own room better, and slept in the plane. In the morning I rose early to the song of America, jets, birds, and automobiles, and rode the motorcycle through dogwood blossoms up a long road to the ridge of Signal Mountain, where I looked down on the city.

There I ran in a five-mile race. Ruthlessly, I overtook boys who should have been more fit; they staggered behind. I finished fourth. I like to race: there's not much luck to it, you live tough and alone with yourself, and when you pass someone and pull away up the long hill, there is nothing in the world that he can do. It's lonely and difficult, but so am I. In the early morning the sun flickered through the trees and cast circles of light out ahead on the pavement, and I followed.

It was a bright gauzy day, under the pines at the Signal Mountain School Dogwood Festival. What a delightful morning! I sat on the steps of the sixty-year-old school talking with Norbert Kier and dazzlingly beautiful PTA mothers about their school and their children and their life on the mountain above Chattanooga.

"Lookout Mountain is old money," said one mom. "Signal Mountain is no money." Not quite.

"Ninety percent of our parents are college graduates," Kier said. "Houses range from $50,000 up to $250,000."

A solemn architect came up to talk policy with the principal. He towed a big-eyed kid with a confetti egg. "Hit Mr. Kier with that," his dad said without a smile. The eyes got bigger. "Go on. Go on." Kier grinned. The kid couldn't do it. He broke the egg on his dad's leg. The confetti was shredded office paper.

"Where did they get the confetti?" someone asked.

"The CIA," someone else answered.

"No," someone said more seriously. "TVA."

The secrets of the controlled valley littered the schoolyard. "It'll be gone by fall," Kier said.

I bought a barbecue sandwich.

"Slow or not?" the woman said.

"Ah, excuse me?"

"It's good slow."

"Ah, yeah."

She scooped a ball of cole slaw on the plate. She was right. It was good.

"Got down in the forties last night," Kier said. "The last cold spell. Mountain people call it blackberry winter. Before air-conditioning, people used to come up here in the summer to get away. You can feel the heat as you go down that hill."

"When you hear the thunder clap you know you're on the mountain," said the PTA president. "You hear reverberations."

There was a fortune-teller, T-shirts sponsored by a Coca-Cola bottling company, a petting zoo with a raccoon, goats, and a rabbit. You could buy a $15 portrait, or buy balloons, or sit and eat under awnings furnished by the Chattanooga Funeral Home. In Tennessee extra public school programs depend on parent fund-raising; this event would raise about $15,000. Recent PTA fund-raising projects air-conditioned the school and provided a part-time physical education instructor, a library clerk, and academic supplies.

"It's unique up here," said a co-chairwoman of the festival. "A lot of upwardly mobile corporate people come in and out. It's almost like living in a little fairyland up here."

Shows were performed in the parking lot: beginning clog dancers, a singing group, and kids demonstrating karate in cute white uniforms. They trotted gently through their paces and were gently applauded by parents murmuring in the shade: darling little ballerinas in their diaphanous fairy wings, pretty pre-nubile chicklets in their little red bathing suits, throwing batons. It was sweet and gentle and kind, and white.

Then Flippo Morris and his boys walked onto the tarmac stage.

He was black. The boys were black, all nine of them. They were barefoot. I could see no black faces in the crowd. The boys laid thin pads on the tarmac. I was about to go into the school building for a guided tour with Kier, but when the boys began to tumble we both stopped. It was as if there had been a clap of thunder.

Gentleness and sweetness were gone. Serious, powerful, intent, the boys leaped and tumbled. They were nine to eighteen years old. Two by two, three by three, three over three, they ran, bounded, rolled. Morris directed them fiercely, silently, using sign language. A loud-speaker played the theme from *Mission Impossible*. The boys dove and rolled over red traffic cones, and over pyramids made of each other. They landed hard on the ground, *SMACK!* They leaped to their feet and ran, without smiling, back to the line to take direction from Morris to leap and tumble again.

The barefoot boys bounded and sprang. One of the older kids hurt his foot on the tarmac at the edge of the mat. He wrapped it with duct tape and got back in line. Flippo grabbed Kier out of the edge of the crowd and stood him at the edge of the pads. The boys ran, bounded off a little trampoline, flew over his head and put straw hats on it, one at a time. Then they flew overhead again and took them off, one at a time. They had done the same thing once, in Atlanta, to Ted Turner. It was spectacular, dramatic. The murmuring under the trees dwindled. The white faces turned and watched, and could not tear away. The heat had come up the mountain.

Flippo Morris dreamed, when he was a kid, of flying. He would be running, running, running, swift as a cat, and he would trip—and glide. No scuffed knees, no bite of the ground. I had those dreams, too, and made mine come true with a machine. Flippo Morris taught his body to fly.

He was tumbling before he was four. "You stop turning those somersaults," his grandfather would say. "You're going to tear your liver up." Flippo's parents were deaf mutes. His grandfather whopped him for somersaulting, but later his father paid him nickels and pennies to entertain his friends. He had a few gymnastics lessons in the segregated schools of the fifties and early sixties, but mostly he taught himself, and slowly learned how to stay off the ground, how to run and skip and glide.

"It gives me a free sensation," Flippo said later, when I went to see him down the mountain. "Free from problems, troubles, everything. The tumbling takes it away from you. And it gives me something to give of myself."

In high school and college he ran cross-country and track. "I was the type of person who had a lot on my mind," he said. "I would just run it out."

In Chattanooga if you are black, there are things to weigh on your mind. One hundred and seventy thousand people live in the city of Chattanooga. Thirty-two percent of them are black. The people of Chattanooga are proud of their river and their mountains. The long, folded Paleozoic sediments of the Valley and Ridge Province embrace the city, and the tamed Tennessee River curls languidly through town as if reluctant to leave this charming place. A brochure sent me by the Chamber of Commerce called the town *"the natural choice!"* But to the black people of Chattanooga the landscape is barrier and oppression. The blacks don't have much choice. In Chattanooga elevation is stature, and black people don't live on the mountain.

In the official face the community presents to the outside, they scarcely live at all. In the two slick four-color brochures on the town I received from the Chamber, there were 123 recognizable faces in posed photographs of orchestras, board rooms, surveyors, typists, welders, moms and children. Two of the faces were black: 1.6 percent.

"There is no opportunity here," Morris said, "even for me."

"Why?"

"You really want me to be honest with you? We got a system set up here and you can't beat a system. Those people up on Lookout Mountain, they run the show."

When he directs his own show, Morris is fierce. His face is serious, hard, wrapped up in the music and the force of what he and the boys are doing. At the end of many of the routines, he runs and tumbles and leaps, and only his own son could fly farther above the Earth. He still had a lot on his mind.

"They are not going to let you get no higher than they want you to get," he said. "Like myself. I have been doing this for years. They know I am down here. They're always talking about youth gangs and children getting into problems but they don't want to do anything about it. Here is a fellow living right here in Chattanooga, Tennessee, born and raised here, willing to give his time and his money if necessary to help any kids—give them a change in environment, give them a new lease on life, give them self-worth. But he ain't got no backing. They want to bring in outsiders to protect their homes. It's law enforcement; they're talking about Guardian Angels that come in and do all this stuff. Why is that so necessary? Why can't people go into these places where these kids are and *help* these kids? They say there's no money. There is enough money to do all this construction work and build these multimillion-dollar buildings, these spacious places, these beautiful buildings, but there is no money for the kids."

Morris drives a school bus for a living, and donations to the Flippo Morris Tumblers drift in, coming in small bursts after appearances on show like NBC's *Real People*. But too often proposed gifts come with strings. "They want to contribute the money, but they want to tell me what to do. I can't handle that. You do not tell a man what to do."

He had avoided one subject, so I asked:

"How much of it has to do with race?"

He paused. He seemed reluctant to awaken the beast.

"That is basically one— That's probably the main problem. I am going to be honest with you. There are just no opportunities for black people. I could have stayed up North somewhere and got me a job teaching kids something, coaching track or whatever. But I chose to come home. This is my home. What can I do? My mother, she is here, my sisters and brothers are here. Why should I take off and go a thousand miles away from here to try to make a decent living? I don't want to leave my home."

So Flippo Morris stays, chasing the dream of helping kids, of making the tumblers part of a whole community, on and under the mountain.

"I don't regret anything," he said. "If I can help these kids be good citizens. That's not no jive talk. That's not no cornball talk. That's real talk."

So he stays: "Bus driver, director, instructor, manager, first-aid man, everything. One man recreation department. I'll keep doing it until I feel the pull of gravity."

But what about the boys who go to the old Chattanooga YMCA every day to work with Morris, to tumble, to learn discipline, to go out into the mountaintops and stun the people with their edge, their power, their concentration? What happens to them? Do they become the vital part of Chattanooga that their energy might provide? No. They join the Army; they go away to college. They chase their glory elsewhere. They take their promise, and they leave. They know how to fly.

That day after the dogwood festival I jogged over to Signal Point, on the mountain. It looked out over the river and the city. There was a sound of wind and automobiles. Warm, oxygen-rich air rose up the slope. A young nuclear engineer named Ken Wingo sat on a stone wall reading *The Stone Monkey: An Alternative Chinese-Scientific Reality*, by Bruce Holbrook. "I like it here," Wingo said wryly. "I like to come here and get some sunshine and read Chinese philosophy." Holbrook worked for TVA. When I asked people why they liked where they lived they always talked about the landscape, and then how near they were to somewhere else. Wingo was the same. "I've got the mountains, and if I want water, I've got the Tennessee. And If I want more water, Florida's not far."

At Signal Point I also met Robert N. McCurdy, a professor and computer programmer who drove me in the early evening to the northeast of Chattanooga, where people who didn't like the high ridge lines and small lots of Signal Mountain or Lookout Mountain built pillared homes on lower hills. "Chattanooga is very congested," he said. "This is where the open land is." We passed a log-cabin bank: warm wood, lathed to fit, and computer terminals. We passed Choo Choo Customs, a company that customizes Chevy vans. Acres of gaudy machines gleamed in the late sun, all the colors of the rainbow of desire. McCurdy gave me a tour of Southern College of Seventh-Day Adventists. The college, McCurdy said, focused on theology, accounting, nursing, and physics. Quarks, spreadsheets, bedpans, and the mercy of God. He had taught there for twelve years.

McCurdy wanted to show me the college organ. We went into the chapel, but a recital occupied the tall room. It was Saturday, the Sabbath. We peered through a window in a door. There was the organ. It was a tracker organ, a vast array of oak pipes with mechanical connections all the way from each key to each valve on the pipe. It was the largest tracker organ in the world. I stood looking through the little window. Here, too, was a machine of dreams. Ah, to play that organ! To sit at that console, with the pipes standing around you like a forest of music, and call forth the thunder and the glory of praise!

It was at a church that Flippo Morris was most hurt by the people of Chattanooga. It was a black church. He and the kids had gone to the church to give a free show, to return favors for a friend, but while the kids sweated and ran and tumbled, the spectators just wandered around, and hardly paid attention. "I was so frustrated and disgusted," Morris remembered. "I just eased out of the way. My oldest son took over the show. I went and changed clothes and sat in the van shaking my head."

He figured it was the hometown problem, the prophet in his own country: Aw, we've seen this before. So, one hot Fourth of July, he thought it might happen again. It was one of the few times he let the kids see pessimism in him. He was driving his team home from a hard day on the road, to the third show of the day. They'd started in Dalton, Georgia, gone down to South Pittsburgh, and now were going home to do a show in Miller Park, in downtown Chattanooga. South Pittsburgh had been great: a parade through town, cheers, fireworks. But now they were going home, and Flippo was worried.

"I don't like to be negative like that," he remembered, "I like to keep their spirits up. But I was exhausted already, and anything was liable to come out of of my mouth."

"You all," he said to the kids, "we're about five minutes late, but I'm tired, and I don't feel like pushing it. These folks ain't going to pay us any attention no way, 'cause this is home."

"It was hot," he remembered later, "we had been sweating, and everybody had been bumping into each other, and everybody was smelly, and I had about twenty kids with me, me by myself. We got to Chattanooga, and I didn't have a bit of energy left."

There were ten thousand people in Miller Park that day. Flippo parked the van, and he and the kids got out, took their pads and their traffic cones, and went to do the show, indifference or no indifference. They were strong, they were hard-edged, they were fierce, the next generation of black men, who will, when they come back to this land between mountains, at last have power. They would perform, in spite of the disdain of the mountain. Glory danced in the heat like a mirage.

The announcer was ready for them. But was the crowd?

"Ladies and gentlemen, boys and girls," he boomed. *"The Flippo Morris Tumblers!"*

"We are out there to seek their love," Flippo said once. "And we want people to love us like we love them." Tired, sweaty, intent, Flippo and the boys ran out in front of the people of home.

The crowd roared. The sound rolled through Chattanooga. It echoed off the fancy buildings, and off the mountains that stood like levees around the hopes of men and women, but would not stand that way forever.

"The crowd *roared!*" Flippo remembered. "They did. They cheered for us. They were glad to see us. We got a standing ovation there in Miller Park. I never felt that way before. I turned into Superman."

CHAPTER SIXTEEN

I awoke to a still, sunny Sunday morning in Chattanooga, restless and lonely, wishing to be somewhere else. Where? Somewhere familiar. I looked at the maps and drawings of the northern Rockies in my filing cabinet, and wished to be there. I also examined figures on the frequency of tornadoes, hail, and electric storms. Yes. The West would be a nice place to be. All those exuberances of nature were heaviest in the area to which I was about to return: the Gulf Coastal plains—the Mississippi Valley and the south. There was a big dark splotch of electric storms permanently installed on Florida, where I'd be in three days. Oh, boy, here we go.

Late in the afternoon I took off over America's ecumenical house of worship, a shopping mall. This one was opened early in the mornings so joggers could trot up and down between shop windows in the manufactured coolness, stimulating their muscles and their materialism all at once. Far to the east lay the edges of the Smoky Mountains, pretty as the Chattanooga brochure: *the natural choice!* Great Smoky Mountains National Park is almost entirely covered on my chart by the Snowbird One Military Operations Area. Shoot 'em up; shoot 'em down. In the Smoky Mountains the forest are dying, maybe because of acid rain, maybe because of lead, maybe because of clouds laden with ammonia sulfate, maybe because people choose not to see the smoke.

I slipped away south into Alabama. ADMIT, Macho Irene demanded, twenty-five miles south of Chattanooga. I'll admit it. I'm lonely. On the loran, Debbie and the Rockies were 1,400 miles away, and getting farther.

The Tennessee Valley was tidy. The controlled river was straight. The mountains were straight. Regular wooded slopes rose up to even flat fields above, fields with trees between them. Those long parallel ridges must order the lives of the people. Scottsboro fit the tidy landscape: the high school football field stands were painted several colors, and the school had an all-weather track. Four baseball diamonds all had grass infields. A prosperous place! Big factories lay tidy and quiet down to the southeast of Scottsboro; no sign of activity on that Sunday afternoon. No steam, no sacrilege.

I landed at the small strip at Guntersville, drawn down by the green dusk, and went for a run up and down the empty runway, in warm moist air, among fireflies.

Tony Owens, a charter pilot, came in. He had been flying bass fishermen all over Lake Guntersville. Bass fishermen didn't hesitate to go to work in the Alabama landscape on a Sunday afternoon. "Bass tournament starts tomorrow," he said. "They were looking for weed beds along the creeks that feed into the Tennessee channel." He was impressed. "Those bass fishermen really do it up. They had charts of the lake, and they were marking them with different color felt pens."

Guntersville was a great place to sleep: the airport rotating beacon was broken, and didn't flash on my windows. My kind of airport. It turned out also that as far as the mosquitoes of Guntersville's burgeoning spring hatch were concerned, I was their kind of flesh.

Lake Guntersville is known for its heavy growth of Eurasian milfoil, weeds in which bait, bream, and bass hang out. In the morning bass fishermen roamed all over the lake. One fished from a johnboat right at the end of the runway as I took off. I saw his face look up and his lure splash the water. Did my shadow disturb his luck? After I passed the fisherman stood up in the boat, shook his fist, and slowly toppled over backward. Ploosh! Well, maybe he did. I didn't look back.

Bass fishermen were everywhere. Bass fishermen were anchored near a set of tall towers where power lines looped across the lake. Bass fishermen lay back in the inlets; bass fishermen snuggled right up next to the woods, bass fishermen motored to secret holes by the old river channel, detected from the air. Wakes mingled and clashed. Bass fishermen looked at their charts and cast their secret buzz baits into the milfoil. It was a bad day for bass.

Slowly, Six Zero One took me southwest: the Coosa River wound through Gadsden like a child's drawing of boobies, two round curves with a straight line between them. I flew across shopping malls and landed at Birmingham.

Birmingham seemed to snooze in history. I rode my motorcycle into town and looked for the Tutwiler Hotel, where Charles Lindbergh spoke and stayed in 1927. Perhaps my ghosts would become more substantial if I placed them in context once in a while. Lindbergh and Keyhoe had spent too much time in hotels. Of course Keyhoe might be jumpy in an old familiar hotel; that solemn young man the crowd idolized was not safe to live with. Once in a hotel like this Lindbergh had dumped a bottle of gift perfume all over the jackets of Keyhoe and of Phil Love, the pilot of the chase plane. "In spite of the heroic efforts of hotel valets," Keyhoe said, wincing, "Phil and I traveled for a time in a rose-scented world of our own." Another time Lindbergh made a rule that members of the party should be in bed by ten-thirty, and when Keyhoe was late he found all the apertures of his clothes sewed shut. "It was almost an hour before I could dress." And Lindbergh was always eyeing Keyhoe's hat and that little mustache. He found ways to accidentally sit on the hat once in a while, but for a long time he didn't figure out how to get at the mustache.

I found the Tutwiler. It was clean and elegant, complete with its famous terra-cotta cornice. The Tutwiler remembered Lindbergh. It had a Lindbergh room. The management of the Tutwiler even published a newsletter with a photo of Lindbergh on the back. But it turned out that the original hotel had been blown up and torn down in 1973. The new one was a renovated block of apartments. The famous Tutwiler cornice was a replica made of Fiberglas. The newsletter called it "Tutwiler's Crowning Glory."

The landscape of Birmingham was soft and rolling, and hidden in oak and pine and hickory trees. I ran from the airport through the trees to East Lake Park. It occupies about sixty acres: tennis courts, an area of picnic tables, a white gravel sidewalk around a lake with flocks of domestic geese in it. Signs inform you that you have to have a state fishing license to fish there. Many people were fishing. There was no division of races among the fishermen. I could see bluegill nosing around in the rocks beside the shore. I stopped to ask a man whether he had caught anything.

"No, but that man down there caught about an eighteen-inch bass." I looked down there. Holy smoke! I couldn't believe it. Those guys up at Lake Guntersville would have been splashing all over each other to get at this thing. It was a huge largemouth. It looked like something you might see in a museum, or in ads for thousand-dollar guided bass trips in Arkansas: big, green, shiny.

The fish was lying in the water. It didn't have any fight left in it. The angler had hooked it some time before and now was letting it swim sadly beside the rocks for a while. But this wasn't a fluke. He had another almost as large in a plastic grocery-store fruit bag.

When I got there he was putting the big one in the bag; it was all tangled up with monofilament line. The fisherman had a small crowd around him.

"How did you catch it?"

"Snagged him," he muttered.

"Look at the mouth on that thing," another spectator said. "You could put your whole hand in there." Another said:

"You could put your *foot* in there."

The fisherman was there with his wife and small child. They all seemed strangely calm and unexcited about taking such huge fish out of a city park lake. I ran around the lake on the path, and passed them a couple of times; they were taking a quiet victory lap with those two vast fish in the sack.

The whole park was like those three calm people. Few runners crunched on the limestone gravel, but hundreds of people walked. It was a peaceful place. There was no haste on the path around the lake. In Lindbergh's time the park was a resort, with a huge hotel and a swimming pool the size of the football field. But that zest for activity had faded and the park had languished until 1978, when the city parks department began a three-year renovation. Now it was one of the most heavily used parks in the city. "Not scheduled activities," said the park system's Walter Garrett. "Passive-type recreation."

All Birmingham seemed passive. It seemed to doze, remembering. Downtown, at Kelly-Ingram Park, where Martin Luther King once rallied brave people for days of pain and glory, there was only deep green shade under the trees, a statue of King, and a policeman on horseback riding slowly across the lawn.

In the Southern Museum of Flight, next to the airport, a blind man sat in a chair and remembered flying. He was Glenn Messer, who is credited with giving Charles Lindbergh his final instruction before he soloed at the Americus, Georgia, airport in 1923. He was ninety-two. He had been blind for only about five years. He had been flying until the year he lost his sight. He seemed reluctant to go over the old ground of the Lindbergh story, but when I spoke of the West he smiled. He looked into his darkness and saw mountains.

"I'll tell you one thing," he said. "That area south of Grangeville down to the Salmon River, I believe that's the roughest piece of land there is in the U.S." Messer flew the first comprehensive aerial photography missions over that empty country of the Idaho batholith, the Snake and Columbia plateaus, the Cascade Mountains, and the Basin and Range, from Montana to Idaho to Oregon to Nevada. He could fly only on clear days, and on clear days over Oregon at twenty-eight thousand feet he could see the coast and count volcanoes from Mount Rainier down to California.

"You know," he said, "there were a lot of planes lost up there in that country during the war. They'd go down in there, and of course there was no way to get them out. People would walk out, and some were killed. But while we were mapping we were asked to make a report on any plane we saw that was down anyplace. Got to be so many around there that they sent the Coast and Geodetic survey boys out to paint big yellow crosses on those that were already located, so we wouldn't be reporting them again." He laughed, seeing crosses in the woods.

He had learned to fly in 1911, in the days when an airplane was a freak show. You put it in a rail car, shipped it to a town, charged people admission to see it, flew it for twelve minutes if you were lucky, then put it back in the rail car and shipped it to another town. The guy who ran the show hired the pilot, and if you didn't manage to fly the thing for the full twelve minutes you didn't get the full price. Messer had paid $400, all the money he had, for four hours of flying lessons, but he had never soloed when he signed on as pilot with one of these shows.

"How I got the job I never did understand," he said. "I sure didn't know what I was doing. They didn't know that, though. I was desperate. I had run out of money and I had to do something. The mechanic that was in charge of the airplane took me under his arm and gave me a lot of good advice. He saved my neck. I was supposed to fly on the eleventh of May, but the wind was so high he wouldn't let me fly it. That was on Thursday. On Friday we were supposed to fly again, but we couldn't. On Saturday the wind died down some and we took the airplane out. I got my full twelve minutes that day; I got up there and was afraid to come down.

"Some way I got back down on the ground. I don't know how. It wasn't because of my ability, I am sure of that. The Old Master wasn't very busy that day. He had time to take care of me."

➤ In the afternoon I rode the motorcycle to a mall, on noisy roads. When I got back to the airport, I ran over to East Lake Park again, and found myself at home. No wonder people came here just to walk. It was a soothing place: the blue lake, the trees, sound of distant music, the soft crunch of footsteps on the limestone gravel, and the sound of voices.

I stood by the water, and felt like Glenn Messer, waiting in the dark, listening for the passage of lives through the landscape. There was the noise of the freeway, and a closer screech of tires. A pack of dogs yipped and hollered. A faint brittle music came and went: a girl walking by in a headset with the sound turned up too loud. There was the faster tread of a jogger, the faint scratching sound of a kid going past on a bicycle, then the rolling of a baby carriage. A distant cheer came from the tennis court. There were long and short steps together: a guy striding past with a little dog running like hell to keep up; then a patter of very fast, light footsteps: white ducks, geese, pigeons.

I joined the stroll. I was not out of place; many walked alone. A group of chubby men passed, jogging in jeans. I passed parents and a child feeding geese. *Plish!* A kid in an olive-drab T-shirt fished with a plastic worm. I wished him an enormous bass. An anorexic girl walked past with her whole fat family. I could see how she caught her delusion.

Clouds of gnats danced in front of my eyes. People waved the bugs away and grinned at each other. Drive you crazy! Yeah! The girl with the headset came around again. She was reading a psychology text-book. I walked and watched. The freeway murmured the song of America, and a plane roared off into the sky, but the footsteps were more clear: a peaceful, steady movement of people among the trees. There was something European about this place. Maybe it was be-cause this was a place where all things seemed accepted. People walked here; they did not run. When they caught big fish they did not cheer and boast. They had abandoned the chase. Here was simply an unhurried progression through the landscape; no rush, no drama, no glory; people had settled into the circle of life, generation after genera-tion, footsteps sounding softly on the long path. Suddenly it frightened me. I ran back to the plane.

➤ I left Birmingham that night, and saw East Lake Park as I rose, low lights reflecting in the lake. But other things were more promi-nent. A refinery belched flame. A lighted freeway intersection lay like a neon crucifix among suburban homes whose windows flickered through the leaves. The sky glowed redly. I passed right over Vulcan Vortac. Behind, Birmingham looked like a small town, compared to the expanse of light that I had flown over in Texas a few days before. Birmingham shone up against the base of the layer of haze. The glow was orange. That was the color of the haze. I had asked Glenn Messer what the landscape looked like from the air sixty years ago.

"I have thought of that many times," he said. "There wasn't as much smoke."

CHAPTER SEVENTEEN

In the dark and the deepening haze, I flew south. Right below was a fire among trees. To the left two stacks were outlined against a smoky collection of orange lights. The plane moved on, over a mine; a dragline working into the night, its big lights gazing on a patch of soil. It swung slowly through an arc, casting its bucket like a lure. Nearby was another power plant; gold light on a tall cooling tower with a bloom of steam. In the strange light, the stack looked as insubstantial as the steam, or the steam as solid as the tower.

Off to the south, a column of flashing strobes, a radio tower, stood very tall out of the scattered farm lights. Five miles past it another column of strobes flashed. Stunningly, uncannily, the second column flashed at exactly the same frequency as the tall tower to the north of it. They seemed connected. I looked up the nearer tower on the chart. Its top was 2,675 feet above sea level. It was 2,000 feet high.

Ahead of me rode Orion, high and clear, with a flashing light just to his left, an aircraft going past him. Night was complete; the red line of twilight was gone. There was not much difference between earth and sky. The horizon was lost in haze. Stars hung above, and villages floated below. Parris, Oakman, Berry, New Lexington. They were no closer to me than galaxies. Chicken sheds forcing life to burgeon without sun threw light out in rows like space stations. Air Force traffic flowed past me, quickly, a red light beacon flashing away to the southeast, bound for Mars. In the dark I renewed my freedom. Among loose exploding flecks of lights, I traveled in the universe.

The haze grew. At midnight in Columbus, Mississippi, I landed and drove down the road about a mile to find supper, but just got a packet of American cheese and some ice and Rice Krispies at a quick mart; I didn't like the look of the old deli sandwiches in the cooler. I was back down in the Gulf Coast Plains; Birmingham is 800 feet above sea level; Columbus is 188. It was so hot that my plastic bowl was warm to the touch. The gallon jug of water I carried was warm. My toothpaste was warm. I slept under a K Mart sheet on top of my sleeping bag, sweating, dreaming of heat and smoke. I woke up once in the night; after the roar of the airport at Birmingham, Columbus was too quiet. I lay there and listened to the slow grind and grumble of the airport beacon.

The haze thickened. In the morning the cloudless sky looked milky. I took off and flew over Columbus Lock and Dam, a piece of the Tennessee-Tombigbee Waterway. The Tenn-Tom was the greatest, one of the most controversial, and probably the last of the U.S. Army Corps of Engineers' massive canals, a 235-mile waterway that connects the Tennessee and Tombigbee rivers to the Gulf. It has just been finished. The new lake was scruffy; old roads ran out into it and sank. It had straggly islands and a shoreline like a scab. It was a junky little lake. Perhaps with time and trees it will become as pretty as Lake Murray up in Arkansas, but now it seemed spiritless. There was a visitor center down there with lots of parking spaces and no parked cars. Nobody was interested. What had happened? Where was the fascination with great dams and canals and earthworks? Where was the glory? Here was a big lock, and no barges in sight. A sailboat was coming up the river, and a single fishing skiff was going down. That was all there was to the Tenn-Tom, after all the fury.

As if to mock the angular achievement of the Corps, the most dramatic sight from the air was the swirl of color in the trees. As I flew south along the Tombigbee, looking in vain for barge traffic, I flew over broad curves and swirls of different colors of green: forests planted along the river as if by a profligate artist, in vast and graceful patterns. The greens were groves of different trees—hickory, pine, cypress—growing in patterns made along the river by the swirls of old riverbeds, where now there was swamp, flat ground, or an imperceptible rise. The channelized river drove downstream like a being blinded by narrow purpose, but all along the way it threw off these blithe, useless, extravagant gestures. I loved it.

The log of the *Spirit of St. Louis* has a curious entry here: "Birmingham to Jackson, Mississippi. (Flew via Columbus, Starkville, Maben, Mathiston, Miss.)" I could understand Columbus and Starkville, but it took me forever just to find Maben and Mathiston on the chart. Why had Lindbergh picked those two villages out of the many he could have flown over on this route?

The two towns were about three miles apart, higher than Columbus; next to Maben was a hill that rose to 510 feet above sea level. Maben was a dusty town: a big lumberyard, a sprawling junkyard to the south. The ball park had a dirt infield; the high school track was dirt and not perfectly oval. Most of the roads were tan earth. The railroad went through town, making a curve to go down across the highway and along between wooded banks and then south toward Jackson, but there were no rails.

Mathiston seemed greener and less dusty. Homes were tucked into the shade. They had big lawns and tire swings. The school was the biggest industry in town. Suddenly I was awash with longing to be there, at home in that tree-shaded child-noisy landscape. I had not felt that way since New Mexico.

Lindbergh had a good reason to come here. Pilots are fascinated with places where they have crashed. In 1922 he had just bought his new Jenny, and after Glenn Messer helped him learn to fly it, he headed for Texas to barnstorm. He was on his way. He must have been elated. But his drugstore map got him lost and he landed in a field to find out where he was. Ah, vanity.

My phantom Lindbergh grinned. It was, he said, "the shortest landing I had yet accomplished." I understood that pride. "I felt highly professional," he went on.

He whipped the tail around, gunned the engine, and taxied the Jenny into a ditch.

"I had barely time to pull the throttle shut. There was the crash of wood as my wheels dropped in and the propeller struck the ground. The tail rose, like seesaw run amuck, until it was almost vertical in air. I thought my Jenny was turning upside down. Then it settled back to an angle of some forty-five degrees.

"I climbed out of the cockpit down to the wing, and then to the ground, and surveyed my damaged plane. It was splattered with mud, but I could find nothing broken aside from the propeller." He was stuck, halfway between Maben and Mathiston, Mississippi. Mississippi? He had thought he was in Louisiana.

Wooden propellers are handy. When you hit the ground with them they break before the crankshaft bends. I should know. Lindbergh had another prop expressed to Maben, and stayed there for two weeks, making the first money of his short barnstorming career. So that was why he came back in his triumph: to circle the meadow where he had felt like a fool.

We all have our Mabens and Mathistons. Mine's in Iowa. I was drawing closer to it every day. But for now I could smile at Lindbergh, and turn south, to follow a road built like the Fiberglas cornice of the new Tutwiler Hotel, to approximate the past. I flew down the Natchez Trace, where a veneer has been made across four hundred miles of modern human endeavour, so that a driver might think he was in an image of heaven.

The Natchez Trace is a long, narrow road drawn down from Nashville, Tennessee, through a corner of Alabama, and down the face of Mississippi. It's a national parkway, administered by the National Park Service. It follows—roughly—the route of the old trail from Natchez to the Tennessee Valley, where boatmen who had floated down the river walked home.

I looked for the Trace out of Mathiston, and picked it up right away. No mistake. It doesn't look like any other road I've followed. Among the right-angle turns and straight edges of the Mississippi grid, the Trace slithers south like a long pale vine laid in the trees; not a sharp turn in a hundred miles. But most impressive is the corridor it occupies. On either side of the road a strip of woods and fields is protected as part of the park. Outside this strip all the activity of the American landscape proceeds, but within it trees grow tall and deep, fields are lush with grass, and if you look carefully, you might see wolves slip through the underbrush, sniffing for the droves of swine driven by Hernando DeSoto on his way to El Rio del Espiritu Santo in 1541.

I liked this place. It was strange and artificial. I descended to get closer to it, and the sky pounded me. I clunked along at 2,500 feet. This rolling edge of the Gulf Coastal Plain is about four hundred feet above sea level, and much of it is forested. On either side of the Natchez Corridor were small fields, dirt roads, woods, and clear-cuts. Inside the corridor were tidy little turnouts, rest rooms, picnic areas, and nature trails.

Outside the corridor the land was worked but empty. Houses were far apart. Once I saw an estate, a big dark-roofed house in trees with a swimming pool two hundred feet away. A recluse. It is tree-farm country; rectangles on the grid of clear-cuts, second growth, or young trees. From above, the woods looked scruffy, like a face badly shaved. Except along the Trace.

"We try to maintain the rural atmosphere," said Dale Smith, chief of interpretation for the Natchez Trace Parkway. "We try to give the traveling visitor a variety of scenes—forest, cotton fields, soybeans. We give agricultural leases to farmers who have property beside the corridor. We ask them to stay with traditional crops. We try to screen out the communities and man-made types of intrusions."

I saw highways, cuts made by pipelines and transmission lines, dirt roads, the parkway. The only line through the country that I couldn't see was the sunken trail of the original Natchez Trace, where the last true remnant of the old world of heat and sweat and bugs and thieves and yellow fever was thatched over and hidden.

The landscape bustled: slash smoldered in clear-cuts, and Highway 12 rumbled with trucks. All the forests were managed; every field was plowed. Ross Barnett Reservoir lay out on the horizon, its upper reaches bearded by dead, flooded trees. This was the American countryside; this is how it looks: used.

But we don't want to see that. The new Trace ran south ahead of me, sanitized like the autobiography of a despot, with its languid curves, its cloak of woods, and its pretty scenes unsullied by man-made intrusions. We build veneers. The land that nurtures us also reflects us, naked. Shocked, we cover the mirror.

➤ I landed at Kosciusko, Mississippi. This place was high-class. It had grass infields in all its baseball parks. I saw a track through a clear-cut to the Trace, and chased down it on the motorcycle. The day was hot. Five trees were burning near the airport. It looked like a calamity. A man stood beside the fire, just watching.

I rode down from the airport on an eroded, beat-up red-dirt road, through the clear-cut. The road was deeply eroded. I was surrounded by slash. The cut wasn't entirely clear. A few smaller trees still stood, their trunks gashed and oozing. It was as if the cutting had been done with bombs. Bits of pine trees, some raising limp tufts of needles, lay around like body parts. Two posts stood at the edge of the cut, posts splashed with yellow paint. I went between the posts.

It was like stepping through a magic wardrobe into a child's fantasy world where God is a lion. I passed through a hall of green and somber light and came out on the Trace.

It was as quiet as a river. It flowed gently between trees and meadows. Birds sang. Fences were overgrown with vines. There was a perfect stand of southern pine on the east side of the road, and mixed pine and white oak and hickory on the west side, making a barrier. Beyond the barrier was the blasted wasteland and State Highway 12. Like the plumbing behind the drywall, Highway 12 carried the log trucks and the milk trucks and the hogs. I could hear it: there is no escaping the song. But I couldn't see it. At last I could pretend that it wasn't there.

I rode along for a while. Screens were planted to hide the big metal building of the Sheller-Globe Corporation, but not the little rusty-roofed sharecropper cottage next to its half-acre field. No sharecropper had lived in it for years, but it looked right. It was a bucolic and tidy world that had never existed.

I spent the night in Kosciusko, in a motel for once, off the Trace, doing laundry. My ghostly passengers remained at the plane, except for Phil, who joined me in some motorcycle maintenance and told me a story about riding from Casper, Wyoming, to Worland. "I'd repaired the distributor rotor with wax and string, and it seemed to be working all right until we got out on the highway, and then it must have got warmed up. . . ." That led to a pleasant afternoon of cleanliness and memory.

In the evening I ran to one of those sets of baseball diamonds with the grass infields. An asphalt track circled one of them. I ran it a few times, then went over to where people were playing softball. One man was practicing his underhand pitching from a mound. A couple of others were hitting softballs in a batting cage. On another diamond, a male coach hit fungoes for a women's team. The women were wonderfully inept. It seemed almost as if they were practicing at kicking grounders and panicking at fly balls. It looked planned. A group drifted over from a parking lot, the men carrying bats, and started to loosen up, men and women, on the grass infield.

I hung around. I stretched for a long time. I watched the people warming up and laughing. The man catching the pitcher was urging him to get it over the plate; he threw wildly. I couldn't hear what other people were saying, but it was a cheerful little banter that seemed as natural in this landscape as the sound of the birds. I wandered around, and asked people innocuous questions. I wanted somebody to say, "Hey, we're short a right fielder." I wanted to be folded into the banter of this special American landscape until I blended. I wanted to throw a softball. I wanted to PLAY. But it didn't happen. The people answered my questions politely, and turned back to what they were doing. I was being foolish. So I trotted back to the motel, among the warm trees.

Baseball was happening everywhere. I could see glimpses of men hitting balls behind houses for children, and children hitting balls in the street. Finally I passed a house where a couple of slender teenagers were playing basketball, and that changed the spell a little, but didn't break it. It was summer in Mississippi, at the very beginning of May, under the hickory and oak and pine, in the rich thick air. I ran on back on the quiet streets, with the summer night deep and warm above, and the sky muddy as the river. High and far above were the dim reflections of clouds.

In the morning I rode back to the plane on the Natchez Trace. On the way I got to looking at the roadbed. It had been recently resurfaced with a luminous white chert gravel. The white and the dark tarmac beneath it made the road look blue. Good Lord!

I stopped and got off the motorcycle. I looked back and forth. Yup. It was truly blue. Help! I was in somebody else's territory. I was in the wrong book. The Natchez Trace was a Blue Highway. It was time to get back in the air.

CHAPTER EIGHTEEN

"Caution," the radio said as I flew into New Orleans, "for sudden loss of horizon departing over the lake."

I flew into New Orleans from Bogalusa, over winding roads to oil wells. Subdivisions and shopping malls and then cities grew out of the haze. They slipped past below, insubstantial, even from three thousand feet. The haze faded the world. "Six Zero One," New Orleans Approach said, looking at a smudge on his screen, "you have an area of weather at twelve miles, intensity unknown." I couldn't see twelve miles.

I followed the triple bridges across Lake Pontchartrain. In the haze the calm water mixed with the sky. Boats floated in the air: skiffs, barges, tugs, space stations. My friend Macho Irene was at work again: out east by Biloxi was MUDDA intersection, and, over the lake, WAVEZ.

I landed and rode down to the post office in New Orleans along Lakeshore Drive and Elysian Fields. I got lost. A black guy on a bicycle told me how to get there. We waited together at a stoplight.

"Montana?" he said, from my license plate.

"Sure."

"Hey, I know you didn't ride that all the way. RV?"

"Sort of."

"I'd like to get a bigger bike and go to Canada, myself." Oddly, he was one of the few Americans I met who seemed to want to go somewhere. Almost thirty years before, when John Steinbeck roamed the country in his camper, "Rocinante," almost everyone he met wanted to go along. Maybe it's because I'm in an airplane.

The light changed. He wandered away down the street. I got my mail. I ran a race and won. I stopped and talked to Dick Polgar,

Aldeen Kadelbach, and John Long, who were working on a bridge over the river. The span leaped up out of the city in an ebullient sweep of steel and concrete, high into the air. Unfinished, it looked like a launching ramp.

"Had a guy fall off last week," Polgar said cheerfully. "His lanyard caught him. Said he didn't remember whether it hurt or not."

I stopped in the French Quarter and watched a group of black men playing basketball at an outdoor park. "Hey, let the white boy play," one said. I ran, I shot, I missed, I rebounded, I passed. I felt blended. Then a couple of other men came and sat in the shadows of a spray-painted pavilion next to the dry wading pool and the court and watched me, and hung close to the paper bag they brought, as if it contained a precious powder.

The mood changed. A quietness, a watchfulness came over the game. Players eyed me oddly. The men in the shadows watched me. I wasn't blended anymore. I precipitated out.

Back up Elysian Fields there was a convenience store: Soft Drinks, Checks Cashed. The place was a fort. Inside all the merchandise was racked behind three-eighths-inch Plexiglas walls; these walls, framed by two-by-fours, had vertical nails and barbed wire at the top. If you cashed a check (with ID and $5.00 of the check), a two-eyed camera photographed you and the check at the same time. Two pictures like that were posted on the wall beside the little slot in the glass through which you put your check.

A young man was cashing a check when I was waiting.

"Hurry up, babe," he said to the woman behind the counter. "I've got a date."

"Social security number?"

He rattled it off, and added, "Five-five, one hundred and fifty pounds, brown eyes, brown—"

"Yeah, *okay*, babe," she said, but friendly.

I bought an Orange Crush. She put it in a little roundhouse made of Plexiglas and spun it around to me. "There y'are, babe." I rode up under the big freeway underpass for Interstate 610, parked on a slab of grass in the shade of the concrete, and drank the Crush while an ambulance honked and whined, trying to get through a clot of traffic.

When I got back to the plane there was a crisis at the airport. A pilot was on the radio:

"This is Douglas Niner Niner Four Two Six, transmitting in the blind. We have a partial electrical failure."

An aircraft emergency can evolve slowly, like an accumulation of floodwater upstream. The Douglas was fifteen miles out. He could talk, but he couldn't hear; his cockpit was neck deep in darkness, instruments gone blind. "If you read me, Tower, could you turn your runway lights up, approach lights all the way, sir?" The lights brightened. Looking down through the haze, he knew the tower could hear. At a time like that, there is only one glory: the ground. But it seems as elusive as the rainbow.

"This is 99426. As we turn base we'll be looking for a green light for landing clearance."

I went outside on the pavement with a line boy. He was about twenty-five. Out on the runway a small plane moved slowly down toward us and lifted off with hardly a sound, the mumble of its engine floating down to us only after the miracle of flight had come to pass. Out to the west the moon was sinking—a young crescent stained bloody by the haze. The air was warm. Not much breeze. Not enough breeze. Tires whacked on the seams in the bridge next to the airport; the song the bridge sang had a Cajun beat. The strobe approach lights blinked in rhythm. *Tick, tick, tick, tick.* Slowly out of the background hum of the American machine emerged a deeper rumble. Radial engines: a rattling roar; the sound of a lion gargling.

The Douglas still had navigation lights. The lights curved over the field, turned final, and drifted down to the runway. There was a distant squeak. The ground had been achieved.

The plane taxied slowly into the lights by the hangars, an old and weary assemblage of metal and engines, like a tramp freighter limping into Hong Kong after the typhoon. It was a Douglas Invader, a big old twin-engined plane, with a high wing and stout nacelles. It pulled to a stop and shut down. Smoke poured from the port engine.

"Normal for a radial," said the line boy. I wasn't so sure. The pilot slid back the window to say something. The line boy spoke first. He had noticed something else.

"There's fire in the starboard engine," he said.

We ran over there. The plane's door popped open and three men came out. The pilot was last. He must have weighed three hundred pounds. He came rolling out of there like a deployed jeep. The starboard engine was dripping small bright flames. The line boy ran for an extinguisher, but by the time he got back the flames had stopped. It had been oil dripping from the engine and lighting up on the exhaust manifold on the way down. Now it was a hot black pool on the concrete.

"Quite a trip," the pilot said. They had come from Texas, ferrying the old plane to a buyer somewhere up north. His copilot and his passenger were very quiet. The passenger was a tall blond young man from Vancouver, British Columbia, who had just hitched a ride for the fun of it.

"I love these things," said the line boy, looking up at the hulk. "If I was rated for this aircraft, I would go fly it right now."

The pilot looked at him. He raised his heavy hand:

"Here are the keys," he said.

Inside the cool room of the office, the tall Canadian finally spoke. He said, very seriously:

"I am never going to fly again."

As I left New Orleans I saw something unusual from the air: people. I had missed the New Orleans Jazz and Heritage Festival, so on my way out of town I thought I'd drop by. It was a short visit. Departure Control let me fly over at about two thousand feet, going north toward Achafalaya. I crossed the waterfront, where I had ridden the motorcycle the day before, past the brick walls of Brook Tarpaulin Company, established in 1840; past Dietrich & Wiltz Warehouse, which was for sale; past rows of broken-down houses where black people sat on porches, watching me ride past; past one billboard that advertised insectides to kill fire ants and one that reminded me of Chattanooga. "I have been to the mountaintop," it said, "Martin Luther King."

The fairgrounds was a fenced oval, which looked like the levee-walled city of New Orleans in miniature. It was full of green-and-red-striped tents and throngs of people. I had never seen crowds from the air before. They were strange. The people were jammed into huge groups, thousands in each, listening to concerts—John Lee Hooker, Bonnie Raitt, or Duke Robillard. For some reason the crowds looked pink. Maybe everyone had on a red shirt and a white hat. Maybe there was some other reason. It was delightful. It looked as if they were all standing out there, in the sweet moist sweaty Louisiana air, stark naked.

"Attention all aircraft," the radio said as I left New Orleans. "Convective Sigmet Five Five Charlie is current for an area of severe storms moving from the southwest at twenty knots. Hail to two inches, wind gusts to sixty knots possible." That sounded familiar.

Threat and danger. Haze, Hazy, Hazier. The sky conjugated particulates and moisture into a blue-gray thickness. Who knew what hid within? Above the smoky blue in which I traveled were faint blossoms of cloud, like domes of cathedrals sketched far above the street in chalk. The land below was somber. Standing water looked like dusty slate. Trees looked like olive-drab fog. In the haze the Lake Pontchartrain Causeway flew out and vanished into blue distance, a bridge into space. I crossed CLUNK intersection near Slaughter outside of Baton Rouge, and late in the hot afternoon circled over the enormous concrete structures erected by the Corps of Engineers against the tide of nature and the power of the Mississippi River.

The place is called Old River. Journalists who care about the land come here as if on pilgrimage, following their colleagues to stare at the place in trepidation and awe. Here you can forget patience. You can forget the endless slow tick of geologic time, which moves a pebble in a generation. You can forget the contemplation of grains of sand and the effect of wind, rain, and centuries on stone. This is *Geology Today*, in short paragraphs. This is the Mount St. Helens of water. Here, within our lifetimes, dramatic geological change will probably occur. This is the place where the Mississippi plans to take a shortcut to the sea.

Baton Rouge Approach Control gave me vectors to Old River. Once I got to it I had to fly another five miles up the Mississippi to find the Corps' concrete battalions arrayed against fate. But even in the murk of that threatening day it was not hard to find.

In the dim sky the sun appeared, at first a disk hardly brighter than the moon. It was an orange moon. Then it became a blaze, red as a wood fire. It looked as if it was smoking; a wood fire started with crude oil. I crabbed along above the levee, being thrown north by the wind.

There it was. Below, the wall of the river breached west in a fork. Brown water swept out of the Mississippi and drained away through two Corps of Engineers gates into the Achafalaya. The gates were, literally, fingers in the dike.

The problem was simple: In a delta system a river builds up the land through which it travels by dropping silt as it slows; when it builds one area it wants to move to another. Over millennia a river roams its delta, dropping silt and moving on. If you played the years back fast, it would look, in the words of *The New Yorker* magazine master of metaphor, John McPhee, "like a pianist playing with one hand." The Mississippi, constrained in the past century by the levees, has built itself up higher than its neighbor, the Achafalaya. Until 1963 more and more of the Mississippi was diverting to the Achafalaya through a former meander called Old River. In 1963 the corps built the first of its dike plugs. In 1973 this gate, called Old River Control, was damaged by a flood. The Corps has now finished a new structure, called Old River Control Auxiliary Structure.

That's what I came to see, having read McPhee about it: "[I]n grandeur and in profile it would not shame a pharaoh." McPhee also wrote, however: "Viewed from five or six thousand feet in the air, the structures at Old River inspire less confidence than they do up close. They seem temporary, fragile, vastly outmatched by the natural world—a lesion in the side of the Mississippi butterflied with surgical tape."

I was only two thousand feet above the gates, and from that altitude they looked more substantial: six huge white-topped gates, with muddy water foaming out behind them, monuments to that ultimate glory that Roosevelt had talked about in anointing the TVA: human control of nature. But the river looked exactly as McPhee had described it from the ground: "It was odd to look out toward the main-stem Mississippi, scarcely half a mile away, and see its contents spilling sideways, like cornmeal pouring from a hole in a burlap bag."

I circled the complex for fifteen minutes, trying to come up with a better metaphor. No luck. Blood and bandages, grain in the sack; McPhee had covered the territory. But there was something else. What was it? The red sun gleamed off the cowling as I circled slowly in the wind. The river hardly seemed to move. It pressed down with the weight of half a continent. In that expanse of slow water the control structure simply looked—temporary.

I turned my back on it, put the livid sun over my right shoulder, and flew down the Achafalaya, into the haze, into the swamp. Half an hour later I was deep in the wilderness, windblown, flying free like a shuttle loose in the weave, back and forth in time.

At first it looked just like the Mississippi, which, of course, it will someday be. Fields lay in the flood plain between the levees, and farmhouses and more fields stood behind the embankments, out of sight of the water. The brown river flowed south in orderly bends. On the west side of the river a road ran along the top of the bank. I glanced down at it and got worried.

A sports car and tanker truck hurtled toward each other, brewing dust. The road looked too narrow, but they hurtled on. They roared. They accelerated. They drew closer. Like God, helpless before folly, I watched the fateful human trajectory. Look out! Oh no, oh *no*!

Zip. Dust in your face, buddy. No contact. Whew.

Baton Rouge Approach Control was my friend, watching me through the smoke, which did not cloud his radar. He watched me from Simmesport to Melville to Krotz Spring, towns where white-painted pipelines suspended by cables were stretched across the river. They looked like mooring ropes, holding the restless banks together. Homes crouched behind the levees. A tank farm smelled of gas. When I checked in with Approach again, he said, "I'm about to terminate you."

What could I do, plead for mercy? Roger, I submit.

My life as a blip ended. I slid off his screen and was alone, and the levees opened out and vanished into the haze. The red sun leaned in under the wing to gaze in an elderly way at my face. It reflected distantly off square fields of water: crawfish ponds. A group of egrets drifted over the river in an oblique white line. Interstate 10 crossed the river and the wet forests on stilts, a straight line dissolving away into the darkening haze on either side of me. Then the modern world backed away from the Achafalaya. The receding levees held back the flood of civilization.

The dim red light was prehistoric, or maybe it was the light of the future; the end of the world. The bits of human life in this vast swamp were tattered. The brown river flowed between low, cusped banks, but water was everywhere, in gleaming sheets beneath the cypress trees, or in lakes smeared with algae and hyacinths and splattered with stumps. The best of the cypress was gone, and the long canals where the lumbermen had come to log it out were wide and empty.

Here and there stood white-painted tanks, speckled with rust, or dirt roads built up on berms of fill. Crawfish fishermen's floating camp shacks huddled up against the banks.

The haze and then the world snuffed the sun. I floated against a steady, calm wind, in the evening, low across the swamp. I liked this place. This was the landscape's natural state, but to a person from the high country, it looked dramatic. It looked like a natural disaster. Surely there had been some catastrophe here, a soft, still, endless, terrible catastrophe of water. It was wonderful. I let the plane slide closer to the swamp. I rested the tips of my fingers on the wheel and felt the damp softness of the air.

The water dissolved the Earth. The reflection of hazy twilight below made the world seem endlessly deep, or as shallow as a membrane. It was surface tension stretched across night. Trees and water, trees and water, in a thousand shades of trees and water. Trees leaned over the water, narcissistic; water seeped among the trees, subversive. The river channel divided, then came back together, so low and slow and strong it had no need to rush. The water changed color in swirls. It was slowly letting go of the load it had carried for a thousand miles. All along the edges were thin sand banks, where the silt had fallen out. This river, too, was moving its bed. Here was the Mississippi before the levees, and the Mississippi after the levees, once more playing out the single-handed symphony of the flood.

The river grew wider with the darkness, like the expanding pupil of the eye of night. Far ahead of me, a red flame burst up from the trees, flared, and vanished. Another blossomed to my left. Swamp lights. Three; five. They were the same red color as the vanished sun. Spirits of fire. At night I was still reading *Lord of the Rings* to my children. I knew what that was: the candles of the dead.

No. It was the blaze of industry.

I had gone through the swamp. I had escaped the slippage of time. People were flaring gas in the oil fields. I landed at Patterson, near Morgan City, where the Corps has built a twenty-two-foot concrete wall around the city for the day when the great flood comes through. The proprietor of the charter service at Patterson made me a sandwich. Times were hard in oil country.

"A few years ago anybody who could scrape together fifty thousand could get a line of credit for a million," he said. "They could affect the cowboy attitude; big belt buckle, big mouth." Not anymore. The belt buckles were pawned. The mouths were shut.

All night the air thickened. Slowly the stars receded to the top of the sky, then faded away, and as I got ready to sleep the crescent moon dissolved. The beacon threw a thick urgent beam around the airport. Off to the west the fog glowed yellow from sodium vapor lamps; from that direction came a constant rumble of engines, like the sound of a diesel train coming. But it never came.

In the foggy morning I ran on a levee: shotgun shells, oyster shells, and deep, sloped fields of clover. I stood beside a bayou, watching willow cotton blow back and forth on the innocent dark skin of the water. Pending calamities built up in my mind. The wind made little swirls of brightness on the surface like the ghosts of fish or the dreams of glory.

Storms were brewing, so I flew out of there, and crossed a patch of long narrow fields near the town of Des Allemands. It reminded me of the narrow fields near Santa Fe: an old drawing of the human need to possess the land. On instruments, I climbed up through billows of thunderstorms being born. At eleven thousand feet, above them all, I looked down on heaps, canyons, and shreds of cloud, and, between them, a deep blue nothingness. I was two miles up, and the visibility down through the atmosphere was not two miles.

Ahead a cloud rose, grew, towered—and dissolved. Just like that. An explosion in slow motion; a poof of cotton. I crossed New Orleans and never saw the city, and headed east across Mississippi Sound for Florida. My next checkpoint on the flight plan was an intersection over Cat Island. It was called DOGMA.

PART

CHAPTER NINETEEN

To be dogmatic: Florida is the future. Some people promise that it is, and others are afraid that it may be.

I hit the state north of Pensacola, by BRATT, and found myself in hot pursuit of all kinds of glory. "Caution," the chart said down on the coast by Bon Secour National Wildlife Refuge, "High volume of rotary and fixed-wing training surface to 17,500." Caution, the chart might as well have read: Revolt fomented here. Nearby, at Elgin Air Force Base, commandos once trained for the disastrous Iranian rescue of 1980; here Nicaraguan Contras are said also to have worked out in the woods. But the countryside was not used just to practice war. The pine forests were logged in huge bald chunks, and grown back in huge combed chunks. From eleven thousand feet the abundant chicken factories looked like train cars thrown around the landscape by a giant brat. Three of them were at least twice as long as regular chicken sheds: great long particle accelerators; fire an egg at a neutron.

Artifacts of violence weren't hard to find. At Tallahassee I ran into friends, Gary Karasik and Karen Cunningham, who were moving there, and went house hunting with them. One of the houses was owned by a man who liked to shoot deer with a .357 Magnum revolver. Gary was impressed. When he is visibly impressed, it's a good idea to be wary. He asked the guy how he did it.

"Just pop 'em in the neck," the shootist said proudly, "and down they go."

"Really?" said Gary, looking up at a five-point head on the wall.

We went into the next room, where a set of antlers was bolted to a board.

"Very impressive," Gary murmured. "Just blew his head right off."

I left Tallahassee and headed down the coast. Lindbergh had flown due east from here to Jacksonville in 1927, but I couldn't resist the corners of the country. I had been north of Seattle; I would fly to the northeast tip of Maine. I wasn't going to miss Key West. So I flew south to where the trees dwindled away before the salt wind, and the land turned to open fields, ponds, canals, and salt marsh. There, at last, where a thousand inlets let the tide in to caress the grass, the land subsided beneath the waters of the Gulf to make a subtle and endearing coast.

The place was utterly without people; it was the St. Marks National Wildlife Refuge. It was clean and empty. It was what Florida was like in 1773, when John Bertram, a naturalist, came to visit. To him it was a "blessed unviolated spot of earth."

Bertram was my kind of guy. He liked the landscape; he liked adjectives:

"This world," he wrote, "as a glorious apartment of the boundless palace of the sovereign Creator, is furnished with an infinite variety of animated scenes, inexpressibly beautiful and pleasing, equally free to the inspection and enjoyment of all his creatures."

I descended to fifteen hundred feet and flew south, and it seemed that the west coast of Florida reeled by as a picture of the whole state's past. The landscape began as empty as Bertram's *Elysium*. Then, slowly, as the miles moved, glorious apartments showed up, followed by boundless palaces.

The first sign of people were four little boats sitting offshore about three or four miles, near a streak of foam in the water. It was flat calm. It was Juan Ponce de León and company rowing ashore in 1513, chasing the glory of the Fountain of Youth. (Ponce de León was fifty when he left home.) A few minutes later I passed a place marked on the chart as "Camp": a group of boats tied up deep in the little creek; a grid of six parallel roads. This first settlement was a tiny patch in a long, utterly flat stretch of coastline where ground and water met each other without disturbance; no surf, no waves, no cliffs; just an intricate woven mesh of inlets, sand, sea, and grass.

The first European settlement, built by Protestant Huguenots on the St. Johns River on the opposite coast, must not have looked any more impressive than this in 1565, when it represented white folks and their pursuit of religious righteousness for the first time in Florida. For all its insignificance, that first settlement drew too much attention; if religion was its source of strength, it was also its nemesis. That year members of a Spanish expedition, inflamed by godliness, massacred the infidels and established a nearby town they called St. Augustine. An auspicious start.

Flying low, just offshore, I curved back and forth with the coast. The settlements became more frequent: Keaton Beach, Fish Creek, Steinhatchee, Jena, and Horseshoe Beach—a pack of houses on a point. Florida was growing. It wasn't 1565 or 1773 anymore. It was more like 1827, when Ralph Waldo Emerson came down from New England ill with consumption, chasing health. St. Augustine had barely more than a thousand residents, "Yet," Emerson wrote in a poem named for the city, "much is here/That can beguile the months of banishment."

In the same poem he made the place a symbol of the country:

> *Here is the old land of America*
> *And here in this sea-girt nook, the infant steps,*
> *First foot-prints of that Genius giant-grown*
> *That daunts the nations with his power to-day.*

Like a dragonfly dipping close to the water, I made my way south, but it seemed that I stood in one place above the planet while time instead of coastline moved past beneath. Settlements grew along the water's edge: Suwannee was a thriving town on the bank of the mouth of the river, where tea-colored water flowed out to sea, and incredibly thin sand islands advanced like a line of foam upon the shore. Cedar Key was all elegant houses, each with a patrician's stretch of shore, on an island with a runway. The airport was reached by a causeway that hopped islands like stepping-stones. It reminded me of the railroads that bounded into Florida after the Civil War. Then, as tourism was just beginning, writers were already making Florida a symbol of paradise and of loss.

In the late nineteenth century both Washington Irving and a black poet named Albery Whitman wrote about the destruction of the Seminoles earlier in the century. Irving wrote semifictional sketches about the governor who led much of the assault on the Seminoles. The story ended with the worthy triumph of the white man over the romantic, doomed Indian. Whitman had a grimmer view. The Seminoles lived in Eden:

> *Say, when their flow'ry landscapes could allure,*
> *What peaceful seasons did to them return*
> *And how requited labour filled his golden urn!*

But Eden was wantonly destroyed. The Seminoles were shaken from the land they loved like a bug off a branch. They were killed or sent to Oklahoma in the name of religion or the name of commerce. Whitman went on:

> The man who blesses and the man who kills,
> Oft have a kindred purpose after all,
> A purpose that will ring in Mammon's tills;
> And that has ne'er unheeded made a call,
> Since Eve and Adam trod the thistles of their Fall.

The epic poem was called *The Rape of Florida.* That wasn't the last time around for that idea, either. But it didn't occur to most visitors to Florida. Most of them didn't read Albery Whitman. They read the stuff produced by writers hired by railroad companies to write of warm December mornings. The trains south were long and loaded.

On the water below me boats multiplied like cells in a dish of pond water. The four open boats of Ponce de León had become a hundred, then a thousand, some growing sails like mayflies, some turning into blocks like low-rent apartments, trailing great white wakes. I floated serenely apart above them, my white wings blended with the pale, soft, hazy sky. The boundaries of the world were soft, too: between land and sea, sky and surface, surface and the sea's floor. All blended, like this flow of time. I could see the shadows of boats, and beneath them, like the petroglyphs on the desert, strange straight lines drawn on the bottom. They were intricate and layered, one drawn over another. Some were too straight to be organic; some bent around in perfect French curves. They were the tracks of shrimp fishermen, the scratches where they drew their trawls. They crisscrossed like bars of shadow, in depth; old lines fading, new lines prominent. They were more substantial marks than the ruffles of wind and wakes on the Gulf's skin. They made the world abstract.

Everything was wispy: the patterns on the beach, the patterns of small waves on the water, the patterns on the bottom, the bright hazy swirl of cloud above. I looked right, away from the land. Out there the Gulf blended away into a blue haze. There was no horizon. Blue faded into blue. Vertigo ran through me like a prickle of heat. I wasn't sure of my position in the sky. All Florida was as insubstantial as a glory.

In 1873 journalist Edward King reported that a quarter of Florida's growing crowds of visitors came for their health. "[T]he others," he wrote, "are crusading to find the phantom Pleasure." Riding the edge of the crusade like a wave, I tumbled into the twentieth century.

Buildings, buildings, buildings. Boats, boats, boats. What, I asked Skip Livingston, were all those people fishing for off Homosassa?

"Cocaine," he said. "Or pot."

I had met Livingston in Tallahassee. His full name is Dr. Robert J. Livingston. He is a biologist and director of an organization cheerfully named CARRMA: Center for Aquatic Research and Resource Management. He is a stocky, forthright person who had an office in the basement of a building at Florida State University. He had sat there in a room full of files, wearing shorts and a short-sleeved shirt in the spring heat, doing battle with an air conditioner that sounded like a large piece of earth-moving equipment with loose tracks.

"The facilities here are terrible," he had shouted. "We live like pigs."

The air conditioner had roared and rattled like Six Zero One after a hard day. So though I couldn't get Livingston up in the plane with me physically, I took him along in spirit, at least, by asking him to comment later on some of the things I had seen on the face of Florida.

He seemed willing. So his phantom joined the others. South of Homosassa, as the coastline became more and more encrusted by buildings, I saw a net staked out from a sandy beach in a wide loop with a narrow opening at the south end, and a skiff in attendance.

"Beach seines," Livingston said brusquely. "They use them to catch mullet."

"What," I asked, thinking of nicknames, "do they call the people who do that for a living?"

"Mullet fishermen."

"Can you make a decent living fishing for mullet that way?"

"Decent," he said, "is dependent on who it is that's doing the living."

But Livingston's interest wasn't in being a tour guide. He was cool and brusque, but inflamed. He wanted me to see the signs of disaster. He wanted to get me into modern times.

As I approached Tampa Bay I crossed thousands of islands, which were set about in water that looked six inches deep—wonderful wide green and yellow flats. Trawlers' tracks ran parallel to one another here, as if they fished in squads. Then the haze grew thicker, and out of it emerged a vast rectangular settlement, line after line of houses built on the edge of the water. But this was now a different kind of link between water and land.

This northern edge of the complex of cities that began here at Hudson and never completely ended until I passed Marco Island, over 150 air miles south, was a turning point. It was the place at which the land stopped controlling where the houses and roads were; where the people started controlling the land. Until I got to Hudson, the little towns stood on the edges of inlets, and harbors were adjusted to the way the land and the sea chose to mingle. Here the water met the land in the angular confines of endless marinas. Here was the Florida of the boom-and-bust 1920s. Railroads had opened up the landscape, and now bulldozers changed it completely. Now it was as if someone had taken all those winding and myriad inlets, those mysterious linkages of earth and sky and sea and living things, and ironed them flat.

Macho Irene called the intersection here ENDED. Livingston felt that way too. From here, Florida was over. He was like a guardian angel at my shoulder, making sure that I should not be too charmed by the rose-colored light of the sun shining through the haze:

"In Florida we have had massive deterioration in many of our natural systems," he said. "In a hundred years we have lost half our wetlands. The Everglades were wiped out. The Kissimmee River was wiped out. Lake Okeechobee now is souring. The St. Johns River is a cesspool."

Even in this modern complaint there was still slippage to the past. We were hardly into the century. Henry James visited Florida briefly during his tour of America in 1904 and saw beauty and human destruction enough to infuriate him. He kept writing about the "velvet air," but oddly, in this free and open climate, what he saw of people made him think of enclosures; glass jars and fishbowls. At Palm Beach, he wrote, "as nowhere else, in America, one would find Vanity Fair in full blast—and Vanity Fair not scattered, not discriminated and parcelled out, as among the comparative privacies and ancientries of Newport, but compressed under one vast cover, enclosed in a single huge *vitrine*." The girls of Palm Beach "were as perfectly in their element as goldfish in a crystal jar: a form of exhibition suggesting but one question or mystery. Was it they who had invented it, or had it inscrutably invented *them*?"

Off Tarpon Springs I saw an inscrutable invention: a rectangular, manufactured island beach. It stood a mile offshore, at the end of a long sweep of magnificent road. Most of the road was causeway. The island was a perfect rectangle of sand, perhaps a thousand feet by five hundred feet, fully half of it covered by a parking lot with spaces for 425 cars, blocked at each end by groins of rock, planted with tidy rows of palm trees. A few dozen cars were parked out there, and I could see umbrellas and blankets flowering on the white sand. It was the Fred Howard Park beach, built up out of a sandbar in the late 1960s by the Pinellas County Park Department. The causeway had recently been shored up with slag. It was a place where a million people a year came to lie in the sun and listen to the lush flow of the sea and pretend they were somewhere natural.

The place didn't look like a beach. With its long handle of a road, its boxiness, and the mesh of perfect trees and parking spaces, it looked like something else. It looked like huge popcorn popper. Shake it on a hot Sunday afternoon and watch 'em fly. *Pow! Zing!* There goes Aunt Martha! *Bzzzz-BANG!* Well, I'll be; sounded like Joe. *Pop-pop-pop-pop-popopopop-blooey!* There go those kids again!

"I have a feeling that in the last fifty years a very blue-collar resort has developed," John Jackson mused, as we flew down the coast looking at beaches crammed with houses. "It's usually on a beach or at a dam. I was aware of it for the first time in Texas. It was at an artificial lake, and it was just as tawdry as it could be, but you could see that it represented pleasure and leisure and everything else."

"I used to love South Florida," Livingston said. Livingston was not an observer. He was a flagrant participant. If a place became tawdry, he was an injured party. "I used to visit from New Jersey many years ago, when Route 1 was the only way to get south. Then it was a paradise, it was an actual paradise. It is being systematically destroyed." At Clearwater and St. Petersburg I fought haze and smoke, and reports of traffic that came at my face like flies, but I emerged over wonderful patterns of blues, greens, and golds in the water's flow past Egmont Key at the Bay's mouth. It was impossible to sorrow. I grinned and rocked the wings at a catamaran that ripped a hiss off the edge of a wave.

"The public is indifferent," Skip Livingston said. No. I was not indifferent. That accusation will never be among those that hang black on my grave. It was just easy to see those long beaches, to love them, and to imagine that all was clean and beautiful, and strong, and part of another time. The Florida air is full of rainbows.

A thunderhead bloomed up ahead, a hard storm. Tampa Bay relaxed its encrusted perimeter, and opened. Egmont Key was a crescent, a leaf spun at the entrance, a wildlife refuge with ruins, old foundations, pinewoods, and palms. Here again sand ran down into water, and water ran through sand. I could see the sand move; I could see the long elegant curves of color shift and change as the dust of rivers renegotiated its pact with the sea. A sailboat ran before the breeze, chasing its shadow.

Visibility improved south of Sarasota, but still both coast and the barrier islands were laden with homes and apartments and tall hotels. People hung in the high porches like laundry. Bright lights danced in the water below the buildings: sunlight reflected off windows down onto the sea. But the better visibility revealed the background. It was no longer muddied by haze. It was no longer a vaguely patterned green place. The landscape rose up and was seen. It was the great pattern. It was The Wheel of Life. It was *The Rotonda.*

The Rotonda was a huge subdivision, a circle three miles in diameter, ten miles around. It was a circle made of roads and waterways. Two narrow wedges were jammed with houses. The rest of the long curve was empty. Even in the improved visibility, this great wheel vanished off into the distance. It was large, but it looked enormous. You could get on that outer rim road, lock the steering wheel down, and sell hot dogs out of the trunk. You'd get home about sundown. If you had a boat up one of those labyrinthine marina channels, you could take on supplies, motor all the way out to Charlotte Harbor, sight the Gulf in the distance, motor back in, reassure your heirs, get on the *Today* show, and write a book about the experience. No wonder I saw so many houseboats here; you had to spend a couple of weeks on the water just to get out of the suburbs.

This was a large place. It was, I thought, one of the largest single pieces of work I had ever seen on the landscape. Then Fort Meyers Approach asked me to climb to avoid his airspace, and I saw I was wrong.

The chart called these geometrical spaces Street Patterns. Many already had canals between their empty streets. They were nothing like the street patterns I had seen on the desert at Albuquerque. Those were as sheets of lined paper lost in this hurricane of plats. One single rectangle of streets that I measured on the chart covered at least three hundred square miles. Whenever you read about Florida you hear of these subdivisions, but the difference between studying the acreage figures and flying close above the acres was the difference between reading about the thousand-pound man and holding him in your lap. Skip Livingston appeared at my shoulder, the air conditioner clacking behind him. Modern times. Here we were at last. This was today in Florida.

"Florida is now the third-largest state in the country," he said above all the American noise. "We just overtook Pennsylvania. By the turn of the century we will be one of the major states. We will have fifteen to sixteen million people, and they will have overrun most of our natural resources."

Livingston was not the complete pessimist. He had been working for years to help preserve and protect large chunks of the Apalachicola Estuary, which was being accomplished by the state's purchase of threatened land. To that end he had produced almost single-handedly—photos, charts, drawings, text—a magnificent resource atlas of the estuary system. He was still fired up, still energetic, but in the end, he thought, he would leave the state rather than see the degradation complete.

I refueled at Naples, flew southeast between Irene's handiwork—GOODY and DEEDS—to get out of the way of military warning area W174G, and let the land disappear beneath the columns of the day's Everglades storms. I climbed high into the afternoon, gave myself up to the many sweet blues of sea and sky, and set a course for Key West.

Between the archipelago and the mainland I punched the coordinates of home into the loran. While a line of islands disappeared under the storm, and I rose beyond reach of land whichever way I might glide, the counter clicked from 1,999 nautical miles to 2,000. Magic number, I thought. As this civilization approaches that number in its arbitrary counting of years, how many people will expect the planet to self-destruct on the hour? That's a wisp of strange light to chase around a corner.

Key West was the only city on the whole trip farther than two thousand nautical miles from home. I slipped in there like a man on the lam, stunned by the difference between what I had always thought of the Keys and what they looked like. I had imagined a long, ragged archipelago surrounded by the sea, but what I saw was a fat thumb of land extending from the peninsula. The water was so clear and shallow that it seemed mere chance—an afternoon rainshower, perhaps—that had temporarily submerged most of the land and left only these tufts of islands showing—islands tufted themselves with palm trees and buildings. This is what a lot of Florida would look like if the sea level rose a few feet.

"Fly over the Florida Keys and see how they are developing the Keys," said the spirit of Skip Livingston. Here again! "There the development has destroyed, oh, a tremendous amount of potential habitat. The offshore reefs continue to be under pressure. They are being destroyed simply by the weight of people right now who are going off and running boats over them and picking chunks of coral."

I landed at Key West and went for a run in the velvet air that Henry James admired, and I looked down into clear water at a yellow bottom. I was looking for fish; I saw newspapers and beer cans. Key West was a scuffed place. Still, Skip Livingston, I could not grieve. It was one of those rare hours in life in which the whole beauty of the world seems revealed and you can do nothing but watch.

"Wondrous sea life!" "Brilliant Beaches!" Everywhere I went racks of brochures framed the landscape in superlatives that exaggerated the entertainment but were impossibly short of the truth. I was ecstatic just to see the world. I ran laps on the high school track, but it was just an excuse. We sneak our looks at the world, hiding our interest in something less awful, less dramatic, than this big spin, because occasionally in all these excuses we happen to get a glance into the face of the queen, and once in a great while we see her eyes, and it takes our breath away.

It was nothing spectacular: the clear water; the expanse of blue horizon; the light shining through a miniature thunderstorm that came down on the high school track as I ran laps on the oval. But for some reason it was overwhelming. Bits of warm rain fell, and I flew across the tarmac, swept along by joy.

I awoke at Key West, sweating, to the sound of rain. I lifted the corner of a curtain. Low, bulky clouds were lit by the city lights; hard rain rang on the aluminum. It made the tarmac shine. I lay awake in the heat, my skin like slime.

I left in the early light, looking out for Fat Albert and his deadly string. Fat Albert was officially an Air Force aerostat balloon. He hung up there at the end of a steel cable, fourteen thousand feet in the air. He looked down over the horizon 150 miles, past Cuba, his radar package eyeing drug runners. The cable was about the diameter of a fifty-cent piece, but to a plane it was as invisible as pain. "Worse than weather," said a sign at the airport, "run into the tether."

This morning I could grieve. There is nothing more subtle and magnificent to be seen in the world from an airplane than the Everglades. Livingston's ghost and I left the Keys near Macho Irene's favorite wet intersection, DROWN, and moved north across the expanse. Florida had already been a view of the many intricate ways for water and land to meet, and here was the masterpiece. In the calm of the morning the green-brown bottom rose softly to greet the green-brown land, and I had to look carefully to see where the sea ended and the great swamp began. I flew at about two thousand feet above the surface, and met the coast at Flamingo: a little dock and an official-looking campground. Beyond began the long sweep of the Everglades, utterly flat, wound about with waterways. The water was dark in the greens and grays and browns of sawgrass, cypress, and fern. The flow pattern ran almost imperceptibly to the southwest. Hammocks of trees stood in the sea of grass, and the subtle flow diverted around them. I marked my directions well here; over the national park I had to watch out: "Alert area," the chart said. "Concentrated flight training."

Skip Livingston murmured flatly in my ear, "The Everglades is now simply a bunch of tubes, diverting water in various directions. It is probably the biggest environmental scandal in the country because there is no such system anywhere else in the northern hemisphere, and they have virtually destroyed it in thirty years."

"They?"

"You have private interests such as the agriculturists who get their congressmen to force legislation that will favor them, you get federal agencies such as the Army Corps of Engineers using public moneys to destroy public resources for these private interests. You get massive cover-ups or just plain ignorance by the press, and you get massive indifference by the public. You roll it all up, and the Everglades are gone."

Well, they weren't gone. They were right there below me, suffering drought and flood at the wrong times, in the wrong seasons, or to artificial excess. They weren't gone. But then a great line came across the state: the Tamiami Canal, which moves so much of that water that should drain slowly through the swamp. Suddenly, in a few miles, The American Grid was back, and the Everglades had indeed disappeared, replaced first by a sawgrass prairie covered with an enormously criss-crossed and tangled skein of vehicle tracks. Then vast uniform fields of vegetables and sugar cane took over and stretched from haze to haze on each side of the plane.

"The Everglades was actually a sort of an idea in a lot of people's minds," Livingston said. "It had always seemed mysterious and somehow dangerous, and something to be conquered. Which they did, relatively easily. Now it is suddenly dawning on us that it was a repository for literally hundreds of species of birds, for instance, that are no longer able to survive there; that it's a vast interconnected system, from the Kissimmee all the way to the Florida Bay. But the best they can do now is to spend hundreds of millions of dollars and try to redo the piping system. It would always be an artificial system."

Ah. The future of Florida: artifice. I landed for fuel beside Lake Okeechobee. Three boats passing in the lake had stirred up a faint cloud of algae brewing in water made too rich by manure-fed runoff. The tarmac at the airport was trenched by the feet of crop-duster helicopters that landed in the soft black hydrocarbon mud on summer days. On the wall inside the office were twenty-one photographs of tornadoes and funnel clouds, all taken right from the door. Every weekend, the guy there said, there were bass-fishing tournaments in the lake. He was a great person. He let me use the shower.

Henry James, Skip Livingston, and Charles Lindbergh could have sat out there on the Okefenokee levee in the velvet air and sung their century's lament. They would have harmonized. "Florida for James," wrote Anne E. Rowe, "was a vision of all that was potentially good and beautiful in America and all that was ultimately wrong." (Rowe, an English teacher at FSU, was the author of *The Idea of Florida in the American Literary Imagination*, a book included in my airborne library.) Would Livingston have said it any differently? The three thought in terms of the blood of the land.

"Many things contribute to the problem," Livingston said. "Any one of them by itself may seem almost innocuous, but we put them all together and it culminates in the destruction of the natural resource. I call it 'The Death from the Thousand Cuts.' " "Within a fraction of my lifetime," Lindbergh said, "I saw New York parking space disappear, the waters of Long Island Sound become polluted, and the coasts of Maine and Florida packed to the shoreline with houses and motels." James, disheartened by the American effect on Florida and other places in which he had hoped to be stirred by beauty, wrote about it on the train back north. Once again, Florida was a symbol for the nation. James addressed his country directly, bitterly: "It wouldn't be to *you* I should be looking in any degree for beauty or for charm. Beauty and charm would be for me in the solitude you have ravaged, and I should owe you my grudge for every disfigurement and every violence, for every wound with which you have caused the face of the land to bleed."

➤ "And it is also in Florida," Anne Rowe wrote, "that the largest embodiments of fantasy and technology—Disney World and Epcot—have been created out of the very swamps and barrens of Florida that Henry James despaired of, suggesting that even if Florida the real is finally lost, a man-made paradise will take its place." I left Okeechobee and flew north, past Cape Canaveral, shrouded in clouds, toward Orlando and the future.

Very early in this journey I had visited Antarctica. I was in San Diego, before I even felt that the trip was under way, and I went to the Sea World penguin exhibit. I was saying farewell, in a way, to previous work, a book about that frozen continent. I hadn't thought the visit would have much to do with my journeys around America, but now, over Florida, as I glanced down between clouds at spaces of landscape paved from cloud edge to cloud edge by identical subdivision blocks, I thought maybe it did. Here was Orlando, the greatest concentration of artificial landscapes in the world, including another Sea World and another Penguin Encounter. It didn't make any difference if the two places were a continent apart; they were part of our common scene.

It was a sunny day when I went to visit Antarctica. The big opening to the Penguin Encounter was dark. I walked past the sign that explains the sponsorship of Hubbs Sea World Institute and the National Science Foundation, and found myself in the Gerlache Strait, in the Antarctic Peninsula just north of Palmer Station. This was a stylized Gerlache Strait, not the place I remembered from my own journeys. The wall was covered with a vast photograph of ice-covered mountains, surrounded by the tinkling glitter of hundreds of shiny Reflecto disks on a black background, multiplied in mirrors and shallow black pools. In the background was the faint discordant howling that wind makes in movies, and an eerie whine of violins. The people loved it.

I followed the path into a dim room against a window, where I and about thirty other people were carried past a wall of windows on moving sidewalk that is speeded up when the place is crowded—three million visitors ride past these windows every year. On the other side of the windows, living on concrete ice and on snow made behind the exhibit in a machine and sprayed out by fire hose, were about 350 penguins: Adélie, gentoo, chin strap, king, macaroni, and rock hopper. They strutted like elderly porters and waved their wings, and dove into the pool. The people behind the glass saw their transplanted natural behavior more closely than they ever could in the real world. People on the moving floor waved at a penguin that was flapping its wings on the artificial ice, and laughed.

I was more fortunate than most: I was invited to walk around inside the exhibit itself with Frank Todd, the energetic, redheaded scientist who had created the exhibit. He had recently returned from his annual expedition to Antarctica to collect eggs for Orlando.

We crunched around on the snow and guano in front of a painting of mountains that were improbable even for Antarctica. Penguins tugged at his pants legs with their beaks like kids asking to play, or to go to the bathroom, or wondering when they would get to go home. "We're trying to create an ecosystem," he said. "We're trying to make a window into the Antarctic." The big window is cleaned regularly with a substance called Rain-X, or it would fog. It snows in the exhibit: twelve thousand pounds of manufactured snow is blown in every day. Light in the exhibit is controlled to give the penguins the impression that they are still in the southern hemisphere; as the days get shorter in the northern hemisphere, they lengthen in the exhibit; in the long nights of December, the penguins shuffle through the snow and laugh and raise young in a perpetual electric day created out back of the exhibit by a cogeneration plant fired by natural gas. The exhibit consumes 338,000 kilowatt hours of power each month. While we were inside the electricity went off temporarily, and emergency lamps went on above the ice. The treadmill moving people past the window stopped briefly, and the people thought they were trapped. They were scared. The penguins couldn't see past the window into America, or they might have had a strange idea about what America was like.

Outside the exhibit was the Penguin Encounter store, which stood near a display of a Jeep and a Renault provided by car dealer, not far from Cap'n Kids' World, where children played like penguins. Near the store a pine tree played light rock music. In the store were penguin mugs, penguin nameplates, penguin bibs. I asked a salesperson named Susan Brown what the public, emerging from Antarctica, most liked to purchase to remind them of this visit to the planet's strange southern landscape.

"Puffins," she said. "They like the puffin stuff."

Puffins are cute, exotic birds. They live only in the north. There are no puffins in Antarctica.

Now, weeks later, I descended into haze out of five thousand feet, down into a gently rolling country of small lakes, catfish farms, interstate highways, and artificial landscapes. I wondered if, in the next century, beyond that magic number by which the world will not be destroyed, most landscapes people see will be like the Penguin Encounter: artistic renditions of something whose reality has been forgotten. People will ride moving sidewalks past pieces of the prairie, and the trackless desert, and the American farm. We will have indoor landscapes that are sheer fantasy, and outdoor landscapes that are manipulated to match some natural ideal that never existed.

It is already happening. San Diego, which has a magnificent natural landscape, lures visitors with African zoo scenes and Antarctica. Arizona is swamped by water-park hotels. Vast natural landscapes, like the scene along the Natchez Trace, are being managed to promote illusion, even in wilderness. The best white-water rafting in the country, in the Grand Canyon and on the Middle Fork of Idaho's Salmon River, is restricted; rafters operate on a reservation system and on timetables, like trains, so that each group has the impression it is on the river alone. In my own state there's a proposal to consolidate a number of ranches into a vast single piece of land in which fences would be removed and the landscape turned over to bison, antelope, and elk; where people could come in and shoot and pretend they were out there with Theodore Roosevelt. It's to be called The Big Open. You'd have to pay to get in.

In these places there will be an increasingly vivid separation of classes: spectators, who are vague, half distracted, in awe; the curators, who are cocky, possessed of special magical knowledge about how the cogenerators work and where the bathrooms are concealed, and who move the spectators around like sheep. In time curators will become an elite, with a prescribed ritual of outward deference and internal disdain, and special schools for their young. Spectators will never be quite sure if curators really can turn off the sun, but they will obey all the signs, just in case.

One thing would be certain. Never, in a landscape like that, would you ever suddenly become transformed by wonder, as I was at Key

West. You would never be utterly captivated, utterly in love with the world. Living among artificial landscapes would be like painting a bull's-eye glory on a piece of tin, and carrying it around with me to cocktail parties to boast that I'd finally caught it.

Orlando Approach directed me out of the way of his incoming jets and over the theme parks. I crossed hotels. I crossed a water slide and a rectangular chlorinated pond with a white beach at one end: the inland complement to Fred Howard Park beach. There, at last, was Epcot Center: a glittering ball, a parking lot, a tidy little fake lake, little red walkways, little Eiffel tower, a little circular railroad. Everything was miniature, so much smaller than life.

CHAPTER TWENTY

Skip Livingston left me with a warning. Why do we ignore the subtle damage we do to the land, the thousand wounds that bleed so quietly, but so long?

"What we are waiting for," he said, "is a calamity."

I flew north toward Jacksonville and Georgia. The world seemed aflame. Armageddon was upon us. A red ball of fire raced with me across the country as it had in the Achafalaya basin—the sun reflecting off water between trees. Macho Irene had been here. She'd been depressed too. WORMS was the first intersection, GUANO the next.

One of Irene's associates in the office was trying to impress her. She'd nicknamed him too. He was WIMPY Joe, who was in charge of naming all the military operations areas. He didn't dare cut loose as often as Irene, but when he did he thought he'd make her eyes wilt with his tough language. So up ahead, in a cloud of restricted areas that surrounded Savannah, was Gator Low MOA, which was pretty daring for Wimpy Joe. But he had really hung it out on the line a little farther north. Here it was Quick Thrust. Joe thought this was great. Every chunk of airspace for miles got the name, with alphabet tags to tell them apart. Quick Thrust J, Quick Thrust E, Quick Thrust G. There, thought Joe. Unngh!

Irene was unimpressed. On her way to Macon on Victor 243 she glanced over her shoulder with disdain. "DUMMY," she said.

I left Florida in murk. There was no glory in this shadowy world. I fueled at Jacksonville and took off after a 747 landed, all smoke and thunder. The air stank of burned rubber. Beside the runway, so close its beak must have buzzed, stood an egret in a pond.

The haze closed in like twilight. It was early afternoon. Above the haze the edges of clouds towered, but I could barely see them. It was like looking up at cliffs from under muddy water. I crossed a corner of the Okefenokee Swamp and saw two canoes tied up next to a mound of dry land, and wished to be down there with the moss and the hyacinths and the swamp mist instead of up here in this heavy sky. At the north edge of the Okefenokee pale roads rode the backs of dirt causeways into the swamp, and great swatches were torn down for pulp logs for what a forester called Pampers paper. Drainage trenches began to appear, light weals in the green edged by alternating humps of dirt, like the scars of sutures. At the edge of my visibility to the northeast, about five miles, a red gash of fire burned in a logged field, along a trench, and it looked like war.

At Waycross, Georgia, the town was somewhere off in the haze, but all I saw was a rusty spreading of rails. The sun glinted below me in the trees, finding water I couldn't otherwise see. This was still the vast Coastal Plains Province; the flat land, the wet land; where the sea will come when the sea rises. In this Armageddon smoke, I was still thinking of calamity.

Real farms began to appear now among the logged trees: larger fields, cows in a group; splotches of brown where they were fed hay this winter. Woods opened gracefully into light green pecan orchards. At the town of Nichols there was a ball park with a dirt infield, with kids playing on it. The Ocmulgee River wound its way across my path, fields began to turn from gray to Georgia red, and a voice said to someone else on the unicom frequency:

"Just talkin' to one of our people up in Chester, and he said there was some pretty high winds and rain up there. Looks like it was coming our way." Another red cornrow of fire ran like a Civil War battle line across my path, with the thunderstorm behind it. I turned and circled and landed at McRae.

McRae was an old town and a quiet town, slumbering in the haze. When people saw people they knew, or people they didn't know, in McRae, they said "Hey!" They were being friendly. McRae made its old fortunes on cotton and Naval Stores, a strange name for resin and its products that were once milked all over the South from loblolly pine and slash pine like maple syrup. In McRae it still is. "Yankees call it R-E-S-I-N," one man told me. "We call it tar." Getting it out of living trees is called dippin' tar.

"There's some families in this area couldn't spend all their money if they tried to," someone in McRae told me. "They made it with dippin' tar—cheap labor." That was years ago, but still in the woods around

McRae you can come upon stands of pines and every fourth or fifth pine has a rectangular tin cup hung below the streak of the cat face, with the tears of sticky juice falling slow as night into the tin.

The airport was a good paved strip with parking room for a dozen planes, with three tied down. While I was looking around and waiting for the rain an old car drove up to me beside the plane. In it was a long-faced, dark-faced white man with pale eyes. He had a paper cup of liquid on the seat. That cup was important to him. He stopped, took a sip, and leaned out the window.

"Hey!"

"Hello."

"Gonna tie down here tonight?"

"If that's all right."

"No objection." He took a sip, and put out a hand.

"Johnny Kearce."

"Mike Parfit."

I told him I'd be sleeping in the plane.

"Hey, you can sleep in that little building there. Got a couch in there." A sign on the little building said "Welcome to McRae. GA Elv 197."

That was all right. I said I sure appreciate it. I didn't say I liked my home in the plane.

Johnny took a sip. Just standing there, by plane and car, we got talking. We talked about flying, and we talked about agriculture.

"Agriculture's about faded away here," Johnny said.

"When did that happen?"

"In the late seventies when the farmers began to get too big, too fast." Sip. "A guy's coming down to look at my old blue Ag Truck tomorrow." It was a crop duster sitting next to me on the apron.

"You getting out of the business?"

Sip. Long stare.

"I paint airplanes now." Sip. He dug out a card. Tri-State Aero. Long pause. Sip. "I have been in aviation for twenty years, Mike. I've got fifteen thousand hours of flying, and I'm wore out."

A drop of rain hit my wing like a gong. Johnny Kearce grinned out of those cool pale eyes.

"I'm going to be out here around dawn-thirty," he said, starting the car. "You take advantage of that little house there. Got a hot shower."

The rain came on. I was sweaty. I put my running shorts and singlet on and left the plane, and ran and ran in the dark afternoon, relishing the coolness. In five minutes I was completely wet. I ran across the empty highway to Little Ocmulgee State Park: a golf course and a reservoir. I trotted through the park, past two men fishing on a pier into an arm of an empty lake. The lake had been drained to kill weeds, to improve the fishing. The men looked as if they were fishing in mud.

I ran on past a sign to a group camp, to where the sign said "Oak Ridge Trail." I ran out that trail on white sand, in pouring rain, with the branches bent into my path splashing me with water cooler than the rain. It was wonderful; pines and maples and live oaks and big-leafed post oaks, and flies that kept up with me and goaded me to speed. It was wet and cool and lonely, though there were many tracks of motorcycles in the wide sand trail, and lots of little cups of anthills. Then I ran downhill and out a little bridge to a platform at the edge of the upper end of the lake and stopped.

It was a bridge to a million years ago, to a swamp that made oil. The place was black muck, under huge round hyacinth leaves that lay folded on the muck. A small stream of dark water trickled down to a darker brown rill through the muck and the leaves. The only sign of human life was a pair of footprints in the muck, where someone had gotten squelchy dirty wading out to a clump of grass to fish in the rill; and strange metal shields on about fifty trees around the end of the lake. The park naturalist had put them up to keep ferrets out of the wood duck nests. But these things did not matter. They did not seem real, like artifacts my memory put up to try to tell me I had not gone back in time. Dinosaurs were dying deep in the muck, and the trees were full of vultures.

I started counting vultures, and stopped at fifty, then saw the shapes of as many more birds standing on the ground. It was misty and rainy, and they sat in the trees around the end of the swampy lake, a hundred hunch-shouldered turkey vultures with their puny heads and their black silhouettes, smelling the mud and the carrion.

I stood there captivated by this abundance of life and the death that must attract it. Then the frogs in the woods began to creak. They made a wild chorus of a high, metallic *cheat-cheat-cheat-cheat*. It sounded like a whole fleet of cars riding around on bent rims. It was very loud. As it went on, vultures took off in black clouds and soared over me, their feathers ratty, their airborne silhouettes sharp-edged and wicked. The woods went *cheat-cheat-cheat*, and then the lake frogs began banging pans with their rubber feet. *Cheat-cheat-cheat; tank-tank-tank-tank.* The only silent creatures were the vultures, as they flew and watched, and waited, for somebody's calamity.

I ran back, listening to the woods, and went out on the dam, where brown water swirled down over brown concrete and made a dark brown pool. This was a strange place. Rain fell softly, and on the edge of the dam seven people stood in the falling rain and fished. Three were on the bank, casting rubber worms and slowly retrieving. Four—a black family—stood close together on a shallow reef with long bamboo poles held low over the water in the current. No one moved except to cast and retrieve. No one caught anything. Far out in the many narrow and dwindling channels of this lake, two men floated in a johnboat. And on the far side, one man waded away, through little stretches of water, up onto land, and down through stretches of water again, walking on and on, as if putting as much space as possible between himself and something that made him afraid.

I watched the rain fall on the fishermen, then looked over into the pool where the Little Ocmulgee flowed from the lake. There bait fish jumped, and a large angry bass chased them with slashes at the surface. I looked back at the fishermen, watched this hungry fish, and decided that something was going on here that I did not quite grasp. I ran slowly back to the plane on the soft fairways of the golf course, and came back to find that the rain was leaking through the roof all over my cardboard file cabinet.

I fixed the leak—for good, I thought. In the middle of the night the rain stopped, and someone came along and started a fire just outside my window. Fire? Fire! Calamity!

I opened the door.

"What's going on out here?"

It was a kid working at something by his airplane. I must have shocked him. Planes don't usually come alive and ask loud questions in the night. The fire in my head was his big wooden match.

"Ah, just lighting a lantern mantle, sir."

Oh. He was a long-faced, blue-eyed kid who looked like Johnny Kearce twenty years ago, who had come out to work on his airplane, carrying the light to shine on his glory.

"Oh. Okay. Be careful with that flame." I sounded like a grumpy old fart. "Good night."

"Good night, sir."

For an hour, from midnight to 1 A.M., the kid carefully changed the brake shoes on his Cessna 150, the cheapest, most basic plane you can buy. If you had a friendly banker, you could buy a plane like that for fifty bucks a month, and fix it up with the help of a licensed mechanic for no more than it would cost you to work on an old car. This kid was happy. The hiss of the lantern and the clink of tools were the only sounds, but for the faint hum of the American Song out on the highway. I didn't mind it at all, lying on my back thinking about Phil Timm tinkering with an engine in his shop, and listening to the friendly sounds of a young guy and his machine on a hot night in Georgia.

But the haze held close and deep to the earth that night, and the next and the next and the day and night after that, and would not go away.

CHAPTER TWENTY-ONE

It seemed as if I had never seen the air clear. I had lived forever in this red soup. At Key West, one afternoon and one morning had seemed free of haze, but that was all. Even there, lines of smoke had hung along the blue horizon. Ever since I left Texas in the dark and then rode up out of Oklahoma into the hills of the Ozark Province, the air had been stained around me. Now it became oppressive.

I could have escaped it. I could have climbed high, up to where cumulus clouds floated in the top of the murk like globs of sherbet in a sulphurous punch. Every day other planes reported the "Top of the Haze Layer" at four or five thousand feet in the mornings, and ten to twelve thousand in the afternoons. I knew how those pilots felt as they rose: released, free, clean. But up there I would lose the landscape; at the bottom of two miles of this atmospheric sludge it would be a brown shadow of itself; a faint accumulation of patterns and, here and there, the smoky gleam of a city.

So I remained low, down in it, making short hops, counting off Lindbergh's cities one by one. Now my determination to share his flight was a chore, but I knew if that route wasn't there to make me zigzag I'd climb out and head for Maine. Here was where the slow accumulation of miles would count for something, would stitch the land together. And now I was chasing a special kind of glory, hidden in the back of the mind, and far ahead, in Virginia. I wanted to find Donald Keyhoe.

Vidalia, the land of onions, was rolling fields and pecan trees, swimming pools, a factory, ballparks with grass infields, and Quick Thrust L MOA. I crossed the fall line, that long edge of stone between the Coastal Plains Province and the Piedmont, but I noticed it only on the chart. The land rose, and I rose with it, keeping a discreet half mile in the air. Up out of the swamps the land was tidier, but still deeply forested. Lime kilns and steeples showed white among the trees. In the haze the towns materialized a few miles ahead, lived below me briefly, then dissolved behind. Seven miles visibility was reported at Atlanta. People on the ground thought it was a nice day; the sun was shining, and it was warm. Only if they looked at the edge of a shadow on concrete, or where the sun hit a white curtain, would they see: the sunlight was too yellow. It was stained.

I roamed restlessly through the corrupted light. Atlanta was a string of air traffic commands, fuel at Dekalb-Peachtree airport, water tower after water tower, and the strange, whale's-back granite dome of Stone Mountain, where Lindbergh and Keyhoe had encountered violent turbulence beside the mountain while looking at the Civil War memorial then under construction. There was the big pit of a rock quarry near the mountain, as if it was necessary to balance out the rise of stone with a hole. At Athens, someone on the unicom frequency said, "Tower is only operational during football games." *During* football games? They must have a dangerous passing attack.

I spent a night at Spartanburg, South Carolina, and another night at Winston-Salem, North Carolina. In between were tobacco fields and orchards. No grid here. I was back in the colonies: metes and bounds still drew the landscape, just as it was in the days of revolution; the patchwork landscape of freedom.

The fields rolled up out of the brown air, and rolled past. I wandered along the western edge of the Piedmont Province, with the foothills of the Blue Ridge Province almost invisible out the left window. At Gaffney, South Carolina, the water tower was a vast peach, leaf and all. I flew on. Kings Mountain. Salisbury. Salisbury had a baseball diamond with a dirt infield and a dirt outfield. A basic kind of place. Who needs *grass*? Near Lexington, Greensboro Approach kept asking inbound pilots: "You *do* see the antenna? Is that *affirmative?*" A few miles west of Lexington three towers stood over a thousand feet tall, almost invisible in the haze in spite of their strobes, spreading guy wires like a gillnet strung across the muddy wind.

I flew on. I wanted to slow down this swift passage through the thick air, but I kept moving. Don Keyhoe drew me on. I was looking ahead. Someone had told me he thought Lindbergh's old companion was still alive. I was hoping to find him.

"I think he lives somewhere out by Luray," the man had said. I asked Luray directory assistance for Keyhoe, Donald. "I'm sorry," she said. "There is a listing, but it's not listed." That was enough for me. I would try to find him.

I flew on. I flew at night. "Traffic at two o'clock," Atlanta Center said, "altitude unknown." I looked at two o'clock and there was the moon—my glory!—big and red, way out beyond me. I slept restlessly in the heat, and flew on in the deep pale haze of morning. I made myself stop at South Boston, and walked down to the Dan River through black fields of broken cornstalks that stank of recent floods: dead animals, flies, rot, mud. The Dan River didn't hold me long. It was the color of the air.

I did laundry in one town. A couple sat there. They were in their fifties. He had been to Montana. No, it was Wyoming. He'd never forget it. Went out to work there one winter. They had the darndest things there. Kind of like a jackrabbit, but they had antlers.

"Jackalope," I said, not mentioning the rest: that they are made by taxidermists out of rabbits and antelope antlers.

"Yeah," he said. "Jackalope. Thought they were a joke till I seen one alive."

The haze thickened. I flew on. And finally, one hot afternoon, I went up on top of the pink sherbet clouds and came back down into the Shenandoah Valley, between long ridges, into a pool of haze, and touched down on the runway at Luray, Virginia.

Then everything I did seemed to happen slowly, and carefully, and with patience.

Why did it seem to matter so much, finding Don Keyhoe? Lindbergh still would not be such an old man, if he had lived. Almost everyone in my own parents' generation remembered the Paris flight, and many had seen Lindbergh on the grand tour. But I had been living with Keyhoe. I had seen his big ears almost every morning as I thumbed his book trying to find clues about where Lindbergh had sewed his clothes shut or poured the perfume on his dress jacket, or reminding myself of the next long zigzag on the tour. He wasn't the great hero. He wasn't the giant. He was the guy I talked to and complained at when the zags got too long, and sympathized with when Lindbergh got him up at midnight to go fly out of Santa Fe. He was my friend of these wonderful but lonely days. I would give a lot to sit across from him, just to say, "Hey, wasn't Crater Lake spectacular?'' ''Air's still rough at Stone Mountain,'' and, ''Those days! What was the color of the sky?''

I took my notebook and rode up to Luray Caverns and went into the gift store. The first person I talked to had no idea. Donald *Who*? But the second was a small quiet woman with gray hair and a secretive air, as if she knew more than she was saying.

''Yes, as far as I know he's still alive. He's not well, you know. Now let me think—I know where their house is, but I can't tell you how to get there. It's somewhere out 340 South.'' She gave me a small, secret smile.

I rode into town in the hot afternoon air. Cows stood up to their shoulders in ponds along the road. I rode through town and south on the highway. A man and his wife were mowing a large lawn. I stopped and took off my helmet.

''I'm sorry to bother you. I'm trying to find a gentleman named Donald Keyhoe.''

''Oh, sure,'' the woman said. She looked like the kind of capable person who knows where everyone lives. ''You go on out here three miles. On the right. Up the hill. He's not very well.''

I told her what I was doing. ''Do you think they'll mind me barging in?''

''No, no. Just you go ahead.''

I rode on up the road. Summer, summer, summer. Bees hummed in the flowers by the road. Hawksbill Creek rippled down the valley on the left. Two boys were swimming with inner tubes in a pool. I missed the turn the first time, and came back to it. The driveway was too steep for the motorcycle. It struggled and quit. I pushed it up the hill. The house stood on the slope, looking out across the valley toward Shenandoah National Park. The haze made the view soft. Very faintly from the hills, echoing up from the highway below, came the murmur of the American Song.

I am not a hardened journalist. Long ago I wished to be that way, but it never worked. I took the helmet off. I left it at the motorcycle. I walked up a brick path between great bushy green boxwood hedges. Who was I to call unasked at this long-closed door to history? The door was white, behind a screen. I walked up, and pushed the bell. It chimed faintly inside.

I waited. There was a whisper of footsteps.

Slowly the white door opened. Donald Keyhoe stood there behind the screen.

I knew him immediately. Those big ears. The lean face. Those serious eyes I imagined being slightly bewildered by the romping, mercurial, joshing pilots all around him. He was small. He was gaunt. He was old. But to me he didn't look different at all. I prickled all over, spun again on the wheel of vertigo.

And now I should say something.

I said nothing. I stood looking at the face behind the screen. Keyhoe was softened by the gray mesh, as if I saw him through the haze of years.

There were no words to be found in my life.

"Yes," Keyhoe said, as if he knew why I was there. His voice was high and sharp and familiar.

I almost said what I was thinking:

"I knew you when you were young."

I didn't. I got back in control. It was like concentrating on the instruments when you suddenly find yourself tumbled in the clouds. Trust what you see. Trust the machines. Level off. Check the gyro.

"Hello," I said. "I am traveling—flying the route you and Charles Lindbergh flew sixty years ago. I—ah—wondered if I could talk to you."

"Who?"

I knew what he meant.

"Charles Lindbergh."

Keyhoe smiled. "Yes, yes," he said. "I could tell you a few things about him. I knew him, you know."

A face appeared behind him. Younger, stronger, sharper with life. Don Keyhoe slipped into the shadows. It was his wife. I explained, with all the words now back at my command, and she was friendly. He was not well, and later someone was coming over. But maybe tomorrow, if he was up to it. Call about noon. In the background Don Keyhoe gave me a smile and a little salute. The white door closed on the screen, and I was walking away down the brick path between the overflowing exuberant green plants, and raising my hands high in jubilation.

I had found him! I had moved time, or time had moved me. My glory haloed the day. I had found my old friend, and made the journey real.

The inside of the plane smelled like a locker room. I had hung my towel in there to dry, but it had just stewed. Fireflies glowed mistily. In the sultry darkness the quick airport beacon poured its white and green light through a haze so thick I could see only the brightest stars straight up, and a faint ridge line of the hills. They would be a sharp black edge against the whole range of stars at home. The grass was deep beside the plane, deep and wet. Frogs made a sharp sound like the passage of a whip. Orange lights of farms shone in the mist, and a white glow of the signs to the caverns glowed above the divided road.

When I am moved I look to the land for help or reassurance or celebration, so in the morning I went for a long run in the valley, along the river whose name itself is a benediction: Shenandoah. Mile after mile I ran along the river, thinking about Donald Keyhoe. Great warm oak woods hung over the road. The river was wide and shallow. At last I got thirsty, and stopped at a farm. Luke Kibler was there. I know his name because he showed me his pilot's license, dated July 1972. He was about seventy. He wore loose jeans held up by suspenders, rimless glasses, about seven days' white beard, and a brown pith helmet. His top row of teeth looked like last year's corn field. He was working on the sickle mower attached to an old Ford 9N tractor.

"Best water on the place," he said, "is in that old pitcher pump over there."

The pump was near the ground. I worked the handle. The water was near the pump. It gushed into a trough. Pea hens and chickens ran around, pecking.

"This place goes from the river to the top," Kibler said. "See that knob up there? Goes right up there."

The water was cool and clean.

"You graze it?"

"No. It's timber land. Used to. When I was a boy, we'd just turn them loose and put a bell on one of 'em so you could find 'em."

How we got to flying I can't remember. I must have told him about Keyhoe.

"I used to fly a J-3 Cub," Kibler said. "Got in a storm up there couldn't tell which way was front. I said, 'If I get my feet on the ground again, I'm going to keep them there.' Say, if I could get the truck running, I'd give you a ride to town."

I gave the pump a last lick and poured cool glitter all over my face. On the way back I stopped at a grocery and bait store for a drink from a hose. A dog came out as if to bite off my hand, and a woman yelled it off. There were two brand-new poultry barns right next to the place.

"Page County doesn't have any regulations about these things yet," she said, "so people are trying to get them built first."

"Does the smell bother you?"

"Naw. Only occasionally when it is hot and muggy like this, you get a little bit. But I figure I can always get an air freshener or burn a scent candle. But these fields! When they fertilize these fields, put a load or two on a hundred acres around here, that'll knock you *over!*"

Before I went to see Keyhoe I went to the Luray Library and looked up his books. The library had three: *Flying Saucers from Outer Space*, 1953; *The Flying Saucer Conspiracy*, 1955; and *Aliens from Space: The Real Story of Unidentified Flying Objects*, 1973. They all made the same point: UFOs had visited the earth frequently, but their presence had been covered up by the U.S. government because they were representatives of an alien civilization.

I called his wife. She wasn't sure he could help me. She tried to hint that he didn't remember much. I could come over anyway, that was fine. "You're lucky," she said. "You're young. You have your life ahead of you."

So in the afternoon I rode back out the long road south of town, and pushed the motorcycle back up the hill, and once more rang the bell at the screened door. The young nurse who opened the door for me wasn't coy. "He's pretty senile," she said. She was wrong. The forgetfulness of his ninety years had touched him lightly, and left him his grace.

The room was dark: paneling, a piano. On the piano were songbooks: Nelson Eddy and Jeanette MacDonald. The last time I had seen those songbooks was on my grandmother's piano in 1962. Keyhoe sat lost in a big chair, such a small man, with his big ears and his gaunt face, and a little rattle in his mouth when he talked. His wife, Helen, and the nurse sat nearby, poised, edgy, as if waiting for calamity.

"Trouble was," Keyhoe said, "so much information kept pouring into me, and I knew darn well it wasn't all correct."

I didn't know what he meant. Oh—he thought I had come to talk about UFOs. Made sense; that had been his life. But then Helen brought out a large framed photograph of Lindbergh. It was a shot Keyhoe had taken in Canada in 1927. Lindbergh had that wicked, happy grin. "This was Anne Lindbergh's favorite," Helen said. "She told us."

"It was very good working with him," Keyhoe said. "He was a brilliant man. He checked on me for about two weeks to make sure I wasn't going to cause him any trouble, and then he gave me all the information he had."

I showed him the map of the journey in his book.

"That looks familiar," he said, and laughed.

"That western part of the country must have been pretty empty in those days," I said.

"It was kind of thin."

But it was Lindbergh he wanted to talk about.

"He kind of braced himself up-standing," Keyhoe said. "People were all the time wanting to pull him off somewhere and use him, you know. Finally he built up a list of what to do and what not to do. All he would do is just say, here's a copy."

He paused. He worked his teeth together briefly. He was looking out over my shoulder past the picture of the young Lindbergh and that wonderful grin.

"He was a great guy," Keyhoe said quietly. "We went around the United States together."

Another silence. I wanted to ask him about his crushed hats, but didn't.

"You were on time every time!" I said. "That was impressive."

"We were very lucky," Keyhoe said. "We insisted on getting planned a month ahead if we could. Several times people tried to use us. I said no. I said *no*. And they'd get mad as the devil at me." He laughed. When he laughed he seemed to wake up a little and come closer to us, not staring beyond the photo. Then he'd drift out there again and Helen would fill in the silence.

"I flew with Lindbergh over Washington," she said. "That was a big thrill. He looked down, he had a light blue shirt like yours, and he smiled, and he had the happiest smile."

"After all those crowds," I said, "it must have been a relief for him to get back in the airplane and go fly."

"Yes it was," Keyhoe said quickly. "He lived on that."

There was a silence.

"He was a great pilot," Keyhoe began.

"They invited you up to Hopewell, didn't they?" Helen said. "And Anne sang to the baby, 'You must have been a beautiful baby, because look at you now.' "

Helen turned half to me, talking past Keyhoe, who was thinking about something else.

"Somebody peeped in the window while Major Keyhoe was there," she said, "a Peeping Tom, and he wanted to say, and he's regretted ever since—he wanted to say, 'You should have something on the windows to protect him.' And that was just before the kidnapping."

She turned back to Don. "I remember you said, the baby took your hand and wrapped his fingers around your fingers."

This didn't seem to reach him. He shook it off with a little toss of his head like a pitcher shaking off a sign. I had a sudden pain that a man should lose such a memory. But he was concentrating. He was thinking about the man.

"He was an excellent pilot. One of the best. I flew with him a couple of times at the start, and I was a little uneasy, because he was doing things that I wasn't doing, and not many people were doing. Finally I said to him, you mind if I copy what you're doing? He said no, go right ahead."

He paused. His teeth made their little rattle.

"One thing you already know, obviously. Lindbergh had a tremendous mind. He was terrific. Anyone who tried to pull a fast one on him, he lost out in a hurry." He laughed.

Listening to him, I knew I could never reach him now, never talk to him about the journey, never close the years between us. Time and Charles Lindbergh intervened. I didn't know much about Keyhoe's life, which had been filled with UFO reports and disputes, and some people revering him, and some people laughing at him. But there Lindbergh stood, the special man of his generation, first worshiping science, then losing his faith in it when the technology it had produced increased the evils of war, then reaching through mysticism, religion, and primitive cultures for ideas to frame the world, to brace up his hope for the future of human life that he had thought was so bright when he was young.

No. Lindbergh stood there between us, and all those years. And there were places in Keyhoe's mind where the memories just didn't seem to be anymore.

"I don't try to start reworking a lot of the history," he said finally. "It's too much. I can remember it, but to start using it again, building it up, I . . ." His voice drifted away.

But once, late in our conversation, there was a moment.

"You had some bad weather along there," I said. "I know out near Butte, it sounded pretty bad. Clouds down on the mountains; rain. It was bad going into Seattle too. Were you ever worried?"

Ah. Keyhoe grinned. His glance woke up. Just for a second or two the poised women weren't there. For a moment he and I were sitting over a beer somewhere halfway between my youth and his age, in a bar down around 1955. He grinned, and he got a light in his eye.

"Sometimes it was bad," he said with that grin. "We got to the point where we weren't scared, but we were serious."

We laughed, and we looked at one another, and we knew what we were talking about, and in our heads we bought each other another round, and then Keyhoe was old again, and I had to leave him and get back into the thickening sky.

CHAPTER TWENTY-TWO

From the Piedmont to the sea, the whole East Coast was a valley of smoke. I fluttered around inside it like a moth in a jar.

I ran in Luray in the morning. It was hot. Embedded in the tar near the airport was the skeleton of a possum. I felt the breath of extinction. The Shenandoah shone red against the sun as I left Don Keyhoe's valley. As I climbed, the river disappeared into the haze.

I flew over Keyhoe's house, by Hawksbill Creek. It was a lovely little gray-roofed home, with a pond out back, and green awnings and a white fence around an upstairs deck, and white fence posts. It looked anachronistic in this urban sky. I was at two thousand feet above it and already the house was disappearing in the terrible murk. By the time I crossed the ridge of Shenandoah National Park the land had faded away beneath. A scattering of ponds reflecting the sun looked like flames.

I crossed the mountain ridge by BLUES. Yeah, Irene, I know. A Delta Airlines L-1011 came up out of the murk below: landing lights and a black trail of smoke. It grew into a shark and climbed out of the dirty aquarium. Lines of houses lay like parked cars on the bottom of the tank. On city maps the mass of houses and freeways and shopping malls and banks of tall apartments below was resolved into separate towns: Manassas, Fairfax, Herndon, Bethesda, Gaithersburg, Silver Spring. In this real world of haze, there were no differences. Mile after mile, it was all the same.

Another airliner swam by below. The urban complex of the Washington, D.C., area turned imperceptibly into the urban complex of Baltimore. Baltimore Approach turned me away from his city to keep me out of the way of the sharks, and all I saw of it were great pale slabs of factories attended by hundreds of trucks suckling up to their freight docks like piglets.

Was this flight? This wasn't air. It was some other gas, made up of arsenic, benzene, cadmium, chlorine, carbon monoxide, hydrocarbons, formaldehyde, hydrogen sulfide, mercury, nitric acid, sulphuric acid, manganese, nickel, nitrogen dioxide, ozone, lead, silicon tetrafluoride, and sulphur dioxide. It was the regional haze, manufactured on the Ohio River, in Atlanta, in Chicago, on the Tennessee River, or in New Jersey. It was made by chemical factories, by coal-fired power plants, by burning forests, by refineries, by air conditioners, by automobiles, by Six Zero One and me. It was the video of the American Song.

I groped along. My navigation radios told me where I was in the sky, but though the land was there in front of me, it had withdrawn from the picture. Patterns were haphazard and meaningless. Lakes and waterways appeared in red when the sun found them, then vanished. Roads showed up below me, but led only a few miles out into the gritty atmosphere before they turned to ghosts. The sun set red and the moon rose red. Night brought no relief. Days were somber, and even the noon sun looked tired. The sky was frightening. It was the end of the world; the day in which the system finally became overloaded, the rain could handle it no more, the wind was full of soot, and the bad air blew around the world. It was the doom of humankind, to be shut in a room full of poisonous air and be unable to rise above it; to choke amid the sounds of engines. But no television station spoke of danger, and no newspaper headlined the thickening of the air. People here were used to it.

For days I flew from airport to airport in the haze. The journey became episodic, scattered. I missed the grid. I missed the landscape. It was as if the tapestry had rotted and come apart in my hands. In Florida I had asked Skip Livingston how he thought his state was going to look in twenty years. "You want to know what it will look like?" he said. "Just go up the Jersey shoreline." But when I got to the Jersey shoreline I could hardly see it.

I landed at Atlantic City in the dark, bouncing down on final approach over hot air blown up by the casinos. I could see the breakers shining in their light. I slept badly in the glow of the neon and the roar of the roads, and woke to see a stranger's face peering in around my curtains. I glared at the face. It went away.

I jogged into town and along the boardwalk. The hotel where Lindbergh had spent the night was now condominiums. The hotel in which he had made his speech was a hole in the ground. The Tropicana Hotel and Resort was explanding into the pit. The expansion was called Trop World. It was going to include six restaurants and lounges, a convention and exhibit center, a health club and indoor swimming pool, and, a billboard said, "two acres of indoor Disney-inspired theme park." Even the beach people were turning away from the outdoors into an artificial world. Just in time. A few days before thirty-five miles of the state's beaches had been closed when a vast brown slick made up of dead algae and lumps of grease the size of golf balls from an offshore dump threatened to wash ashore. Skip Livingston would ask: How long before that happens every day?

The boardwalk was crowded. I walked out on the beach. A fake fur jacket and a running shoe were washed up on the sand. No grease balls. I found my way to an empty place. It was the space under the pilings of Ocean One, a vast shopping mall on a pier. I liked it under there. It was cool. Condensation dripped from the concrete ceiling. The American Song rumbled distantly. The sea was louder, working at the pilings. An older footing lay broken up in the surf, rusted rebar sticking up out of it. Pigeons flickered in the dim light like huge bats. Bits of Styrofoam, weathered like bone, washed back and forth in the waves. It was the underside, the support, the reality behind the image. It was the back of the set. The crowds shied away from this glimpse of the world as it was, as if it were dangerous.

The air was foul. I left Atlantic City and struggled across New Jersey. The air was so thick it seemed to slow the plane. I passed the Salem and Hope Creek nuclear power plants on the shore of the Delaware River. The cooling tower, just on the edge of vision, about four miles away, was a huge eggcup brewing death. I knew it was benign, at least for today, but I saw it silhouetted against the somber water beyond, and its tiny cloud of red-gray steam looked malevolent in the heavy sky.

I landed on a grass strip at Salem, New Jersey, and found my way to the Salem Oak, under which, in 1675, John Fenwick bought a couple of counties from the Lenni-Lenape Indians for four guns, 336 gallons of rum, coats, shirts, and other goodies. The tree, which hung over a quarter acre of the Friends Burial Ground, was strung about with cables like a suspension bridge, to hold up its weary limbs. Beyond it the sun sank, a red dwarf, as if it would never rise again. As it went down, all the sirens in the world began to cry.

So. Calamity had come. I stood under the old tree among short gravestones, and waited. The sirens howled. The red sun drifted downward in the sky. The sirens grew louder. They were moving, gathering power, calling out the guard, the militia, the riders of doom. They were of several voices: some deep wails of anguish, others screams of pain. The sirens moved as a group somewhere nearby, but invisibly, germinating fear. They called urgently. It has come! It has come! The missiles are launched, fire advances across the earth, the very air is dying around us!

Life in Salem seemed suspended. Everything awaited the delivery of the message. Nothing was going on. The road seemed deserted. The sun sank lower. On the electronic clock and thermometer at the Franklin Bank the lights flashed: 7:34 P.M.; 95 degrees. A few doors opened, and people came out to stand and listen and look at the sky. The sirens grew louder.

Around the corner by a convenience store, at the end of Broadway, just down from the Delaware Memorial Bridge, came every fire truck and police car in Salem. They howled and they wailed, but they were going very slowly. They were covered with teenage boys. The boys were shorts and singlets, and had numbers pinned on their chests. They were shouting and waving their arms. That afternoon, for the first time in its history, the Salem High School track team had won the state championship.

The next night, in Philadelphia, I revised my instrument approach charts, replacing about four dozen charts with new ones mailed me by the chart publishing company. I sat in the plane under the bright lights of the vast airport. Cones of light hung down from the sodium vapor lamps in the haze. The whole place roared: jets landing; jets taking off; jets taxiing to the gates. I wore my earplugs, but they didn't shut it all off. They did nothing to mask the stench of burned jet fuel that seeped into the plane.

I flipped through the pages of charts, touring the United States again through the loose-leaf books, once in a while tearing out a page and putting in a new one. Arkansas, California, Florida, Georgia, Idaho, Montana, New Jersey. I had never seen many of the towns and airports I revised. I would not see them on this journey: when it came down to it, even the broad wanderings of my twenty-five thousand miles covered only a fraction of the country. But many of those strange diagrams of procedure turns and precision descents reminded me of places that were important to me: on this night I thought mostly of the nature of their air.

A revised approach to Eugene, Oregon, reminded me of sleeping there in the wonderful cool aroma of Douglas fir trees, mixed with the smell of pulp mills. For Miles City, Montana, I remembered waiting out the clean, cold blast of a blizzard for two days, then exuberantly racing low past an Amtrak passenger train along the Yellowstone River. That day I could see from Billings into the Rockies; close to a hundred miles. There was Yuma, Arizona, the place that smelled of lemons and jet fuel. There was Fort Worth, Texas, and a flat night landscape spinning into a galaxy and filling the haze layer with light. There was New Orleans, and the Pontchartrain bridge flying off into space. Here was Portland, Maine, the single town at which Lindbergh missed his schedule, because of fog, and where I would soon run into the same problem. Here was a new approach into Spartanburg, South Carolina, where just a few days before I had landed in the haze and had gone into town and seen the quintessential small-town-America landscape from the corner of Main and Forest by George's Home Style Coin-op Laundry: In one view looking west were Dave Edwards AMC-Jeep-Renault, Spartanburg Grain & Feed, a wooded park, the office of the Spartanburg *Herald*, a small valley with a creek in it, Brown Rogers Paxon Wholesale Hardware, the Spartanburg Water Works water tower, and, beyond the low roof of the U.S. Post Office, the thin white spire of the Bethel United Methodist Church, where ministers J. Chadwick Davis, Joel E. Cannon, and Gary Hyndman shared the dispensation of the grace of God. But there, too, beyond the spire, the sky had been tan.

This was normal. This was modern life. This was America, coming up on the twenty-first century. When I put in pages that reminded me of open sky and an endless view—Reno, Nevada; St. George, Utah; Mojave, California; Bismarck, North Dakota—I seemed to be remembering the past.

In the morning I rode the train into Philadelphia. It had rained in the night, but the haze had not broken. The sunshine on the sidewalks was orange. Small summery clouds floated overhead, but you could hardly see them. Nobody seemed to mind. If you didn't know what clear sunlight really looked like, you'd never notice. To them it was a nice day. The visibility, the newspaper said, was expected to go up to five miles.

People in Philadelphia were outdoors, enjoying it. Women and children swam in the Logan Circle fountain, and high school kids newly freed for the summer were wandering the streets. One of them, a young girl carrying a video camera on her shoulder, came up to me like an attack journalist, microphone stuck out ahead of her like a sword.

"What do you think of the Flyers?" she said, sticking the microphone in my face.

"Too bad they lost," I said. At least I'd read the paper.

"What are you doing?" she asked, the red light flickering on the camera. The lens bobbed around in my face. You could get seasick watching this tape.

"Flying twenty-five thousand miles around the United States."

"Oh, wow," she said. She turned off the camera.

She was a student at Friends Select School, which occupied a brick building along Benjamin Franklin Parkway. She was doing this for a class. Well, it was a makeup, really. School was already out, but she had to get this done to avoid an incomplete. She was supposed to interview people in the street and make an edited video.

"People answer the *dumbest* questions," she said. " 'What color is your bathroom wall?' 'Sort of orange.' 'What did you eat for breakfast today?' 'Eggs and ketchup.' "

"What's your name?" I asked, with my own version of the video camera, my notebook, ready to go in my hand.

"Why?"

"*You* don't answer questions."

"Oh, no," she said. "Forget it. I've lived in this city all my life. I don't know who to trust." She grabbed the camera and the mike, and she fled.

The thick sky hung over the city like a pall, but nobody noticed. At the Museum of Art, Michael J. Dougherty spent all day out on the steps setting fire to a pool of gasoline in a metal basin. It burned in great smoky bursts of flame. Over and over he put it out with various kinds of fire extinguishers to instruct groups of museum employees. On the edge of the Schuylkill River, near a memorial honoring the first municipal waterworks, Frank Flowers spent the day fishing for channel catfish, accompanied for a while by Fred Thomas, who kept his fishing floats clipped to the spokes of his ten-speed bicycle. Fred liked fishing, and hated water.

"I almost drowned in a bathtub once," he said. "I'm afraid of a fire hydrant." Up at the edge of the Piedmont Province where you could draw a mark in the dirt right at the fall line, three boys—Ken Carhart, Shane Lafty, and Jim Henderson—spent part of the day swinging from a rope and dropping into Wissahickon Creek, where they swam around in a pool with brown foam, an old tire, and bits of Styrofoam. If you didn't know what clean water was, it wouldn't bother you.

All day the haze colored the sun. The visibility went up to five miles and then back down to four, then three, That night the amber lights at the airport again cast cones of light through the haze, and in the middle of the next day when I flew to Teterboro Airport, just outside New York City, I had to fly on instruments, though the sun peered down through the haze and tried to shine.

Teterboro Airport seemed tame after the tumult and the fuel smell of Philadelphia. In the evening I stood outside the plane listening to the familiar low rumble of the American Song. One small twin-engined plane wound itself up and took off on Runway Six, then a corporate jet passed low on a practice instrument approach. In the distance off the end of Runway Six was a very bright glow in the haze. It was the Meadowlands Racetrack, Giants Stadium, and a collection of new buildings going up in the New Jersey Meadowlands, where only a few years ago the landscape was mostly polluted bog and garbage dumps. The Meadowlands was booming; the soft wet underbelly of land that had lain undeveloped and dark next to New York City for centuries was giving way to offices, condominiums, and sporting arenas. Companies were moving big chunks of their operations from Manhattan to new office buildings built on hundred-foot pilings driven into the muck of the Hackensack River Estuary.

It wasn't just buildings. People were manufacturing nature there too. Among the recent projects was the construction of a sixty-three-acre salt marsh in a previously unproductive area of the Meadowlands to make up for other marsh turned into high rises. The natural vegetation was sprayed with herbicide, then channels were dredged to let the tide flow in, and—presto!—sandpipers and ducks. The new marsh cost Hartz Mountain Industries $5 million.

A little farther away was another blossom of light: the city itself. At Teterboro pilots gauge distance by those lights or the daytime silhouettes: the Empire State Building is seven miles away. Tonight the visibility was not seven miles. The glow was shapeless. But it was dazzling. It shamed the red light of the rising moon. There it was, shining like a cauldron of gold: the hungriest city in the world.

Once I flew over New York City, looking for the field Lindbergh left in the early morning of May 20, 1927: Roosevelt Field. It was not there. It had vanished long ago beneath buildings. But Mitchel Field was still there. It was the airport to which the *Spirit of St. Louis* returned after the forty-eight-state tour. It was still there, but it lay beneath new uses. Freeways looped around it. A shopping mall and a stadium stood on its old aprons. A long stretch of runway lay there, half buried. Beside it were a covered stadium, a few acres of parking lot, and a half-dozen baseball diamonds. Only half had grass infields.

That night I rode the bus into the city for dinner with friends. On the way, the bus passed a sign that announced "This is the place where Aaron Burr shot Alexander Hamilton." A chill went through me. The setting was perfect: grass, trees, river, heavy light. It seemed familiar. Years before I had read a story of the duel by Gore Vidal. Now the place seemed just the way it was then. Nothing makes human life and history seem real except to place it in its landscape. It seemed that I remembered the spot, not as the place I had read about, but the place I had been on that day: the shooting, the groans, the air of humidity and disaster.

I rode back to Teterboro on the midnight bus, waiting in the terminal while people asked for money, then riding out of town, and there was the night skyline that I had wanted to see. I sat and watched the lighted city pass. I was suffused with affection for the people on the bus, as the driver fought the balky door and jerky brakes, and people dozed and gazed through the windows. There was no laughter on this bus. We were like used-up husks, drifting out of New York City against the great tide that pours into that place and is consumed there: the gifts of the land—stone, gravel, wood, the translated falling water in those lights—the gifts of human life and talent. The city is like a thundercloud, taking its power from the land, soaring, dominating, alive with drama. How long, how many hours or centuries before the storm is spent? When I got out of the bus at the airport, I could hear the city rumble. Strobe lights on stacks and antennas flickered like lightning. The city was its own glory, eating the sky.

I walked a half mile back to the plane behind a woman who had disembarked ahead of me, and who walked so fast I knew that I scared her. There was nothing I could say or do to ease the fear, so I just stopped by a fence for a few minutes and let her get far ahead. She had to do this every night. So I walked on alone in the humming world, looking out at the surrounding glow. The New York skyline had gone back into the haze.

That evening I discussed New York briefly with my companions. To Lindbergh, it was a place of personal conflict:

"New York, symbolizing power, always brought my mind and intuition into conflict. When I first flew eastward to the city . . . I was repulsed by its bigness, luxury, and artificial life, fascinated by the stupendous forces it commanded and by its influence in the material accomplishments of man." This was the serious face of Lindbergh, reading from his *Autobiography of Values*. "To take part in the development of aviation," he went on, "New York was the best headquarters I could choose. But on returning to the city from my frequent flights, I always felt I was leaving a better life behind me. Sometimes I circled to delay my landing. I would bank and let a wing blot out the expanse of buildings below while I looked westward to the mountains or eastward to the sea. . . . When I lifted my wing again, what difference did it make whether it had blanked out a forest or a city? The basic qualities of life would continue."

John Jackson eyed the vast city with speculation. He had ridden his motorcycle through here. The city had affected him, too, but he didn't choose to think of it that way. Yet the conclusions were similar.

"As a man-made environment every city has three functions to fulfill," he said. "It must be a just and efficient social institution; it must be a biologically wholesome habitat; and it must be a continually satisfying esthetic-sensory experience. Up to the present we have given all thought to the first of these. These are signs that the second will receive its due attention before long. . . . But the third will be realized only when we ourselves are enlightened: when we learn once again to see nature in its entirety; not just as a remote object to be worshipped or ignored as it suits us, but as part of ourselves."

To me, New York City was adventure. To bring a light plane into the big city through clouds and traffic: adventure. It was all adventure, this life—the thunderstorm at Abilene; the long, low run down the Arkansas River; the dim light of the Achafalaya, the water and the sky at Key West; and my glory always running ahead of me in a bright and elusive dazzle I can never attain, and never give up.

It was even adventure to sit in my plane on the vast expanse of the Teterboro airport, watching a Lear jet taxi to the runway in the glowing night. The American Song was so loud I wore my earplugs.

But I was content, at peace, at home, here on the ground with my feet up and the cooling moist air between rainstorms breezing through my little room.

Within the adventure was the knowledge of risk. A few minutes before, I had talked to Debbie in Montana. The call had left me with a familiar feeling. An undercurrent of fear ran through me that somehow in the flying of the next day, or in their driving, one of us would die, and those words we had spoken to each other would be elevated to the importance of the final connection. Good-byes always contain a germ of that fear, since sometimes, very occasionally, it happens. I remember waving to my grandfather from a train when I left his home for the summer in 1964. I wondered then, as any young person will at the farewell to an older one, if that would be the last time. It was. When I say good-bye to my parents, who are in their seventies and very healthy, the same chill strikes. When I talk to Debbie and the children, it is more the other way around: I fear something may happen to me, and that this wonderful thing that I do, taking to the air, will end up taking me from them.

Is that vanity? Am I that important to anyone? I know only that with all this traveling, in this plane or someone else's airliner, or someone's car or train, or on the motorcycle, I take that extra little risk, and open myself to odds that are an inch or two beyond normal. And I see my family vulnerable to the loss.

But I think the reason that these things go through everyone's head is that there is too much melodrama reported in the world. It seems contagious, so you think you are going to catch some and create a classic sorrow. You think that you will fly off into the night and vanish forever, when in fact you will probably die querulous and forgetful, surrounded by people who will say, "It must be a relief to him," meaning it is a relief to them. So! I'll ride the air on this aluminum horse, and will not get off until I'm ready.

I read to the children, typed my journal into the computer, tucked the sheet around me, and went to sleep in command of my life and destiny. At 3:00 A.M. the melodrama began. I half woke. I vaguely heard the rattle of rain on the aluminum. I went right back to sleep. At 3:20 A.M., while I slept unaware, the roof began to leak. Water gathered along a seam in the aluminum skin, seeped down into the wing, and collected in a pool on the plastic headliner. At 3:22 A.M. it started to build up against its surface tension. It built up a long pool. At 3:25

A.M. the surface tension broke. Half a cup of water was released. The water poured through the ceiling onto my right leg.

At 3:25:30 A.M. anyone passing in the street might have heard a parked airplane utter expletives.

I was glad it was 3:30. It was likely, in fact, that no one was around. In my T-shirt and running shorts, I must have looked stark naked, a bare bozo emerging full of wet energy from a parked airplane, trying to climb on its roof. My repairs at McRae were not permanent after all.

I had a tube of bathtub silicone in the pocket of one of the seats. Before I got it out the roof cut loose again and splooshed down my neck. I scrambled around inside and tore my curtains down from their Velcro fasteners. *Rip*. I became tangled in the curtains. The roof dumped another load. I found the silicone and climbed back on the wing. The silicone refused to stick to anything wet. I clambered back inside. *Rip*. Down came a curtain. I stuck it back up. For some reason, in my wide-awake angry sleepiness, it was very important to take care of my leak in privacy.

I thrashed around some more trying to get the overhead headliner open, pulling down the back curtain. *Rip*. I had to contort to get it back up again, and got a cramp in my left calf. Oww! The sound of tearing Velcro became widespread. I got the curtains up again. I swung back outside into the rain and looked at the aluminum. Nothing to do out there. Then I tried to get at the toolbox for a tube of gasket sealant that had worked once before. No luck. The toolbox was buried up forward on the pilot's seat under all the junk that occupied the bed in the daytime. Filing cabinets, briefcases, boxes of charts, my camera case. Now I had to get all the way out. I stood on the ramp wet-footed, getting soaked, moving furniture. I pushed the seat back, got out the gasket sealant, and bashed around inside. *Riiip*. I feverishly put the curtain back up, through my naked legs were sticking out into the rain in the view of any who cared to see. I opened the gasket sealant. The sealant was black; I knew that I would have a cleanup job, now I couldn't find a rag. *Riiip*. A curtain presented itself as rag. No; that was a short-term solution. The T-shirt would have to do.

I held the flashlight under one arm. I applied black gobs of gunk to the inside of the wing skin. Water ran down my arm. I dropped the flashlight. It went out. *Drip. Rip*. Towel? T-shirt! My wet feet dried themselves on the inside of the sleeping bag.

At last! Big silver drops stopped emerging from the aluminum as if they were squeezed out of the metal.

I looked outside. It was because the rain had stopped. I applied more gunk, feverishly. *Riiip*. I put up the curtain with an unblackened hand.

At last, the task was done. Rain began again. I watched the new seal, lay down on the damp sleeping bag, then got up to watch it again. *Rip*. The rain was heavy. The seal held. Sounds of dripping and gurgling water came from all over the airplane except right there. But if my sleeping bag and my little computer could stay dry, then things would be all right.

It was five in the morning. It was time to try to get some sleep. Ah, sleep. At last. It was going to feel great. Sleep.

Come on, sleep.

Sleep!

Alas. All that water. Now I had to pee.

Later that early morning, sleep abandoned for the day, I sat in the open door of Six Zero One, watching the distant glow and the slow red growth of dawn. The ground itself rumbled with the American Song. But then, through all the noise of machines, there came a different sound. It was a patient, intent, eternal kind of noise, a sound that tells you the seasons are again changing and things are the same in the world. I often heard it at home in the spring and fall. It was the wonderful, steady, airborne honking of geese. I stepped away from the plane and looked for the sound. Surely, I thought, it must come from a recording. What cruel soul would play geese to a homesick Montanan? Then I saw them.

At least fifty birds, silhouetted against the glow, streamed across the city in a long line, honking as they moved north. What were they doing here, in this thick sky? Had the lights, or the impenetrable air, or the poison smoke confused them? Or had they been attracted by that five-million-dollar Meadowlands marsh? They did not seem bewildered. They seemed in control of their lives. They were like spies, infiltrating occupied territory to see how long it would be before the free world could return. But John Jackson's voice reminded me gently that this life was not a war. "Which comes first," he said again, "the blessing or the prayer?" It was not easy, even in this landscape, "to separate the role of man from the role of nature." The geese flew the length of Runway Six and off into the north. I stood still and listened until the welcome sound was gone.

PART 6

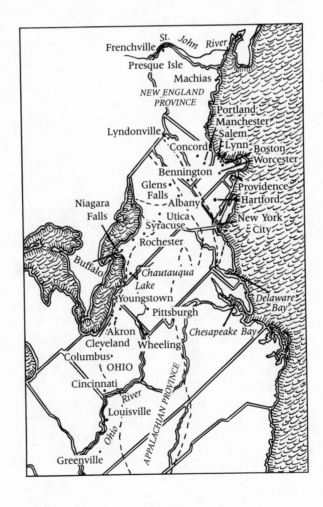

CHAPTER TWENTY-THREE

In rain and smoke and cloud, I followed the geese north. All this journey I had been looking forward to the New England Province, to the granite hills and the rugged coastline, where the flat land of the Coastal Plain Province vanished beneath the sea, and New England rocks made cliffs at the water's edge. But New England was cloaked and muffled. I landed in rain at Hartford, and ran to a city park in the rain, and watched men play soccer in the rain. In the rain I rode my motorcycle from the plane to the fuel office.

"Hey! You can't take that thing on the ramp!"

I turned around. Someone in a yellow raincoat advanced on me from the corporate terminal.

"Why not?"

"You can't!"

I went inside and called the tower on the phone.

"No problem with us as long as you stay on the ramp and not on the runway," the tower said. Yellow Raincoat was not placated.

"I don't care what the tower says. You can't drive that thing here."

"Why not?"

"If Preston catches you, he'll jerk your license."

Which license? I thought. It would be amazing to lose my pilot's license for riding a baby motorcycle. That would be a story to tell Don Smith back in Helena.

"Who's Preston?"

"The guy that drives around here."

"Does he drive on the ramp?"

"Yeah."

Well. Time to leave Hartford.

I went on in the haze. I had lunch on a hazy afternoon in Providence, and had a radio problem fixed at Worcester. At Worcester the guy who ran the radio repair station was also a pilot. He was the first person in weeks to mention the haze.

"Don't let anybody tell you that those plants in the Midwest aren't putting anything into the air," he said. "It's changed a lot just since I was flying around here when I was a kid. It's like soup now."

Late on a murky afternoon, after the five o'clock rush at Logan Airport, I flew high over Boston, and was given a tour by Boston Approach. By controllers' standards, he was loquacious.

"There's downtown right below you."

I could see the shadows of high-rise buildings on the water, but not the buildings themselves. Near the water, stacks poured smoke over a harbor full of the little toothpick hors d'oeuvres of sailboats.

"There's Lynn, just off your left wing." Lindbergh had dropped a message on Lynn. It was a tight-packed town up a slope from the bay.

"Looks like a pretty place," I said to the controller.

"Must be hazy," he said. "It isn't pretty, usually."

There was Salem, too, just up the coastline: a maze of buildings that was indistinguishable from the rest, except for the invisible airway intersection Macho Irene had named almost right above it: WITCH.

Northwest of Boston all the country roads had houses every thirty or fifty yards, but woods behind them. In the haze reservoirs shone like pools of lava. Cars on the interstates glittered, dots of light hurrying along, like a Disney model of electricity.

Manchester Approach was also chatty.

"I hope you enjoy your observations," he said. "We've got a lovely bit of country up here for you to see." But the country was all smoke. The Merrimack River Valley was full of it. It lay in long gray lines along the water and over the cities. Beyond it the granite hills of New Hampshire rose in somber procession. I could see farther now, but all the view revealed was more valleys full of smoke. Then I turned for Portland, Maine, and fog slid under me like a whisper of the past.

In 1927, Lindbergh was due at Portland at 2 P.M. He left Boston and flew north, but the fog blocked off the city. He circled for two hours, with plenty of fuel in those big tanks, then turned back and landed at Concord. Now Portland Approach wanted to know what I was going to do if I couldn't get into his city. Naturally: "Go to Concord."

But I had equipment that Lindbergh hadn't dreamed of in 1927. Three gyroscopes, two navigational radios, a glide-slope receiver to keep me descending at the right rate, and a localizer needle to keep me pointed straight at the runway. When Lindbergh had been trapped above fog during his days as a mail pilot, he had bailed out and let the plane crash. Now an instrument approach was routine. Yet it still seemed to me like a miracle.

Approach Control vectored me around to the final approach course. I connected to the glide slope like a car approaching a freeway off ramp. It was still high above the fog. I sank toward it. The late sunshine was behind me to the right. As I dropped toward the white blanket my glory appeared upon it, a luminous spot of light embracing my shadow, racing ahead of me. I hadn't seen it for weeks. I grinned, and went down to meet it. The circle of light opened to receive me and then vanished just as I reached it in a burst of brightness, and the outside world was erased.

Flight on instruments is mysterious and satisfying. The windows became useless. All sense of travel disappears. You thump and bump around in the air, but the only indication that you are moving from one place to another is in the movement of needles in the instruments in front of you. You play the needles with throttle, stick, and rudders like an organ. The glide-slope needle rises, you add a little power to slow the descent. The localizer needle tilts to the right, so you gently push the rudder and change the compass heading five degrees. The needles return to the center. You watch the altimeter. You wait for the beeping of the marker that announces that you have come far enough and it's time to give up the approach, and every once in a while you glance out the window to see if the airport has materialized out of nothing.

An instrument approach is an abstract business, but it links you inextricably to the machine. You live inside a vast mechanical contrivance that mirrors your movements and pumps your blood out through cables into its distant aluminum fingers. Breath, heartbeat, the roar of the engine, the whine of the gyroscopes, the clatter of communication that runs through the radios, even the flow of the air outside that affects all your movements, are all one part of this maneuver that seems so mechanical but is so closely connected to life.

I had hit the fog around a thousand feet with a bump and a change in the wind that pushed me off the localizer beam. I kicked my way back onto it, and held to the glide slope like an aerial tram running down a wire. Outside the light changed from the dazzle of the top of the cloud to a slowly darkening gray. The altimeter slid around the face of the dial. "Keep an eye on that little jewel," Phil Timm said. It approached the minimum altitude. My life depended upon that machine made of a diaphragm and a dial to keep me out of the trees.

The beep of the middle marker began to filter into the headset. One hundred feet to go. Fifty feet to go. Now I was two hundred feet above the ground. The marker was beeping. I advanced the throttle to begin my missed-approach procedure and head for Concord. But there it was: approach lights and runway threshold, and beyond it a vast black sheet of tarred landscape ready to welcome me back to earth.

I landed. It was so foggy I couldn't see the full length of the runway. The tower was invisible.

"Ha!" I said aloud to myself. "I did it!" But you can't sound excited on the radio. It is necessary to treat even a triumph with apparent boredom. Pilots fly around day and night thrilled and astonished at the earth and the things they can do and then talk on the radio as if they'd rather have taken the bus. I pushed the mike button and said somberly, "Tower, this is Six Zero One. We're on the ground."

"Roger. Turn left next intersection. Contact Ground Control on 121.9." An amazing technological feat had been accomplished. "Taxi to parking," Ground said.

I parked and got out. The air was cool. A line boy in his young twenties came out to help me tie down.

"Hey," I said, as if I came from McRae, Georgia, "it smells nice here. It smells like salt and moisture. It smells great." The kid was taciturn. He nodded. We tied the wings to the ground. I went on and on, analyzing the scent, the welcome coolness of the air, the freshness. The kid watched and listened. He didn't have anything better to do. Pleased to have executed the instrument approach so well, and glad to be here, I talked about the aroma of trees, of fresh oxygen, of the lack of the stink of jet fuel, of spring. Finally I ran down. "What is it," I said, "that makes this place feel so *good*?"

"Smells like a sea breeze to me," the kid said.

Late that night the fog grew so thick that the airport closed down. I sat in the plane and listened. It was quiet. It was truly quiet. The American Song was muffled by the weight of the fog. I could barely hear it, just above the sound of the blood in my ears. There was a profound lack of noise. It was as quiet as I had heard it since leaving Montana. This was the American Song of a century ago. Except in the cities or in the factories, when you stopped moving, or stopped your horses, this must have been what met you: silence. Sometimes you heard the sea, or wind, or the sound of a river, but mostly it was quiet.

It was wonderful. I slept deeply. In the morning when I awoke the sky was clean.

CHAPTER TWENTY-FOUR

On a day so beautiful that it would take a broken heart to break your heart, I flew the coast of Maine. Wind off the Atlantic blew clean air far inland. The sea crinkled itself up to smooch with the rock. Sun shone on slow breakers. Sun shone on the white walls of houses in villages: Boothbay Harbor, New Harbor, Port Clyde, Rockland, Camden. Islands and coastline were scuffed by centuries of wind. White sails leaned in unison, crossing bays. I could see forty miles out to sea, far past the edge of a barrier cut by a long sharp edge of blue on the chart, Warning Area W-103: "Operations hazardous to the flight of aircraft conducted within this area."

That was not the only danger. Everywhere was the hazard of beauty: the enchantment of open sea, rocky shorelines, forests, islands, flowing water, silence, clear light, and a clean wind. Beauty: of all the glories in the world, it is the most seductive, the most elusive. I always yield; I always pursue.

I diverted again from Lindbergh's route. Where he turned southwest from Portland, I went north, reaching out to touch the last of the nation's four corners. On the way, I flew for hours immersed in beauty, dazzled by it.

The landscape of America is beautiful everywhere. It is impossible to hide from it. Everywhere I had flown, even deep in the haze, there was beauty—the great limbs of the Salem Oak; the geese at Teterboro; the shine of the red sun on the Shenandoah, and on the water of Chesapeake Bay; the neon glow of the casino lights on the breakers at Atlantic City. But there are places, like this coastline, that are so magnificent they become haloed in our minds.

These places are islands. They are not always separated from the rest of the landscape by water, but something about them sets them aside.

Every state has its islands of beauty, places where the quality of the landscape makes it special, either in the way humans have shaped it with cleared fields and old bridges, or the way rivers and frost have arranged it into cliffs and spires. People come to see it, to save their lives. Sad, tired, lonely, bewildered, restless, they flock to these places, chasing relief, or hope, or satisfaction in the shape and color of these lands. And when they go, they pay, and pay, and pay, and so these places have become professionally beautiful. When that happens the beauty remains, and the visitors still find spiritual uplift in its contemplation, but something else is lost.

Once I flew to visit an island where I had lived as a child. The place was like this Maine coast: a stony beach, trees to the water's edge. I circled the familiar beauty, trying to embrace it with my wings, and landed on the new airport in the middle of the island. I climbed out of Six Zero One into the old familiar scent of fresh water and cedar trees. The grass beside the runway was deep and lush, and buried in it was an understory of wild strawberries. I found a single tiny fruit under a leaf and carried it like a gem over to the rustic airport terminal building. The building was empty but for a young woman in a uniform whose business was renting bicycles. I smiled at her and showed her the little lovely red fruit in my palm.

She glanced at it with boredom and contempt.

"Oh, yeah," she said. "They're all over the place."

I had forgotten that this was a tourist island. I had forgotten the endless assault of eager people who went chasing up there from Chicago, Detroit, Buffalo, New York City, or Toronto to pluck the wildflowers or the strawberries, and then leave. I had forgotten that when I lived there as a kid, the tourists were like a herd of stupid cattle that stampeded onto the island during the season, then fled with rolling eyes at the first touch of frost; they weren't human. I had forgotten what a woman had said to me once on the other side of the country as we sat next to an escarpment of rocks that rose out of a long glacial valley in tier upon tier of stone up to fields of snow and clean distance:

"All I care about tourists is their money," she said. "I know it sounds terrible, but by the end of the season you dislike everybody who walks in through the door. You can answer the same question forty times a day, and they still ask it. People look out the windows and say, 'Are those mountains *real*?'" I had forgotten what it was like to be a curator, and see the place you cherish slavered over, poked, elbowed, and carelessly hurt. I took my little wild strawberry back outside and ate it.

➤ On that beautiful morning in Maine, I flew on up the coast. There were islands here too: Vinalhaven, Deer Isle, Mount Desert Island. A few small farm fields were cut out of the trees inland. Were there tourists there too? Maine farmers as well as townspeople are trying to cash in on the beauty and on the fact that agriculture is a curiosity. A group of them had recently formed the Maine Farm Vacation and Bed and Breakfast Association.

"We want to get people to farms to see rural life and farm life," a spokesman told a reporter, "and we want them to leave money behind."

Farms selected for the program were elegant or simple, but all, he said, were clean.

"Tourists want to see agriculture," he said, "but they don't want to get it between their toes."

I turned the corner of Maine by a promonotory covered with antennas: "26 towers forming 2 stars," the chart said. The towers were painted with red and white stripes, and linked with a web of wires. It was a naval communications station, chatting with ships and submarines far over the horizon.

I had now flown coast-to-coast, from the Naval Air Station on North Island in San Diego to the end of Maine. The armed forces were still with me. They had been my constant companions. It struck me again how hidden they are on the ground, and how familiar in the air. When you drive in the United States you hardly see them—once in a while you pass a convoy on the highway, or a sign that points to a base behind a line of trees. But from the air over open country the bases and the invisible fences of military airspace are as common as the steeples in the towns.

I turned north and passed well clear of Wimpy Joe's Deepwoods Military Operations Area. In the landscapes of beauty the marching band played on.

As the day waned I followed the St. Croix and then the St. John River Valley north past Houlton, looking west across woods and lakes at the outline of Mount Katahdin, where, it is said, the morning sun first strikes the United States. Haze shimmered in the evening sun around the base of Katahdin; the mountain looked like a wall between the haze of civilization and northern Maine, making Aroostook

County an island of clarity in the smoke. In that light the long lakes shone, but everything else—roads, houses, farms, logging cuts—was shadowed and invisible. For fifty miles between Katahdin and me it looked as if there were only white pines, spruce, oak, aspen, and fir, and as I passed Presque Isle and Loring Air Force Base and began a descent into Northern Aroostook airport for the night, I thought, I have seen the great Northeast forest as it once was—unbroken, vast, wet, dense, magnificent, terrible.

The airport was on a ridge. It was quiet there, but for the distant murmur of the American Song. At least I thought at first it was distant. Then I found out the rumble came from an incinerator building right next to the airport. It burned cleanly, but it rumbled. So I spent the night listening to the hum of Aroostook County garbage.

In the morning I made the turn west at the top of Maine, nineteen hundred miles from home. The air was cool there at the last of the four corners of my journey. This was the kind of country in which people like to say they have two seasons: winter and the Fourth of July. At Frenchville people had two-story houses with steep roofs. They owned four-wheel-drive pickups. Their cafe had a big vestibule with a bench for removing coats and boots. Moose antlers were nailed up on shed doors, and the sweet smell of cedar smoke hung in the air. Even now, in early June, paper IGA grocery bags covered the tomato plants in the early morning.

I liked Frenchville. It was a beautiful place, but there weren't many tourists. It wasn't spectacular, just a lumbering town on a river. I went into town, wishing to be a part of it. It was a tight little bilingual community in which people wrote letters to the editor decrying the Americanization of French names. Pelletier, they argued, should not rhyme with beer. In the cafe the language was French. I ate a sweet roll and watched a middle-aged man who sat in a booth with his wife with his back to the door. He was like a talisman, a lucky stone. Almost everyone who came in reached over and tapped him. A woman came in and patted his shoulder. A man came in and pinched his ear. Mr. Lucky laughed when it happened, and looked gratified by the friendship, but when the door creaked open again he flinched. This time the man who came in clouted him gently on the side of the head. Then his wife reached over and swatted his forehead, trying to tame his hair.

That was it. Without losing his smile, he paid the bill, took his wife by the arm, and left. I did too. The quiet language, the friendship in the cafe, reminded me that this was not my place. The beauty was not mine to capture, or even to understand.

Under a cloudy, darkening sky, I filled my motorcycle at a gas station in Frenchville. The young man there asked what I was doing here with a Montana license plate, and then looked up at the sky.

"You are not flying today?" he said.

"Sure. Why not?"

"Dangerous, today," he said.

But it was dangerous only if you loved beauty. As I began the zigzag journey west I passed more tourists. They were running the St. John River in kayaks. They and their craft were bright toothpicks swirling down the river between the rocks, chasing adventure, chasing wilderness. The landscape mocked them. It looked like the Natchez Trace Parkway. Down on the river, the kayakers paddled through what must have seemed a wild and pristine country: the big empty river, the heavily wooded banks, and no roads for miles. Did they sense a mystical connection between wilderness and life? It was a veneer: a hundred yards up the banks on either side were huge clear-cuts in the forests, sliced by pale dirt roads and littered with mounds of slash.

➤ Beauty and illusion: I spent the night at Lyndonville, Vermont, with long windblown smooth clouds lying across the night sky, and a bright light from a hangar shining in my window, by the grass in the still evening. Pleasant town, Lyndonville; I drove through the little winding streets, crossed the covered bridges, looked at the clear water beneath, listened to the Vermont voices, ate at the Miss Lyndonville Diner, enjoyed the deep shade of the trees and the white houses; and then went up a hill on one of those little roads, and saw, above, two huge bridges carrying Interstate 5 along past the hillside. I looked up at the green steel beams and the curve of elevated concrete, and listened to the singing of the cars that I could not see, and suddenly felt as if all these little houses and streets were models, a replica with people in costume of the late twentieth century, and the road was an amusement-park ride into the past.

On a day of scattered showers I tumbled straight down the chart along the border of New Hampshire and Vermont, and the mountains became wormy. Among lakes and forests, they rose in humps of Precambrian granite, but their wooded slopes looked eaten away, like pecky cedar. They were striped with ski slopes. The farther south I flew, more of the mountains looked as if they had been attacked by this disease of vertical stripes. Logging roads and clear-cuts were almost insignificant, but everywhere I looked, ski runs drained down hillsides.

Clusters of buildings were all piled up at the bases of these striped hills. They looked like mounds of debris that had broken off from the tops of the mountains and slid slowly down the sides, carving out the stripes, and piled up at the bottom. They were groups of condominiums. They were entire communities built where only woods had been ten years before. They were, *The New York Times* reported, "brand-new 'villages' designed to look antiquated, with clock towers and quaint architecture." From them people could ski right over to the lifts.

They reminded me of Epcot. They reminded their owners of Disney World. "We want to give our skiers a highly concentrated, urban-entertainment environment," said a developer. "We want to be throwing a nonstop party."

But among these same hills, in the valley along the upper Connecticut River, under the Yankee One Military Operations Area, were passive solar houses with red barns, white fences, goats in the yards, and fields too small for serious farming. They were exurban homes like those I had seen in Arkansas and Alabama and anywhere the land had charm, where people had come, not just to see the beauty for a day or week, but to grasp it, to own it, to make it part of their lives.

I once spent three weeks in an archipelago much like the islands of Maine, or the islands of the St. Lawrence, or the islands of Lake Huron's Georgian Bay, or these inland islands between the mountains and the river, where beauty was life and death and property.

The archipelago was on the other side of the country. It was the San Juan Islands of northwest Washington. Like all these other islands, it attracted tourists. They came by ferry, crossing the space between their urban lives and this rural scenery in the meditative peace of a ship. Then, as if the ship bottled them up rather than soothing them, they poured out onto the landing and into town. "It's like an eruption," one merchant told me. "It's like one big dripping ice-cream cone moving up Spring Street." But this place was more than that. It was like the land along the Connecticut River. Here people chose to live, to find answers for their lives in the shape of the land.

People moved here, enchanted. They saw beauty everywhere, in their windows and in their sleep. At a museum in one of the towns I asked a young woman why she had abandoned good work in a city to come here and work for minimum wage.

"Need you ask?" she said. It needed no saying. In the windowless room, her eyes were brighter than her rouged cheeks. She came to capture the beauty: the lightness of land on water, the silver of the underleaves of the cedar trees, and the alder, turned by the wind; the yellow flame of the autumn poplars, burning themselves out against the dark wall of the firs; the red skin of the madrone; the pale blue sky; the white of the driftwood on the beaches and the white of the waves breaking against the black cliffs; the black fin of the whale; the bold silent deer; the eagles and the gulls; and everywhere the sea, surging around the points and through the passes. "Need you ask?"

"Of course not," I said. I glanced at the man who had introduced us, who had been here longer. He said nothing. Only in his eyes was there a hint of a smile.

There was never a need to ask. People come to live in these places to chase the beauty, to own it. I often heard a phrase, credited to a man whose real name was Sam Buck. Buck, some thought, chased only his name. He was a real estate developer, an eager, earnest man. "Nobody gets transferred to these islands," he said. Life histories here tended to echo that of Eleanor Howard, who was chairperson of the county commissioners and was seen by some as an archenemy of Sam Buck: "I came here from Detroit on a sailing cruise in 1956. I went back knowing this was where I was going to live."

How many people had fallen in love here, had first felt the longing to forever behold these serene views? When Robert Moran, a wealthy shipbuilder, came to the islands in 1904 and built his mansion on island rock, he was under a physician's prescribed doom, to die within the year. The people who owned the mansion when I was there, and all its attendant resort paraphernalia, liked to point out that Moran lived another forty years. How many others, resting here in rooms that fill the eye with nothing but water, forests, and stars, have imagined for themselves the same relief? Give me beauty! Give me life!

On the islands there was a national historical park, named to honor a conflict that almost erupted here in 1859 between the British and the Americans. The only casualty was a hog. Not far from the British Camp section of that park was one of Sam Buck's subdivisions. It could also be the site of a monument to honor the latter-day conflict a newspaperman called the Land Wars. These wars were hardly unique to this place: In every island of beauty, from Mount Desert Island to the Green Mountains of Vermont, to Georgia, to Idaho, to San Diego, to Seattle they have been fought for twenty years. They were the wars between those who wanted to sell the beauty and those who wanted to protect the piece of it they felt they owned.

"I helped agitate for planning," Sam Buck said, with frustration. "But we were sold a bill of goods." We sat in a back room of his building, a renovated bank. In adjacent rooms, agents listed property: "Westside waterfront home with 180 degree marine view . . . $495,000." "SPECIAL. 790 feet high bank waterfront with over 16 acres of beautifully terraced woods and spectacular building sites. High potential for imaginative development of fresh water resources . . . $175,000." Buck was burly, friendly, eager. He was born here in 1927. His gray-blue shirt was open at the collar and unbuttoned at the cuffs. He had been a dry-goods merchant, an insurance agent, a newspaper publisher.

"In the old days here you did a lot of things to make a living." He didn't always make a living.

"Went broke twice, left twice, and came back." He was back, and in the right business, in time for the real estate boom of the 1970s, when total land sales in this island county rose from around one thousand transactions a year to two thousand a year, and the population doubled to its present level of almost eight thousand. It was happening everywhere. Here it was resorts like Buck's Carefree planned-unit development, where people could look out at the sea; in Vermont it was those new ski resort condominiums. Suddenly there was wealth in the San Juans; but something else happened too.

"The people here opened their arms to let people come in," Buck said, "but those people felt they could take care of things better than the islanders."

"There was Sam Buck carving up farmland and selling it to people from California and Seattle," said the publisher of the weekly newspaper. He delighted in irony, and there was enough of it in the land wars. He continued, with relish, "And suddenly it was pretty obvious that Sam and company had imported too many people who had different ideas about how to do things." The people had come for the beauty: To have it! To hold it! And as soon as they bought a piece of it, they became afraid that someone else was going to sell it away.

I stood with the publisher in the back of the newspaper's offices, in a comfortable, busy room full of the sweet-and-sour smell of ink. We looked through old issues of his newspaper. The boar hog of the land wars is the County Comprehensive Land Use Plan, and a succession of headlines recalled various ways people had tried either to fatten it, emasculate it, or turn it into ham. The publisher grinned as we flipped through years of invective. "Ah," he said, "those were heady times."

The publisher stopped turning pages at August 2, 1978. The page was dominated by a photograph of a young, dark-haired woman holding up a sheet of paper. "There it is," he said. The woman, who, had been angered by the county government's attempts to shoot down the plan, had started a recall of one of the three county commissioners. Two years earlier, the commissioner, a lifetime islander, had been elected unopposed with 2,316 votes. On the day of the photograph, the woman turned in 1,488 signatures demanding his removal. The publisher stood looking at the photo.

"That's when the county changed," he said. "There she is, holding up those petitions, showing the county what had happened, and the county hasn't recovered yet."

Buck had said an odd thing before I left him. "You can't shut down the graveyard because you don't want anyone else to die," he said. "You know they're coming. You have to prepare a place."

I traveled among the islands with Father Edward Leche, the Episcopal priest, in a motorboat he called *Archangel*. He preached in big churches and small churches, depending on the size of the island. "The fundamental work of the church is to tell people that there is help in the time of need," he said, standing under a huge figure of Christ who bore a metal halo and bloodless wounds. Christ's hands and feet seemed enormous; they were painted a deep reddish-brown. After the service Father Leche hurried back to the *Archangel* and headed for another island, through squally winds. He docked the boat, wiped the salt water off his face, and grinned. "Well," he said happily, "it's a job." There was a pile of roofing slate beside the next church, waiting for volunteers. "The fundamental work of the church is to tell people that there is help in the time of need," Father Leche said again. "The purpose of existence, according to the Bible, is to enjoy a kind of dynamic harmony with God."

We went back out into the harmony of the beautiful world. There are times when you think you have caught it. The rain fell, the wind eased, the bays settled. The sky and sea were gray. The islands were so dark blue-green they were almost black. A flock of gulls worked on a school of herring in the distance. The birds looked like the fizz dancing above a glass of champagne.

In the morning, a chill wind blew out of the southeast. Clouds ran with it, and the sea was gray. In the dining room at the resort at which

I was staying, wind howled at the windows, and I wondered if it was a manifestation of the ghost of the place, the late wife of a previous owner, who was said to haunt the teak-paneled halls of the mansion in the same scarlet nightgown she used to wear when she rode her motorcycle into town to visit her friends at the tavern.

The wind kicked up whitecaps even in the sheltered bays, and there was a taste of rain in the air, but it was homecoming, so I went to the parade.

I had asked Sam Buck what he liked about the islands. He thought a long time, and then he said, "It's the extended family." The family was gathered outside the high school, and when the hour struck it marched down the road to the clang of a wheeled bell and the sound of poster paper tearing in the wind. Four girls in blue-and-white cheerleader uniforms wheeled the bell, followed by a trailer load of seniors behind a truck from Valley Propane, and juniors in a '56 Chevy pickup whose driver persisted in revving up huge clouds of black smoke. A kid on the pickup's running board shouted anxiously, "Don't blow it up before we get down the hill!" "Burn the Braves!" shouted the sophomores. The four homecoming-queen candidates rode in an El Camino, hair tousled and noses red in the wind, all wearing dresses that could have been designed for the summer solstice dance at the University of Arizona. Behind them all clattered the Booster Club's single roller skate, made out of a go-cart whose driver was entirely sheltered from the elements by a large white boot. "Roll over the Braves!" The go-cart sounded as if four or five extra rods were clattering around in its single cylinder.

"Complete chaos," said a teacher on the parade route, with affection. The parade rolled down past Bilbo's restaurant, past Acres Real Estate, past Eastsound Square, with its charming gift stores for tourists, then turned around and went back up to the school again, the four chilled cheerleaders clanging away on the bell like soldiers, the queen candidates rubbing their bare arms and laughing with their bundled-up parents and neighbors on the sidewalk, the sophomores chanting, and, at last, the roller skate.

As the clang and clatter faded, I met a young county commissioner candidate named Gary Franco, who was handing out brochures near the market. He wore a sweater and jeans, a day's stubble, and an anxious smile. The brochure spoke of Political Harmony, Affordable Electricity, A Diversified Economic Base, Proven Leadership, Foresight and Conviction. On its back was a Celsius to Fahrenheit temperature conversion scale. Franco said he thought the comprehensive plan was too restrictive. I asked him about the temperature scale. "My wife didn't think we should waste the space," he said.

It was a day for the family. I wandered around in it, out of place; the door into this part of island life was shut. And yet, who is to say the closed door was unfair? It wasn't even intentional. The people here were like the people at Frenchville. The beauty they had made took years to put together, and years to understand. For a little while that day the small town had simply been shut to the world that peers with such awe upon its setting, closed to allow it to celebrate in the wind that other kind of beauty that the outside always misses in its demand for clock towers and quaint architecture: the extended family, the beauty that cannot be caught on film or in the net of property, that cannot be grasped or protected, that can only be lived and remembered.

Ah, the beauty, the merciless beauty. "A lot of people come here as some kind of escape," said Lance Sobel, the county psychologist. "Then they confront themselves." When I had talked to him in his office at the Community Services Center, the psychologist looked so happy that he seemed to be constantly working to restrain himself from dying his beard purple and leaping down Spring Street shouting for joy.

Sobel's story was like Eleanor Howard's. He came, he fell. In 1975 he moved to the San Juans from Chicago with his wife and son to write. They lived in a wood-heated cabin. Their water supply was a rainwater cistern. "For the first month, it was like paradise," he said. "Then, beginning in October, it rained four days out of five. I was a city boy. Learning how to keep that cabin warm took most of that year. I remember sitting at the table with two kerosene lanterns, typing in my gloves, wearing a down jacket. I remember wheeling a car battery in a wheelbarrow a mile and a half to get my car started. I think I came close to losing my mind. Here the stresses, rather than being tied to the outside world, consisted of me dealing with myself and my family. I came face-to-face with myself, with my son, with my wife. I was not used to spending twenty-four hours a day with her." He grinned as if hopelessly happy to have had the experience. His dark eyes shone. He looked around his office. "Those are the kinds of things that bring people in here."

"If you come here because your marriage is in trouble and you think you need a change," said Father Leche, "you get here and in two weeks you're divorced. You come here because you're an alcoholic, and in two weeks they're carrying you away."

I walked down the hill from the county offices past the tavern. There, in a corner with four other men, was Sam Buck, dealing cards. The tavern was an island institution. Buck had been sitting there one day when an old friend spoke up. "You know," the man said, "nothing has changed in this goddamn place 'cept the faces. Still a bunch of old guys sitting around in Herb's, only we're them."

But changes swarmed in the street. What with the comprehensive plan, and all the people who bought land, things had changed enormously. Although the 1980 census counted almost eight thousand residents, it also reported that at least thirty percent of the homes on the islands were seasonally vacant. When, as predicted, there are 13,000 people here at the turn of the next century, how many more of those homes that tantalize you from the ferry will be empty most of the year? The islands are slowly becoming a village of visitors who come on occasion to turn their eyes self-consciously upon the beauty, and who don't even know that the extended family exists. If there was one phrase I heard as often as "I fell in love with the place," it was "I don't recognize everyone on the street anymore." And if there was one common irony, in these islands and all the rest, it was that the bitterness of the fight to save the physical beauty, the land wars, was destroying the other beauty, the extended family, the real warmth of the islands.

Was it already getting colder? One afternoon, waiting for the ferry, I watched a young couple in a battered Volkswagen with California plates drive off onto the island. Right there in front of cars lined up to board, in front of a group of waiting passengers, the car stalled. It choked, coughed, roared, stalled again, then sat there shaking helplessly as others drove around it, but no one came to help.

There were two killings in the islands the year I was there. A man was shot while mistakenly borrowing the wrong boat, and an alleged prowler was killed by a San Juan resident. Two deaths don't make a trend, but when the sheriff told me about them, he shook his head. "It would be different if we were in a bad urban area. But here there's no reason for that kind of paranoia."

Every year the beauty drives people away. Honoring it for years from a distance, they come to clasp it at last, and they find the bag they purchased empty, the savior just a model with great red wounded feet, the beauty a ghost in a scarlet nightgown. "It seems like the turnover of people is very great," said one resident. "People come to places like this, and they get pulled up by reality." They are here for a year or two and then they're gone. They are seen on the streets briefly, themselves ghostly, like faces seen on one frame of a long film. But in that brief time of their presence here and their departure, they had reached for the glory and grasped it and found that the light was gone.

A man drove to the islands from Minnesota. In the last city before the ferry he bought a hose and clamps. He rode the ferry across the still water to the islands and drove up to the state park. There, among the slender fir trees, with the water of the lake shining and the little deer grazing in the campgrounds, he attached the hose to his exhaust and took his life.

There was a young woman who loved the islands. "A very beautiful trip," she wrote after one visit. "Images of the intertidal still flowing over me. Camping on cliffs above the waves. Warm days and rainy nights." In a ferry on the way to Friday Harbor, she shot herself.

If I ask the beauty to make me happy, and I still despair, what? The people who survive on all these islands of America are the ones who march in the homecoming parade in the cold wind, who let living get between their toes, and who let the terrible beauty drive them into each other's arms.

I left Vermont, as I had left the San Juans, in the dark. As Six Zero One climbed out, I was startled by the abrupt appearance of the lights of the cities that surrounded the cherished beauty. They rose with me out of the horizon like vast, golden cupped hands. The glow was all around, on the ground, against the clouds. Only in the center, here where the loveliness lived, was a pool of precious darkness. Was it always this way, that the beauty was separate from our daily lives? Has the landscape we admire always been so isolated that we have to chase it, and, in the clamor of pursuit, lose its silent and natural presence, its reassuring background to our lives? When you have to protect the beauty, and praise it with self-conscious noise, is it already gone? Or is the beauty of the land like any glory that crosses a cloud: forever enticing, forever out of reach?

I flew on through the darkness toward the city lights. The night was so beautiful it broke my heart.

CHAPTER TWENTY-FIVE

"Were you ever afraid?" people used to ask Lindbergh. "Did you ever think you were going to die?" He would brush off the question. Now people ask me the same thing: "You flew twenty-five thousand miles in a small airplane? Weren't you ever scared?"

Yes. Once. In Pittsburgh.

From Vermont it took me two days to get there. If I had known, I would have taken longer. I wandered around in the ski-striped mountains of the New England Province, looking down at towns through curtains of rain. In the cool, misty, unsettled day, New England felt like a memory even as I saw it. Its streams were bottled up everywhere by dams, and interstate highways flowed big as rivers in the valleys, but the deciduous forests of southern New Hampshire and Vermont were deep and mysterious, and only subtly touched by the chain saw. I crossed granite mines in New Hampshire, and mountain farms in Vermont. Closer to Massachusetts and New York, I began to see as many golf courses as ski hills. The fairways were cut in strips through trees, so they looked as if they had caught the same disease as the hills. It was a pity the mountains couldn't be used year-round for both sports. What a pleasure it would be to blast a golf ball off the top of the lift at Mount Snow, halfway across Windham County.

Clouds jammed me down into the haze over Albany, but it wasn't murky enough. I had the mixed fortune to get a glimpse of the New York State office buildings: a huge reflecting pool, pompous towers, and a strange squashed-egg performing arts building. The arrangement of three vents on top of the egg made it look like a huge electric socket. It was the home of the Governor Nelson A. Rockefeller Empire State Plaza Performing Arts Corporation, better known as GNARESPPAC.

"Rockefeller's Imperial Capital," said D. W. Meinig, the noted geographer, when I talked to him a few hours later in Syracuse. "That's a brutal intrusion on a historic city." My visit in Syracuse was brief. Meinig sent me off cheerfully:

"Americans aren't much interested in their ordinary landscapes," he said. "They'd rather have a theme park."

Hastening on my unknowing way to meet fate at Pittsburgh, I crossed Rochester, where the reflection of the sun suddenly went raging through a huge parking lot like a glory, throwing off sparks of red, blue, orange, pink, and gold. I passed Fairport, Spencerport, Brockport, Middleport, and Lockport. They were all inland, and looked landlocked, but they were all on the Erie Canal. At Lockport trailer houses stood in dense packs, tight as piano keys. The town hung under a pall of dust from a nearby gravel pit. This was not unusual: Like prisons and military bases, only more numerous than both, gravel pits are seldom seen from the highway but are everywhere when you look down from the air. They splatter the country with holes.

The sun hung in the sky long enough to paint a rainbow in a cloud of mist at Niagara Falls, which looked pinched by the development around it, as if it had to erode its way through houses and overlooks just to get to the rocks. In the low sun Buffalo looked golden and handsome, all roads converging on its noble city hall, capital of the country still called the Niagara Frontier. Offshore, a fleet of boats caught the sun in their sails.

I rushed on down the coast of Lake Erie, where coal-fired power plants on the shoreline threw sulphurous plumes toward Canada across the water, as unfriendly as someone pouring dirt in your drink. Out over the water were Macho Irene's intersections: DOLFN, ANGLR, GILLS, and PHISH.

"If you see a shore around here that doesn't have a building on it, you know something's wrong," Meinig had said. Nothing wrong with these shores; they were packed with houses. I followed Lindbergh's route over Lake Chautauqua, where a thousand private docks looked like protozoan cilia, paddling the lake across the rolling twilit expanse of the Appalachian Plateaus Province. Once again the sun sank red, and the full moon materialized out of the dusk, as if it had been sitting there all day just waiting for its competition to die. I spent the night at Erie International Airport, where fuel cost $2.03 a gallon, the highest of the journey. Near the airport was a stadium, and I went to bed listening to the whine of mosquitoes, the steady hum of the American

Song from Interstate 20 beside the field, and the distant cheers of baseball fans. In the morning I clung to the shoreline over the milky green of the lake as long as I could, then flew south across the working-class dirt infields of Cleveland and the huge dark Goodyear Airdock of Akron, which was built in 1929 and can hold one blimp or seven football fields. The parking lots near the hangar and attendant factories shone like interstates dammed up to make reservoirs of cars.

From there the route took me south and east, to meet my destiny.

Canton, Alliance, Youngstown, the coal mines of New Castle, all passed beneath. The route stuck to the west edge of the rolling hills of the Appalachian Plateaus, as if Lindbergh and Keyhoe had been reluctant to move into the vast Central Lowland. Between the cities, fields of houses were planted in rows like corn, next to golf courses and farms. Smoke lay in white wreaths in the bottom of the Ohio River valley, but from fifteen miles north I could pick out the course of the river by following the line of power-plant stacks.

I landed at Pittsburgh Metro Airport, which sounded grand but turned out to be a narrow, weedy field on a ridgetop, one hell of a long way from town. And town was where I wanted to go. Without premonition I unloaded the motorcycle and poured some aviation gas into it from the wing. That didn't fire it up much. The motorcycle beats walking, but it's very small. That's useful when it comes to putting it in the plane, but when I take it out it doesn't exactly snort and paw the ground. It stands there, embarrassed, looking like a horse that just realized it was a miniature, and stands seven hands high. It thinks like a skateboard. It admires the grand style of bicycles. It has 49 cubic centimeters in its single cylinder; downhill it rips along at twenty-five miles an hour. Uphill, I have to pull over to let joggers pass. But eventually it gets me there. I thought it would get me to Pittsburgh.

I took back roads for fifteen miles. Then I got lost. I was down by the fork where the Allegheny and the Monongahela join to form the Ohio, in a part of town called West End. Geographically, I looked out at a major landmark, the joining of great waterways just west of the Allegheny Front and the long even lines of the Valley and Ridge Province. Forts had occupied the point between the rivers since 1754. Across the water was Three Rivers Stadium, where there was a grass infield made of plastic. But none of that helped now. I had to find a bridge.

The road I was on came to an end at the Ohio, just downstream of the confluence. I turned right. This was West Carson Street. It was wide and quiet. I buzzed along. Occasional trucks passed, large as warehouses. Ahead and above was the graceful single arch of a bridge. An innocuous ramp led up to the right toward the bridge. I puttered up the ramp. The ramp swung around to the left toward the bridge and downtown Pittsburgh. This looked like the right way to go. I cranked the machine up and leaned forward into the gentle breeze stirred up by its speed. The ramp lifted me onto the bridge.

Then it happened. I got scared. I became very afraid. I thought I was going to die.

The ramp tossed me out onto the bridge's left lane. But this wasn't just a bridge. Behind me a hole opened in the hillside: the mouth of a tunnel. Out of the tunnel emerged the entire howling river of Interstate 279. I was now part of it, but that participation was going to be brief. In a moment or two the motorcycle and I would be either a small grease mark under the thundering wheels, or over the side and down in the last hundred yards of the Monongahela River, blending soul, body, oil, and the last wisp of living into the Ohio.

I looked back. Yup. Everything was gaining on me. There they were: cars, station wagons, delivery vans, U-Haul trucks, tractor-trailers, M-1 assault tanks, all bearing down at eighty miles an hour.

This was the American Scream. From a mile up I had admired the interstate highway system. It was beautiful. It was graceful. It drew sinuous curves through the abrupt landscape of the grid. For drivers and passengers embarked upon it, it was a glide. But the perspective today was different. When you face a stampede on a short-legged pony, you change your mind about the romance of the range.

The bridge shook. Huge metal creatures roared past, swerving around me. If I did not get off this thing at the next exit, it looked as if I would be condemned to five miles of being a twenty-five-mile-an-hour sitting duck. I changed lanes, one to the right.

I have read descriptions of World War I, of the way large artillery shells howled as they blasted overhead on their way to cause damage elsewhere. The noise reminded those who heard it of the other shells that were even now howling in their direction. This was the roar I now heard as a truck blasted by on the left, and a car whizzed past on the right. When would the earth erupt in my trench, and cover my face with dirt and silence? I changed lanes again.

Alive! I was still alive! The off ramp approached. It shone in my view ahead. Would I ever attain it? Would I survive? A grille grew

large in my rearview mirror. The grille was the size of a barn door. If it
hit me, I would lodge like a fly in its chrome smile. It was the grille of
retribution. Repent this hour thine iniquity! Thou hast passed where
pedestrians are prohibited; yea, even where motor-driven cycles are
not allowed. The grille thundered down upon me. It shook the earth
with wrath.

I slipped down the ramp and was saved. Suddenly the thunder
receded, and turned into an innocent hum and rumble. I stopped on a
side road and looked back at the bridge. Vehicles moved sedately
across it. But I knew better. It had been like opening a door, stepping
for a moment out into chaos, then stepping back and closing it again.

The whole experience had taken about ten seconds. Later I took
look in a mirror. No, my hair had not turned white. A few hours later
I sneaked out of Pittsburgh by a quieter bridge, pushed the demoral-
ized motorcycle up steep residential hills, and made it back to the
airport. Half an hour before sunset I climbed gratefully back into the
safety of the sky.

I followed the stacks downstream. A boat towing someone on
an inner tube drew a winding wake in the muddy Ohio River by
Sewickley, a suburban boomtown twelve miles down from Pittsburgh.
Warehouses, train tracks and dead steel mills lined the river, then
suddenly there was a patch of homes and a dirt baseball diamond with
two teenagers playing on it. I was low enough to see the arc of the ball
in the last sunlight, shining like the swift toss of a glory from one to
another: the dream to play someday on the plastic infield. On the
instructions of Pittsburgh Approach I was only about a thousand feet
above the ground; farther downstream I floated almost level with the
tops of two stacks of a coal-fired power plant. The stacks threw a long
plume of smoke into the west wind. I looked down the length of the
plume. It was bright red-brown, the same color, condensed, as the
haze I had lived in for days along the coast.

I landed at Wheeling on the top of the ridge. Late that night I sat in
the airport after everyone else had gone, talking with Jim Nagy, who
was there to clean the place. Jim was battered and scarred. He limped.
His right arm was almost useless; he swung his body to give his hand
momentum to lift it up to be grasped by his left. It was hard for him to
move the vacuum around the floor. But he came up here every night,
bringing his young daughter, who slept on the couch, to be janitor at
the airport, because once he had come up here every day to fly.

"I can't believe it," he said. "I was getting paid to fly." When I talked about Lindbergh, he told me about a guy he met recently who was going to ferry a Cardinal to Paris. He told me about once flying a Cessna 206, the pickup truck of the air, to Dallas to pick up a pump.

"I just barely got it in the plane," he said, grinning. "It weighed fourteen hundred pounds." Pilots are always talking about the heavy loads they managed to pry into the air; I told him about Phil Timm loading half a beef into a smaller Cessna and then having to use full-forward stick the whole trip to keep the plane level.

"I just loved to fly," Nagy said, "and I got hurt in a darn automobile." The wreck had left him almost dead. "The car was in two pieces." Years later he was still recovering, but he could no longer fly. He looked at me over the top of his glasses and grinned. Not a flicker of bitterness, not a shadow of pain.

"The night before it happened," he said, "I did a trip to Springfield, Vermont, and back. Five and a half hours. That's pretty up there."

His eyes were bright. It was as if it were joy enough for him now to come out to the airport and hear the sound of the engines, and talk to people who could still fly.

Nagy was about my age. When he was a kid he had run a paper route. When he had saved up $9.00 he went up to the airport and paid for an hour of flight. He climbed into the airplane like a steel baron. "Take me to Pennsylvania," he had said. It was about twenty miles.

Now we stood at the wall chart of the United States. We looked at the chart and talked about places we had flown. In the background, by the sleeping child, the public television station was running an old history of the space program. The show worked its way relentlessly toward the explosion of the space shuttle Challenger. There were clips of the selection of the teacher who would ride in it, and clips of the crew grinning about their projects. The narrator took slow, calm steps toward the tragedy, as if he didn't know it was coming.

It gave me a chill. For a moment revulsion passed through me like a shudder. Machines! They maim us; they kill us. Like something foul in my gut, the fear I had eaten on that bridge had not left me.

Jim Nagy hitched his body and swung his bad arm up. He had a short fringe of hair. It made him look like a boy. He clasped his right hand in his left. He smiled.

"I loved to fly low down around Elkins," he said. "They have white rocks down there, down below those mountains."

I told him what I was doing, and described my schedule for the next months. "I hope to be done by '86," I said, then caught it. "By '88, I mean."

"Yes, I know what you're thinking," Nagy said, with another grin. "I'm still back in '79, when I got hurt."

We looked up at the map. On the television the Challenger climbed slowly away from the gantry and exploded. I winced. The narrator talked steadily of recovery, sacrifice, perseverance, and bravery. If I didn't know all about those things, Jim Nagy did.

He was looking up at the top of the country.

"That Georgian Bay," he said, his eyes all lit up. "That's the most beautiful sight in the world."

Oh, yes. I, too, had flown high across that northern expanse of Lake Huron, on a clean, calm, misty day in which each island seemed to float in the sky, and my glory was a wisp of brightness sailing ahead, subtle and kind as hope. I looked up at the chart. Fear dissolved in the memory.

Nagy was still grinning at me from under that happy-kid fringe of hair. The Georgian Bay floated before us both, up on the wall. "I just can't get it out of my mind," he said.

It was midnight. He had to finish his work, and I had to sleep and get on to other places in the morning. Much later he sent me letters; one had a clipping of an article on a Ford Trimotor that had stopped at Wheeling. He had taken a ride in it. He was thrilled. He dotted the *i* in Jim with a round happy face, and on my Christmas card he drew a picture of a classic old Beechcraft twin-engine plane with grins on its nose and engines. "I'm still a janitor," he wrote. "For now."

"Well, you have a good time," he said that night at Wheeling. "Toodle-do." He limped back to work.

I glanced up once before I went to sleep. The ridgetop airport seemed desolate, high above the valleys full of lights and life. The airport was dark, but the office was still lighted. I could see them in there as if they were on television themselves: the child sleeping on the couch, the man pushing the vacuum, towing his ruined arm along with him from office to office, thinking of flight and the Georgian Bay.

CHAPTER TWENTY-SIX

Jay Lehr ran up the paved road. A woman's voice whispered in his ear:

"Eight minutes, thirty-two seconds," she said.

A short time later she said, "Eight minutes, fifty-one seconds."

"You probably would have called me a fanatic then!" Jay Lehr shouted, puffing slightly, referring to the last time I had visited him, a year or two before. "That's nothing to what I am now!"

The woman's voice came to him in his headset from a box he wore on his belt. A radar device like a cop's speeder gun looked out of the box at the passing ground, and calculated Lehr's speed. The box was also connected to electrodes stuck to his chest and to a headset that rested on his ears. The synthesized woman inside told him his speed per mile. If he asked her, by pushing a button on the box, she would tell him his pulse and the distance he had already covered.

"I'm like a kid with a new toy!" Lehr yelled. "The new toy is my body!"

I had left Wheeling in pouring rain. By the time I got the plane untied and ready to go, I was as wet as a rat. I was in the clouds almost all the way to Columbus, fogging up the windows as I steamed. I had emerged over country roads and condominiums north of the city, where the city was exploding outward, and the whole landscape looked unfinished, like a house framed but not yet sided, with studs scattered in the yard and Skillsaws making a bagpipe wail in the background of the American Song. I made a sloppy approach, landed, and got back on the little horse.

Jay Lehr's office was in a growing suburban town, about three miles from the field. It was beside the Scioto River. It had a basketball court, canoes, a volleyball court, horseshoe pits, and pieces of rock from every province in the country on shelves inside: lava from the Snake-Columbia River Plateaus, Cococino sandstone from the Colorado Plateau, fine-grained sandstone from the western edge of the Great Plains, in Deaf Smith County, Texas. There were hundred-pound sacks of birdseed in a closet for the squirrels.

"When you've got a crazy boss," said Jay Lehr's secretary, "you've got crazy surroundings."

We had gone out to dinner and a movie the night before. We got up at six to run. It was a six-mile trot through the neighborhood. For him it was a warm-up for the day. I, too, wore a black box, which was called a Nike Monitor. The company had given Lehr two demonstration monitors because he had earned fame running year after year in the Ironman Triathlon in Hawaii.

But Jay Lehr's most notable achievements were not in the Ironman, nor in the lacrosse coaching he did for several years at Ohio State University. Twenty years before, in college, he had spent his days with his nose pressed against the Plexiglas walls of boxes of sand, watching dyed water flow slowly between the grains, or sitting alone at the bottom of a swimming pool, wearing a mask and a scuba tank, thinking about what he had seen. All this immersion had added up to the United States' first Ph.D. in the study of underground water. Now he was the executive director of the National Water Well Association, and had become a world authority on the way water flows within the earth.

Ground water is the invisible life of the planet, but you see its effects everywhere from the air. You see it where it emerges in springs: miraculous patches of green in the desert, or a sudden glitter among trees. You see it in those thousands of gravel pits outside of towns from El Monte, California, to Connecticut. You see it lying blue-green, the color of copper ore, in the bottom of the mile-deep open-pit mine in Butte, Montana.

In the great plains of the Dakotas, Kansas, Colorado, or Texas, and in southern Idaho and eastern Washington, and so many other arid and semiarid lands, round irrigated fields bloom in rows far from any river or canal, nourished by water drawn up from the ground like blood. In limestone country, in the rolling landscape called karst, you see rivers burst full-grown from hillsides. This seems so strange to people who don't know how limestone caves collect and channel rainwater that they think up fables to account for it: there's a big spring in Arkansas whose owners claim it is fed by water from Crater Lake, Oregon.

I have flown low through the Hagerman Valley in southern Idaho, at a place called Thousand Springs, where for twenty miles clear water pours out of cliffs in waterfalls or emerges from beneath them in crystal streams. The water comes from rivers and irrigation water that sink into lava desert far to the northeast. There is enough of it to raise almost all the restaurant trout in the country. I have stood in the spray of artesian wells in California's Owens Valley. Fifty years ago people pushed wells down in that valley's desert floor. Boom! Water pressurized by its seep from mountains above burst up out of the pipes in sudden fountains. The fountains have run ever since, spilling their wealth in profligate abandon into a parched landscape. Ground water is commonplace magic, like birds.

Jay Lehr explains ground water to everyone he meets. He's crazy about it. He gives lectures on ground water. He offers seminars on ground water. He shows slides of those Plexiglas tanks he watched for so long in college, demonstrating the way the water moves through pores in earth, gravel, sand, and rock at about one-seventieth of the speed of a snail, the way wells draw the level of the water down in cones of depression, and the way water poured into one end of a lone aquifer will raise the level at the other end, even though the water itself takes hundreds of years to flow through. He publishes journals and writes editorials about ground water. He relentlessly attacks the durable business of water witching, which feeds on the public's ignorance and awe.

"I go out of my *mind* over this mystery and occult of ground water!" he told me once, shortly before taking off on a routine sixty-mile bicycle training ride. "Ground water is just real simple! It's funny for something so simple to be mysterious!"

But ground water, like all the beautiful mysteries of this planet, is in danger. Ground water is restless. It moves slowly, but it never stops. When rain hits the earth and sinks in, it picks up whatever may dissolve in it and takes it along. In the unturbulent flow of ground water, plumes of waste may drift for years, and who knows what system they may ruin, in whose generation? In the early 1960s everybody thought organic chemicals would not trouble the ground, that the earth would take care of them. But then they started popping up— solvents, degreasers, septic-tank cleaners people had been releasing since they were invented. Among them was the popular solvent tetrachloroethylene, better known as TCE, a carcinogen that has become one of the most widespread of all detected ground-water pollutants. TCE was impossible to even see in the water until recent technology found it. What else remains unseen?

Jay Lehr sees everything. It is as if he sees right into the earth and feels the way the water moves. In a way he is like Skip Livingston, looking at a whole system that is under stress. But in other ways he is not like Skip Livingston at all. He is never discouraged, never pessimistic, always possessed by a vast and ebullient hope. Being around him is like watching an inexorable natural force, but he doesn't move like ground water. He moves like a flood pouring over rocks. Look around, and he's half a mile downstream. He doesn't just talk, he shouts. It's not the volume; it's the tone.

To Lehr all the concern over ground-water problems today doesn't mean that the land's life blood is becoming fatally poisoned. It means that ground water is at last getting the attention it deserves.

"In 1968 people couldn't spell ground water!" he shouted one Saturday at a small airport near Columbus. He was sitting shirtless at a picnic table in his shorts, the marks of his parachute harness still on his shoulders. He had just completed his 230th career jump, riding cheerfully down on his reserve after his main chute failed. "They thought it was water in a puddle! Today it is hard to pick up a newspaper without finding a ground-water story! I really believe eighty-eight percent of the people know about ground-water pollution! I think as many people know about ground-water pollution as could name you the President! Public attention is almost universal! Man, we have won a huge victory! We got the country's attention!"

Talking to Jay Lehr involves pursuit. You chase him around the landscape. On another occasion we had talked beside an Olympic-sized pool filled with ground water. He was about to embark on a two-mile swim in his element.

"There are no insoluble ground-water problems!" he yelled enthusiastically that day. "None! There are problems that may get out of hand. But they're being addressed. Biological reclamation is going well! We're learning to activate the natural bacteria, and it will eat most of the pollutants! We're getting better at siting septic systems, at managing pipelines! Landfills are much better than they were! We're reducing effluent in the ground to ten percent of what it was ten years ago! The wheels are in motion! Agricultural chemicals are becoming one of the biggest concerns! But already we're handling our chemicals better! They're finally not wasting as much water out in Texas on the Ogallala Aquifer! They're doing sensible irrigation! I'm the most optimistic person in the country! No one will be able to sell a crisis in 1990! There will be plenty of water! Now that we have the attention, we'll get it done!"

When I stopped by during my journey, he was skinnier than I had ever seen him. He had lost thirty-three pounds in eleven weeks. "I decided to give up exhibition eating!" he shouted as we ran. He no longer ate a quart of ice cream and a whole bag of Oreos for dessert. "I got stronger as I lost weight! Now I'm as gung ho on body building as I am on the Ironman! I can count all my abs now!" He looked at the ripples of muscle in his abdomen. "I never knew there were eight of them!"

We finished the run and went back to his house. I shot a few baskets in the hall, where a full-height basket hangs over the hardwood floor. Lehr bounced his body a couple of times on the living-room floor, which is a trampoline.

He headed upstairs to pack. He was off to Israel the next day to run an international workshop on "Behavior of Pollutants in Porous Media."

"We have a long way to go in water management in this country!" he shouted when he came back down. "We still have so damn much of it! We should study Israel and how they handle their little amount of water! The problems here are people problems, not resource problems! This country has accessible well-water reserves twenty to thirty times greater than all surface-water supplies! And yet the nation uses three times more surface water than ground water! That's crazy." The drive to flatten nature, to chase the glory of making each year just like the last by building vast dams and aqueducts, was, to him, nonsense.

"We have to develop the confidence to take water out of the bank account—the ground water—knowing that nature will put it back in! In the drought period we want to pump the hell out of our ground water! By using it we make room in the bank for another deposit that comes in the flood! But we don't work with nature! We're stupid!"

He went downstairs and started bench-pressing weights: four sets of eight lifts of 140 pounds.

"People think I'm an obsessive-compulsive person!" he yelled. The weights went *clank!* "But if so, I'm the most laid-back obsessive person in the world!" *Clank!* "I'm not punishing my body! It likes it!" *Clank! Clank!* "Nothing bothers me!" *Clank!* "I never worry about things!" *Clank!* "I think it's those parachute malfunctions I've had!"

➤ I had come out of the Appalachian Plateaus Province on my way from Wheeling to Columbus. I was now in the vast Central Lowland. In this expanse, geographer Charles B. Hunt wrote, "[T]he low altitude and lack of relief results in scenery that is as plain as the plain is extensive." It wasn't plain to me. When Jay Lehr took off for Israel, I took off for Dayton, Cincinnati, Louisville, and Muhlenberg County, and the scenery was dramatic.

Most of it was in the sky. Every day of summer these plains build spectacles of violence out of heat and moisture. Every day on the radio I heard the familiar warning for some part of the plains: "Sigmet Charlie Alpha Two is current, for an area of thunderstorms forty miles wide extending from St. Louis to Springfield, Illinois, moving southeast at twenty knots. Tops to fifty-five thousand. Possible tornadoes, wind gusts to sixty knots, hail to two inches."

I was used to these warnings. But I couldn't ignore them. Each one was a dispatch from headquarters, routine but vital, giving the daily coordinates and estimates of power of the enemy fleet. You couldn't go out on patrol without it.

So far I'd managed to stay out of their way, but summer was advancing. The white ships were becoming more abundant in the sultry afternoons. Soon there would be an engagement.

I climbed out of the haze and leveled off on top of a scattered layer of small cumulus clouds that floated like popcorn on dirty dishwater. In the distance great towers of cloud rode slowly across the sky. Below, the landscape was dominated by fields. It was the first serious agriculture I'd seen since those sugar-cane and winter-vegetable fields south of Okeechobee. I crossed the Ohio River again at Cincinnati. It was crowded with boats. It was a muddy green, almost the same color as the infield grass in the stadium. I kept going, at 10,500 feet. Once more the river's course was marked by the stacks of power plants. I now had a whole list of things drivers seldom saw that I noticed everywhere: prisons, gravel pits, military bases, power plants, haze.

Below me, south of Cincinnati, in the haze, the visibility was about ten miles. But up here I could see a hundred. I was free of all that stuff down there. What went on on the ground was academic. It was part of my world, but it was mine to appreciate or ignore. The Earth was like those models of aquifers under Plexiglas; at any point I could turn away and get on with real things: clouds, sunshine, clean air, and freedom. My engine roared. Earth and sky were under my dominion. I could stride the planet, heedless of the footprints I left in disturbed ground. I could build dams and aqueducts with a sweep of my hand. I could pee on the ground, and let the mystery beneath the ground cleanse itself. I had control; I had the power.

Illusions die hard. The last time I flew this route, in almost exactly this weather, feeling just this free of Earth, the radio had suddenly begun to squawk on the Unicom frequency.

"Mayday," said a male voice. "Mayday, mayday!"

I grabbed a pencil and the mike, and was about to answer when he spoke again:

"Roger, roger," he said. "I'm losing power. I can't get the power on."

Someone closer had answered. But there was static in the background: other planes that couldn't hear the distress call were giving reports and asking for airport conditions. Someone else broke in:

"Hey, fellas, get off the radio. We've got a mayday on the frequency."

The static drained out of the background, like blood out of a face. In the quiet a crowd gathered around, a stilled and anxious audience at all elevations in the amphitheater of the sky.

The first voice came back on:

"I'm near Greenwood Lake. . . . Roger. Greenwood Lake. The power just isn't there."

Silence. Then:

"Roger. Tried carb heat. Don't make any difference."

Silence.

"Roger. Lots of gas."

Silence. The only Greenwood Lake I knew about was down in South Carolina, over three hundred miles from where I was flying. It would be possible to hear him across that distance. But that was wooded country; small farms and large forests. The thought chilled me. Where would he put it down?

All the listeners had the same thought. We all knew, from our training, what it was like to be sitting in the air with a quiet engine. It was like starting down a ten-mile incline in a car and suddenly finding out you had no brakes. We were all there in the cockpit with him, banking right and left as if to avoid the sweep of this sword of silence. We all looked down, searching for open space and looking out for wires and towers, remembering rusty procedures, watching the swift rise of Earth.

"I've got a small field. I've got a small field," the voice said. It was as if he possessed the patch of open land, like a passport, and was waving it at the implacable agent of gravity. See, see! I'm legal. I can get back into the nation of life.

But no one was there to check his credentials and show him through the gate. A small field, he had said. I had seen that country. I could see the field. It was two hundred yards long. It was not level. It would demand attention, precision, and luck. If he guessed wrong about the wind, he would come in short and hit the steep slope at the field's end, and turn himself into a mixture of aluminum and blood. If he overshot, he would start a forest fire and have to be identified by his teeth. I could see that patch of ground among the trees, glowing in his head. I could see him make his turn as the plane sank, swift as a leaf, toward the bottom of the sky. Now he had to be smarter than he had ever been. He had to work with nature.

I was an optimist. I was like Jay Lehr. I thought he'd land and make it. I wanted to call on the radio, as if saying it would make it come true: "You'll be okay! You'll be all right! You'll get it done!"

His voice was calmer now. Silently, the audience praised him. Silently, we most earnestly wished him well. The drama would soon end.

The sound of the radio began to break up. He was getting lower. Hills were interfering with his voice. He was very low. He had a minute left in the air.

". . . near end of . . . lake."

Silence.

". . . no power."

Silence.

". . . can't . . ."

Silence.

". . . power."

Silence.

". . . power."

That was all.

The frequency was quiet for several minutes. Then we all realized we would hear no more from Greenwood Lake. Voices began to return. "Dayton General Unicom, request airport advisory." "Vinton County, Vinton County, can you give me the winds down there?"

Months later I called the National Transportation Safety Board to try to find out what had happened. If the pilot had been killed, the board would have investigated. There was no record. That afternoon the flier and Earth had come to an agreement about life. They had forged a truce, and his life had continued. But was he crippled? Did he walk away and laugh? Life had gone on, but I'd never know the quality of what his negotiations with the air and the land had saved.

The frequency hummed and crackled again. No one mentioned the mayday. We let the illusion creep back, like the static. We were in control here. We could do what we pleased with sky and Earth. We had the power.

➤ Warships moved across the horizon, their white sails spread, firing volleys that rattled through the AM frequencies of my direction-finder radio. Muhlenberg County drew me on. I still lived with Charles Lindbergh and Donald Keyhoe, but I was making my own journey. Muhlenberg County Airport, at Greenville, Kentucky, was not in Lindbergh's log, but I went there anyway. It extends south from Louisville out of the Central Lowland and up into the Interior Low Plateaus Province, south of the edge of the ancient glaciers that covered most of the Lowland. The Low Plateaus, Hunt wrote, are noted for "tobacco, corn, coal, bourbon, and Kentucky colonels." I went there chasing the lyric of a song:

> Daddy, won't you take me back to Muhlenberg County,
> Down by the Green River where Paradise lay.
> I'm sorry, my son, but you're too late in askin'
> Mr. Peabody's coal train has hauled it away.

Muhlenberg County was the land of strip mines. It was the land of draglines the size of hotels, of piled overburden, of the removal of the black bituminous aquifer to power plants along the Ohio River. John Prine wrote the song to lament the spread of the mines, and it has been sung and the lyrics repeated everywhere where the same kind of mining promised to forever change the landscape. Muhlenberg County was a landscape fabled for its devastation, and I ducked around the black keels of the storms, avoided the flicker of depth charges, and, too busy to look around, ducked into Muhlenberg County Airport just behind the rain.

The airport was surrounded by deep, green fields of corn. The grass between the runways and beside the apron was lush. The air smelled of moisture and green life. What had I expected? Gray dust and blackened hills? I hadn't found it. In the warm moist evening mead-owlarks walked around in the deep grass, eating bugs. As the day faded, fireflies shone. In Greenville a happy crowd listened to blue-grass music under big old oak trees in the park.

Late that night I went to use the outdoor airport phone, and as I stood there in the completely deserted airport, waiting to make the call, I watched a frog.

The frog sat on the concrete. I had thought about my son, David, when I saw the frog, which hopped away from me when I walked to the phone. David likes frogs. He catches them, massages their little muscles for a while, and lets them go. Now, as I talked to Debbie's sister, Julie, the frog just sat on the pavement, utterly still. For ten minutes as I talked to Julie it did not move. It was a stone frog.

Then a drama began to unfold. As I watched the frog I noticed a very small moth walking down the concrete toward it. This moth was in trouble. It wandered along on the rough man-made stone, as if the coarse grain of this pitted plain made it hard work to get around. It walked straight toward the frog.

The moth didn't have much time left. A minute, maybe two. It had six inches to go. Off in its distance sat the frog. It must have looked like the Sphinx. The bug's trail was on the side of a crease in the concrete, and there at the end of the crease the frog was poised, with a vast and inscrutable face. The moth had time here, to make a judgment, to turn away, perhaps to fly, to go land in a field. It kept walking ahead. Now it closed with the Sphinx. Another two inches were all that bug had left of life. Quick! Find a field! You can get it done!

One inch.

Half an inch.

The Sphinx struck. Vast jaws blasted open, and a great sticky plank moved like thunder. That bug was history. Life had become death, and I was still laughing with Julie on the phone.

I climbed into heaven in the morning and took a good look at Muhlenberg County. Yes. The whole damn thing had been mined. Right below me, near the airport, was the cutting edge. The topsoil was orange. Peeled back, it revealed gray. Beneath that was the black shelf of coal. The coal weeped ground water. Yellow draglines and coal shovels worked deliberately at the face. Slurry pipelines crossed the landscape to a tipple at the Green River. In the river, lines of barges filled with coal rode deep in the water. There were stacks in the distance.

But most of the mined land had been reclaimed. It looked as if Mr. Peabody's coal trains had hauled back the landscape. Except where the draglines made their patient casts, the ragged trenches had been filled in with dirt or with water, making domed fields or long, narrow bass ponds. On the domes of the remade landscape, trees had been planted in rows.

Some of the land was pasture. One stock pond was a perfect circle. Another was a triangle. The land looked like a ruined face that had been repaired by a team of surgeons. You could see the grafts and the molding, but expression had returned. If there was pain in that expression, it was masked.

There was just one odd patch. It was a small cemetery, and had not, out of respect for the dead, been mined. It was the only piece of land that had not been remade in the image of a new America. It looked out of place, like a wart.

I had appointments farther down the line. My detour had set my schedule back. I flew over another power plant and left Muhlenberg County. I thought about Jay Lehr. Before we went our different ways he had taken me from his house to see a sewage treatment plant. The pretty, rolling, new land of Muhlenberg County now reminded me of the plant.

Lehr had taken me there on his motorcycle. The machine was an enormous Yamaha, the opposite end of the spectrum from my miniature. Its chrome shone. The whole thing gleamed with the colors of the rainbow. To Lehr it had a special halo.

"This is the last of the things that I wanted!" he shouted. "I didn't buy it for fifteen years, at first because I couldn't afford it, and then in the last five years when I could afford it I knew it was the last thing I wanted so I thought I might get depressed if I bought it! But I bought it, and I don't feel depressed!"

The motorcycle was about the size of a Mercedes sedan. It was like an elephant: if it ever fell over, you'd have to shoot it. Lehr came charging out of the house, shirtless, in his shorts, on the way to the office.

"Come on!" he shouted. "Let's go!"

We jumped on the vast machine and roared off, stopping on the way to visit the treatment plant. It was elegant. It looked like a park.

"It's gorgeous!" Lehr shouted, as we walked around the grounds. "You'd want to retire here! We've got to stop this stuff about 'Not in *my* backyard!' Let them spend their money in tangible improvements instead of legal battles! People have to accept that waste is a part of life! Let's not fight shadows and bogeymen! I want *everything* in my backyard, but I want it to look nice!" Jay Lehr was a man of the twenty-first century.

We left. He had to go to the office, then catch his plane. We pulled out on the interstate on the huge motorcycle, and the American Song roared and thundered around us. New construction was going up everywhere: condos, apartments, single-family homes, built on land that had been bulldozed flat and would soon be landscaped over from the beginning. We joined right in the flow of trucks and automobiles, and the motorcycle did some singing of its own. Jay Lehr shouted in the wind:

"I love being outdoors!"

PART 7

CHAPTER TWENTY-SEVEN

The wind blew hard out of the north. I fought it. I chased memory across the heart of the Lowland Province, with the winds of Earth and time in my face. It was Sunday morning. I demanded of the landscape: Take me back to the last place I saw God. It was four hundred miles north.

At Troy I crossed the Ohio again: a sheen of water, and the smudging of the sky by stack plumes. The haze layer was bronze. West of Ferdinand, Indiana, by Interstate 64, the chart was marked "Seminary" on one side of the big road and "Convent" on the other. The road between played the American Hymn. At Bloomington the guy who sold me fuel also flew charters for the feds, looking for marijuana plantations in the woods. Indianapolis was an All-American city: the speedway, domed arenas, a building bearing a vast flag, a brassy, shining, glass skyscraper, a parking lot with a couple of hundred parked school buses, and the small downtowns of old cities on the periphery standing out among endless suburbs like barns in a flood. The center of Indianapolis was lost behind me in the haze before I came to the edge of the metropolis and found Westfield, a separate town, all by itself beside Interstate 31.

Even in the unifying order of the grid, towns were more individual from the air than from the ground. From above there were no repeating McDonald's signs and Sears-centered malls to make them run together in the mind. Kokomo was a tidy city with a big factory and a tank covered with red checkers. Huntington had a handsome county courthouse and a big hole in the ground: another gravel pit. Gravel pits looked profound; they were the only elevation change in the enormous flatness. They looked like holes where odd-shaped giants had fallen off of beanstalks.

Fort Wayne was heavily wooded, a shadow of a city among the pale greens and browns of the surrounding fields. Southeast of Toledo the earth was pied, mottled depths of brown in the plowed ground, mottled greens in the crops, clay showing through the topsoil lost to wind. Toledo was dominated by a huge circular parking lot with a mall that looked like a giant bird. It made the whole city look symmetrical. At Detroit the morning praise had risen from the steeples and now it looked as if the whole population of that sweltering city had headed for the water: Lake Michigan and Lake St. Clair were clouded with sails and by the white streamers of foam pulled by power boats, and west of town, out by circular and serpentine automobile proving grounds, one small lake I crossed was so churned up by crisscrossing wakes that it looked like a Jacuzzi.

The opposing wind grew. I continued north. The cities dropped away. Forests spread. I became disoriented on the face of America, looking down on the expanse of trees. Where was I? Three-quarters of the way through my journey, land forms were starting to remind me of other land forms. Was I south of Presque Isle, Maine, or north of Saginaw, Michigan? Let's see: trees and distant coastline; a forceful wind; an Air Force base; purple outlines on the chart of vast Military Operations Areas. It was all familiar. It might have been Maine. It might have been Louisiana.

A clue: Here the roads all ran straight and at right angles to one another. I was on the grid. This was Michigan, not Maine. And up there ahead on the horizon, where the fine threads of the suspension bridge between the peninsulas of Michigan was outlined against the burnished lake, was Mackinac Island, where the wild strawberries grew in the grass.

With the wind against me I moved across the straits so slowly that my approach did not seem real, a steady airborne movement toward a place that existed for me only in the past. I landed again on the airport in the middle of the island, stepped out of the plane, and, in that aroma of cedar trees and fresh water, was assailed with premonition.

This was the last time for me here, I thought. I would never come again. It was over.

For a second the thought gave me a catch, a fear. This day in which we live is too short for these losses.

But, no. I refused it. Clairvoyance is a handy literary device, but in real life it doesn't work. I have often been overcome by eerie and profound premonitions, and none has come true. But in spite of denial the thought clung to the back of my mind, as I walked and jogged through the streets of the place that was once home. It was natural to listen to these instinctive voices of unreason here, because this was the place where I had been taught, again and again, to honor the rumors broadcast by the mind. They were, I was told, the voice of God.

Landscapes remind you of the past as powerfully as scent and music. This island was layered with sentiment. On top of my own memory was an institutionalized nostalgia. For the sake of history and tourism no automobiles were allowed on the island. An old fort was maintained by men and women wearing the costumes of 1812. Horses pulled carriages through the streets; even now the smell of horse manure takes me back to the island.

I walked down dirt roads toward the tiny town and its fudge shops and carriage-ride concessions. The cedar and birch woods were full of green leaves, ferns, flowers, and ghosts. I must have looked as if I still belonged here: a couple of tourists stopped me and asked:

"Sir, do you know where Tranquil Lane is?"

"Sorry," I said, and thought, That place has escaped me all my life. The only tranquility when I lived here was once in a while on the surface of the lake, and even that didn't happen often.

I lived on the island as a child. It was children I remembered. We were six, ten, twelve, fourteen, sixteen, seventeen years old here. It was children I missed, and the child I was. I visited a former teacher, for whom I had been trouble. She was distantly friendly, but I left wishing I had not gone. She had been cool, and I understood it. Coming back to a place where you have lived is worse than being a tourist. People forget you, or recall you vaguely, and when you return they can't help resenting you. They have had this setting for themselves all these years, piling life upon life on the artifacts of the past you revere. Then you come charging in, lamenting the changes, making your claims of nostalgia on a setting that holds their real present.

I was sorry I had gone to see her. I went back to being a ghost, and chased the glory of memory all the way back, and saw my friends as they were in the faces of children on the street.

The school I had attended was now a museum. There was the stone wall where we played marbles. I learned about ownership there, and gambling, and competition, and teasing. There was the hotel where my parents were married, in a festival of joy right after the war. There was the window from which I watched the first snowfall I can remember. There was the place that was an infirmary, where I once lay with blood poisoning, listening to rock music blaring from ferries crossing to the mainland. There was the road we sledded on homemade bob-sleds with conduit for runners. Four Boy Scouts were half riding, half pushing a cart down it now, shouting at each other.

"You've got to go *fast*!"

"I was trying."

"You weren't."

Time and memory. No wonder our minds embrace mysticism: the view we have of our own existence is so gloriously baffling. Five years before this visit I had come back to the island, and I ran in a race around its perimeter road: eight miles. The last five island residents who had been part of the religious and ideological organization in which I was raised came out to cheer me in front of their house, which was two miles along the course. As I passed, deep in concentra-tion of competition, I heard a voice:

"Go, Eric!" it shouted. My father's name is Eric.

It was Shelley, one of the kindest men I have known. After the race he apologized. "I'm sorry," he said. "You're the spitting image of the Eric I worked with for fifteen years." He had done just what I was doing now. The passionate camaraderie of the organization had been gone from the island for more than a decade, but once in a while he saw a face that made him think those days had returned.

I found my way to the theater the group had built on the island when its founder had decided this was the American headquarters for his organization. God had told him to build here, and there were Indian myths that made the choice seem ordained. The theater was silent. I sat in the balcony. Someone was hammering slowly back-stage. The sound echoed faintly, but the place roared with ghosts. My mother had acted on that stage. I had acted on that stage. But we had not just been acting. We had been preaching, praising, exhorting, pleading, and proselytizing; promoting the word of God. We thought there was only one way for human beings to behave righteously: to adhere to the four absolute moral standards the founder described, and, every morning and at any point in the day in which decision was required, to stop and listen and wait for the slow percolation into the mind of celestial truth.

The group was called Moral Re-Armament. Most people of my parents' generation remember it. It was founded by Frank Buchman, and was also called Buchmanism, and The Oxford Group. For a while it had an influence on the politics and outlook of the people of the globe: From about the time of Lindbergh's flight until the mid-1960s, a period of upheaval on this planet that may stamp this century as the age of ideology, the group made a stir. But the stated goal was more grand than mere influence. Buchman's goal—ascribed to God—was to remake the world. Long before Star Wars, the people in the group called themselves The Force.

I can remember, at the age of thirteen, walking among those cedar trees and looking out at the calm water of Lake Huron and being certain beyond doubt that this loveliness was evidence of God's work, and that I knew what He wanted of me.

At fourteen I lost that assurance. I had become so wrapped up in guiding my life through the whims of intuition that I became almost paralyzed looking for signs that what I thought I heard from God was real. In this place, surrounded by a wonderful changeless, peaceful setting of water and trees, the more bizarre your thought, or the more painful, the more likely it was considered by others to have sprung from heaven. There were infinite numbers of rules, but all were unwritten and subjective, and they changed by the day, according to whoever could more fearfully wield the voice that morning. I became lost in this amorphous structure of behavior and belief. I became desperate. Then suddenly, almost in the course of a single day, I looked around and saw the trees and tasted the wind, and loved the planet, and thought: There are other ways to live.

It felt like being born into reality. I have never since been as certain of anything as I was of God's voice at thirteen, and glad I am of it. Awe of the mystery makes life and the Earth a greater wonder. But my uncertainties of those years troubled others in the group, and until I was twenty-one and split with the group forever, we fought. They would try to get me to go to meeting after meeting, where my unfortunate friends would have to stand and bare the trauma in their lives. But I would escape to run through those woods and dream of being a wolf who could travel from island to island in the winter on the ice. Or I'd find my way to the shoreline in an autumn storm and let the spray lash my face, and look out at the wild water of Lake Huron and believe it was evidence of something I did not yet know: freedom. I was not the only one to see escape in the landscape: I remember watching a thirty-year-old convert poring over charts.

"One of these days," he said, "I'm going to get out of here. That's where I'm going." He pointed to the islands of the Georgian Bay. One day, when he disappeared, we hoped we knew where he had gone.

In a way the place was a prison camp; in a way it was a monastery; in a way it was wonderful. It was the closest community I have ever experienced; it was the fiercest. Buchman had chosen his place well. Lost on this remote landscape, people had only each other and The Force. Surrounded by beauty, people chased the glory there, a grand, magnificent glory. To change the world! They chased it. They were on fire.

That *was* a time. Like war, that was a time. Through all those years, while my friends and I grew up instinctively battling the effort to control our minds, we were close to one another in a way I have not known since.

I walked down to the big central hall where the meetings that I had schemed to avoid once took place. People I cared about had stood there year after year in front of strangers and their best friends, and confessed, cajoled, or called out to heaven. Prominent visitors had stood there and said they were changed forever, and cried. Men had admitted hate, corruption, and masturbation. Couples had announced engagements, solutions of strife, and vows of sexual abstinence. Buchman, it was once said, "had a Napoleonic gift of making people want to do hard things." In that room people had stood joyfully embracing decisions that would make them feel lonely, poor, and in pain, but blessed.

Now the buildings put up to change the world had become a hotel. The Force had evaporated from this landscape. In one of the meeting rooms I heard a voice speaking before a crowd:

"Do you stretch before you warm up?" it said. "Or do you warm up before you stretch?"

In the evening I sat at the end of the airport in the twilight and looked out over the lake at the lights of the mainland. The lake was utterly calm; new leaves on the birch trees rattled in just a breath of breeze. There was the sound of distant horses' hooves, and of girls giggling as they passed on bicycles. In the distance lay the edge of the continental haze: a line of red down on the southern horizon. It was inflamed. As the twilight faded it turned darker red: dangerous, heavy, smothering the world. I looked down toward it and felt apart from it up here; safe in the past. But I remembered how it was to feel the power to make things change.

I crushed cedar leaves between my fingers and smelled them. Once a friend and I, thinking tobacco itself was a mortal sin, had rolled dried cedar leaves in brown paper and smoked them in the basement of the place that was now a hotel. We caught hell.

The lake was unmoved. Lights glimmered in the distance. The scene was indifferent to me. But I was not indifferent to the scene. It held those hours for me, beautiful, inaccessible, unblemished, as in a jar.

An outboard motorboat buzzed by. A long time after the roar had passed, I could hear small waves wash on the stony beach; the boat's wake coming to shore.

I prowled around in the grass and flowers at the edge of the runway and found four wild strawberries. All over this country people have sayings about the things that make their home countryside appealing, the things that draw people back. Once you eat the cranberries of western Oregon, once you put your feet in the red water of Oklahoma, once you eat Texas chili, once you drink Tennessee moonshine, you will return, you will return. So I sat there in the dusk, looking down toward the hazy world we had not saved, and ate the wild strawberries of Mackinac Island.

CHAPTER TWENTY-EIGHT

Six Zero One was in trouble. I could not push it much farther without repair. On the island, when I pulled the prop before starting the engine, one of the cylinders was soft. I knew what it was: the lead in the fuel was clogging the valves, and one was sticking. I flew south, listening to the beat of the engine, waiting for a stumble.

Drought dusted Michigan. Along the west edge of the Southern Peninsula lines of trees beside fields made the landscape look gardened, but the garden wilted. People had hooked big nozzles to wells and were doing emergency irrigation, but most of the land looked dry as Arizona. The controller at Kalamazoo said, "Yeah, my yard's almost dead." There were grass infields on the baseball diamonds in Kalamazoo, but they were brown.

From Benton Harbor to Chicago I flew the coast of Lake Michigan: from sand dunes and little houses with trails down to the beach, to buildings as tall as radio towers, all lining the unpredictable blue water. Would the lake rise as high as it was in the seventeenth century, and wash the buildings away? Or would it shrink, dried up by the greenhouse we have made of the planet, and leave the shoreline far from shore? The water wasn't giving many hints. In thirty years the lake had risen almost five feet, but in the previous year it had gone back down eighteen inches.

In the clearer air of the Midwest, the city crowded around Lake Michigan's southern bend looked larger than New York; from Gary to Chicago, and west to the horizon, streets shone as if polished, lying straight out to the horizon like the tracks of a harrow, raising their crop of stone.

"Numerous jets behind you," Chicago Approach said cheerfully after I passed the center of the city, where cars flowed and glittered like rivers of marbles rolling to the furnace. "They're descending out of ten thousand."

I looked back. No jets. They were invisible, like torpedoes. But the look of Chicago had changed in the changing light. Now the line of buildings stood in a black line against the pale blue lake. They looked like battlements, a ragged fortress. They held back the pagan tide. But which tide? Of unpredictable water, or of more buildings?

West out of Chicago, it was the same old story. There was Aurora, a town with an abundance of bridges over the Fox River, whose Chamber of Commerce sends out brochures with the slogan "Come Share the Wealth!" Aurora was barely outside the growing city, right outside the edge of Du Page County, whose population has grown from 300,000 in 1960 to 700,000 today. Du Page looked all city; Aurora was the first separate town outside the flood of buildings. I turned south there, and, feeling foreign in this expanse of structure, punched in home on the loran: 1,205 nautical miles, on a heading of 297 degrees. One long night's flight. I could abandon all intention and chase home, and get there at dawn. I'd ride the motorcycle up the long hill as the sun came over the mountains, and knock gently on the door.

"Hello, Debbie."

"Mike!"

No. I flew south. Past Joliet, the spread of the city ended abruptly. Suddenly there were no suburbs, no dribbles of exurban homes along the county roads. This was farm country. Everything was fields. The grid took over. The crops took over. Every half section there was a farmhouse, a barn, and a silo. Each field was individual; its own shape and color, but in the wide view everything was uniform, like a wool coat with imperfections in the fabric, but tidy, well-knit, pressed.

The fields were plowed and seeded right up to the back door. This land was valuable. Corn and soybeans; soybeans and corn. It looked as if people put up two-story houses so they'd save a few extra square feet for the crops. This was serious agriculture. So the kid wants a yard for his swings? A sandbox for his toy tractors? Forget it!

I crossed an airport called Headacres and touched down at Peoria in the early dusk. I turned off on the taxiway. There was a faint pop. The plane swerved to the right and came to a grinding stop.

"Uh, Six Zero One," the tower said, "do you need assistance?"

"Roger."

It was a flat tire. An ignominious distress. In an airplane you can't just get out and put on the spare. Six Zero One and I sat on the taxiway in the lurch until a mechanic came out with a tractor, put the deflated side up on a little trailer, and towed us in. But I took advantage of the repair time necessary, and arranged to have the lead reamed out of my exhaust valve guides while I visited Peoria, the headquarters of a group that remade the world: the Caterpillar Tractor Company.

"If you want to talk to somebody about the interaction between man and the environment," said Tom Biederbeck, a public affairs official for the company, "I guess you've come to the right place."

Back in the late twenties, when Lindbergh was the hero of the globe, and Frank Buchman was assembling his Force, the Caterpillar Tractor Company made its big move. Its specialized approach to the land had started in 1904 when Benjamin Holt put tracks on a tractor to keep it from sinking in the soft reclaimed land of the Sacramento Delta. The idea caught on; Holt's crawlers were used for such tasks as hauling supplies for the construction of the Los Angeles Aqueduct as early as 1908. But mostly they were made and used for farming.

Then, shortly after Holt's company merged with another to form the Caterpillar Tractor Company, the new company bought Russell Grader Manufacturing Company of Minneapolis, which specialized in road-building and maintenance equipment. That was the turning point.

"Our customers were taking these crawlers off of the farm and were pulling different types of construction tools with them," said Gilbert Nolde, public information manager for the company. "So we said, 'Gee! Here is a whole new field for us, and doesn't it make sense for us to get into the road machinery business?' "

Between Lindbergh's flight and mine, Caterpillar built the equipment that changed the landscape. In 1935 it presented the world with a machine with a powerful diesel engine and a big blade. The machine became known as the D8, the classic Cat. From then on, if you had looked down from your open-cockpit airplane on projects that involved moving dirt, you would have seen Cats working—on levees, canals, mines, logging roads, dams, highways, and, eventually, interstates. During the planning for the interstate system, Caterpillar practiced what might be called the Pork Barrel Shuffle, which is performed best today by the defense industry.

"We very actively promoted the interstate highway system," said Nolde, who joined Caterpillar in 1955 at about the time the first bills were passed to get the interstate system started. "We promoted it for a lot of reasons. Number one, we felt that it was needed. Number two, for straight old commercial Caterpillar reasons, we knew that when that system was built, we were going to be the prime suppliers of equipment to build it."

Caterpillar and its crawling machines became a symbol, first for the success of American salesmanship in the stories and movie about Alexander Botts, who represented the "Earthworm Tractor Company," and then as a clanking force of oppression in the movie of *The Grapes of Wrath*. Since then Cats have become superhuman. In the American imagination they rumble across the landscape, driverless, changing it. To anyone who has ever pioneered a road along a hillside with a Cat they're stronger than elephants and more versatile. To people who like the way the land looked before roads, they rise up in nightmares, chewing, clawing, ripping down trees, draining the Everglades, building dams that flood Eden, burying rose gardens and orphans' homes.

In the afternoon, while I waited for Six Zero One to be healed, Caterpillars rose up out of trees in a noisy yellow dream. It was the dance of tractors. A hundred people sat in grandstands at Caterpillar's Edwards Sales Demonstration Area, outside Peoria. The grandstands turned to face segments of the stage. The stage was an arena of yellow-brown earth. The great machines rose up from behind a dirt slope in a parade of blades, each one larger than the next: D5H LDP, D6H, D8N, D10N. They carved and pushed and leveled, while Don Stretch narrated:

"Notice the D5H LDP has got real wide tracks on it. This actually gets you down to three point eight PSIs ground pressure, which is less than anybody in this audience walking on the ground. So this machine works very well in soft underfoot conditions.

"The D6H has a logging and petroleum undercarriage on it, which is set back further for draw-bar-type work. Log skidding, pulling implements, pulling trucks, whatever. The D8N is our latest in technology in terms of how we get the power from the engine to the undercarriage to the ground. This machine has differential steer, which gives us live power to both tracks at all times." The D8N lowered its blade and carved a layer off the slope.

It was followed by a machine that could make one pass and turn your house to kindling: the D10N. The D10N could dig a dozen stock ponds before breakfast. You could play tennis on its blade. It was the second largest Cat.

Stretch sounded like a baseball coach at spring training showing off his new roster of kids and veterans to a group of sportswriters. It was all familiar: the Midwestern drawl, the easy familiarity with the equipment, the syntax. The D8N was Stretch's tough, wiry, veteran batting champ. The D10N was his promising new hulk, his future designated hitter.

"The D10N is a product that hasn't went into full production yet," Stretch said. "It will go into full production about October of this year. It will replace the D9L in our current family of track-type machines."

The stage rumbled and turned. It was an in-house crowd—accountants, salespeople—hauled up from the Caterpillar offices in Peoria in buses to learn something about the machines. They flinched when the stands stirred beneath them.

"Notice we've elevated the sprocket on this machine," Stretch said. "This machine is really designed for serviceability and rebuildability."

The D10N ripped a swath through the ground, casually pushed up a heap of dirt big enough to bury a logging truck, walked up over it, and rumbled away over the edge of the hill, as if going back to its lair. The grandstands turned again. A wheel loader variation called an integrated tool carrier carried a box across the field. It was a workmanlike leadoff hitter, and was followed by another tool carrier using a rotary broom, sweeping the plate.

"There's a lot of ways to move dirt," Stretch drawled, "to load trucks and that. Excavators is a good example of a machine in our lineup that really has true versatility in its range of applications that it does."

The grandstands turned. Two enormous excavators came into view on top of a slope. They leaned downhill with their buckets like kids reaching for nickels in a wishing well, scooped up heaps of dirt, and dropped them into a twenty-five-ton dump truck.

"The Nine Thirty-six has the new Caterpillar Penetration Bucket on it. Notice it's got a flat four flush-mounted, weld-on teeth. This bucket is designed to give you added versatility in stripping- and grading-type applications. It's an ideal machine to strip sod, asphalt, and do precise grading work with. Formerly we did not offer teeth on our loose-material bucket. We do today because oftentimes even though the material's loose it may be limestone, which kind of cements up, or it may be frozen in the wintertime."

Stretch does several demonstrations a week. The day before he had put on a show to a group from the People's Republic of China. "We get a lot of PRC people," he had said earlier. We had driven around the seven hundred acres of the sales area, which also included a three-quarter-acre indoor arena with thirty-foot ceilings. Most of the seven hundred acres was still wooded. "Notice," Stretch said, "We haven't tore up much of the area. We try to keep it looking nice." Last year the company found six stands built by trespassing hunters who came onto the land to shoot Caterpillar deer. Caterpillar Tractor Company likes the deer; it doesn't like being a part of people's nightmares of savaged forests. "There is a hell of a big difference between modern logging and land rape," Gilbert Nolde had said. "One has to do with the destruction of hills and mountains and the other has to do with selective logging and replanting and reforestation. We also make the machines that do the reforestation most adequately, so what the hell?"

At the arena, looking out at the excavators, Stretch now sounded like the coach giving tips on how to hit a slow curve.

"You know, material has to kind of cooperate with you a little bit. It's got to stand up fairly straight. It's got to support the machine on top, and you don't want too steep of an angle of repose or you can't reach the hauling unit. But where you have those conditions right, this is the most effective way to topload material."

The grandstand groaned again, and moved its people. A vast wheeled loader appeared, the 690-horsepower 922C. The 922C had a 13.5-cubic-yard bucket. You could swim laps in this bucket. This was Stretch's cleanup hitter.

"It is not uncommon for this bucket to average a forty-five-thousand-pound-bucket payload," he said. "Think about that a little bit. The average car on the marketplace today weighs about three thousand pounds. Which means we can get approximately the weight of fifteen automobiles in the bucket of that machine. That machine, when it's loading, will develop up to 147,000 pounds of breakout force."

The heavy hitter strolled over to the mountain left by the D10N, scooped it up, and dropped it in the back of an eighty-five-ton dump truck. It took three swings and the truck was full.

The dump truck backed up, drove up a ramp of dirt, and roared along the top.

"Of course a most important aspect of truck design is brakes," Stretch said. The dump truck brought its tonnage to a quick stop. The audience was impressed. Stretch and the five drivers who ran to and from the twenty-eight machines in the demonstration knew their cues.

"Let's say you're working in this mine," Stretch went on smugly, "and you've got three or four miles of ten percent downgrade to negotiate with highwall dropping off a thousand feet on each side. There are only two ways to stop that vehicle. One is with the brakes and one is when you hit the ground."

The show went on. A small excavator put down its outriggers, raised itself entirely off the ground, and tilted itself backward like the team's mascot sitting up to beg, so the audience could see its clean belly. The EL300 excavator that had been digging at the hillside now carried a 13,050-pound pipe over to the slope and lowered the pipe over the edge of the hill. It was the utility infielder.

"This is important to the underground utilities market," Stretch said, "which is a big part of the excavator market. Also, look at the length of stick in that machine. It's got a good digging envelope."

A water truck drove past, spraying from its eight-thousand-gallon tank, knocking the dust down on the dirt infield. There was no tarmac on the arena, but a machine designed to peel up roads, break up the material, and lay it back down as base for a new surface rolled out to demonstrate itself. It was followed by a far smaller machine that trotted up like a batboy and cut an edge around a manhole cover thrown on the dirt. "Used to have two guys with a jackhammer out there doing that," Stretch said.

A group of earth scrapers emerged. They were long low machines, like catchers, squatting over the ground.

"Here's kind of the ultimate system in terms of moving material with scrapers," Stretch said. "These are tandem. There's an engine on the front, and an engine on the rear. A very good machine for soft underfoot conditions, steep grades, designed for those really tough jobs."

Two 657E scrapers hooked themselves together and scraped about sixty cubic yards of dirt from the center of the arena. "What we have on that cutting edge working for us right now is fourteen hundred horsepower," Stretch said, "to force that cutting edge through the material and load the bowl. Watch the positive loading action as the material flows into the bowl of that second unit." The two scrapers disconnected, returned to the hole, laid the dirt back in it, and drove away. A compactor came out and stamped around on the dirt, like a third-base coach, with its knobby wheels. It was followed by two road graders that smoothed everything out. "Productivity," Stretch said, "is load times speed."

The whole arena, dug up, loaded, dumped, moved from one place to another, packed and smoothed, had been returned to the way it was when the fans had filed into the seats. But there was one more act in the show.

"Now," Stretch said. "How about the most recent step toward technology that Caterpillar has achieved? You've all seen it in the paper, you've read about it, but here it is!"

A small vehicle zipped across the arena. It was compact, streamlined, and ran light-footed on rubber tracks. It swept around the arena, then hooked itself up to an array of disks. It was Caterpillar's new advance: its step into the future. This swift little machine even had a name. Forget D8s, and D10Ns, and LL235Bs. This was called the Challenger 65. But it wasn't in the same sport. It didn't have anything to do with road construction, maintenance, or replacement. It didn't mash or move earth. It didn't shove or pull logs through woods. It didn't lift six-ton pipes. Among these burly ball players, it was a miler.

This little machine was Caterpillar's recognition that the times have changed. The company had been shaken into the realization. In the early 1980s, Caterpillar, faced with tougher overseas competition and changes in the patterns of development in the United States, began to get a sinking feeling like that experienced by a bulldozer operator who finds his machine disappearing into quicksand. In Peoria it had to cut its 36,000-person work force to 18,000, and suddenly it began making management changes and looking at new procedures like Just in Time parts delivery, which saves warehouse space and inventory cost. But the new little machine was also a symbol of the understanding that, in the United States, at least, the great earthworks are finished.

During my journey I had seen the last enormous Army Corps of Engineers project: the Tennessee-Tombigbee Waterway. I had seen Cat scrapers working on the last great water distribution system: the Central Arizona Project. The history of Caterpillar had spanned the days of major water diversion, from the building of the Los Angeles Aqueduct to the Arizona Project. The United States Department of the Interior had recently announced that its Bureau of Reclamation, which had hired a few thousand Cat skinners in its day, would change "from a construction company to a resource management organization," more involved in pollution control than the building of dams and ditches. I had seen interstate highways curving gracefully across the grid, across the mountains, linking the provinces with their song. But only a few highway stubs had pointed off into the woods where, slowly, roads would be driven to make the last connections. The grid ran almost intact from Ohio to the Pacific. The county roads were cut. The fields were leveled. The country had been remade.

Caterpillar's grandest job was done. There would always be gravel pits and mines, and there would be refinements and repairs. But the glory was over.

Now Caterpillar had come back around to where it started. Its hot new machine, the Challenger 65, was a farm tractor.

PART *8*

CHAPTER TWENTY-NINE

As I crossed Springfield, Illinois, eating Grandma's Old Time Molasses Cookies and drinking O-Jay pasteurized orange juice from machines at Peoria, the fleet of storms at last stood across my path.

Like battleship after white battleship, they lined the horizon seventy-five miles southwest, out past St. Louis. They moved slowly, relentlessly. The radio squawked with warnings. They generated a fluster of reports from the federal command center, the FAA. It was the same old story: "Attention all aircraft: Convective Sigmet 61 Charlie is current, for a line of severe thunderstorms from four-five miles southwest of St. Louis to three-zero miles northwest of Springfield, twenty miles wide, moving southeast at twenty knots. Tops to forty-five thousand. Possible tornadoes, hail to two inches, and winds to sixty knots." This time the line was right across my path.

One fleet stood in view, and another, named by another sigmet, lay waiting over the horizon. I could hear the salvos on the AM frequencies in the headset. But I would not turn back. I would not divert. Today I would address the hazard head-on. I had a promise to keep out there at the edge of the West.

Don Keyhoe's line made its longest zigzag here. The distance between Chicago and Milwaukee is less than one hundred air miles. But Keyhoe took Lindbergh from Chicago west to St. Louis, Kansas City, and Wichita, and then back to Milwaukee via Moline Airport at the Tri Cities on the Mississippi. The round trip was about eight hundred miles.

Keyhoe had no complaint from Lindbergh. Any extra time in the plane was great. I was glad about it too. A kid I'll call Huck, who had once lived with me as a son and who had traveled on my northernmost adventures, was now in Wichita. At last I'd get to see him, if he hadn't gone and disappeared again.

I crossed Springfield and climbed. I cast off the Earth. I rose into the other world of my life—the planet above the surface. The land grew faint and remote below. When I looked west toward the sun, there was only a white world of haze and clouds. Eleven thousand feet passed. I leveled off at 12,500. I would need altitude today.

At two miles down, the Central Lowland Province lay in dusty distance. It did not seem real. The grid, the fields, the interstate highways were just patterns stenciled in the air. Ahead, under bright white towers, the low air blackened. As I approached St. Louis, the approach controller reported battlegrounds all over town: bursts of heavy precipitation that showed on the radar screen. Ahead, piles of cumulus clouds blossomed to about fifteen thousand feet. Behind and above them were strange smooth clouds, lying flat on the air, with soft waves in them. And behind them . . . I looked up and up. Suddenly 12,500 feet seemed very low. Behind them in walls of looming darkness stood the big guns.

Water glittered below between the slow explosions of cloud. I looked straight down a five-thousand-foot white cliff and saw a familiar friend, the Mississippi. It was good to see again that moving, restless, wandering, unhurried, powerful river. The Mississippi was like a thread of character running through the personality of America. Sometimes the landscape seemed unpredictable, or corrupted, or cryptic, or capricious, but then I'd cross the Mississippi again, and remember how much of the land was influenced by that river. For all its dams and levees, the Mississippi was a dominant trait.

Before his flight, Lindbergh once dipped the wheels of a biplane in the Mississippi near St. Louis, racing a speedboat under bridges. The river was part of his blood too. He grinned. "I ran my tires through the wave tops," he said. "and flew so low over a launch that one of the crewmen jumped overboard." We looked down upon the big river with affection. "How it wound in and out through my life, like the seasons!" he said. "I grew up on its banks, swam through its rapids, portaged its headwaters with my father."

Now it wound right back out of our lives again. The white swirl of a sandbar stood out in a shaft of sun, then disappeared. Lightning crashed even in the VHF frequency. The smaller clouds stumbled out ahead of the rolling darkness. But the air was strangely undisturbed. I expected turmoil, the shudder of thunder against my aluminum skin, the heave and slap of the quaking air. But, eerily, I rode the very edges of the violence in utter calm.

But I could not go through. I would be blasted. I told Approach that I would divert, and he approved quickly, as if relieved at my good judgment. I slid away north, glancing down at houses packed together beside the flat roof of a shopping mall. Lambert Field, where Lindbergh had flown the mail, was hidden in the storm's shadow. I had been there just a few months before. I had stood under the replica of the *Spirit of St. Louis* that hung in the entrance to concourses C and D, along with a replica of the center-engine prop from a Ford Trimotor that made the first flight for TWA's forty-eight-hour rail-plane trip across the United States. The plane hung above the TWA flight information kiosk, with its tail in a forest of plants. It hung near the Ozark Country Shop, below the Lone Eagle Pub. Crowds bustled past. Beneath it a young woman handed out books on mysticism translated from Sanskrit; she liked to stop the boys in uniform. Only the old people looked up at the plane.

Outside, jets roared an endless, full-throated American chorus. Inside, the *Spirit*, with its stitched-on tires, its thin little rocker-box covers, its tiny window, its anemometer airspeed indicator with three cups on a pipe, looked like an artifact, hanging above heedless crowds on their way to go fly somewhere. It was like a dusty piece of bone and leather, tied together with stitches made of sinew; a relic left accidentally by our ancestors, showing the way we came.

Now, on this Missouri afternoon, I saw no more of the city Lindbergh returned to as if to a home in the summer of '27. It was guarded by hail and lightning. I swung north around it past a sentinel of the advancing storm, a narrow column of cloud that rose high out of the low haze, standing on the black tower of its shadow. Ahead, the battle line of the storm stood against me.

The windswept tops of the clouds hung overhead, blocking the sun. To the west another tower blossomed and burst like a rude, swift flower out of its side, like Mount St. Helens. An anvil stood north of it; could I sneak between that hammer and that iron? It did not look promising. A wall of cloud loomed bright white ahead. In this somber weather it was the only light thing, but its light was livid, white heat rising up into a deep, bruised, gray-blue sky.

But I had an ally. St. Louis Approach handed me off to Kansas City Center, who sat in his dim room before his radar screen and watched the slow drift of the enemy across the land. Few aircraft fought this afternoon's battle, but all were in the same situation: jet or Cardinal, none wished to tempt the wind and the hail inside those towers. So the formality of the radio communications dissolved into a friendly sharing of advice and counsel.

"Yes, sir, I got through at twenty-five thousand, one-five DME south of the Jacksonville VOR."

"Six Zero One, I'm showing that cell over St. Louis and another just south of Foristell. There's a line that starts about two-zero miles south of Pittsfield. You might be able to get through to the north."

"Roger. I'll go take a look."

It was dark ahead. I climbed. Thirteen thousand. Fourteen thousand. At 14,500 I turned toward the wall. Gaps a few miles wide showed between the frigates and the battleships of clouds. On the other side of the gaps were more clouds. It might be a corridor. It might be a trap. Slow as a moth, I flew inside.

It looked like a vast gray room. It looked like a cavern. I felt the tumble of white rocks across the entrance behind. Light rain sprayed the windshield. The day darkened. The clouds closed around. A light but urgent turbulence began, like the first breaks in the water at the top of a rapids. I heard another Cessna talking to Kansas City Center from somewhere behind me. Had anyone else out there made it through? I wasn't going to offer any advice. Give me a few more minutes, friend, and then I'll let you know.

⤖ We have grown too accustomed to the miracle. We have to go to strange places to see the world. A thunderstorm is the most dramatic thing on the planet, but we're blinded by familiarity to the power and beauty in our neighborhood lover's face. We have to go to Antarctica or Alaska to marvel. When Huck was sixteen years old he and I flew in Six Zero One down the Yukon River under low clouds, between walls of rock, and it was like that afternoon by St. Louis: marvelous and uncertain. But we thought it far more important than clouds.

Huck was very quiet that day. He never said much when he was scared. He was the bravest kid I have known. Back when he was eleven and I was twenty-six we used to hike out in the wonderful open sagebrush country of central Idaho, where we ran and laughed like coyote brothers and rolled rocks off remote cliffs. Huck's father was long gone. His mother wasn't awake enough to put the dog out. He grew up wild, ignorant, afraid. But he was smart, though he never knew it, and he was tough. One day in that high desert he tripped and fell straight into a cactus. His belly was stuck full of spines. He winced, and said nothing. No tear escaped his eyes. He sat down and I pulled them out, one by one. Later, when misfortune stuck him full of slings and arrows, and he needed a home, he came to live with Debbie and me. Then I saw silence come on him more than once, from much harder pain. I tried to relieve that, too, but I failed him.

Huck and I will always have Alaska to share. Alaska wasn't part of Lindbergh's landscape until a few years after his tour, but it will always be part of ours. Like other strange and almost mythical places that you visit, it became part of the background against which we evaluated everywhere else. We started at Sitka, down in the Coastal Mountain Province, which Alaska shares with Canada, and we got as far north as the Brooks Range before we sneaked out down the Yukon and then east down the Alaska Highway.

We flew into Sitka in an airliner, because the weather was too foggy in the southeast for Six Zero One. The plane descended through clouds and intermittent rain. From the windows of the jet the landscape appeared in glimpses, like flashes of a dream: a fjord, a lake, a crease of snow, a pewter sheen of water, the gray shapes of mountains swirling in the sky like headlands in fog and wind. We roared with reverse thrust beside a shimmer of fishing-boat masts and stopped near the end of the runway. Huck was pressed to the window. But he never liked to be thought eager. So he leaned back in the seat, paused, unlatched his seat belt, and said; "This is the first time I've ever been out of the United States."

We were a strange pair, as we traveled that state: me with my notebooks and political questions, doing research on national parks and wilderness, and Huck, who could barely read, watching a landscape that he had never imagined unfold. I was immersed in arguments over the value of untouched country to the American soul and the American economy; Huck was curious about the bears.

"You ever seen those bears?" he asked Cliff Lobaugh, a dentist from Juneau, one night as we camped in a small cabin on Admiralty Island.

"A few," Lobaugh said. "But you generally don't like to see them."

"Not even for the first time?" Huck was wistful.

"Maybe for the first time."

"I keep hoping I'll look out here and see one," Huck said.

"Possibly," Lobaugh answered. "There's a trail just back of the cabin. The bears walk in the same footprints year after year. On the ridges, even in the rock, you can almost see the steps." Huck listened, agog. But Lobaugh turned the edge of the conversation back to his message. "That alone is worth saving the whole island."

Later Huck and I flew far back into the interior, to a ghost town called McCarthy that was reviving on tourism, where the same debate was going on. Someone had used a D9 Cat to draw these words in one-hundred-foot letters in gravel near McCarthy: SIERRA CLUB GO TO HELL.

One of McCarthy's attractions was that the automobile bridge connecting it to a very bad road to Anchorage was washed out several years before. If you didn't fly to McCarthy, you had to drive to the end of that road, park, cross the roaring waters of Kennicott Creek on a hand-pulled cable tram, then walk the last quarter mile into town. This barrier, physically insignificant, was psychologically vast. Huck was fascinated.

"How far's the nearest town?" he asked Jerry Miller, who owned the McCarthy Lodge.

"You mean with a telephone? One hundred miles."

"Wow. They got electricity out here?"

"No."

"Wow."

Huck spent much of his time there helping pull people back and forth across the creek on the tram, enthralled by this primitive link and barrier. Then, later, we flew even farther back into the country, around a ridge from McCarthy and up the Chitistone Canyon, over the sign bulldozed in the gravel, and up to a tributary canyon called Glacier Creek. Where the creek entered the Chitistone there was a small airstrip, two thousand feet of reasonably even gravel. I dried my palms on my jeans and managed to set the plane down on the stony threshold, and as the engine stopped and the gyroscopes did their little song of sleep, I exulted: this was the most remote place I had ever been in my life. I told Huck, but he was not impressed. I realized he had been very quiet during the whole approach and landing. Remote? So? He was still thanking God he was alive.

All around us mountains boomed. It was a country of no compromise: everything was either flat or on end. The brown rock, interspersed with zones bearing copper, jutted up from streambeds that filled a mile of wide valley with naked gravel. These valley floors were flat, planed by the seasonal blade of the flood, and where the water roared every year nothing grew. It was just gravel and sand, and when we walked across it looking for the river in a braided maze of false channels, we found the day-old footprints of a small bear. Out there, away from the softening influence of the town, the land was crude, almost brutal in its power. It was all slabs and folds and uplifts. It was a country still being carved; the chips were on the floor.

We hiked on up the valley of Glacier Creek. An old road dipped through washes and out again and ended at a cut where the water had washed it away. Two cables, the remains of a passenger tram like McCarthy's, led across the racing stream. They crossed about seventy-five feet. Huck looked at me. He grinned. If he had not been there, I would have turned back.

"Okay," I said. "If you go first."

We walked across the stream on the wires, dipping and swaying with each step. Watching me cross, Huck laughed and laughed.

On the other side of Glacier Creek was a deserted homestead. The old cabin was surrounded by oil drums, old saw blades, a bundle of mining bits bound together by a thick wire, a full box of blasting caps, and a mound of old newspapers. The cabin was locked by a hinge nailed to the door and the frame. On the door was a letter from an attorney: "Notice is hereby given that the undersigned Martin Radovan on the Ninth day of October 1970, staked 70 lode mining claims known as the Binocular Group in Radovan Gulch . . ." Near it was a message scrawled on cardboard and tacked to the door. It was dated September 15, 1971: "Please do not break in my home. I will be Back in a few days. Martin F. Radovan."

Huck and I hiked farther up the creek. A road pioneered by a Cat lead up to another shed about two miles up a hillside. This was truly remote. This was farther back in than that airstrip. We were beyond the edge of the known world. We were free, sprung by distance out of the constraints of our pasts. Is that wilderness? The freedom to feel new?

Huck dug around in the heaps of mine tailings. I went into the shed. It had been someone's home. On a shelf were a pile of unopened soap bars and a stack of old magazines. The roof had been broken, and several years of snowfall had softened up the magazines. Their covers were unrecognizable white pulp. I picked one up. All its pages had been pasted together by the years of moisture, all but one. The magazine could open in the middle. I opened it.

A jolt ran through my blood. It was like a shock of electricity. My skin prickled. The magazine was *National Geographic*. I had opened on a feature story of Idaho. I had opened at the one photo in that magazine of the landscape of Custer County, Idaho, where Huck and I had lived. I sat there in that Alaskan hut, with the magazine open on my lap, looking at the bare brown hills of sagebrush where we had run and laughed when he was eleven. There was no escape.

⤙ We flew on, to the Eskimo town of Bethel, far west of Anchorage on the Kuskokwim River delta. In four hours of flight we traded a vertical landscape for a horizontal one. Coming down from the mountains, it seemed as if the open sky of Bethel curved way down around the side of the Earth. We could see the tops of clouds on the horizon. It was like flying from Colorado to Louisiana. The Kuskokwim rolled through the city like the Achafalaya, in lazy gray swirls, divided and joined by channels that curled between banks of rich, dark silt. But there were no trees. From the water a dense brush of willow and alder fenced off the land.

Huck didn't like this place. He was already getting into some of the patterns of living that would trouble him later. The adventure of the street was always his nemesis. In Anchorage he had prowled Fourth Avenue, where he could snuffle around the outsides of joints like the Booby Trap and the insides of pawn shops ("Hoc it to me"). It made him feel urban and tough, so when we got to Bethel he went looking for the same experience. But he came back and sat silently in a skiff while I took a tour of Bethel's myriad waterways. He had just encountered an Eskimo child who laughed at him, never having seen a redhead before.

In Bethel people bought pizza to go with their sun-dried salmon. We rode around in the skiff with Showalter Smith, an Eskimo who had been away to college. On the shoreline were rows of split salmon hung to dry; they were a deep red, and the meat was sliced repeatedly across the fish to speed drying, so the wide strips looked ragged. Huck recovered from his bad mood to be fascinated again. At first these racks of fish looked odd to us, as if we had been driving across Iowa and had suddenly passed a farmhouse with several dozen beef halves hanging from the eaves. But he got used to the sight: the racks of salmon were everywhere, thousands of pounds of red meat, absorbing the sun, perspiring moisture, shrinking, toughening, ripening for winter. It was an ancient way of living. But partway through our tour, Smith had to stop the boat, lift the engine, and disentangle a red and white checked plastic bread wrapper from the prop.

We stopped at a fish camp. The people there were angling for whitefish from the shore with rod and line. We clambered up a bank and there was a middle-aged woman carrying a ladle made of a number ten can nailed to a stick. Smith spoke to her in Yupik and they laughed. "I was telling her that I'd brought along a couple of *gussuks* to take pictures of her in the steam bath." Behind the nearest canvas building was a low structure roofed of tin, with a stovepipe—the steam bath; you would have to sit low to get in it.

"I took three, four steam baths when I got back from college," Smith said, "but I got too used to the All-American shower. I go take a shower at the National Guard Armory now."

In a building a woman was eating fish. They were winter pike, caught through the ice and smoked. She ate them as if they were corn on the cob or chicken legs. In front of her was a Wesson Oil jar half full of seal oil. The woman chewed the pike meat off the curled skin. A transistor radio played John Denver singing "I Wanna Live." There were radios all over Bethel, and almost every house had a television. Commentator Paul Harvey was on the radio at 9 A.M. and noon. "Paul Harvey is very good," one resident told me. "This community is very Paul Harvey-oriented."

There was no escape. Huck looked around curiously, with longing. Young white people not unlike him were moving into the wilderness upstream on the Kuskokwim, moving in to squat, often illegally, on native or federal ground in search of new ways of life. It was like subways passing in the dark. As the natives rumbled along, reluctantly, toward the capitalist system, the kids were driving back, demanding simplicity of themselves and subsistence from the land.

"They come in with added tools and knowledge," said another Eskimo, who was earning his Ph.D. at Stanford University. "They put extreme competition on the limited resources. They say they want a simpler way of life, that's why they're coming. But they're adding to the complexity."

To the people of the United States, Alaska has been the landscape of hope. Since the grid's net of order closed over the lower forty-eight states, Alaska has been The Territories. It was the place you could light out for. Huck was smart, but ignorant, restless, tough, lonely, in constant trouble with the Aunt Pollys of the world. He was about due to light out. Would Alaska give him enough hope, and a place to grow?

We flew north from Bethel. Huck slept, head against hand against window. I felt immensely alone. The flatness of western Alaska rolled before us. There was one village of fifty eskimos thirty-five miles east of Bethel. We flew across huge untraveled plains that were swirled like finger paintings by oxbow lakes, oxbow muskegs, oxbow meadows. Black spruce mingled with alder and balsam poplar in shadings of light and dark like cloud shadows. "Numerous small lakes," the chart said, a message of despair from the cartographer.

Then we reached the Yukon: two thousand miles of river. From the canyons of the Canadian territory that bears its name, across the lake-spangled flats of the north, where the Porcupine River joins it in a thousand meanders, down through the bluffs at Rampart, past the hills at Tanana, curving south at Koyukuk, rolling between marsh and sand into the delta country north of Bethel, turning north at last and fanning out at Alakanuk, Emangak, and Kotlik into that perfect gush of silt and channel that, from the air, makes a delta look so much like a cross section of a brain, the Yukon is power.

As I crossed it, I thought of the others. The Colorado, the Mississippi, the Missouri, the Columbia. The creek that runs in my backyard flows into the Columbia. But the Columbia is plugged up like an old man; it walks down concrete stairs to a striped umbrella by the sea; nurses attend it, stifle its every whim, dissipate its restlessness on a treadmill to sell its strength, coax it into gentle death. The Colorado is half trapped, living in bursts between lakes, like a prisoner playing angry football in the yard, busting knees. The Missouri stops at its first dam barely forty miles downstream from its start. The Mississippi is trained to domestic tricks like a lion; dangerous but caged, for now. Only the Yukon is alive, robust, free.

After a fuel stop in Galena, a place to which our navigation radio was drawn by the sound of a baseball game between the Chicago White Sox and the California Angels, we continued north, and abandoned the Yukon until our last flight down through the gorge at Rampart. We landed at Bettles, north of the Arctic Circle, and chartered a float plane to take us deep into the Brooks Range, America's most remote wilderness, to a place called Wild Lake. I was drawn there by a long correspondence, and Huck just came along because he couldn't stay in Bettles. But Wild Lake became the place he would remember best.

The letters were from a man named Fred Meader and, later, from his wife, Elaine. I had met them in Los Angeles years before where they had been showing a film they had made about their life in the Arctic. Wilderness living, they told groups of students in auditoriums and classrooms, was the answer to the nihilism of civilization. "The only life worth living is the necessary life," Fred said. "The cost of living in civilization is too high. Continual personal involvement with the necessities of life—food, shelter, fuel, and clothing—is still the only way in which we maintain lasting meaning in life." On the bottom of Meader's stationery was printed the familiar quotation from Thoreau: "In Wildness Is the Preservation of the World." Sometimes Fred crossed out the middle words with a slash of a pen, so the sentence more clearly expressed the writer's belief: "In Wildness *Is* the World."

To me, living at the time in Los Angeles, his words were instantly appealing, so I got to know the Meaders. I corresponded with them, saw them again when they came down to refine their film—and each year told them that next summer I would come up to Alaska to see them.

As the float plane rumbled north and I was, for once, just a passenger, I thought about Fred's words the last time I saw him, in a house near San Francisco: "There is no hope for man except that those few individuals go back and live that way of life so that when the catastrophe comes we may have some of that ancient wisdom." Before it's too late! Before it's too late! The calamity comes! Now Huck and I at last had reached the Brooks Range, to see the place where Fred had lived, and to talk to Elaine. But it was too late for Fred. The technology of the civilization he had rejected had killed him.

Fred Meader did not come to his perspective by way of wilderness philosophers like Joseph Wood Krutch, David Brower, or Aldo Leopold. His was a raw journey, through a more fundamental darkness. "We realize that urban man, with his messy instincts and his archaic beliefs of freedom, independence, self-reliance, dignity of the individual . . . is essentially an anachronism," he wrote.

Meader, son of an A&P manager in upstate New York, turned to philosophy in college after his mother got cancer. It did not soothe him. Finally, after searching in vain for a place "to find a niche in this domestic culture," Meader wound up, at the age of thirty, with Elaine and their baby boy, Dion, in the Brooks Range, on a homestead at the peak of the long lake. For five years Meader, Elaine, and their son, who was three when they moved there, nestled in isolation. But somehow, even in the wilderness, Fred Meader's restlessness was not slaked. He finally could not keep hidden the answer he had found. He had to show it to the civilization he spurned.

"The most influential thinker in my life has been Friedrich Nietzsche," he wrote once. "The writings of C. G. Jung and Rainer Maria Rilke have also been very important in building my philosophy, but none of these men have analyzed the domestication-civilization-slavery-wild complex. That seems to be my task."

The float plane made a long scratch in the polished blue of the lake, and left us on the shore. Huck was stunned. The lake was a long pool in a glacial valley. Green slopes rose to rock on either side. At the lake's head was the Meaders' house, a log house a hundred yards up from the shore. There were five people there: Kip Kermoian and Suzi Lozo, friends of the Meaders who lived a mile across the lake and were both bright with some joy in each other that was so clear and unencumbered it must have been new; Elaine's two children, Heather, four, and Dawn, one; and their mother.

Elaine was thinner than I remembered. She was forty-four now. But her brown hair was just the same, wispy and slightly wild, her voice was as light as down, and her eyes were pale blue, intelligently dazzled, as if everything she saw was aflame. On the walls was all that was left of her men: a portrait of Dion, who drowned in this lake when he was seventeen, and a photo of Fred taken an hour before he was killed in Bettles getting out of an airplane. He had walked into the prop.

Huck took to the water in Elaine's canoe. She and I sat on the beach, talking. We sat on a bleached stick of driftwood. Dawn played in the sand. The child was naked, and the coarse pale grains stuck to her bottom. Her blond hair was in straggly curls, and her skin was lumped here and there by mosquito bites. Elaine waved in the air around her daughter to keep the bugs away.

"It's very difficult to talk about these things," she said slowly. "I think of the Earth as not only an organism, but that it has a total spirit as an organism. It just can't take it anymore; it's too sick. Now we have this huge lesson we must learn—we just can't exist by ourselves anywhere—we've got to find a way the Earth can become healthy or we're going to disappear."

All of the Meaders' life at the lake in the Brooks Range was spent trying to learn that huge lesson. Their attempts, interrupted by disappointment and tragedy, never ended. One summer I had received a series of letters, describing one such attempt. Four people in their early twenties had moved to the lake to share the wild way of life the

Meaders had by now refined to the point of eating almost no domesticated foods:

June 28, from Fred:

"These young people are as committed to the ideal of elemental living as any young person can be today, but they have many doubts and fears. . . . Right now they are all having a hard time with the exclusive meat-fat diet, but good things are happening, too. . . . You should realize you will not find an idyllic primitive life here."

July 16, from Fred:

"The all-meat diet has been too difficult for everyone except Elaine and myself and they have ordered some civilized food. . . . Other problems have arisen and it is doubtful if all or any of the people who joined us will winter over."

August 1, from Elaine:

"Fred is on the mountain, sheep hunting—indefinitely. . . . It has been an unprecedented summer. What started as positive and full of promise soon broke down into depression. The commitment was too great for the others. . . . These people came with some hope and a big dream that living with the country would be their 'answer.' The dream broke with the reality, and they felt this extreme could not be their answer. . . . So yesterday, on a sudden decision, three of the people left. . . .

"We understand so much better the extreme difficulties of this kind of choice, all the cultural imprinting we must move counter to, and how long it must take to grow into a relationship with the land that is *rooted* in value. Before these new values are rooted in us, we are in a no-man's-land of depression and emptiness. The instincts and feelings that have brought us here are too weak to overcome the homesickness."

Sitting on the shore, I watched Huck out in the canoe. He stood in it like a heron, perfectly reflected. Until we got here he was a spectator in Alaska, interested in Admiralty, charmed at McCarthy, eyeing trouble in Anchorage, offended by Bethel. Here he had slipped into this wild living like a frog into a pond. It was the only place more interesting to him than the street. He spent patient hours in the canoe, hunting northern pike in the shallow water with a bow and arrow or paddling across the bay to talk to Kip, who had shown him how to set a rabbit snare and how to employ maggots to clean the skull of a moose.

"Obviously, most people do not believe it is meaningful to live in a wilderness environment," Fred Meader once wrote. "Even the so-called 'wilderness lovers' would have us all think of the wilderness as a museum. But if a man's relationship to the wilderness is one of 'a visitor who does not remain,' then his relationship is one of sentimentality rather than love, for love cannot exist without perfect intimacy."

The beach was quiet. The ripple waves that broke on the sand made just the sound of breathing. There were small clouds over the mountains to the south. In the tops of the spruce trees white gulls rested, like flame on candles. An Arctic tern slipped past, a slender, whetted bird, on the way to a nest in the reeds. Dawn was at peace now, nursing. There was no other sound. There was no American Song.

"In the early years when I came up here I was really down, really despairing," Elaine said softly. "After living up here a few years and discovering the joy in very simple things, I knew that was the soul of things, that kind of joy."

Far out in the lake, there was the sound of rhythmical splashing. Loons called to each other. One sounded like a cry, the other like a long wail. The splashing ended; they were airborne. Then three of them assembled in the distance and flew across us, long pale bodies with long necks, stretching forward as if passionately hungry for the rush of air, for the next moment of life, for the glory. With each swift beat of wings each bird chimed gently, like something light and silver. The strange, ethereal sound sailed across us and disappeared.

"I can go away now," Elaine said. Her voice was not much louder than the waves. "I don't have to be here all the time to be home. It seems to be inside me now."

We sat on the beach in the silence. Huck stood in the canoe far offshore with his arrow poised, looking down for the pike. The cool air was bright around him. He had no philosophy to drive him, no cause to chase. But he stood there in the glory, calm for a rare moment in his troubled life, calm and quiet and safe.

Then, slowly, subtly, the sound of an engine stole into our lives. It hummed, and then it rumbled. It echoed in the valley, rolling north slowly, as relentless as the tide. It was the sound of the plane coming to get us.

CHAPTER THIRTY

West of St. Louis, in the late afternoon, lightning blasted in my headphones. The walls of the cavern of clouds pressed closer. I glanced down. In the depths, two roads met in a right-angle corner by a bulldozed stock pond. But the sky was so compelling, so dramatic, so powerful, that the land seemed only as important as the floor of the sea. A piece of cloud far below drifted across the scene.

But there was light to the right. I turned, and saw a lower layer of scattered clouds ahead, with sun on it. I would find my glory out there, like the rainbow's promise.

Farther right, tower after tower rose in a line. But I was behind them now.

Slowly the fleet moved on east, while I swam clear, westbound, saluting the enemy. Ahead was blue sky. I was through.

At nine that night I straightened the last kink in the westbound route at Chanute, Kansas, where three ballparks were lighted for softball and Little League. Suddenly, as I looked down on those families and their fun, I thought, I'll bet Huck's not there. He'll be out somewhere, at some bar, or drunk, or out in the street, and I won't find him. He may have left Wichita.

Forty miles northwest, lightning reddened by haze rippled through another line of storms that converged on my route. But I raced the squall line, and slipped into Wichita between it and another cloud that rattled with lightning to the south.

I got there with five minutes to spare. As I was taxiing to park, the wind shifted to the north. Suddenly it was blowing twenty-five knots, gusting to thirty-five. I got out the motorcycle and put on my yellow rain suit. It flapped against me. I got on the little machine and headed for Huck's house five miles away as the plane shook and the first drops hit the aluminum.

⤚ I have often wished I could have put whatever it was he had found at Wild Lake into Huck for good. When I got to thinking about our time there, I realized that it was one of the few times I had ever seen Huck quiet for a long period when he wasn't in pain.

"I felt relaxed," Huck told me much later. "You couldn't get into no trouble there—there wasn't hardly any *way* for you to get in trouble. The people up there don't like cars, or big buildings. They don't have no electricity. They like to see animals; they like to be by themselves, so they can think a lot better. You was free there. When I get to be eighteen, I'm going back to live."

Huck never went back. I did not have what he needed when he was my foster son, and he left us after six months. He spent the rest of his youth in institutions. He was not a criminal, but nobody knew what to do with a wild boy. Now he was in Wichita. He checked in with us every six months or more. Sometimes he had work. Sometimes he needed money. Sometimes he was in trouble with the law. Sometimes he vanished for a year or more. But he never got back to Alaska.

Just as well. The glory he had seen there didn't exist any more. The grid had taken over even Alaska. You couldn't see much of it there, but the lines had been drawn. The most magnificent countryside was national park or official wilderness, where man was legal only as a visitor. It was sad but necessary: by now all the streams that pour into the Yukon have their homesteaders' cabins. Some of the cabins are legal. Some are concealed. People who live up those rivers aren't necessarily friendly. They wish to be alone. They carry arms. One of them went berserk in McCarthy in 1983 and killed six people. There is no escape.

So I rode down through the warm air of the poised storm, while the lightning flashed on the horizon all around. I rode down Maple Street past the empty stores, on dry pavement and then on wet in drizzle, with the smell of dust in the air, thinking of Huck's tiny, drab rental house in the back of another house, with its curtains made of sheets and the stereo and TV, and how the last time I was here we had walked all over Wichita the way we had once walked all over the sagebrush hills of Idaho together. I wondered if he would be scared when I knocked on the door in my yellow suit; would he peer out the curtain and think, Cops! Or could I make him hear the *me* in my voice, and my wish to see him?

I turned down his street, and found that the house seemed too close. Suddenly I was dreading it. Is it unkind to wish to avoid the pain of seeing the damage life has done to someone you love? I stopped at the house and I went around back, and there was a light in a window.

I knocked. No answer.

I called, "Huck! It's Mike."

No answer.

I did the same again. I went around to the window with the light and looked under the blind. Cups. A dish. It was the kitchen.

"Huck!" I shouted. Again I went around to the back. All the places were filled in the carport. The carport looked as if you could lean against one of the posts and bring it down. Huck's place had a van in it. The van didn't have a side door. The garage smelled of beer.

I did not stay there long. I left a note under the door: "I'm at the airport. I'll be here in the morning." And I went back to the airplane. It had drizzled, but the rain had not yet come.

When life gets intense we look to the weather for omens and clues. So I sat a long time in the plane with the door open and waited for what the sky would bring. The storms approached. Lightning surrounded the plane and closed in. It flashed and flickered, and drew close. Tornadoes, hail, wind gusts to sixty-five knots. It would blow and roar and maybe kill.

But it spent all its power and haste on the farms and the empty fields. By midnight the lightning was almost gone, and the wind hardly shook the plane. The rain came at last, but without clamor, to ring softly on the metal and bring sleep.

I awoke to wind rocking the plane again. I looked outside. The airport lawn was tossed by the wind. Sunlight glittered from wind-blown puddles on the ramp. It was one of those hard-light, tough-wind summer days of the plains. I got up, and remembered the flight through the night, with the towers of blackness rising all around, flickering with violence. I remembered sliding down through that avenue of wildness to the runway, five minutes before the wind hit the airport. I grinned, knowing this is the way I have always wanted to live; that close to the storm of the world. Then I remembered Huck.

I thought I'd spend a couple of days in Wichita with him. But by ten in the morning I was back in the sky, fighting the wind north, through bitterly clear air, running straight along a section line that reached out to the sharp edge of the horizon like a track, and took me away from Wichita.

Yes. I'd seen him. But I wished that I had not. In the hard brightness of the early morning I had ridden back down that long street and knocked again.

A shuffle of footsteps. A creak. The door rose and was set aside. It wasn't on its hinges.

He was thin. He just had his old jeans on, bell bottoms with the denim worn through at the heels. He looked tired. His red hair was magnificent. It hung in curls over his bare shoulders. Its beauty mocked his weary face. He had a mustache. He looked handsome but weathered. We embraced. He was silent. He let me in. A motorcycle stood in the living room, in various pieces.

"Huck!" I said. "It's good to see you!"

He gave me a wisp of the old smile.

"I'm supposed to be at work," he said at last.

"Where were you last night?"

"In jail."

"Why?"

"Driving my car without tags."

There were pictures of naked women on the walls, and clothes on the floor. A kid's room. No smell of alcohol inside. It smelled more like motor oil. The motorcycle was like a third person standing there.

Conversation came hard. I told him what I was doing. He listened halfheartedly. I thought about Alaska. I thought about days when he lived with us in Idaho, and how we laughed when we were washing dishes after dinner. The kid was smart; he was sharp, kind, and had a good sense of humor, but I'm the only one who saw those things. Everyone else saw him as sullen, angry, silent. He was ignorant; he had never been civilized. He had slipped through all the cracks, and when I had put out my hand to catch him I hadn't the wit or the understanding or the stamina to hang on.

"I'm stupid," he said suddenly.

"No."

"Look at how stupid I am. I was robbed last week. I brought this girl home and she took all my money. Then three guys rolled me and took my whole wallet. See how stupid I am?"

"No. You've never been stupid." But he was wheedling at me with his story. He wanted money.

"What did that preacher say to you?" Six months earlier he had called me, drunk and in despair, and I'd called around Wichita for counselors and turned up a minister who said he'd be willing to help. Huck had gone to see him weeks later.

"He said he couldn't do anything for me."

"What about drinking and drugs?"

"Yeah. I'm drinking again. I'm not doing no drugs."

Now I said things I'd said before. That thousands of people had said to him before. The preacher had said it to him before.

"Huck, you've got to take hold of yourself. Nobody can do it for you anymore. You're in a rut, and you've got to get out. You're the only one who can do it."

"I can't, Mike," he said. It was a whine.

He had lain back down on his couch. Now he sat back up again.

"See this?"

He held out his wrist. A new scar across it like a welt from a whip.

"Went right to the bone," he said. He looked at me, half proud. I didn't say anything.

He pulled aside his mustache.

"And here, on my mouth," he said. His familiar old smile came again, but it was disfigured by the anger of the knife, now forever recorded in his flesh.

He lay back down.

The scars did it. In the back of my mind was the old rule offered those who wish to intervene in the lives of loved ones under the influence of chemicals, that the alcoholic has to hit bottom before he seeks help. Interveners are taught to create a false bottom. I thought, in the back of my mind, to give him that shaking. But looking back on it, I think that was just an excuse for me at last to vent my despair.

It was the cuts that did it. I could not bear to see him carved away.

I stood up, half blind.

"Huck, I'm leaving."

"Why?" It was almost a cry.

"I can't stand it. I can't stand it. I don't want to be around when somebody kills you."

I got up to leave. It was hard to see. "Give me a hug, Huck."

He didn't get up from the couch, where he was lying on his back. He just put up his arms. I leaned over and put my arms around him, my head in his long hair. He was silent. I hugged him for a long time, feeling his body slight and cool, and feeling that I could lift him and carry him away, as if the weight of life had already gone and I was the one asked to carry what remained of him to the grave.

So I fled, and by ten-thirty I was forty miles north, and the vast regimented kaleidoscope of the American Midwest spread out ahead of me. When I had told him what I was doing, he had said, seriously, "Take me with you." He, too, wished to recapture those days of traveling in the clean far spaces of Alaska, where there were no people, and nothing but the fish and the bears, and no way to get into trouble. But I told him no. I couldn't give him that ticket anymore. It didn't exist.

So I flew north. Vanity of vanities! All is vanity. Who are you in this life if you cannot give hope to the brother of your heart? I went on looking at the landscape—the straight lines, the stock ponds, the green and brown—but I thought, What did the American landscape matter to him?

Then I thought, Everything. He belonged out there beyond the edge of the grid where they didn't have electricity. He belonged somewhere where it mattered if you could learn how to clean the skull of a moose, where you could save yourself with a rabbit snare, where you could live a necessary life. He belonged where you could run and laugh like a coyote, where you could stand in silence and think better. But the grid was everywhere. The Song was everywhere. America was all kenneled up. There were no more territories.

I was okay. I was tamed enough. I had my airplane. I knew how to coexist with the rule of order. I had the sky. But in all this world there was no glory for my wild American boy, Huckleberry Finn.

PART *9*

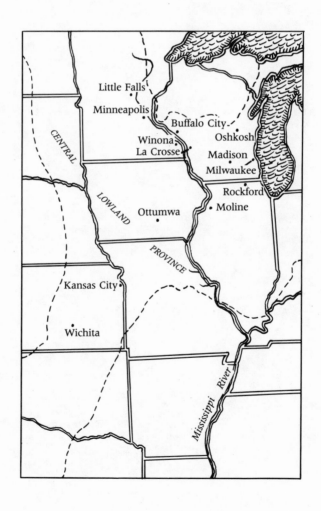

CHAPTER THIRTY-ONE

Somewhere between Kansas and Wisconsin stood a mountain range. It was tall and snow-covered. I would need altitude and judgment and luck. Around it were deadly winds and shifting cornices. It hung there in the back of my mind, blue slopes and white ridges, as I flew back east and counted off Lindbergh's towns without seeing them: Junction City, Fort Riley and Fort Leavenworth, Kansas; St. Joseph, Missouri.

I knew there was no mountain range, but there it was, a worry. I thought about downdrafts. I thought about the rough air in the lee of the ridges. I flew on and on over flat ground. In the loneliness of leaving Wichita, I could not rid myself of the illusion of a cliff ahead.

It took me half the day to persuade myself that the mountain range that troubled me had, literally, evaporated. It was the line of thunderstorms I had crossed going west. Except in my mind, that whole huge range of danger, which held threats as final as any cliff of stone, was gone. Just as strangely and magically as it had grown up ahead of me, with those ridges and passes and caves moving and blossoming all around, now it had disappeared as strangely, like a Precambrian mountain range that had been ground into loess overnight.

Late that day I flew into Oshkosh, Wisconsin, after a sunny day over flat, flat land. But an odd thing happened as I descended. The sun was sinking, and as it came down to rest its edge on the horizon, the flat land took on a roll. Shadows appeared in long pools, and suddenly hills ran across the landscape. They were long, low, even, smooth swells. They were the tracks of glaciers, old furrows smoothed by the centuries. The roll in the grid went on only a few minutes, like the passing of a ship's wake, then the sun sank into the haze and once more the land was ironed.

I parked under a big amber light, which shone like a hazy sun into the plane all night. DC-3 airplanes owned by Basler Flight Services of Oshkosh stood on the tarmac all around me. Even parked, a DC-3 looks poised, like a football player in the stance: ass down, head up, waiting for the call to glory.

I was back in a countryside of mechanical nostalgia and sporting metaphor. This was my sanctuary from sadness: a noble old machine. I'd left Caterpillar Tractor Company, to go see Huck; I'd come back to another piece of equipment to ease the loss. I was no Cat skinner: tractors were strange to me. But the Douglas was more familiar than church. Like the Cat, the DC-3 had also transformed the way we think about Earth. When the television program *NOVA* did a documentary on the DC-3, it called it "The Airplane That Changed the World."

Late at night, in the amber shine of the big lamps, I walked around the airplanes. The DC-3 is boxy and graceful, all at once: a long smooth taper of fuselage after from the snub nose; the authoritative tail; the two big main tires and a hefty tail wheel; muscular engine nacelles, each with a round open ring of cowl flaps, like a skirt; the long, tapered wing, slanting upward at almost a seven-degree dihedral; the ailerons and empennage skinned not with aluminum, but with fabric, drawn tight as a drum. In the red-gold light, the thousands of round-headed rivets on the wing looked like drops of dew.

Back in 1935, the year that Charles Lindbergh took his family to live in Great Britain after the kidnapping of his child, about the time Phil Timm turned from building his Model T to designing and putting together this own plane in high school workshop, nobody knew what a working aircraft ought to look like. People thought maybe it should hang down from a big flat wing. They thought maybe it should have an engine on each wing and one on the nose. The specs that TWA gave Douglas that eventually led to the DC-3 demanded three engines. But in December 1935, the same year that Caterpillar introduced the D8 and showed us what a bulldozer ought to look like, Douglas Aircraft Company, of Santa Monica, California, rolled out the DC-3, and then everybody knew.

After all these years, the DC-3 is still the essence of a useful aircraft. Dakota, DC-3, C-47, Gooney Bird, whatever it is called, there is nothing like it. A year before my journey, when I was visiting Idaho, a U.S. Forest Service pilot walked out from under that big, rivet-studded wing where he had been draining fuel and said, "The only replacement for the DC-3 is another DC-3."

"I have it on good authority," Ken Lemon said, listening critically to the clatter of the two old engines, "that when Christ comes back, He is coming in a DC-3. He can land anywhere, and He knows He will get there too."

A little while later, as the big old plane he was flying rumbled above the Lowland Province, he said something else:

"You," he said, pointing abruptly at where I sat in the jump seat behind the pilots, "are going to fly us back."

It was a cargo run for auto parts out of Oshkosh. This was the era, as Caterpillar Tractor Company had learned, of Just in Time parts delivery, and now Ford needed five thousand pounds of parts in Kansas City before sundown. I had gone along for the ride chasing an old glory: to fly the world's first and greatest working airplane.

This was a dream I shared with millions. You don't have to be a trained aviator to long to fly a DC-3. The thought has run through generations. *Tapocketa, pocketa, pocketa.* "To hell with the ice, Junior. We're going through." I fly small single-engine planes; for me to dream of flying a DC-3 was like a model-train driver wanting to be engineer on the Orient Express. But now, since Lemon was a certified instructor, it was going to happen.

Lemon poured a cup of coffee out of a thermos labeled "Radioactive: Handle Carefully." He put the coffee up on the top of the instrument panel, in the corner made by the DC-3's two flat windscreens. The coffee vibrated gently, in rings. Lemon's copilot, Scott McCulla, was flying the plane.

The two of them were a likely pair. They fit the world through which DC-3s fly today: In their faded glory, the old planes clunk here and there around the world, flying fish in Alaska, weapons in Central America, car parts in the United States. Lemon and McCulla reminded me of two men I had met in El Paso. They had been flying north from Chihuahua, Mexico, with a load of seat covers for Chrysler: one was a veteran, one a kid.

Lemon was forty-four, large, balding, deliberate. He talked steadily in the headphones as we traveled. McCulla was twenty. He had a fair face, tousled fair hair, fair stubble. He wore a T-shirt printed "Old Rhinebeck Aerodrome." His father was an airline pilot. McCulla had gone directly from flying tiny Cessna 150s into the DC-3 copilot's seat. "You always see these airplanes in movies," he said.

"Scott is the right age for this," Lemon said. "He's the age of the guys who flew the C-47 in World War II. Me, I'm way too old. I should have progressed on to something else way before now." McCulla had been flying for two years. He had a thousand hours of flight time, total. Lemon had thousands more.

"I've been flying for a living for almost nineteen years," Lemon said. "I've finally gotten up to the heavy iron." He paused to sip carefully from the coffee cup. The air was bumpy. The land was bumpy. It was the Driftless Section of the Central Lowland, between Madison and Minneapolis. This was higher, rolling country where the glaciers' vast blade of ice hadn't leveled the land. The hills and valleys were covered with contour-plowed fields, white silos, and black-and-white cows. We flew at six thousand feet, down there among the humps of land and air. *Clunk, bang, thump.* It was as if we were in a two-mile-long truck, bumping along over a corrugated landscape. It was great. Lemon thought so too.

"You can either have fun until you're sixty years old," Lemon said, "and then not have any fun when you retire because you don't have any money, or you can have a boring job until you're sixty and then have fun because you have a lot of money." His choice was obvious. "No one gets rich doing this kind of flying," he said, "except the man that owns the airplane."

The radio squawked. Lemon checked in with Minneapolis Approach while McCulla flew the plane. "I have to admit," he said, "when I wake up in the morning I smile because I get to go to work."

The old plane rumbled slowly northwest through a howling head-wind. It would take forever to get to Minneapolis. But all that time would go in the pilots' logs. "This is how we get paid," Lemon said.

The plane's registration number was N97BF—November Niner Seven Bravo Foxtrot. It was a converted military C-47 that Basler Flight Services had bought from the French Air Force. It still had a dome on top for the navigator to get sun sights. It still had plastic grommets in the passenger windows for troops to stick their rifles through and fire at the enemy. "You had to train the troops not to shoot the airplane," Warren Basler, the head of the company, had said earlier. The plane was powered by two Pratt & Whitney R-1830 radial engines rated at 1,200 takeoff horsepower each. Now, over western Wisconsin, the turbulent air slugged the plane around, but the old engines rumbled reassuringly on.

At least I thought the rumble was reassuring. Lemon and McCulla kept looking out their windows at the engine nacelles and observing with apparent skepticism, "My side's still dry." They were looking for the gush of oil that might give warning of engine failure.

DC-3 pilots once had a slogan for their faith in these engines: "Trust in God and Pratt & Whitney." But all those DC-3 engines are ancient now, and have been rebuilt again and again. The plane itself goes on and on, but the engines are getting tired. There are no new cases. "The only thing that will stop the DC-3 from flying is the cases," the chief mechanic for Provincetown-Boston Airlines, the only company that flies scheduled passenger service in DC-3s, had told me when I dropped into his shop in Florida. Shops that repair them are becoming fewer.

"They show you an engine like this in school," another mechanic once told me. "They tell you—'This is a radial engine. You aren't going to see any of them.' " And some of the shops aren't much good. For a while the U.S. Forest Service in Utah and Idaho averaged only four hundred hours between failures.

Once, when one of the Forest Service DC-3s was flying over that magnificent Idaho wilderness, two of those engines quit at about the same time. One of them fell off the airplane. A friend of mine was copilot on that trip. I used to ski with him. He skied with utter grace. You never would have known that one of his legs was artificial.

A photographer hiking in the woods that day took an amazing photo: It showed the engine falling out of the sky like a meteor, and the unmistakable silhouette of the DC-3 in the distance, still level and aloft. The plane looked confident and stalwart, in spite of its wound. That big DC-3 wing gives the plane a long glide. It was once even tested as a glider. My friend and his captain needed that capability now. After the second engine quit, they flew the plane for about five more minutes, looking for a flat place along the Selway River. They almost found it.

A backpacker who was walking along the side of the canyon saw the big plane go past, still level at about two hundred feet above the river. It was eerily quiet, he said later. It made only the sound of wind. Inside, someone testified later, there was no singing, no praying. It was quiet there too. "We're going in," one of the pilots said. "Link arms." The smooth river lay ahead. But the plane caught a wing on a tree. The backpacker heard the sound of a crash. After a while he saw bits of fuselage swirling down the river. The only survivors were two people and a dog who were sitting in the back of the plane.

Basler Flight Services gets sixteen hundred hours out of an engine, and, like any aggressive employer, tries to replace it before it quits on its own. Still, sometimes the reassuring rumble clanks into chaos.

"If you fly these long enough," Lemon said, "you don't have to wonder if you're going to lose an engine. You just wonder when. You fly with the assumption in the back of your mind that an engine is going to quit at the most inopportune time." This was one of the reasons Lemon wasn't one of the pilots from the company that recently flew several DC-3s back to the United States from New Caledonia.

"I have mixed feelings about flying fifty-year-old airplanes over large bodies of water," he said. "I'm old enough now I don't have to prove that I'm brave, so I'm willing to admit that I'm not. Not that I'm afraid of flying. I'm afraid of dying."

This led to a discussion of Lindbergh, and of another pilot who had recently flown a single-engined Mooney across the Atlantic to honor Lindbergh's flight.

"Man like that," Lemon said, "puts his testicles in his pants with a shoehorn."

But the DC-3 has balls too. It'll fly all day on one engine. I wouldn't have been riding there looking out at Iowa over Lemon's shiny head if it had been any less capable: When I was twelve years old I was sitting at the window of a DC-3 at night over the jungle of Brazil when flames started pouring out of the engine on my side. I was not very happy then, and was less so when stewardesses came running back through the cabin, looking through the windows as if searching for a place to jump out. Phil Timm has a phrase for what happens to you when your airplane goes wrong: Your face gets so long you could eat out of the bottom of a butter churn. That's how I felt when the propeller stopped. The cabin became very quiet. In the next half hour that DC-3 *became* a church. But forty minutes later the plane found the glory we had chased in prayer, and drifted easily down into the haloed lights of São Paulo.

The wind was gusting to twenty knots at Minneapolis. As we descended McCulla fought the wheel. The ailerons on a DC-3 are as long as the whole wing on the trainer he was flying only a few months before, and there's no power assist. The rudder stands up there like a barn door. "In a crosswind," Lemon said, "that rudder can be a heavy mother." This was a crosswind.

"How come," McCulla said, "I always get these landings?" Lemon just grinned. Minneapolis came bouncing up toward us, its dark jagged skyline out the right side, its airport a big clearing in the forest

beside the Mississippi. "Gear down," McCulla said. On modern airplanes the landing-gear lever is a switch. In the DC-3 it is a pair of
metal bars that Lemon compared to an oversize screen-door latch. He
worked it like a handbrake.

"I have a main," said Lemon, looking out the window.

"I have a main," said McCulla.

"Full Flaps."

"Full Flaps."

McCulla landed straight down the runway, dancing a jitterbug on
the rudder pedals. We taxied up to the freight gate. With the tail on
the ground the DC-3 was as tall as a 747. We looked in second-story
windows at people sitting at desks. Looking at them, we felt fortunate
in life.

"I sit higher in this than my dad does in his DC-9s," McCulla said.

He and Lemon jumped out and helped load the plane. The pallets of
parts were strapped down in the big hollow tube of the fuselage. They
weighed five thousand pounds. The Pratt & Whitneys started with
puffs of blue smoke. We took off for Kansas City. We had been just
ten minutes on the ground.

Lemon was flying now, so McCulla handled the radio. The radio did
the same thing to him that it did to all of us. Once he pushed that
transmission button the eager kid was transformed into an old man,
the bored captain of ten thousand flights.

"Good evening, Minneapolis Center," he said. "Dakota Niner Seven
Bravo Foxtrot with you."

He didn't say "Niner Seven Bravo Foxtrot is flying south on a
beautiful evening, with the last clouds fading from the sky and the
land becoming golden beneath us, and there is nowhere else in the
world we would rather be." But that's what was happening. The
engines rumbled along without a cough, the nacelles were dry, and
the flat rich land of Iowa slipped under the plane. To modern jets, the
landscape is a faded view, smothered by altitude and haze, but to
Lindbergh, and to the pilots of DC-3s past and present, it was part of
the nature of flight.

"In summer," Ernest K. Gann wrote in *Fate Is the Hunter*, "the
prevailing westerly winds brush across the yellow grain in the fields,
the hedgerows, and the tops of trees in such a playful manner the
whole region appears to be alive and in rippling motion. In autumn,
when the colors turn and become even more jolly, the welcome of the
land is almost audible." In the DC-3's days of glory, when radios were

rudimentary and unreliable, the land was loved for its grandeur and loveliness, and for the landmarks it offered: that ridge of trees, that junction of rivers, that island shaped like a dolphin, or, for Gann, the coast of the lake that led you safely through snowfall to Erie. The plane that changed the world was on intimate terms with the landscape. It touched you; you touched it.

"I hit a duck once," Lemon said, munching on a sandwich. "Right here." He pointed to the left window. "Didn't even crack it. I went IFR with blood and guts all over the windshield." He paused, and sipped his coffee. "You don't hit geese. They fly faster than a DC-3."

We passed a few miles south of Mason City, Iowa. This was familiar country to me. This was familiar to me the way Maben and Mathiston had been to Charles Lindbergh. I had made a memorable mistake here.

"I landed wheels-up on a road around here somewhere," I said on the intercom.

There was relative quiet in the DC-3 for a minute. I was remembering how much I had enjoyed the fact that the wheels of the tiny, ancient, wooden plane I had just bought tucked up into its wings after takeoff just like the big boys. I was remembering how I got lost in that tiny airplane somewhere over Iowa.

I have never been truly lost in an airplane, and I wasn't then, if I had just trusted my compass course and studied the chart under the line I had drawn across it. The town I was circling was right there where it ought to have been. But it was getting dark, I was running low on fuel, and I didn't make the connection. I kept looking for a name on a roof or a water tower. Nothing. Modest damn town.

When Lindbergh toured the country he agreed to fly over some of the smaller towns if the towns' names were painted on roofs to guide future pilots. When I followed the tour later those signs were gone; the roofs had fallen to rust and progress. The only sign I saw was a bright new sign on a barn near Moline, Illinois. It read "ITSABOY."

A few months after the tour Lindbergh must have wished he had made the same agreement with towns in Mexico. He got lost on his long December flight to Mexico City and began circling communities, flying low over railroad stations, looking for a sign. Sure enough, he found one. I could see him give that grin again, that smile of delight:

"A sign was on the end of the station, as I expected—smaller than ours in the United States, but easily read. The name of the village was CABALLEROS. I unfolded my map as I climbed. But I could find no

Caballeros. Too small a place, I thought. I flew over cactus-bordered tracks to the next village. It's name was CABALLEROS, too! I tried a small town, with the same result. All the stations in Mexico appeared to be named alike. Slowly, after my sleepless night, I realized that 'Caballeros' marked a convenient place for men."

When I got lost I just decided to land and ask someone where I was. There were no airports in sight, but the grid has provided aviators with endless country landing strips, as long as they look out for fence posts, mailboxes, wires, and traffic. So I confidently selected a dirt road, made a low pass to look for obstacles, executed a careful landing pattern, and came in to touch down. My approach was impeccable. My glide was long and smooth. I swept gently down over the road, pulled gently back on the stick, and touched down as delicately as a feather.

Skrunch!

The plane stopped. The road was empty. It was very peaceful in the Iowa dusk. I sat there. I thought, Hmm. That was a loud landing. Then I thought, The plane sure didn't take long to stop. Then I thought, I am sitting very close to the ground. Then I looked ahead and saw my wooden propeller. It looked as if it was made of straw. Then my face got so long I could eat out of the bottom of a butter churn. I had forgotten to lower the wheels.

I left the plane in the middle of the road with its lights on, so it wouldn't get run over, and walked to town. A cafe stood on a paved highway on which one car passed about every ten minutes. About ten people were sitting in the cafe. They were very quiet. The waitress stood in a corner, slowly making a dinner salad. One tomato slice, two tomato slices. One customer was reading a paper. It was a weekly, about four days old. When I entered all eyes moved slowly over to me. I was a stranger. I walked up to the counter, and sat down on a stool. The eyes retreated. The hope faded out of them. I was not going to be that big a deal after all. But they were wrong. I said to the waitress:

"Hi. I just crashed my airplane up the road."

The plane hadn't been badly damaged. It was fixed in a few days, and I'd just as soon forget the landing. But I'll remember that cafe a long time. Everyone had heard what I said. The whole place sighed. In a moment I became a movie star. I became a prince. I was the hero of the month. It was all those people could do to keep from cheering. Something had happened there at last.

Back in the DC-3, Lemon chuckled.

"If you see the place," he said, "let us know. We'll fly around it."

We didn't see it. We rumbled on down into Missouri. The little office in the sky was peaceful. In the cooling afternoon, the air had become calm. The radio burbled along in the background, hardly louder than the engines. ". . . the DC-3," Gann wrote, "is an amiable cow, grazing placidly in the higher pasture-lands. . . ." As we drifted south across this vast American pasture, conversation was languid, and contented.

"We're close to where I was born," Lemon said. "Chillicothe, Missouri." The plane rumbled on for a minute or two.

"I didn't live there very long."

Several square miles of the grid passed below.

"I didn't get to make my mark in Chillicothe."

North of Kansas City farm ponds appeared in a rumpled landscape. There were hundreds of them. Below us they were blue and green and gray-green patches of water, depending on their depth and chemistry; to the west, reflecting the sun, they were red-gold coins scattered across the land. This was another mark Caterpillar's machines had made on America: over two million stock tanks, fishing holes, and farm ponds scraped out of marshes, meadows, and farm fields across the country. As we rumbled south over the countryside, new ponds shone up into the sun while others faded; the land was a conveyor belt carrying pieces of water north.

"They were crying in Pittsburgh when I left," McCulla said.

"Especially the women," Lemon said.

McCulla just smiled. The two men glanced at their engines. Still dry.

"I thought I would have to get a big stick to beat them off when I got my pilot's license," Lemon said.

The radio told Seven Bravo Foxtrot to begin its descent into Kansas City. McCulla sounded old and bored: "Roger. Seven Bravo Fox." He loved it.

We crossed the Missouri, that beautiful, wide, patient river, the river that is born far west, near my home, in a strange sort of inverted delta of winding waters and bottomlands, made of the Jefferson, the Madison, and the Gallatin rivers. Up there it looks from the air as if the land had cupped its two hands around those three streams and let the Missouri run out between its wrists. The three forks that make the Missouri are trout streams, but right where the Missouri begins is a big gravel pit, with cliffs cut away in terraces, and dusty rock crushers; a reminder that this river is an engine of industry.

Lemon pulled gently back on two knob-headed levers at his right hand. The noise diminished slightly. The DC-3's nose declined a few degrees against the horizon. Our shadow moved among the racing shadows of clouds, its halo flickering across fields and across the wide, flat roofs of prisons and shopping malls.

"Of course," Lemon said, "I was old when I got my license. I was twenty-three."

I was forty years old when I first flew a DC-3. Kansas City stood emblazoned by the setting sun as I got into the pilot's seat. It looked like every other American town: glass, concrete, steel. Phil Timm built his Model T at his father's farm on the outskirts of Kansas City. His father delivered produce to the wealthy of Kansas City, including Harry Truman. When Lindbergh flew into Kansas City Phil's mother took him into town to see the famous man. This was at about the time he made a glider with his bicycle and feed sacks and became briefly airborne before the bicycle, the sacks, and the baling wire and the boy became entangled with each other. But when they got to Kansas City the crowd was all going the other way; they had missed Lindbergh by half an hour.

As we prepared to leave Kansas City I climbed up into that chair that seemed so much higher and farther forward than the jump seat I'd been sitting in behind Lemon. I belted in. I was now going to fly a two-story building. Lemon had put on his instructor's hat. It did not hide his shine.

"The controls are the same as you're used to," Lemon said on the intercom. He was didactic now. "Rudder pedals, control wheel, elevators, ailerons. But the airplane will respond much slower to the control inputs than what you're used to. So even though it's a slow airplane, you have to plan further ahead of it. Because it takes much longer to make it do what you want it to do than it does in a more modern airplane.

"It's easier to land than the Cessna 170. But if it gets away, it gets away *larger*. It happens in slow motion. Everything in this airplane happens in slow motion. But the corrections happen in slow motion too. So when it begins to lose directional control on the runway, it does it in slow motion, and it's almost, 'Ha . . . Ha . . . Ha.' "

Lemon's words passed through my mind like the background rumble of the engines. I would not, on this flight, learn enough to work in either seat of a DC-3. But for a little while tonight I would fly in the lap of history. I put my feet on the pedals. I put my hand on the wheel. This was not strange. This was natural. The airplane fit; or I fit the airplane. Nothing inhuman about this machine.

The engines rumbled up. Needles in the instruments moved to their appointed places. The wheel was heavy. It was built like two-thirds of an automobile's steering wheel. It was old-fashioned. It was not a wheel to caress. It was a wheel to do business with.

The plane began to move. It veered slightly to the left. I corrected. I overcorrected. "Ha . . ." The plane veered to the right. ". . . Ha." I danced on the pedals. The plane settled down. I pushed the stick forward. The tail rose. Slowly the DC-3 accelerated. Still on the wheels, we were so far from the ground that eighty-four knots seemed a stroll. But the airspeed was sufficient, so we just strolled up into the air.

We rose, big and buoyant as a blimp. Lemon raised the landing gear. Macho Irene had decreed that this was the West: the first intersection by Kansas City was LASSO.

The setting sun drew a red arc on the outer edges of the propellers. We climbed to eight thousand feet and, with altitude, prolonged day in the evening's high pasture. The fleet of thunderstorms was somewhere over the horizon to the south; we flew near the base of a scattered layer of cumulus clouds that were drying into shreds. West of Ottumwa, we looked up under those clouds as if under a skirt, watching for the secrets of the land revealed, and saw patches of farmland, roads showing short straight pieces like strewn straws, and gently rolling hills. Narrow groves of trees ran in the valleys between fields, outlining the branching veins of the hidden water. The land was hilly now, east of the many jagged arms of Rathbun Reservoir, and the roads and fields were shaped by the land more than by the meridian. It was odd: in this part of Iowa, the straightlaced, straight-edged state, the grid lost its dominance. It was like a government guide for artists that had been subverted by creative personalities to their own expressive ends.

As twilight deepened across Iowa the clouds vanished and the farm lights came out, and slowly the grid became spangled, further losing its order. Only fifteen years ago, when I first flew here, there had been seas of darkness between islands of light. But now the whole landscape glittered with random stars made of mercury vapor and high-pressure sodium.

It was peaceful out there, as we rumbled east. Other aircraft checked in regularly on the radio, but all the voices seemed unhurried, content.

In this early evening, the great passenger liners of the high altitudes were sailing above the world on their long arcs, cleared direct from Denver to Kennedy and getting close to home. The commuter planes were hauling their after-work passengers to Chicago, Kansas City, St. Louis, Omaha. The freighters, the mail planes, and the little bank planes ferrying canceled checks had picked up their cargo and had all taken to the marvelous, clean, calm sky. For a few minutes it seemed as if the whole community of pilots was aloft, each one of us at peace, moving gently across the beauty, engrossed in the world.

The DC-3 and I were comfortable with each other. The little room of the cockpit had become a pleasant and familiar place, with instruments I understood informing me of our collective health, and switches and devices to manipulate that protected my life and gave me joy. I looked back at the long sweep of the port wing, and the engine. It was still dry. The chrome surface of the spinner spun the twilight like wisps of sugar.

"You can do just about anything in a DC-3 on landing," Lemon said, reminding me of what was coming up. "*If* you do it straight."

Flying a DC-3 had become a way of life. This plane was not fast. To a pilot this did not matter. "The difference between a fast plane and a slow plane," Lemon said, "is how much it costs to call home." Patient, glad for all the time the plane would give me, I flew through the history of aviation. Checkpoints passed like birthdays: Ottumwa, Iowa City, the Mississippi River, where there were power-plant stacks and a row of pastel-colored barges. In the twilight the metal golf balls of water towers gleamed softly above the shadowed towns like moons. The old plane passed almost unnoticed above, its song just a low rumble, like the legendary resonance of an aurora.

The DC-3 would always be a legend. One hit a mountain with a wingtip, lost twelve feet of wing, and was flown on to the airport. Once the whole crew of a damaged DC-3 bailed out, thinking it was doomed; it landed itself in a field. Ten thousand DC-3s were built. Twelve hundred of them, in a formation two hundred miles long, dropped paratroopers on the beaches of France on D day. A DC-3 was the first plane to land at the South Pole. A whole generation took to the air in DC-3s, and the world changed. To the passengers the DC-3 made the world smaller. But to the pilots to whom it gave a life in the sky, the DC-3 made the planet whole.

The DC-3 stood alone in history. In that special time between Lindbergh's flight and the war that debased science and technology by the ends of ideology to which they were used, in the days of the D8 Cat and the Tennessee Valley Authority, the DC-3 emerged like a miracle of desire from the long human dream of wings and glory. It *was* the dream. It *was* the glory. To many it still is.

"The Three is certainly the best and best-loved airplane we've ever produced," Donald Douglas told a *New Yorker* writer in 1960. "But the circumstances that made it great just happened. They were not of our making. I doubt whether any airplane will have the same impact, or the same opportunity, again."

We turned north just past GREAS intersection, west of Milwaukee, where city fathers were debating the construction of a giant monument to the city. This was to be a major new addition to the landscape, a Gateway Arch, an Eiffel Tower, a symbol. Among the suggestions had been a one-thousand-foot fountain in Lake Michigan shaped like an *M*, a huge globe, an enormous badger, a statue of Bacchus, a solar-heated geodesic dome over an indoor playground, and a statue of the mayor holding a beer and a bratwurst.

Such are the uses of modern engineering. In the air, a symbol of another kind crossed the stars.

"If it bounces, it's no big deal," Lemon said. "Just catch it." It was full dark as we approached Oshkosh. Lake Winnebago was a pool of blackness edged by lights, a hole in the planet. I turned the grand old airplane onto its final approach to Runway Twenty-seven out over the lake.

"Don't think of control movements," Lemon said, almost to himself. "Think of body pressure. You are physically holding it off. Have you ever seen geese land? Same thing you do with an airplane."

Those twin lines of lights that outline a runway are the pilot's welcome mat. The planet is, after all, glad to have you back. I flew down the middle of the lights, toward the invisible ground. The plane was steady. I danced lightly on the pedals. A pool of moving ground rose in the landing lights. I eased back on the wheel, just a thought of body pressure. This thing was a great hulking piece of complex technology, but I was in control.

My feathers ruffled in the wind. The big tires thumped the pavement, and stayed put. I brought the stick back. The tail settled to the ground. Niner Seven Bravo Foxtrot rolled out and slowed. We turned off the runway. The engines rumbled down and clattered to a stop.

We got out of the plane quietly. Even with the ground beneath your feet it is hard to break the membrane of flight. We left the plane and walked slowly back toward the bright office. We didn't say much. Pilots love to talk about the near misses, but they keep the drama and beauty of their everyday lives to themselves.

The lights of the office brought us back to the dazzle of the real world.

"It's an enjoyable job," Lemon said as he folded up the books and got ready to close the place down, "if you can stand the on-call thing." He told a story about being called in the middle of the night for a bad flight in a snowstorm. He grinned. There was, after all, a reason why he was still doing this kind of work after twenty years as a professional. The DC-3 might not be the glory anymore, but it was still the chase.

"There's still some romance in it," he said. "It's still two guys flying through the night in lousy weather, loading the freight, and flying off somewhere else."

CHAPTER THIRTY-TWO

It was summer in America. I had tasted it first in Texas and Louisiana along the Gulf edge of the Coastal Plains Province in early April. I had watched baseball in Mississippi in May. Now, in June, I had followed it north to Wisconsin. The day after I flew the DC-3 the wind blew summer through the grain in the fields, and drew threads of spume on the lake. On the ramp, Six Zero One rocked in the wind. The old airplane tugged at its tie-down ropes. Six Zero One and I had left home in the winter. What would be the season of our return? I rolled up the sleeping bag, put the motorcycle back in the plane, and chased Charles Lindbergh north into his Minnesota summer childhood.

The warm wind blew and blew. Small cumulus clouds raced before it. Beneath them, the wind ran like ghosts of playing children through the corn, the wheat, the grass along the little rivers. Flustered water glittered. I flew over the austere grounds of still another prison, the Fox Lake Correctional Institution, a state medium-security joint. Two of its three ballparks had grass infields. I looked down on a game. Someone was stealing second base. Fox Lake itself was so low with drought that it looked as if the tide had gone out; all the docks were beached.

I turned north into the face of the wind at Madison. On Lake Mendota sailboats raced. Madison was a city of water; fountains blew in the wind. A forest of thousand-foot radio towers stood at the west end of town. Madison Approach was solicitous.

"Keep all them antennas in sight, if you would," he said.

Into the wind my ground speed slowed. At the Dells a hill had broken out with a modest infestation of the Vermont disease: the first ski hill I'd seen in a couple of thousand zigzag miles. The dairy farms had waste-treatment ponds; their fountains blew foam up into the wind. It was summer in America. Canoes were nosed up against sandbars in the Wisconsin River. Tents fluttered like multicolored flags on a hilltop campground. I bumped down into the valley of the Mississippi and stopped for gas in La Crosse, and as I walked back out to the plane I heard a *whack* from somewhere over in the trees on the other side of the field. Then the sound of cheering voices of men and women floated to me in the summer wind. The cheers floated on and on: home run. Suddenly I was ecstatic to be there below the Mississippi bluffs in this warm breeze on an American Saturday morning, hearing baseball. I grinned. I laughed aloud. I climbed into the airplane and took off as if lifted by the strength of my own joy, and flew low, wings spread like the arms of a running child, close to the great river.

I flew along the edge of the bluffs that line the river all the way from Minneapolis to Dubuque. There were two worlds of human life here: the river people in their towns on the bank, and the hill people on top of the bluffs. I flew precisely at their elevation, looking level across their fields. Their silos were above me. They looked like a tremendous secret, a hidden civilization, out of sight of the people in the bottoms. But the bottoms people had their own secrets.

Near Buffalo City I crossed a light brown question mark built of sand in a wide calm eddy off the river. Next to it was another big sand island, curved into long narrow arms, like some rune intelligible only to the big eyes that watch from outside the galaxy.

What was this? Earth Art? A barge was pulled up to the question mark, and there seemed to be pipe on the top of it. Maybe Don Keyhoe had been right all the time: The government knew about the aliens from outer space, and was communicating with them, using signs made of Mississippi River mud.

It turned out later that this place was called the Weaver Bottoms, which was turned from pastureland to marsh by the construction of Whitman Lock and Dam in the 1930s. The question mark and its cryptic sibling were part of a $5 million cooperative effort by the U.S. Army Corps of Engineers and the U.S. Fish and Wildlife Service to get rid of dredged material, help prevent Weaver Bottoms from silting in, and to provide new wildlife habitat. The islands had been made by piping dredged material over to the Bottoms and making piles. The piles had been pushed into shape by D7 Cats. But why that shape? Who was the artist?

"That's known as using the least amount of sand to get the most shoreline," said Melissa Shortridge, the Winona resident engineer for the Corps. "Habitat along a shoreline is more valuable. It's better than a circular pile of sand."

"We maximized the edge effect," said Richard Berry, of the U.S. Fish and Wildlife Service.

Well. Of course the government would have to have an excuse to be drawing galactic calligraphy in the Mississippi River. But if there's a run of UFO sightings in Buffalo City, Wisconsin, let no one say I didn't give fair warning.

I could knock on every door in the world, but none would open to show Charles Lindbergh behind the screen. He is buried between walls of lava rock two feet thick on the island of Maui. But I chased the memory of him up the Mississippi, charging along into the wind while the land hardly moved beneath, as if I were running up a down escalator. Finally, far north of Minneapolis, I circled a small town on the river's banks. The town embraced the water. It had a pulp mill, a yard full of newly manufactured boats, an old dam. The town's name was on its water tower: Little Falls. This was Lindbergh's home landscape. South of town on the west side of the river was a modest house on wooded land that had once been the Lindbergh family farm. It is now the Charles A. Lindbergh State Park. If there was any place in the world that held the memory of the young man whose route I followed, this was it.

Charles Lindbergh was born in Detroit and spent his childhood in Washington, D.C., and California as well as Minnesota. But he awoke to the glory at Little Falls. The farm was the first place he loved, and one of the places he always loved most. He grew up there wearing blue overalls, with one foot in the Mississippi and the other in the wild past. During those summer days, he sat on a plank in a linden tree, or hung from the high branches of a big red oak in the wind, "with the trunk swaying and the leaves fluttering and white clouds drifting past overhead." He would swim in the river, which was "swift and . . . full of shallow rapids," sliding down through the turbulent water like a seal, then climbing out to dry on a big rock. Twice each summer he watched the men called River Pigs bring their bateaux and wanigans down the river to clear out the logjams. At night his father would tell him stories about life when Minnesota was a wilderness frontier.

"In early nighttime I would often lie on the bed with my father while he told me stories," the phantom Lindbergh said. In his age his smile had matured. It had kindness in it now as well as glee. "So far as I can now remember, they were invariably about his boyhood on the old homestead near Melrose—about his hunting, fishing, and schooling; about the Chippewa Indians who camped and passed nearby; about the dangerous Sioux; about the squeaking wheels of Red River oxcarts, the coming of the railroad, and the farm and household chores."

The farm was his favorite place, but even there other interests split him. He was also fascinated by his grandfather's laboratory in Detroit. "I loved the farm," he said, "with its wooded river and creek banks, its tillage and crops, and its cattle and horses. I was fascinated by the laboratory's magic: the intangible power found in electrified wires, the liquids that could dissolve either metal or stone, the lenses through which one could see the unseeable. Instinctively I was drawn to the farm, intellectually to the laboratory. Here began a conflict between values of instinct and intellect that was carried through my entire life, and that I eventually recognized as inherent in my civilization."

But he didn't have to leave the farm to enjoy the development of technology. He was given his first rifle when he was six. By the time he was about eight he had two .22-caliber rifles, a 12-gauge shotgun he could barely lift, a 10-gauge saluting cannon, a .22 pistol, and responsibility for a .38 revolver. He didn't have much to shoot around the farm—"The plentiful game of my father's boyhood had largely vanished from that part of Minnesota." But the equipment fascinated him. "I spent a great deal of time cleaning and oiling my guns. . . ."

To the children of the young century, the internal combustion engine was the glory. As it was for Phil Timm a few years later, Lindbergh's first romance was with a Model T Ford. Lindbergh's father bought the car in 1912, and his mother called it Maria. Lindbergh still remembered it in detail:

"Maria was a Ford Model T tourabout with Ford's standard foot-pedal gearshift, four-cylinder engine, smooth-faced clincher-rim tires, carbide headlights, hand crank, squeeze rubber-bulb horn, folding waterproof cloth top, and quick fasten-on side curtains for rainy days." Maria was fancier than Phil Timm's car. "For me, Maria brought modern science to our farm, and nothing else attracted me as much, or was as challenging or as symbolic of the future."

He learned to drive at eleven, and would drive his mother into Little Falls to shop. Since neither of them was strong enough to give the engine a vigorous crank, sometimes they'd spend an hour just getting it started. In spite of this, Lindbergh was so fascinated with the process of maintenance and repair that by the time his father bought a new car, a Saxon Six, in 1916, Charles, Jr., took care of it, "including a motor overhaul, replacing piston rings, and grinding valves." When, in his later teens, he managed the farm, his fascination and talent with machinery led him to buy various modern engine-driven instruments for the farm, including a three-wheeled tractor and a milking machine.

Charles A. Lindbergh, Sr., was a congressman for ten years, and during some of his campaign tours he and his son drove the Ford from town to town. Much of the time the boy drove, but when he got sleepy at night his father would take the wheel. The candidate sang to keep awake, with the carbide headlights flickering uncertainly out into the pitch-black Minnesota darkness. "All through the Bay of Biscay," he sang, "that gallant vessel sailed . . ."

"Actually," Lindbergh remembered with another grin, "it was more shouting. He would shout at the top of his voice as we drove through the night."

The century and the boy were in their young teens, and all the symbols of the future were good. So were the artifacts of memory. After he bought the Model T, his father drove Lindbergh back to the homestead site in Melrose more than once with the boy standing on the running board, hanging on to the struts of the roof, feeling the wind in his face and plucking leaves off branches as they passed. At the old homestead his father showed him the hollow in the ground where the house had been, as if to remind him of what mattered, and they walked together by the tracks of the Great Northern Railroad, and in the ruts left by the oxcarts on their way to the Red River Valley. In those days before gasoline engines, his father told him, you could hear the squeaking of the oxcart axles miles away.

Winter and summer, Lindbergh slept on a screened porch that overlooked the river. "There I was in close contact with sun, wind, rain, and stars. . . . On stormy nights rain blown in through the screen would mist it. Some of the valley's treetops rose slightly above its level."

In summer, thunderstorms rolled down the river. When the night sky filled with crackling sheets of light, his mother would take her child inside and put him on a cot in the middle of the dining room.

But when he was older Lindbergh liked the storms. Once he stood on the porch and watched hailstones the size of hens' eggs fall among the sheep. "One of the big hailstones landed on the head of one of them, and he acted as though another buck had rammed him."

Lindbergh seldom described his emotions, though his last book, *Autobiography of Values*, was all about his philosophy. He scrutinized most other parts of his life in prose, but he was either a coolly unemotional person, or he just wasn't comfortable with the vocabulary of passion. It must have been the latter. It was more than a mild affection for land and sky that drove him outside onto that porch to sleep in the dazzling, harsh glory of Minnesota winters.

"I would undress in the warm sewing room," he said, "put on an old fur-lined coat of my father's, open the window, and climb through it onto the bed. The bed was piled high with blankets and quilts. . . . On some very cold winter nights, the stars were extraordinarily bright. I'd lie on my bed and watch the stars curve upward in their courses— the box-like corners of Orion's Belt—Sirius's piercing brilliance—rising over treetops, climbing slowly toward our roof. I would curl up under my blankets and web the constellations into imaginary scenes of celestial magnitude—a flock of geese in westward flight—God's arrow shooting through the sky. . . . There was no roar of an engine in my ears, no sound above the wind in leaves except the occasional whistle of a train, far away across the river."

The sun threw beauty across the Earth like a mantle as I circled to land at Little Falls. The river shone a deep blue. The fields were rich greens and yellows, looking wholesome and valuable. Groves of trees cast dark shadows out into the fields. They looked like forests: robust, mysterious, virgin. The horizon was distant and curved. Thunderstorms towered a hundred miles west, a distant, protective fleet.

Lindbergh left Little Falls for college in 1920. He flew home for the first time in the summer of 1923, when he was twenty-two. As I circled it I could hear him, solemn and elated at this return:

"There it is, lying nakedly below me, river and creek, fields and woodlands—our farm. It has never fully exposed itself to my eyes before. How well I know each detail! How little I've understood the whole! In the past, I've seen our farm as a surgeon views his patient— all parts hidden but the one on which he works. Now, I embrace its entire body in sight and consciousness at once—in a realization which previous generations assigned to birds and God."

➤— I landed in Little Falls, and the landscape disappeared. Flat land throws a sheet over you. Once you're down at its level, you no longer see. For a while after landing you grope around among the trees, thinking that if you could only stand up you would again know where you were in the world.

I took out the motorcycle and found my way into town through the warm air. Along the road a father was playing with his boy and a red wagon under a big burr oak. My children were 750 nautical miles west, playing by themselves.

It was summer. It was time to turn west again, and set a course for Montana. I had flown about twenty thousand miles. I had five thousand more to go. I rode the motorcycle from the airport through the oaks of Little Falls as if I had been traveling this way forever, and suddenly realized that I would not be doing it much longer. This was the last glory of the journey: the place of Lindbergh's childhood. After that the only halo of light on my horizon was home.

I followed signs that pointed toward Lindbergh's home. It felt as if my travels were ending right there. I had wanted to make this journey for so many years, and now it was almost done. I was suddenly conscious of the pacing off of days. In a few more this would be over, and a new mark would be struck across the calendar of my life.

I crossed the young Mississippi on a bridge in the middle of town. The water was dark, the flow small. Traffic rumbled on the short bridge. I looked out at the water, and thought again, Good friend, Mississippi. I have watched you redraw borders. I have watched you lean on the fence like a bull. I have held you in the wide embrace of my wings. Again and again I have crossed you, as I do now on this miniature machine. I have realized you. I have realized the land that nourishes you. Like birds and God, I have realized America.

I got off the bridge and turned left at a light. Had I realized America? Who was I kidding? What vanity it was to suppose that America lay revealed before me like the hundred acres of Lindbergh's farm. Yes, I could now step back from the picture I had made with all those zigzags and view the nation not as a map, but as land, woods, and water: desert rolling up into mountains, mountains to dry plains, dry plains to farmlands, farm to forest, forest to mountains, mountains to swamp and sea. But that was not what memory made of the journey. Memory does not make generalizations. You do not say of a loved one, "I recollect her courage." You say, "Do you remember the day she broke her hand when she fell on the ice outside the grocery store?

Not a peep!" This land was my loved one, and though I had flown the grand picture, I remembered glimpses.

No longer bound by time, these memories rattled together and glittered at random like uncut stones in the palm of my hand. Each bright with the moment, they made curious combinations. Shrimp trawlers drew marks on the bottom offshore of Fred Howard Park beach; prehistoric Americans padded soft patterns of geoglyphs into the California desert, praying; kids drove Caterpillar tractors to make swirled tracks through fields in Texas. I floated high above the corridor of the St. John River in Maine watching kayakers worship wilderness; I stood in the blasted, logged-over clearing beside the Natchez Trace and plugged my ears while a white delta-winged fighter flew low over-head and tore the sky apart. I looked down from Signal Mountain at the steeples of Chattanooga and watched Flippo Morris tumble and fly forever to the music of the mighty Seventh-Day Adventist tracker organ. I awoke, sweating, from nightmares of endless antennas stretching a steel web across my path. The flat roofs and open fields of the prison outside Santa Fe looked just like a shopping mall that was under construction near Syracuse, New York. Arnold Murray stood knee deep in Spavinaw Creek with his hand on the forehead of Jeff Brandon's young son, Keith, while a mountain lion stared with its strange and familiar barred face from a sycamore, hunting penguins through the people exhibit. Praise the Lord! Ken Lemon turned Christ's DC-3 inbound for final approach. The Mississippi rattled the pearly gates of the Achafalaya.

I would never stop riding those few hundred yards of Interstate 279 across the Monongahela at Pittsburgh. I would always hear those geese over Teterboro airport outside New York. Even back in the clear air of the West I would always be haunted by the somber red shine of Delaware Bay seen through the haze of Armageddon. I'd taste the wild strawberries. I'd soar with the bears. I'd fly among white and gray ships of the sky's might, and never hear the thunder. I'd see Don Keyhoe behind the screen. I'd see Huck Finn standing poised and happy in a canoe on a lake in Alaska. Again and again I'd blow east from Santa Fe and watch the grid take over the land like a tide.

The grid, agriculture, reservoirs, haze, cities, gravel pits, interstate highways, the armed forces; in order of importance, those were the manifestations of the human presence upon the land. In the West the clear-cuts that marked the hills with swatches of dark and light were more significant than the canyon-bottom lakes. In the East power-plant stacks were more prominent than interstates. Everywhere the landscape was altered. In the back of my mind Geraldine Page sat on the porch of the Chapman ranch outside of Waxahachie and reached out, like all humans, for the hope of permanence in the landscape, but everywhere I looked I saw change. The rivers wandered, a fresh crack appeared in a hillside in Idaho, the mottled colors of the earth in the Midwest revealed clay beneath the topsoil that was blowing away. Dams filled canyons with water, rivers filled reservoirs with silt. Man and nature drove restlessly on, inseparable. I saw John Brinckerhoff Jackson, his face as new and ancient as his dry landscape. He said again, "Which comes first, the blessing or the prayer?"

Charles Lindbergh returned to Little Falls for the last time in 1973. His life was ending. He had already been treated once for cancer, with apparent success, but he did not yet know that the disease had advanced. He gave a short speech for the dedication of the park's interpretive center. It was the end of September, but it was an Indian summer day in Little Falls. He stood on the steps of the old house, where he had once slept in the cold and looked up at the stars out of a night in which no mercury vapor lights clouded the darkness and in which the American Song was just the single distant melody of a train. He read a short speech full of memories and hope. At the end it seemed as if living itself was the glory he now chased to its end.

"As our civilization advances," he said, "if our follies permit it to advance, I feel sure we will realize that progress can be measured only by the quality of life—all life, not human life alone. The accumulation of knowledge, the discoveries of science, the products of technology, our ideals, our art, our social structures, all the achievements of mankind have value only to the extent that they preserve and improve the quality of life."

I parked the motorcycle near Lindbergh's house, but he was gone. I wandered around the grounds of the old home, but saw no ghosts, and felt no reverberations of the past. It was Sunday morning. There was a religious service on the grounds, and the gentle music of the United Spirit Singers filtered through the trees. I walked all around the house, among the pines and the oaks and the linden trees.

"Bless the Lord, oh my soul," sang the Spirit Singers. A plane flew over. As usual, the songs of God and America clashed and mingled. What were religion and science but metaphors to explain the mystery?

Lindbergh never stopped testing the image against the evidence, as must we all.

Along the river the linden trees bloomed. They smelled of honeysuckle, the aroma of nostalgia, but it didn't take me back to Lindbergh's past. We are accompanied by our own ghosts. Instead it took me back to the day after I watched Jack Barnett, Mike Wray, and their sons fish with such earnest futility in the arena at Lake Murray, Oklahoma. The following morning I ran in the woods near Lake Murray Lodge, on a trail through trees, across gray plank bridges where turtles plopped into the water from logs and the woods were full of honeysuckle blossoms.

That was more than a season ago. It was barely spring when I was in Oklahoma. The trees were turning more green with every hour; the forest thickened like soup. Big squirrels scuffled through leaves. I ran, looking down at the pale sand of the trail, thinking about the world brimming with life, and saw ahead of me the mingled footprints of children and raccoons.

For all the seriousness of Lindbergh's messages to the rest of us, he walked as lightly through the world as the creatures who left those tracks. His words, and maybe his thoughts, were sometimes unbearably heavy, but perhaps life was not. When William Jovanovich visited him just a few days before he died, and helped carry him onto the plane that took him to Maui, Lindbergh asked Jovanovich, "Do you think I am dying well?" He might have asked Donald Hall the same sort of question when they were designing the *Spirit* in San Diego: "Do you think we need more wing area?" He planned and arranged for death as if he were working out a flight he had looked forward to for years. "It's not terrible," he told Anne. "It's very easy and natural."

Maybe it had always been that way. "What justifies the risk of life?" he wrote once. "Some answer, the attainment of knowledge. Some say wealth, or power, is sufficient cause. I believe the risks I take are justified by the sheer love of the life I lead."

How many people are that free? When we were children, all of us followed the footprints of raccoons, just for love. When we were young, we chased the glory all the time. We knew life was desperate and amazing, so we told each other all those things we were so pained and so exalted to perceive. We counted tornadoes from the porch. We learned how to tumble and fly. We went to sleep looking at the winter stars. We swam the rapids. We watched the huge hail conk the sheep.

But when we got older we became comfortable here in this house of living, and now most of the time we say the polite thing, do the accepted thing, and look for the reassurance of stability in a landscape whose very nature is change. We turn away from the storm because it may remind us of how precarious it really is in this thin, tender, blue-green place between rock and space. But when we stop seeing that horror and beauty, and stop knowing the precipice, and stop looking out at the dazzle of the horizon, and stop wanting to see forever and ever, and stop riding on the running board with the wind in our faces, and stop feeling the whirl of vertigo, the gasp of flight, the sheer love—when we stop chasing the glory—then our eyes glaze over and get dull, and all there is left is to hunker down in the basement and wait for the formal nod of physical death, because the angel of life has already gone.

But Lindbergh never hid. He never got off the running board of that Model T. Like his father, he shouted songs in the dark.

⤞ Reeve Lindbergh visited Little Falls shortly after her father died. "When I came, I felt as if I had lost him," she said later. "When I left, I felt as if I had found him."

I flew out of Little Falls on a beautiful afternoon. I let Six Zero One rise a foot off the runway, then held it low, racing down the double white line in the middle of the runway, holding the nose down, taking up the flaps, accelerating, gathering speed like wealth. The old plane felt strong and alive and eager. At last I let it point its nose at the sky and squandered the speed on altitude. We stood up, above the land. We leaped high over the trees, across the Mississippi River. We soared. I was filled with a wild happiness. All the world seemed unfettered. I flew, taking breath on the wing, returning once more to the boisterous element of my home in the sky.

PART *10*

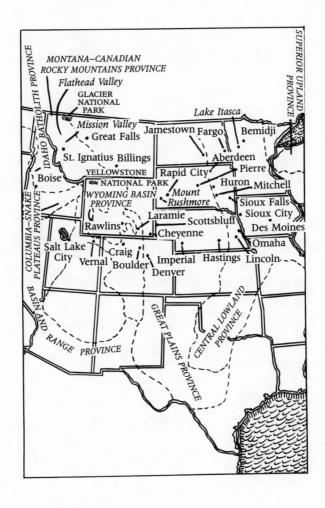

CHAPTER THIRTY-THREE

Two weeks later I sat in silence at Great Falls, Montana, ready for the last leg, but the engine wouldn't start.

Six Zero One was tired. I had raced through the last miles, hardly stopping to sleep, from the Lowland Province up into the Great Plains Province to Denver, then back east on a long Lindbergh zigzag to Pierre, South Dakota, where the vast Missouri River Reservoir called Lake Oahe, which is said to have a longer coastline than California, reminded me of all the stopped-up rivers on this continent. I'd flown back to the Rockies in a day. Just that morning I had left Boise, Idaho, for the longest day, a thousand-mile tangle of zigzags across Idaho and Montana to Billings, Butte, Helena, and Great Falls, before flying over Glacier Park. Lindbergh's Glacier Park route had been a detour: "I flew more than six hours," he said, "to cover no more than the fifty-mile distance between Butte and Helena, Montana, just to have time to think without distraction."

But for several days the plane's starter had been slowly fading away, and now it refused to crank at all. So I was out pulling the prop through by hand, which made Six Zero One even more old-fashioned. But in my urgency to get home I had overprimed the engine, and now I sat in the plane, waiting for the engine to dry out, so I could try again.

I had come a full circle. The trip was almost over.

When I left Little Falls I flew out over Lake Itasca, where the Mississippi begins. The tiny river flows out of the lake over an informal stone dam, just a reminder to the river right at the start from humans: Pay attention, river. When I landed at dusk at Bemidji, Minnesota, four deer and I nearly died when the deer darted out on the runway just as I touched down. I left two streaks of rubber on that runway, but we all survived.

The forest ended near the Minnesota border as if a line had been drawn across the earth. I crossed into North Dakota, and almost four months after the California Winter Fair in El Centro I went to the Stutsman County Fair in Jamestown, North Dakota. When the band called for a jitterbug dance contest it got two teenage girls to compete, but when it came time for the polka the stage was crowded. At Jamestown men and women from the U.S. Fish and Wildlife Service were putting tiny transmitters in mallards and blue-winged teals as part of a major project to find out how to raise more wild ducks on fewer acres while farmers continue to drain more of the post-glacial ponds that speckle the prairie and nurture the birds. As the wetlands diminish, birds and foxes converge on what's left. This is more to the foxes' advantage than the ducks'. But the researchers were doing their best. They were curators, like the employees of Murphy Brothers Enterprise, who ran the fair's big neon rides. They struggled behind the scenes to maintain the amusements.

At Jamestown I got interesting information from a young line boy. He was a chubby, sly, sleepy-looking young guy who came slowly out in the evening to where the plane was parked.

"Need anything?"

"How much is your gas?"

"One-eighty-five."

"No, I guess I got enough fuel. Wind blow like this all the time?"

He shrugged.

"Pretty much. Sometimes it gets . . ." He couldn't bring himself to use the word *calm*. "Sometimes it gets . . . pretty nice."

We talked briefly about my travels. I told him I'd sleep in the plane. It sounded terrible to him.

"I do it all the time," I said.

The kid was watching me with his sleepy eyes.

"What are you doing here?"

"I thought I'd just drop in and see what this town was like," I said.

"Boring." And he looked it too. His eyelids drooped.

"Been here all your life?"

"Pretty much."

"Been bored all your life?"

"Pretty much."

Then, without a change of expression, he modified the analysis:

"The only thing that's not boring about this town is the women," he said.

What? I tried not to sound startled:

"Really?"

"Yeah. The women are fantastic. They're *fantastic.*"

The word animated him at last; he drew it out again: "Fan-*tas*-tic."

"Well," I said. "That must help."

He shrugged his shoulders again. His eyelids drooped once more. "Some of them are going with guys," he said. "Some of them are married." A sleepy, sly smile appeared, and he walked away.

A couple of days later I celebrated the Fourth of July by poking around a vast thunderstorm near Omaha—"Possible tornadoes, wind gusts to sixty knots, hail to two inches." Over a farm near Polk, Nebraska, I saw a kid race out of a farmyard on a four-wheel off-road vehicle, charge out into the dust of the road, and make a big, skidding 360-degree turn, kick up a cloud of dust, then charge back into the farmyard. I remembered that wild skidding car in Oklahoma. Desperation stalks the countryside.

Cattle feedlots appeared among the fields. The chart changed color, from greens to browns, at the two-thousand-foot level, one and a half degrees east of the 100-degree meridian.That was an important place, the symbolic line that marks the eastern edge of the dry land, of what's left of the short-grass prairie, of the Great Plains Province, and of the West. I had been gone a long time.

No visible line marked this great division of America; it looked as if it ran in the middle of the fields between the lines of grid. Like someone making a choice, I stepped across the line and committed myself to the West. Pierre, South Dakota, at the end of the last big zigzag, was about twenty miles west of the 100; so I would not step east across that line again on this journey. It was just an invisible line, less important in real life than state or national boundaries, which most aviators do not highly respect. But it had its effect on the mind. I found myself concerned about how much water I carried, if I should have to land in a field. That was a Western worry.

The Great Plains Province began with an increase in the numbers of polka dots of center-pivot irrigated fields, and then a disruption of the grid by broad pastures that the county roads did not cross. Over western Nebraska I heard other aircraft asking for weather in Chicago, Long Beach, and Cleveland, and suddenly all those fields connected up. They were part of a single landscape, slipping back down behind me, with their rivers and their windblown soil, to Minneapolis, to Des Moines, to St. Louis, to Morgan City, Louisiana. The country seemed whole.

The landscape was green. Summer had not yet drained spring's color. The green spread across the gravel pits and the interstates and mines and the flooded valleys. America lay scarred beneath the haze like a partner of love to whom we have given pain and a virus; it lay there, beautiful; yielding and forgiving and green with hope.

Denver was clear. I had become used to the plains. I took one look at the great wall of mountains, so strange and massive to me now, and rushed back east, on course. The sky was clear all the way back up to Pierre, except for a single sailing ship of cloud with its prow high and its sails tattered and windblown, riding the sky on a keel of rain. I slept in Pierre like a just soul, rocked by a dry prairie wind, and flew back west over the Badlands to see the faces of the Presidents near Rapid City.

I was startled. There was no grandeur in the sculpture. It was the opposite. The famous heads were tiny. All around them rose vaster humps of rock, seamed, bulbous, massive, grim; nightmare faces with unreadable expressions, leaning together under a storm. The white shoulders of the kings of America hid among them, with the curved parking lot full of cars kneeling as if at pews. But the mountains, and the heads of the mountains, rose behind them higher and higher, a crowd of stone faces murmuring their slow story of time in frequencies no human can hear.

I returned to Colorado and crossed the most elegant grass infield I had seen, near Boulder, then flew slowly up into the mountains. It was like stepping reverently into a grove of trees after years in the desert. The mountains were vast, wrinkled, and dry. Craig, Colorado, once a boomtown for the construction of power plants, and for the aborted drive to dig oil shale out of the mountains, was almost a ghost. A huge trailer park south of Craig was empty. Its concrete pads looked like mounting pads for computer chips that had been removed. While I flew over Craig I heard a single ominous observation on the Unicom frequency. It was one pilot talking to another:

"That thing's pumping smoke out the exhaust like a son of a bitch," the voice said. "That's a solid trail of smoke. You're a solid trail of smoke." A pause. "I'm not sure as you hadn't ought to come back." I heard no more.

Except for a final two thousand miles the journey was over. I was back in familiar country, going back over land I had covered on my rush back to Debbie in March. The checkpoints passed. Vernal, Utah. Salt Lake City, with the Jordan Queen restaurant and the pool of blood at Western Zirconium. Burley, Twin Falls, and Boise, all in Idaho. I was almost home. I slept in Boise, and rushed on across the Idaho Batholith, over Yellowstone Park, over Billings.

When I first drew the outline of Lindbergh's trip on my chart on the floor of the office out in the woods near my house, I thought this diversion around via Yellowstone and Glacier Park was enormous. At Billings, halfway through it, it seemed to be nothing compared to some of those other zigzags—Chicago-Wichita-Milwaukee, for instance, or Denver-Pierre-Cheyenne. It was hard to believe now that all that drawing on the chart had turned into a part of the past.

Then I got stuck at Great Falls. For a moment, with home just past the ridge of the Continental Divide, I thought, What time's the bus? But I went back out in front of Six Zero One, thinking of Phil Timm, who once propped a plane with too much throttle and saw the plane taxi swiftly away without him. The plane galloped off on a wide curving trajectory toward a wreck, but Phil cut the corner and caught it. "If you want something outstanding in my life," he said, "that was it." So I tied Six Zero One down and went through my safety routine like an elaborate genuflection—roll up sleeves, plant feet, shuffle to check traction, swing left leg forward, swing it back to carry you away from the prop, and PULL! And I heard, for the last time on this journey, the welcome song of my American machine.

I took off, climbed out of Great Falls, and just kept climbing. I would touch the sky this evening, and bring this trip to an end.

Climbing, I passed strip farms where all the farmed and fallow strips lay parallel, north-south, for mile after mile; to the left were buttes and the Rockies, hazy at forty miles. Old farm buildings stood, bedraggled, at long intervals on the plains. Macho Irene knew about them, as she had known about everything: the intersection south of me was called ABARN.

Climbing, I passed into better weather. The clouds had turned to summer cumulus, with few buildups, and no showers to be seen. In the afternoon sun the creeks and canals that come out of the mountains and flow down into the plains reflected the bright sky as I passed, and drew fine silver lines down the landscape.

Quick, I thought, before this trip ends: Inspiration! Symbolism!

Wisdom! I called, but those old dogs didn't come. I listened, but nobody howled. I couldn't even muster a Summing Up. I had only plains and mountains and shining water; remote ranches and fields; and hard-hearted clouds turning slowly to fluff as the cold front moved away.

Journeys end in various ways, not usually the way they were planned. Lindbergh's trip certainly didn't end in the manner Keyhoe had in mind. Near the end of it, Lindbergh finally organized some assistants, pinned Keyhoe down, and shaved off his little mustache. But Keyhoe had compensation. Late in the trip an important visitor came to one of those many hotels to talk to Lindbergh, who was out. The visitor threw his hat on the couch, and waited. Lindbergh came in. Lindbergh saw the hat. He thought it was Keyhoe's. That grin came across his face. He sat down on the hat. The hat crumpled. The visitor was speechless. Inconspicuously, Keyhoe smiled.

When the tour was over Lindbergh gave engraved watches to each of his companions and walked solemnly away, to chase new glories. But to me the last day felt like leaving home.

Alone, I climbed and climbed. A headwind poured down out of the mountains of my last scene, Glacier National Park. The canyons kept me away from their secrets long enough to lay shadows in the tender places. I climbed, and crossed the park. The air was as jagged as these peaks. I soared above.

The late afternoon light was perfect. It caught the cliffs, shadowed the valleys, gleamed on snow, shone in my eyes. The park was a rage of rock; outrageous rock.

Bang! I bashed my head on the ceiling. The mountains made the sky rough as rapids. I swam among them. In the violence life came in bursts. Downdraft! Updraft! Down again; a serious down. Now there was not enough altitude to make the pass. Turn out. Back on the east side. Climb again. Two rows of glaciers and rock between here and the Flathead Valley. Yellow-gray rock; blue depths. Sheer bands of sediment. Updraft. Ride it. Ride it west. Sun on green slope. Parking lot on ridge. People on Going to the Sun Highway. Lake in shadow. Waterfall.

Keyhoe had chased the glory as he followed Lindbergh in Glacier Park. "Could we but have stopped to enjoy that wonderland!" he wrote."To camp in a serene valley beneath those inspiring peaks. . . . Just to rest and to dream, forgetting the world outside and our suddenly petty troubles." Lindbergh's thoughts are not known. Keyhoe saw him and his airplane far below, swooping and playing in the wild landscape. He was audacious, Keyhoe thought: mischievous. I thought: happy.

I climbed, and climbed. There was the Flathead Valley, whose foot turned into the Mission Valley, and led to the tiny town of St. Ignatius, where I live. I was in my home province, among the great tilted slab rocks of the Montana-Canadian Rockies. But in the late sunlight, I climbed, and climbed, and climbed.

I reached the level of the scattered clouds. I climbed above. The air smoothed out from one moment to the next. The turbulence ended as I passed through twelve thousand feet, as if, right there, I left the province of human conflict. The outside air temperature was two degrees centigrade. The national grid was remote below; the national park was behind me; the last sights were seen, but I had not finished flying. Slowly, slowly, slowly, I turned for home.

But still I climbed. The sky drew me up. Thirteen thousand feet. Hungry Horse Reservoir was below, more deep blue arms of a controlled river. In the distance Flathead Lake was a plate of silver. I climbed through 13,500 feet. On the shoulders of the forested mountains below, the winds had made parallel patterns in the trees, a grain in the forest. Life is layer upon layer. The scattered clouds were far below now, bright. I looked for my glory. I didn't see it. No halo. The whole world shone.

CHAPTER THIRTY-FOUR

I do not let it end. I hang in the sky like a kite. Bird or paper? It doesn't matter. Fourteen thousand feet. I lower the nose to level off. I can feel my heart working as it does when I run. My heart pounds in my head. The air is thin. I sip oxygen from the bottle. There is nothing profound up here. Or maybe everything is profound. Sunlight, moisture, stone.

It is time to descend. I do not descend. I fly slowly at fifteen thousand feet, my haste all used up. Few people live at a greater altitude than I float now above the ground; I am on the high edge of life. The mountaintops below me are stark and barren. The breath through the cabin vent is bitter.

The engine hums the American Song. Heaven is blue, transparent, and empty. If I am still afraid, what? But I am not afraid.

Soon I will make a long slant down through the entire thickness of the place in which human beings live. The air will grow warm. Debbie and the children will be waiting on the summer grass. I will come back from heaven to the only miracle we have. It is more than enough. It is the glory. I will return to our thin and precious home between rock and space. It will take almost no time at all. The glide will last just fifteen minutes, then the wheels will kiss the earth.

INDEX